The New Communisms

The New Communisms

DAN N. JACOBS, Editor
Miami University

Harper & Row, Publishers / *New York, Evanston, and London*

Chapter 1 is based on material drawn from Jan F. Triska and David D. Finley, *Soviet Foreign Policy* (New York: Macmillan, 1968), pp. 154–170. By permission.

Chapter 5, although written for this volume, also appeared in *Bulletin of the Atomic Scientist,* June, 1966, vol. 22, no. 6, pp. 58–65.

THE NEW COMMUNISMS

 For information address Harper & Row, Publishers, Incorporated, 49 East 33rd Street, New York, N.Y. 10016.
Library of Congress Catalog Card Number: 69-10548

To and for and from

Jan

Contents

Preface

As is always the case in a joint effort such as this, there are, putting it as circumspectly as possible, problems of time and coordination.

In this context, I must here express my appreciation to those authors who sent their chapters in on time and apologize to them for having to wait for publication. I also want to thank those who belatedly took assignments and produced extremely worthwhile contributions on comparatively short notice.

In addition to the authors, many cooperative and understanding people in New York, Washington, and Oxford have helped me ready this manuscript for publication. I thank them all. I also express here my appreciation to the Faculty Research Committee of Miami University which provided me with several grants that enabled me to work on the book and defray typing and other costs.

Oxford, Ohio DAN N. JACOBS

Introduction

Dan N. Jacobs

IT IS ONE of the grand ironies of history that communism, which was premised on an inevitably proliferating international spirit and which has from its Marxist inception vigorously proclaimed the victory of internationalism, has, in the last half of the twentieth century—over a century after its prescriptions were first put down and half a century after it first came to power in Petrograd—become encrusted and deflected by the barnacles of a still-proliferating nationalism. In magnificent confusion of wish with fact, Karl Marx averred that "National differences and antagonisms between people, are daily more vanishing . . . (and) the supremacy of the proletariat will cause them to vanish still faster."[1] Yet the story of contemporary communism reads almost completely to the contrary. The period since World War II has witnessed not the disappearance of "national differences and antagonisms" but their enthronement: in Latin America, in Asia, in Africa, in Eastern Europe. Only in Western Europe, in the European Common Market, has there been contrary evidence. And even the development of the ECM, beset by constant obstacles, has been slowed, while its military counterpart NATO has been all but done in chiefly by the slings and arrows of rampant Gaullism.

But, nowhere—not even in those territories where it has played the leading role in smashing colonialism and bringing subject peoples to power in their own countries—have the effects of nationalism been of greater world significance than in and among the Communist coun-

[1] "The Communist Manifesto."

tries and Parties. For what has been witnessed is the *nationalization* of communism and its conversion into whatever, to all intents and purposes, any leadership decides that it should be.

This then is the purpose of this volume: to indicate (a) that the nationalization of communism has taken place; (b) how this has occurred under differing circumstances; (c) the present state of this process and of communism in those continents and countries considered, and (d) the possible consequences of these developments for the immediate and more distant future.

Looking backward from today's vantage point, it seems almost absurd that the strong possibility of what has transpired—the nationalization of communism—was not recognized earlier and generally. For in retrospect, it is evident that the seeds of communism's nationalistic future were present in its founding; and indications of their sprouting and development have been abundantly demonstrated.

Although Marx prognosticated concerning the future and attempted to rip off those blinders which he thought prevented his contemporaries from seeing the present as it was and the direction in which it was leading, he was very much a man of his own times, and those times were, for some men—in particular, for the bourgeoisie, to which Marx belonged—times of great confidence about the future.

When the history of the second millennium A.D. comes to be written, from the perspective of time, I have little doubt that the century from 1750–1850 will be described as the most remarkable period within that thousand years. The technological advances of later eras would be more extensive, but none of these developments, not even the projecting of hitherto earth-bound man to new planets and perhaps even times, would have as profound consequences upon the life and spirit of man as those which derived from the transformations engendered by the industrial revolution. Some men—great numbers of them—were cruelly treated by these changes, it is true. Rooted out of the countryside, foisted on to a city ill-prepared to receive them, they were forced to adjust to what was far greater than ordinary meanness, brutality and corruption. But for other men, discovery and invention brought property, success, and the vision that grew steadily into a conviction that tomorrow would surely be better than today—even as today was, at least for them, undeniably better than yesterday.

The concept of linear progress, of continual uninterrupted progress was extensively developed and gained millions of adherents. If man had suddenly learned to fabricate machines to do his work for him, to send iron horses clattering down tracks at enormous speeds and to propel ships across oceans without the aid of a single zephyr, then what was there that man could not do? And the consequence of the "progress" that was being made was that the future would be "better" than the past, and that man's tomorrow would be happier than his yesterday.

Part of this happiness, certainly not the least part, was that there would be no more wars; and the relative peace of Europe after Napoleon fostered the conviction that man's age-old ideal of universal peace was being achieved. The same formations and uniforms and weapons, and even the same officers and tactics, that had seen service at Waterloo would be called into action at Sevastopol, two score years later. The arts of war were dormant as the productive arts pushed forward at what seemed to be breakneck speed.

The vision of peace adopted by the bourgeois world involved the concept of the fraternity of man, of all men, regardless of nationality, living as brothers in a world devoid of national boundaries and national enmities. This was not a new dream. For centuries it had been, however, a backward-looking dream, to something that had in fact or fancy existed at some past time, to a lofty summit the view from whose heights man had once enjoyed but from which he had subsequently fallen. But now men looked forward not backward—and there was no peak which modern man could not ascend. *Per aspera ad astra.*

This was the prevailing outlook of the nineteenth-century liberal world, and it was an outlook that Marx shared: tomorrow would be better than today, man would be happier than he is now, and the national differences between men would disappear as they should. Hence Marx's internationalism.

As he saw it, the development of capitalism, as it expanded across continents and around the world, would eliminate national barriers and differences. When the revolution came the process would be accelerated —nationalism would disappear together with the bourgeoisie.

For the time being, however, Marx did see a positive implication in nationalism. For it represented a "natural" development intimately involved in the maturation of capitalism and hence contributing to its demise. In this context certain nationalisms—those that favored the growth of larger national units,[2] for example, German nationalism—were to be favored. While other nationalisms—those that favored the disintegration of already existing units, such as that of the Czechs with respect to the Austro-Hungarian Empire—was to be opposed.

However, there is a persistent doubt that Marx, in differentiating between "good" and "bad" nationalism, always operated with complete

[2] The larger the unit, the more "international" it would be.

objectivity. For not only was he a man of his own time, but of his own country, as well. The basic German values were his values. He shared the Hegelian enthronement of the state, specifically of the German state. He favored an enlarged and united Germany, whatever the reason he gave. He clearly valued the culture of the West above all others and looked with ill-concealed distaste, if not contempt, upon that of the Slavs, to name but one. Hence, while Marx became the apostle of internationalism, he did not erase its opposite from himself—nor the prejudices it gave rise to from his writings.

However, not only for Marx personally was nationalism a still-important factor, but for Europe as well. The year 1848 was not, as Marx thought it to be, a victory for internationalism, but of nationalism—and from 1848 on the latter's presence would be experienced more, not less violently.

The unheavals of 1848 signify the overwhelming defeat of nineteenth-century liberalism. Its ideas and values would still persist into the twentieth century, and, indeed, its internationalist components would reach a certain culmination in Wilson's house-of-cards League of Nations. But by that time liberal internationalism would have been further drained by the Franco-Prussian War, by the race for colonies and the carnage of the Great War, whose rivers of blood nourished an already vigorous nationalism.

On the side of revolutionary internationalism, nationalism destroyed not only International I, but International II, as well. In World War I socialism could not withstand the siren's song of national identity. Whatever may have been written and felt about the brotherhood of the international proletariat, once war had begun, the call of the fatherland and motherland proved more powerful than that of fraternal working class solidarity. After the Zimmerwald Conference, it was unmistakably clear that the great majority of socialists were—some reluctantly, others less so—"social chauvinists." International II lost its moral force. It has survived only as an anachronism, a breathing, if hardly living reminder of an ancient dream.

During World War I, Lenin sided neither with the "social chauvinists" nor the "social pacifists" but resumed the position that he had first taken up during the Russo-Japanese War of a decade earlier: the war having begun, it should be converted into a revolutionary situation. The guns of the "exploiters," held by the exploited in the front lines, should be turned against their exploiters who stood behind them forcing them on. Instead of the French *travailleur* firing at the German *arbeiter,* and vice versa, let them each turn one hundred eighty degrees and aim their muzzles at their own bourgeoisie. Thus the war between nations would bcome a revolutionary class war, speeding the revolutionary process.

Lenin's Marxist bias would not permit him to detect a principal lesson to be derived from the experience of proletarian internationalism in World War I, namely: that the proletariat was not very international-minded, but was indeed a hotbed of nationalism. The prevalence of "social chauvinists" in the working class movement was interpreted by Lenin not as a reflection of working class prejudice, but as a result of false and treacherous leadership. The proletariat remained, in Lenin's professed views, as potentially internationally-oriented as ever Marx had said it was, the experience of Zimmerwald notwithstanding.

Although in this episode, Lenin comes off well as an internationalist compared to the majority of his Socialist contemporaries, the existence and persistence of a strong nationalistic strain in Lenin and his fellow Russian revolutionaries was nevertheless to be detected.[3] Of all the socialists, the Russians were the most isolationist. Their interest, however stated, was in revolution *in Russia.* Even in exile, they tended, for whatever reasons, to stay within their own circles. Lenin's unfamiliarity with the general revolutionary scene outside Russia, even when he was abroad, has not gone unnoted. Lurking in the background, and not always very distantly, was the Russian-Lenin-held bias that Russian revolutionaries were the "best" revolutionaries. It is only a very slight overstatement, if any, that Lenin's interest in the revolution elsewhere —in the "countries of the highest development of capitalism," where Marx had said the revolution was to break out—was predicated on his fierce desire to have the revolution spread from there to Russia.

But the revolution did not break out in one of the countries of the highest development of capitalism, but in Russia. Nor, having broken out in Russia, did it spread to more developed countries. (They were not yet "ready," explained the Bolsheviks.) Nor did, as Lenin and the Bolsheviks feared would happen, the most highly developed countries intervene to crush the revolution in Russia.

Lenin, now having achieved power, would endure almost any ideological sacrifice, rather than surrender it. The Western Powers and Japan, had they been willing to make the necessary commitment, could

[3] Lenin's reluctance in the prerevolutionary period to appeal to national interests in Russia for support of revolution is usually cited as an example of his international large-unit-mindedness. It is also likely, however, that Lenin, who had strong Russian identification, rejected appeals to national sentiments, which might lead to the dismemberment of Russia, for nationalist as well as for internationalist reasons, i.e., as a Russian, he wanted Russia kept together.

have overthrown the Bolshevik regime, but they had not done it yet. It was of the first urgency to see that they did not, for it was argued, if the revolution in Russia failed, who knew when the great proletarian cause would have another such opportunity? In this way it became the primary responsibility of all partisans of revolution throughout the world to see that the Revolution remained in power in the country in which it had originated, even at the expense of downgrading the revolutionary priority in all other lands. Thus was born the concept of "socialism in a single country," spawned, by necessity, in the brain of Lenin and institutionalized by Stalin.

But "socialism in a single country" did not replace internationalism, which was too deeply interwoven into Marxism, and still too useful, to be discarded. Rather, "socialism in a single country" was placed *beside* internationalism in a form-and-content relationship, with the latter providing the form and the former the content.

The operating principle for Soviet communism in the international arena came to be that, by definition, what was good for the Soviet Union, i.e. bolshevism (i.e., Stalin), was good for the international movement. Soviet interests had to be paramount, for it was the Bolshevik position that the continued existence of the Soviet state was a precondition for the development of revolution elsewhere. The interests of the Soviet state and thus those of its Party came first. By Congress II of the Comintern, meeting in mid-July of 1920, the chief concern for the Soviet Party was no longer the spread of revolution to Europe and the East, but the control of the Comintern apparatus by the Soviet Party. Soviet experience became the model for all revolutionary development. If there was conflict between Soviet requirements, interests, experiences and those of other countries, the Soviet position always had to receive first consideration.

The disciples of Moscow in the Comintern became adept at the techniques of equating the welfare of the international movement with that of the Soviet Union. Yet many intimates of the Comintern already saw that, whatever the arguments, this was in fact Russian nationalism in practice. Throughout the 1920s, but particularly in the early and late years of that decade, intimates of the Comintern departed or were driven from that organization—for a variety of reasons, prominent among which was opposition to Soviet domination and its insistence upon the the international institutionalization of Soviet Russian experience.

This Russian chauvinism in international Communist clothing doubtlessly was evident to a good many more Party members than those who actually departed the movement, but a wide variety of factors, then and later, were to keep them tied to the Moscow leadership. These considerations included Russian money and, especially in the 1930s, Russian coercion, but even more determining were the multiple implications of the *authority* of the Russian Party, the first *and only* Party to have had a successful revolution. United with such a Party there was hope for the success of your own Party. Outside the movement headed by the Soviet Party, one was deprived of the aura of the latter's success as well as the hope that that success engendered.

While the movement had indeed been captured by Russian nationalism, frank pretensions of that nationalism were studiously avoided. With the advent of Hitler, however, the Soviet regime became openly nationalistic, although still attempting to maintain its internationalist credentials. Whereas in the preceeding decade there may have been a difference between the emphasis of Soviet foreign policy and Comintern policy, though the general intent of both were identical, now both worked overtly to protect the newly rediscovered *rodina,* Mother Russia, against the anticipated Fascist onslaught. The nationalistic trappings of Tsarist Russia were rescued from oblivion and unveiled as the symbols of Communist Russia, as well. One by one, or in entire groups, the previously despised and disestablished heroes of Russian history, Alexander Nevsky, Ivan Grozny, Peter the Great, Suvorov, Kutuzov and so on—all the defenders of the Holy Russian soil—were rehabilitated. The nationalism of the 1934 Soviet leadership outdid that of the general populace. As the danger increased, all the nationalistic stops were pulled out.[4]

Now, in the face of the Hitlerian threat more so than ever, divergence in the international movement had to be guarded against. Any suggestions of differences, no matter how slight, were suspect. Soviet leadership, which, by this time meant Stalin, or very nearly so, acted upon the conviction that even the least shadow of doubt reflected potential active hostility, and therefore had to be ruthlessly removed internationally, as well as domestically, by enforced standards of absolute "orthodoxy." If there existed the possibility that a foreign Party might question the sagacity of Moscow, then that Party had to be supressed, as was done to the Polish Party in the late 1930s, for example, for the sake of Soviet security. Whatever the situation, regardless of the cost to the international movement, what was regarded as the Soviet interest

[4] Earlier, use had been made of the strong Russian love of country, as in mobilizing opposition to the Polish advance of 1920. But this was by no means analagous to the multifaceted appeal to nationalism which came in the mid-1930s.

had priority over even the life and death of all other Communist movements.

Throughout the late 1930s and certainly during World War II, Soviet foreign policy was determined by what was conceived of in Moscow as Russian national interest. In the Far East, as in the West, it was the maintenance of the territorial integrity of Russia that dominated the thinking and motivated the actions of Soviet leaders. If it would serve Russian interests, the Soviets would even sign a treaty with their Nazi archfoes—and live up to it, meticulously—because they believed it would fulfill their purposes. If it would serve Russian interests, hastening the Second Front, even that apotheosis of the international movement, the Comintern would be shut down—as was done in 1943.

Yet, given the nature of fascism and the threat it spelled not only to Communists and liberals but to non–Nazi mankind in general and given that for a considerable length of time the Soviet state comprised the principal opposition to that fascism, the overt turning to nationalism in Russia did not more than casually offend the partisans of the movement throughout the world. Indeed, the strong antifascist position of the Soviet Union contrasted to the flirtations with Hitler on the part of the British and French, served to augment the movement's ranks and to deepen the commitment of its devotees. And while the August, 1939, pact with Germany did result in defections, the June, 1941, German assault upon Russia, engaging the latter in the antifascist battle once again, caused the twenty-two month aberration largely to be forgotten.

The rise of fascism in Germany extended the period that Russian nationalism could hide behind the skirts of Communist internationalism for the Soviets, while defending themselves, seemed to be fighting the battle of free men everywhere. It had been possible to solicit support of the USSR on an even wider-ranging appeal than that of defending the Revolution. With the destruction of fascism, however, the acceptable excuse for exclusive Russian self-serving which fascism had provided came to an end. Moreover, even before the final destruction of Hitler and his Third Reich, Moscow's claim to support and preeminence based upon her Communist uniqueness was on its way to being rendered obsolete.

All over Eastern Europe, Communist states were in the process of coming into being. The emergence of a multiplicity of Communist states, dominated by a Soviet Union oblivious to national interests other than her own, but each of which having its own interests and its own well-rooted pre-Communist history, destined sooner or later to come to the fore, meant that at the very moment of its great victory and prestige, the seeds of the destruction of the monolith which Moscow had assembled were being sown. With the addition to the Soviet Union as the only Communist state of a number of other Communist states, the Stalinist version of proletarian internationalism was fated to come to an end. For a generation, the prestige and power—the *authority*—of the one Communist state and its Party, the relative weakness of other Parties, Soviet leadership in the struggle against fascism, all of these had aided in disguising Soviet intent and in maintaining the myth of Soviet internationalism. But the unmasking was soon to occur.

At first, the new Communist states were, without exception, of no mind to question the leading role of the USSR. The USSR, if it had lost its unique place in the Communist world still remained in every respect, the first Communist country. It had had *the* Revolution. It had overcome the Hitler beast. It had provided sustenance and "guidance" for the new Communist leaders in power in Eastern Europe during the time of their exile. It had put them in power—and it alone, those leaders felt, could keep them in power in their exhausted, war-ravaged lands. And in those countries where communism had not taken over, Communist party leaders profited in prestige and finances from their ties with Moscow. But in power or out of power, who could stand before the horns of Moscow's blazing sun?

One who could and did was Tito of Yugoslavia. The Yugoslav leader had been on the Moscow line all of his adult life. The primacy of Moscow in the Communist world was a simple matter of fact to him and his retinue. Yet when Stalin "advised" the Yugoslav Communists not to make a move for power on their own in 1943, his words were disregarded. Whether conceptualized as such by Tito or not, he was, at this early date, putting the interest of *his* group, *his* Communist Party, and *his* judgement above that of the Soviet Party and of Stalin. Later, after power had been gained, Tito and his followers objected to Stalin's insistence that the Red Army had liberated Yugoslavia, as though the heroic and effective guerrilla efforts of Tito's followers had not taken place or had been of no avail. They objected to the suspicion with which they were treated, to the infiltration of their institutions by Russians, to selling to the Soviet Union at depressed wholesale prices, and buying from the Soviet Union at inflated retail prices. They objected to the Russians' assertion that they knew best what was good for Yugoslavia and its Party. They objected to Russian interests being placed before Yugoslav interests.

Nevertheless, the Communists of Yugoslavia led by Tito did not want the break with the Soviet Union which came in June, 1948. They did not think it could occur and they were dismayed by it when it did occur. To be physically wrenched from Moscow's womb was unthinkable, but it was likewise intolerable to continue to submit to Moscow's demands and insults. Yugoslav Party and national interests, important to Tito in seizing and maintaining power, would not permit it.

The dilemma was solved by Stalin's initiating the break. But the break having once occurred was not repeated elsewhere, at least not at once. The Yugoslav situation was unique: Tito and company had not spent the war years in Moscow and had not been propelled into power by Soviet tanks and planes. The aura of Stalin's position was still such as to preclude further defections. The Yugoslav Party had not sought its independence; its leaders were not prepared to go it alone, much less the leaders of other Parties in power. However, the purge of "Titoists" that took place throughout the satellite world indicated that national opposition to Stalin did exist—or at least Stalin feared that it did and was ruthlessly determined to root it out wherever it did or *might* exist.

The excommunication of the Yugoslav state and Party from the Communist world, shocking though it may have been, was hardly seen at the time as being a model for events elsewhere. The monolith of communism, with the Titoist carbuncle excised and the wound cauterized was thought to be as robust as ever. Indeed, the induction of the People's Republic of China into the camp in 1949 was seen as added proof of its strength and virility. It was only a decade and more later that the debilitating influences of China's presence in the camp began to be significantly recognized. In 1949, there was scarcely any tendency to see China as presenting a threat to the solidarity of the movement —in that most of the leadership of the Chinese Communist Party had admittedly come to communism through nationalism; in that, in developing Maoism, Mao had fundamentally altered Marxism and Leninism; in that in 1950 Stalin had dealt very parsimoniously in negotiating with Mao in Moscow, and so forth. Subsequently, additional instances of pre-1950 Russian–Chinese differences become known. It is doubtful that, even if widely known, they would have altered Communist and non-Communist opinion regarding bloc solidarity. Generally, the facts were there for all to see, but the vision of the unshakeable monolith was as strongly held outside the Soviet world as inside it. The Yugoslav case was treated as an aberration and its implications and those of a China seeking to recapture the glories of its ancient past, to obliterate and avenge the memories of its more recent humiliating international experiences, were all but disregarded. The sweeping iceberg of Communist power with the "genial" Stalin riding on its peak transfixed the popular gaze, East and West.

But then Stalin was dead.

The Soviet world, from the perspective of a later decade, needed change, from the point of view of its effective operations, for at least the last five years of Stalin's life. But Stalin, full of years and satisfied with the perfection he had wrought, was, in most respects, determined to keep the machine as it was. Let no one upset the "red" apple cart. Yet, it seems that even Stalin in the last months of his life became aware of the need to make decisions requiring change that was repugnant to him. It may even be suggested that "the purges of 1953" for which Stalin was laying the groundwork at his death, were in some manner connected with the new conditions with which he had to deal.

In any event, by 1953, economic difficulties were troubling the Soviet Union and her satellites alike. Planning was becoming increasingly complex, and thereby difficult to manipulate satisfactorily; Stalinist techniques adopted for the earlier stages of development were no longer suited to solve the problems of a higher level; industrial growth was slowing down; productivity was not improving sufficiently. Some workers were grumbling—and sometimes striking—particularly in the satellites. In the latter case, the cause of unhappiness could be attributed to native Communist leadership and to the USSR, both of which had been exploiting the Eastern European countries for their own advantage.

To some of Stalin's successors it was already, or soon to become, obvious that changes were going to have to be effected in the area of relations with other Communist states. It was evident, too, that there was something amiss in the economy. Nothing radical, but here, as elsewhere, some tinkering was called for to improve operating efficiency. Tinkering was to be the quality of change, and there was to be a continuing close relationship between developments within and among the individual Communist states.

Some Soviet leaders more than others favored slight modifications of the operating practices of the system. None, however, advocated or possibly even considered extensive modifications. They were all "Stalinists," trained by Stalin and probably had survived because they thought like him. They were not—except by inheritance—revolutionaries or even reformers.

The same was true of the subalterns in command in the satellites. They too were aware of problems. But with few exceptions none sought changes that could even be so extravagantly described as moderate. These men were the products of the Soviet system and its shapers in their own countries. More independence from the USSR might have some advantages, but it was not to be expected and in most instances was not even desired. They continued to require Soviet support to hold on to their thrones.

To the evidence of problems and the reaction to them, one more ingredient must now be added to understand the change that developed in the Communist world in the post-Stalin period, leading to the decentralization of that world and to the new communisms, namely: the struggle for succession taking place within the USSR—which ultimately was going to have an unstabilizing effect.

In much the same way as the scions of Genghis Khan withdrew from Europe into Mongolia to select their father's successor, the Soviet leaders became preoccupied with their own domestic rites of succession. Within the USSR this meant at first collective concern for the "unity" of the Soviet citizenry. While the new leaders themselves had, in a sense, been victimized by Stalin, they had also been the victimizers of the masses. They recalled the bloody aftermath of collectivization and the massive defections that followed the German invasion. Their own lines against the masses had first to be secured: by making concessions, economic ones, if need be. But having made these and discovering that the lid did not blow off—at least immediately—they proceeded to embark upon the sometimes bloody business of determining which of the chief's sons was to succeed to their father's estates. (There is no need here to discuss why in the Soviet contest only one could win rather than several cooperatively.) It was necessary for the competitors to gain support. How? Again, by concessions. Why? Because in such a desperate struggle, aid must be secured from any and all quarters lest it be enlisted by the opposition.

Previously, both Lenin and Stalin had on many occasions made "concessions" under demand; although those of the latter, as he grew older and more sure of his control, fitted almost exclusively into the illusory category. The system had operated on the basis of taking as much from the worker and peasant—and satellite—as possible, and giving back as little as possible. Upon the basis of this system, Soviet power had been founded, maintained and extended. The Soviet Union had grown strong and great. There was little inclination on the part even of a competing Soviet leadership to alter the formula. Whatever the imediate problems and objectives, the primacy of the Soviet Party—centralized control—had to be maintained. A few changes here, a few there, eliminating obstacles to economic progress, raising the public morale, gaining support for the system and for certain leaders. But no more than this, certainly no wholesale revisions of theory and state–individual, not to mention Soviet–satellite, relationships were contemplated.

But they were to occur. Those followers of Stalin—and Pobedonostsev before him—who argued that any change could only lead to increasing and perhaps unlimitable, if not uncontrolled, change, were probably, on the whole, correct where unstable situations prevailed. But to a large degree this begged the issue, for what were the consequences of *withstanding* the changes that grew out of irreversible productive and social developments? Had Stalin lived another decade or had Molotov won out in 1957 instead of Khrushchev, would the estate of international communism be different from what it is today? Perhaps the bourgeoisation (although Stalin was hardly against most bourgeois values) and disintegration of the Communist world could have been prevented through the continued imposition and use of Stalinist means and norms—but at what costs? Perhaps the continuation of the unrelenting Stalinist greyness would have led to even more violent and widespread explosion than did occur in Poland and Hungary in 1956, and still more rapid and extensive changes than have taken place. We will never know. What does seem likely is that, given the stages of Soviet and Eastern European industrialization and urbanization, given the fact that the recollections of the recent World War were occupying a smaller and smaller role in the world's consciousness, given the spread and revivification of nationalistic values—given these it is unlikely that any solution other than that which seems to be developing in the Communist world could have *in the long run* occurred.

Change in Russia in the mid-1950s became more of a political issue than any of the contestants for power would probably have preferred. It is likely that Khrushchev stumbled into using "change" as a vehicle to power. In 1954, he sided with those who opposed Malenkov's advocacy of change. He became its champion only after Malenkov had been removed as Chairman of the Sovmin and Khrushchev had discovered that there was support to be gained from "progressive" measures. This is not to argue that Khrushchev's heart was not in the measures he advocated; it probably was, but he came to the advocacy of change primarily out of political motivation rather than a reformist spirit.

In comprehending the changes which occurred in post-Stalinist Russia and its relations with other Parties and Communist states in power, and in grasping Khrushchev's role in those changes, it is necessary to take into consideration his outlook and style of operation. Khrushchev was an *ad hoc* problem solver. He had no disposition to view the total context from a Kremlinean Olympus, himself remaining aloof from the scene of battle. Khrushchev opted for personal involvement. If something was wrong Khrushchev sought to deal with it personally, on the spot. To a large degree he tended to deal with problems, domestic or foreign, one at a time, often with little consideration of what the "ultimate implications" of the solution might be. Moreover, Khrushchev, in his congenital optimism, seemingly believed in a kind of "hand of God" context, fitting all the pieces together, that this could only lead to a strengthening of Soviet life, the augmentation of the international Communist movement and the spread of communism throughout the world.

In inter-Communist state relations Khrushchev, aware of the need for tinkering and for personal image building, traveled to Peking in 1954, participated in ameliorating the harsh terms set by Stalin four years earlier and placed relations between Russia and China on an "equal footing." The following year, again offering a contrast to the stay-in-the-Kremlin Stalin who had his vassals come to him, Khrushchev traveled to Belgrad to attempt to do what Stalin, with all his threats and scheming, had not been able to accomplish: bring Yugoslavia back into the bloc. Khrushchev placed all the blame for the Soviet-Yugoslav rift on Stalin's minions—not yet on Stalin himself—conceded the existence of multiple paths to communism, and thus opened the way to 1956.

To Khrushchev the radical nature of his concessions was probably, at best, only vaguely apparent. He saw himself as only recognizing the facts of the situation. He wanted the Yugoslavs back in the bloc. He needed such a coup to augment his shaky hold as First Secretary. In truth, it was evident that there was more than one path to power. It was he who wanted something, the Yugoslavs being dubious; therefore, it was he who had to make the concession. And for Khrushchev, this seemed little enough to offer, since he remained convinced of the unassailability of Moscow's over-all position. He was, in fact, giving up very little that seemed important to him, though for another man the abandonment of claims of Muscovite preeminence in this area might have been far more difficult.

There can be no doubt that there is a lineal connection between the confession of multiple paths to power in 1955 and the collapse of empire in 1956. But, it must be cautioned, the latter did not grow out of the former: the former is only a milestone along the way.

There are in the period from 1953–1956 many harbingers of change in the Communist world. In some areas, in some countries, demands for change and change were greater than in others. But with few exceptions movement was slow, the waking of a giant from a deep sleep—until February, 1956, Khrushchev's "Secret Speech," the breaking of the flood walls.

Again, the *direction* in which the Communist world seems headed was probably little affected by 1956, except to make even a temporary return to the past more difficult. But the tempo at which that world moved and the manner of its transition were profoundly affected by what Khrushchev had to say to the closed meeting of Party Congress XX (PC XX) on Washington's Birthday, 1956.

All of the circumstances surrounding Khrushchev's decision to make that "Secret Speech" are not known, and probably never will be. But indications strongly point to Khrushchev's having made the speech almost entirely for domestic purposes, to weaken the opposition by attacking the dead leader with whom they were most closely identified: destroy the Stalinists by destroying Stalin. It is impossible to think that Khrushchev or the others agreeing with his tactic foresaw the ancillary consequences for the international movement which the speech and the release of information which followed in its wake would have. To the extent that they were concerned at all, in the turmoil of the decision to make the speech, with the negative effects that the revelations would have on Communist Parties and countries abroad, they probably concluded that, come what may, they could handle the situation.

And, indeed, as the immediate situation developed, they could for the time being everywhere except in two countries: Poland and Hungary. There, the revelations of Stalin's stupidities and barbarities, the subsequent mounting indications of the implications of local leaders in these, the general dissolution of Soviet authority (who could believe anything they said if their great constantly extolled leader was now revealed to have been a bloody, illiterate paranoic?)—all these served to accelerate the leavening of change that had previously set in. Hitherto suppressed hatreds and frustrations were released and given force. In some cases adulation soured into disenchantment and then resentment. Revolutionary and national traditions, already reemerging, were avidly embraced. In both countries Communist leadership relatively untainted by Stalinist contacts was available. Even so, numerous and multilateral stupidities and the repeated intervention of coincidence were necessary to terminate in the Polish October and the Hungarian November.

From February, 1956, on the pace of change would be greatly

accelerated in the Communist world. One development would lead to another sometimes in dizzying succession. Although only Poland was driven to the brink of revolution, and Hungary to actual revolution, Soviet and indeed Communist credibility was thrown into doubt among Communists everywhere by the "Secret Speech."

Even so, there might have been a far more manipulable reaction had it not been for the Polish and, in particular, the Hungarian developments. The intervention of Soviet forces in Hungary and the strong suppression of resistance there led to a greatly augmented crisis throughout the Communist world. Soviet authority was so far compromised that the Chinese had to be engaged in order to help stabilize it. This the Chinese did in late 1956 and in 1957. But in return for having pulled Moscow's chestnuts out of the fire and helping to restore at least the facade of unity to the international Communist movement, the Chinese anticipated that the USSR would provide world revolutionary leadership. The Chinese themselves aspired to be first, and 1956–1957 gave them the opportunity to experience a growing strength of position within the movement. They still recognized the primacy of Moscow's position, enhanced as it became in the course of 1957, by the successful launching of Sputnik I. The Chinese were for the time being content to follow Moscow, but they sought to determine the direction in which Moscow was to travel. When it became clear that the Soviets were as ever, Russian nationalists, first, with a low revolutionary priority and unprepared, in practice, to assist the Chinese in achieving even junior nuclear partnership, the Chinese began to vent their pique. In the resulting struggle between the two giants of the Communist world, the other Communist powers began to rearrange themselves—internally and in their relations with the rest of the world, Communist and non-Communist.

In part such a development was the effect of the passage of time eroding the unnatural situation which had been imposed after World War II, whereby Russian interests were able to submerge all other national interests. But certainly the continued Moscow–Peking vendetta gave those who wanted it, or came to realize they wanted it, or those who were forced to accept it, much more maneuverability than they might otherwise have had. Within certain limits, more confining for some Communist states than others, each country was increasingly afforded the opportunity to pursue communism in its own way. And in those countries where communism had not taken power, virtually each Communist could decide what kind of communism he would pursue: Russian, Chinese, a native, or even a personal blend.

The monolith of communism had come apart. It was probably

inevitable that this should have happened, but it need not have occurred in the manner nor with the speed that it did.

In retrospect, we realize that the Communist world never was so monolithic as it appeared to be; but it is not at all now. There is no single Communist ideology accepted and observed in fact by all or even nearly all Communists. What exists today is the world of *communisms*—and it is that world that this book is about.

1

The Socialist World System in Search of a Theory

Jan F. Triska

IS THERE A Communist-produced set of ideas linking the several units of the Communist world which may be called a theory? In a 1963 paper we said there was no such theory.[1] Were we wrong? Has anything happened to make us change our mind?

A *theory* may be defined as a generalization asserting that two or more things—activities, situations or events—co-vary under specified conditions[2]; its acceptance depends on its precision and verifiability. Well-confirmed, a theory is called a *law;* not yet confirmed, a *hypothesis;* while the formulation of *concepts* and their linkage into frameworks—just as the construction of *paradigms* or patterns of mutually related questions, propositions and variables—is an analytical exercise which, while useful, may or may not lead to the building of coherent, formal theories.

To start with, the Communists have not made claims to possessing a theory linking the several units of the Communist movement together. The closest they come to describing the mental underpinning of the world Communist system is when they talk of *classical proletarian internationalism,* a set of "principles" which dates back to the "Communist Manifesto" and the Marxian programatic postulate "Workers of the world, unite."[3]

[1] Jan F. Triska, with David O. Beim and Noralou Roos, *The World Communist System* (Stanford: Stanford Studies of the Communist System, 1963), p. 2.

[2] David Easton, *A Systems Analysis of Political Life* (New York: Wiley, 1965), p. 7.

[3] "When a Marxist speaks of proletarian internationalism, the first thing that comes to his mind is the militant revolutionary appeal advanced by Marx and Engels: 'Workers of the world, unite.'" A. K. Azizian, "Proletarskii interna-

Setting aside for the moment the several definitions—which are more stochastic, normative, and hortatory than definitional (such as "proletarian internationalism is the ideology and policy of the brotherhood and friendship of the whole working class"), proletarian internationalism, "the antithesis of bourgeois, capitalistic nationalism," is a mental construct of considerable historical significance. Nationalism had no place in Marx's scale of values: the emancipation of labor was a social, rather than a local or national, problem which embraced all advanced countries. Nationalism was irrelevant to the proletariat's common interests and objectives, which were above any limits imposed by nationalism.

Marx's theory, international in character and purpose, drew on the elements of national experience which it perceived as universal and historically repetitive. It postulated an international or nationless world, but it was not concerned with the in-between developmental stage—the period of transition from the nation to the non-national level.

As a consequence, before the Bolshevik Revolution, Lenin's proletarians had no homeland. Their class enemy was international; ergo, the conditions for their liberation were international:

> Petty bourgeois nationalism proclaims as internationalism the bare recognition of the equality of nations, and nothing more, while (quite apart from the fact that this recognition is purely verbal) preserving national egoism intact; whereas proletarian internationalism demands firstly that the interests of the proletarian struggle in one country be subordinated to the interests of the struggle on a world-wide basis, and secondly that a nation which has achieved victory over the bourgeoisie be able and willing to make the greatest national sacrifice for the sake of the overthrowing of international capital.[4]

In this period only the class solidarity of the proletariat in several countries could express proletarian internationalism, the progress in uniting workers of all countries under the banner of the "Communist Manifesto."

Socialism in a Single Country

After the Bolshevik Revolution the "toilers" had a homeland. But now, as Lenin put it, "the most important thing, both for us and from

---

tionalizm," *Znanie* (Moscow: 1957), p. 98. See also Evgenii L. Korovin, "Proletarskii internatsionalizm i mezhdunarodnoe pravo," *Sovetskii ezhegodnik mezhdunarodnogo prava* (Moscow: 1958), p. 51.

[4] V. I. Lenin, *Sochineniia* (Moscow), 4th ed., vol. XXXI, p. 126, cited by T. Timofeyev, "Certain Aspects of Proletarian Internationalism," *International Affairs* (Moscow), no. 5, May, 1957, p. 46.

the point of view of international socialism, is the *preservation* of Soviet Russia."[5]

Stalin completed the hiatus: "An internationalist is he," he stated, "who unreservedly and without hesitation and without conditions is prepared to defend the USSR because the USSR is the base of the world revolutionary movement, and to defend and to advance this movement without defending the USSR is impossible."[6]

Ending with "the emergence of socialism from the confines of one country," the Soviet stage of development witnessed the testing of proletarian internationalism both horizontally and vertically: *Abroad,* the world movement of workers supported the first Communist Party-state and in turn "the toilers of the USSR supported the latter movement."[7] (This double link was elaborated in a study published by the Soviet Academy of Sciences in 1952: It was the "sacred duty" and "international" obligation of the victorious Soviet proletariat to assist toilers abroad, just as the foreign toilers were obliged to support the USSR. This mutuality of interest and support was coupled with the duties of Communists everywhere to educate the masses in this period in the spirit of proletarian internationalism *as well as* in the spirit of devotion and love to the USSR. One could not exist without the other—not for long, anyway.[8]) *In the USSR,* proletarian internationalism was employed as "a national policy" vis-à-vis nationalities and minorities among and within the Union Republics. The Soviet Union was the first political system—Soviet theorists maintain—to demonstrate empirically the possibilities of developing the model and setting the pattern for the future. An ideal proving ground, it fulfilled its historical mission by bringing to its nationality and minority groups all the fruits and advantages of unity and solidarity on the basis of equality and self-determination. The Soviet pattern was thus "bound" to become a model of international and intergroup cooperation for the post-World War II community of Communist Party-states.[9]

The short-lived Hungarian Soviet Republic of 1919 and the abor-

[5] Lenin, *ibid.,* vol. XXVI, p. 410 (emphasis added).

[6] J. V. Stalin, *Sochineniia* (Moscow), vol. X, p. 51.

[7] I. Potelov, "Razvitie sotsializma i proletarskii internatsionalizm," *Kommunist* (Moscow), no. 1, Jan., 1957, p. 18.

[8] N. P. Vassil'iev, and F. R. Khrustov, eds., *O Sovetskom patriotizme* (Moscow, 1952), p. 142, cited by Wladyslaw W. Kulski, *Peaceful Coexistence* (Chicago: Regnery, 1959) pp. 34–35.

[9] G. I. Tunkin, "Socialist Internationalism and International Law," *New Times* (Moscow), Oct.–Dec., 1957, p. 5. See also his "Novyi tip mezhdunarodnykh otnoshenii i mezhdunarodnoe pravo," *Sovetskoe gosudarstvo i pravo* (Moscow), no. 1, 1959, pp. 81–94.

tive Bavarian Communist takeovers of the same year provided little opportunity for the Soviet government to indulge in Socialist international relations. While a somewhat greater scope for the testing of proletarian internationalism was furnished in relations between Soviet Russia and Outer Mongolia and the Soviet districts in China, it was only after and since World War II that proletarian internationalism could be tested among several Communist Party-states, and between them and the nonruling Communist Parties.

Socialism Emerges from a Single Country

"Socialism in a single country" was Lenin and Stalin's conceptual merger of Marx and Engels with the Soviet state: exclusively Soviet interests were equated with the interests of the Communist movement, and the world revolution was subordinated to the first national Communist revolution. The Soviet Communist Party, by becoming a ruling Party in Russia, came to rule the movement. The primary allegiance of the foreign proletariat was no longer to world revolution but to the USSR. But with World War II, socialism indeed "emerged from the confines of one country" to embrace the several states in Eastern Europe. Socialism was exported there from the USSR as Stalin had predicted. To Stalin, however, the new Soviet allies were not allies —but rather satellites orbiting around the Soviet sun: created by the Soviet Union, they existed to serve it; their sole purpose was to strengthen further the first Socialist country. Under the "socialism in a single country" prescription and assumption, it was a legitimate process to subsume the welfare of all other Communist Parties—and hence the countries to which those Parties were attached—to the welfare of the Soviet Union, as long as the USSR was the *only* socialist base and the *sole* victorious revolutionary country in the world. Now, however, the Soviet Communist Party was merely one of *several* ruling Parties. To be sure, the Soviet Party was the *first* victorious Party; it was the Party of Lenin and the cradle of ruling Communism in the world, and it was the ruling Party of a very *powerful* state. But that was all. The old "socialism in a single country" concept, which would have authorized untrammelled interference into domestic affairs as well as sustained disrespect for the independence and integrity of the new Communist Party-states, was no longer acceptable—precisely because the several Communist Parties became, just as the Soviet Communist Party had become thirty years previously, ruling Parties. "Socialism in a single country" was based on the unique existence of one ruling Communist

Party in the world. With the disappearance of the premise, the concept collapsed. Stalin refused to recognize that the old organizational pattern was no longer workable. Nevertheless, new patterns had to be forged if the catastrophe of many Yugoslavias was to be averted.

As long as Stalin was alive, the alternatives available to the new ruling Parties were limited: either they conformed or, like Tito, they were expelled. Had Khrushchev not condemned Stalin as clearly as he did in 1956, the Soviet abiilty to impose its own rule on others would not have been curtailed so rapidly or so dramatically. But the Soviet quarrel with Peking and the ensuing indiscretions of both became community property. The increasing reluctance of many ruling as well as nonruling Parties to take sides and support either of the contestants—and their ability to remain aloof—gave striking evidence of looseness and slackness of relationships among *all* Parties.

Not that this development could have been either prevented, suppressed, or even significantly retarded. But without Khrushchev's speech before Party Congress (PC) XX in Moscow in 1956, it probably could have been less dysfunctionally and more discreetly managed. Khrushchev's subsequent attempts to patch up here and there was not the kind of substantive overhaul of the organizational machinery that was needed.

To sustain development and growth, large-scale political organizations must keep adapting their theoretical foundation as well as their functional and operational mechanism to the new demands, responsibilities, opportunities and challenges imposed by their very development and growth. In particular, they must constantly relate their *modus operandi* to the increasing ratio of responsibilty, influence, and power which their development entails. Failure to do so, whatever the reason, is bound to lead to a series of reversals which, increasing in significance with time, result in a general slowdown, followed by serious breakdowns in the organizational structures which the frantically squeezed controlling valves barely manage to check. By then, not only further development but the actual existence of the organization is dangerously threatened. Continuous accommodation and checking of new stresses as they recur within as well as without the organization is an enormous but imperative task. The process of disintegration, which in the past reduced and ultimately destroyed all large political organizations in the world without a single exception, has a tendency to sneak in through the back door of stagnation, and frantic insistence on preserving the status quo becomes incompatible with the very dynamism and vitality on which large-scale political organizations depend for their life.

In 1918, the Russian Soviet Federated Socialist Republic (RSFSR) was a highly centralized body politic, the government of which was the culmination of a hierarchy of soviets—central, territorial, regional, area, district—and Party. In 1923, the now-expanded RSFSR became the equally centralized Union of Soviet Socialist Republics, then composed of the original RSFSR and the Ukrainian, Belorussian and Transcaucasian SSRs. In 1936, the USSR consisted of 11 Union Republics (the RSFSR, the Ukrainian, the Belorussian, the Uzbek, the Kazakh, the Turkmen, the Tadjik, the Georgian, the Azerbaijanian, the Armenian, and the Kirghiz SSRs). In 1940, the former Baltic states of Estonia, Latvia and Lithuania became new Soviet Socialist Republics, and, with the acquisition of Bessarabia and Western Bukovina from Romania, the Moldavian Soviet Socialist Republic was created. The Karelo-Finnish SSR "joined" the ranks of the Soviet Union Republics after the Soviet "victory" over Finland in 1940, which increased the number of Union Republics to 16. (The latter, however, was dissolved in 1955.) The Carpatho-Ukraine (formerly part of Czechoslovakia), the Kuriles and Southern Sakhalin (formerly part of Japan), Tanna Tuva, and West Prussia and Königsberg became parts of the USSR after World War II. Soviet growth by armed osmosis continued with the acquisition by Stalin of the eight European (Poland, East Germany, Czechoslavakia, Albania, Bulgaria, Hungary, Romania, and Yugoslavia) and three Far Eastern (Communist China, North Korea, and North Vietnam—Outer Mongolia was an earlier acquisition) satellites. Soviet control grew from one political unit in 1918, to 4 in 1923, to 11 in 1936, to 16 in 1940, to 26 "sovereign states" (16 Union Republics and 11 satellite states [minus Yugoslavia]) after Stalin's death. Within this multinational complex, the Soviet Autonomous Republics became, by definition, "the highest form of political organization attainable by ethnic groups" and "states"; the Union Republics, above them, were "the fruition of statehood for the Soviet nationalities" and, after 1944, "sovereign states" with their own foreign relations and military organizations; and the satellite states, *above them,* were "people's democracies," or even, later, "Socialist states" (Czechoslovakia, Outer Mongolia, Yugoslavia and Rumania), formally separate and "completely independent" from the USSR. The relatively rapid increase in Soviet control, if only because of its extent, was bound to lead to some relaxation of the rigid pattern of centralization insisted upon by Lenin and Stalin. As a matter of fact, denial of autonomy, both at home and in the satellite states, became in time incompatible with the post-Stalin political organization. The formal but not effective homage paid by Stalin to decentralization in 1936 and 1944 was far outmatched by the decentralization scheme effected by Khrushchev in 1957 and 1958 in the USSR and by his statements on behalf of "complete equality"—political, social, economic, and ideological—of all "Socialist states" at PC XXI in 1959.

Soviet organizational development brought about demands for significant operational changes in the international Party relations. Continued insistence upon centralization became unthinkable—it would have brought instant and probably final dissolution of the Communist alliance. "Autonomy," "equality," "sovereignty," and "commonwealth of Socialist nations" became the catchwords employed with great emphasis and frequency from Prague to Pyenyang—in territorial *as well as* in organization terms.

Under Stalin, the Soviet body politic had not only achieved its maximum effective organizational level but, as suggested by the evidence, had already surpassed it. Stalin's success was also his failure: the Soviet organization was beginning to move beyond its own saturation point, where this large-scale political organization ceased to be controllable, with the given safeguard mechanisms now operating within a framework no longer adequate for their purposes. While control, enforcement, and conditioning devices might *eventually* become available to sustain a Stalinist-type regime capable of controlling as much as one-third of humanity living on one-fourth of the world's available space, under the given circumstances the Soviet bite was far too big. Modern science and technology have as yet been unable to supply adequate controls to permit the sustained continuity, let alone further growth, of the large-scale Soviet political organization without far-searching and fundamental revision of the assumptions and premises upon which it was built as well as the complete modernization of its machinery.

The problem then became—and remains—how to construct a rational organization which would produce a minimum of undesirable side effects but bring a maximum of satisfaction compatible with the aims of the organizers.

It is to be noted that the great success of the Soviet organizational system in its charismatic phase eventually came near to destroying the organization. The successful "socialism in a single country" thesis, brought about the organizationally costly antithesis of Yugoslavia-Poland-Hungary-China-Albania-and-Rumania. The synthesis could be either a collective break into fourteen hostile Yugoslavias, Albanias, Chinas or worse—undoubtedly much worse, once the process of disintegration was really rolling—or, hopefully, by means of skillful surgery, it could be a regional organization of "Socialist" but autonomous states. This appeared to be the issue as Khrushchev saw it: faced with an adverse reality, on behalf of the organization, he started an offensive to reconstruct the organization employing the least costly means.

Socialist Internationalism

The "new type" of international relations which emerged with Khrushchev's formation of "the Commonwealth of Socialist Nations" was formulated in 1955, *after* the April Bandung Conference. Like the Bandung Conference, the "Commonwealth" was said to stand for mutual assistance and cooperation, genuine friendly relations, world peace and security for all. In particular, following the Bandung Declaration, the principles of mutual respect for territorial integrity—nonaggression, nonintervention in domestic affairs, sovereign equality, and mutual assistance—were said to link all the Communist Party-states "headed by the Soviet Union." The domestic construction of socialism in the USSR was essential for the development of the Commonwealth "because such construction involved a continuous search for theoretical principles which would guide development and bind Socialist states in true proletarian internationalism."[10] But in effect the emphasis has been on the *Communist Party-states,* not on the world movement; and on the *states,* not on the Parties. *State sovereignty* is said to be the foundation for mutual relations.

Historically, the term "proletarian internationalism" has denoted relations among all units as well as subunits of the world system; it has extended from relations among *individuals,* such as members of different Parties, to relations among the organizations of several *states,* such as the Warsaw Pact or Comecon. But under Khrushchev, a new category, "Socialist internationalism," subordinated to "proletarian internationalism," both in time and space, has emerged as the "new type" of relations pertaining exclusively to Communist Party-states.[11] To use taxonomic categories: if general international relations is the class, then proletarian international relations is the order and Socialist international relations the family—the latter two being governed by the principles of proletarian internationalism and Socialist internationalism, respectively. Thus, proletarian internationalism, which remains the guiding principle of the world Communist movement, is the principal foundation from which

[10] *Kommunist,* no. 14, Oct., 1955, pp. 4–7. See also "On the Principles of Development and Further Strengthening of Friendship and Cooperation Between the Soviet Union and Other Socialist States," *Pravda,* Oct. 31, 1956, p. 1.

[11] Korovin, *op. cit.*

evolve the subsystemic superstructure of inter-Party-state relations, known as "Socialist internationalism."[12]

But Socialist internationalism, in contradistinction to, and as result of, the lesson of the Soviet "socialism in a single country" concept, means socialism in each Communist Party-state as affected by the existence of a multiplicity of socialist countries. While constructing their own "socialisms" in their own single countries and thus following the Soviet model of "socialism in a single country," the members are also utilizing the advantages of membership in the common economic, ideological, political, cultural and military system and thus enhancing the Socialist community. The Communist Party-state system is thus *not* perceived as a mere sum total of a group of states; it is viewed as an economic, ideological, political and military community, counterposed to the capitalist system. Each Party-state, while an independent sovereign entity, is also a component part of a broader social community.[13]

The *substance* of Socialist internationalism is determined by the nature of the social system prevailing in the Communist Party-states. The liquidation of private property and of capitalists produces conditions which are presumed to be ideal for interstate economic ties and relations. The public ownership of the means of production precludes exploitation of man by man and creates conditions for the close association of different peoples with a common purpose, namely, the victory of socialism and communism in their countries, which are all members of one political, social and economic system.[14] There has resulted what is described as a "community of equal and sovereign nations marching along the path of socialism and communism."[15]

Socialist internationalism is said to express the unity of interests, expectations and hopes of the peoples of the Communist Party-states. The principal unifiers of the Communist Party-states are thus assumed to be: (1) common aims—they all struggle for socialism and communism; (2) a common enemy—they all seek to defend themselves against imperialism; (3) common interests—because of their similar political, economic, social and cultural systems, they are closer to each other than to any heterogeneous outsider; and (4) common accomplishments—to build socialism and communism, mutual assistance and cooperation among all the Comunist Party-states is imperative. Hence the Party-states are bound together by (1) the Socialist international division of

[12] Tunkin, *op. cit.*, p. 10.

[13] I. Dudinsky, "A Community of Equal and Sovereign Nations," *International Affairs* (Moscow), no. 11, Nov., 1964, p. 4.

[14] S. Sanakoyev, "Internationalism and Socialist Diplomacy," *International Affairs* (Moscow), no. 5, 1965, p. 22.

[15] *Ibid.*

labor, (2) the Socialist world market, and close (3) political, (4) cultural, and (5) military relations. In other words, the fact that these states are ruled by Communist Parties establishes basic similarities among them, creating a *presumption* of common interests and goals and therefore of military and economic interdependence. It follows that a substantial amount of sustained transactions rationally conducted among all the Party-states should mutually help them all, individually *and* collectively. The 1957 Declaration of the Twelve Communist Parties in Power, while emphasizing equality, territorial sovereignty and noninterference in the domestic affairs of individual Party-states, considers the "most striking" expression of socialist internationalism to be "fraternal mutual aid."[16]

Leonid Brezhnev, the First Secretary of the Communist Party of the Soviet Union (CPSU), in speaking at the celebration in Moscow of the forty-seventh anniversary of the Bolshevik Revolution in 1964, summarized it succinctly:

> The world Socialist system is a social, economic and political community of free and equal peoples. There is every objective condition for the cooperation between Socialist countries to grow increasingly stronger. Our peoples are united by a community of fundamental interests. (1) We have an economic foundation of the same type—the social ownership of the means of production. (2) We have similar state systems—the power of the people, headed by the working class. (3) We have a single ideology—Marxism-Leninism. (4) We have common interests in insuring security, in safeguarding the peace and security of the peoples, and in defending the revolutionary gains from encroachments of the imperialists. [And 5] We have a single great aim —communism.[17]

Proletarian internationalism, in its Socialist internationalism subsystem, has been thus adapted to the realities of "modern" international relations as they are perceived by Communist theoreticians. But, in the process, Socialist internationalism has been deprived of the most potent ingredient of proletarian internationalism. The use of the language of conventional, traditional, and even classic international relations, and, in particular, the growing insistence on state sovereignty as the only basis for mutual relations among Communist Party-states, implies not only formal equality, and nonintervention into the domestic affairs, independence and integrity of the Party-states in their mutual relations— but also signifies very important deviation from and contradiction to

[16] Dudinsky, *op. cit.,* pp. 4, 6.
[17] *The New York Times,* Nov. 7, 1964, p. 8 (translation by TASS).

the commitments of proletarian internationalism. Thus, several problems have been created.

Problems of Socialist Internationalism

The "Peaceful Coexistence" Dilemma

When under the impact of 1956 and the Hungarian Revolution Khrushchev implicitly coupled proletarian internationalism with the principles of Bandung, he had to make a strong disclaimer that proletarian internationalism had anything to do with the concept of peaceful coexistence among Socialist states. If he wanted to reform Socialist state relations on the basis of a new, particular proletarian internationalism, he could not acknowledge the applicability of simple "Peaceful Coexistence" among Socialist states. Had this been done, the concept of a dichotomous world would have been rendered meaningless:

> From the denial of the fact that the world is split into two antagonistic systems and consequently into two camps the conclusion has been deduced that Socialist states allegedly cannot make a distinction in their foreign policy between the Socialist and the bourgeois states. This is a point of view alien to proletarian internationalism; it amounts in fact to undermining the unity among the brotherly Socialist countries.[18]

Coexistence was only for countries with different social systems. "The principle of proletarian internationalism, not simple coexistence, is fundamental and determinant in relations between Socialist countries, within the Socialist system."[19] It is necessary to go beyond formal equality to a "broader, richer and deeper" concept, to proletarian internationalism, which is a lasting phenomenon: "While the principle of Peaceful Coexistence will endure for the historical period of the simultaneous existence in the international arena of two opposed systems, the principles of proletarian internationalism will endure for a longer epoch."[20]

The Party-State Dichotomy

The system concept which thus emerged was state-, rather than Party-based. After the debacle of the Cominform with its increasingly unsuccessful and therefore fewer system-wide Party meetings and com-

[18] Potelov, *op. cit.*

[19] *Ibid.;* see also Timofeyev, *op. cit.*

[20] M. Airepetian and P. Kabanov, *Leninskie printsipy vneshnei politiki Sovetskogo gosudarstva* (Moscow, 1957), p. 65, cited by John N. Hazard, "Soviet Socialism as a Public Order System," *Proceedings of the American Society of International Law,* 1959, p. 41.

munications, the emphasis on state relations over Party relations among the Communist Party-states indeed made for less fuss and strain. But the retrogressive deviation from proletarian internationalism which was implied when state sovereignty was proclaimed as the foundation of Socialist internationalism, marked an un-Marxian return to the Marxian nineteenth-century world in more ways than one. When Khrushchev said, on January 6, 1961, that it was "impossible" and "unnecessary" to lead Communist Parties "from a single center" because "it only creates difficulties" but "spells no advantage to our Party or other Parties," he was only confirming the developmental process within the system to date. It had become "impossible" for the CPSU to accept responsibiilty for and to the other Parties for the diversities which national environment and circumstances had created and which came to require constant and sustained readjustments in the formerly commonly held belief system. And it had become "unnecessary"—as Khrushchev saw it—because of the absolute Soviet primacy within the system as the most powerful Communist Party-state. In subordinating Parties to states, Socialist internationalism began to mean increasingly "socialism in several countries" with all the implications of the growing statism originally displayed by the Soviet model.

In fact, some Soviet authors suggested that differences of views among the (ruling) Parties harmful to Socialist internationalism should not be carried over to relations among the (Socialist) states (!):

> For each Socialist country, possible differences notwithstanding, can make its contribution to the overall victory of socialism if it strictly observes all its commitments to other Socialist countries, extends economic, scientific, technological and cultural cooperation with them, builds up their joint defense capabilities against imperialism, and joins with them in a united front in the international arena.[21]

Moreover, the Bandung principles, praised on the state level, began to enter the *Party* level as well: As the Central Committee of the Rumanian Workers' Party put it in April, 1964, there are no "parent" and "son" Parties—parties that are superior and inferior—but only a family of *completely equal* Parties. Hence Parties must *respect* each other and must not *interfere* in each other's business. No Party has a privileged position nor can it impose its line or opinions on other Parties.[22]

[21]L. Zieleniec and A. Charakchiev, "Milestone in the March of History," *World Marxist Review,* vol. 8, no. 5, May, 1965, p. 22.

[22] "Statement on the Stand of the Rumanian Workers' Party Concerning the Problems of the World Communist and Working-Class Movement, Endorsed by the Large Plenum of the Central Committee of the Rumanian Workers' Party, held in Apr., 1964," *Rumania, Documents, Articles and Information* (Supplement, 1964), p. 50 (emphasis added).

The circle was being closed. Not only should the national Communist Parties be sovereign, but *ideological disagreement* among them should not affect their *good state relations.* Just as the *Party* links among the ruling Parties have significantly contributed to the relations among the states in the past, so now the ideological *differences* among the several ruling Parties were negatively affecting *state relations.* "If in conditions of sharp ideological struggle it is possible to develop normal and good-neighborly relations *between states* of two *opposing* social-economic systems, why must differences *between fraternal Parties* on ideological questions. . . . irrespective of how serious they are, violate the principles of Socialist inter-state relations?"[23]

Sovereignty of National Parties

Serious differences exist within the world Communist movement and in particular among the Communist Party-states on several issues, and "it would be unwise to close our eyes to the differences."[24] During the almost half century of its existence, the Communist movement engendered different forms of unity. In the past, under the generic umbrella of proletarian internationalism, the community of aims and interests which united the movement produced, most of the time, solidarity and specific concerted international action.[25] But changes in stages of development at the present time produced problems and difficulties before the movement has been able to engender the form of unity corresponding most closely to the new stage of development.

Before World War II, the economic and political ties between Communist Party-states were either weak or nonexistent. Also, the economic patterns of these countries were adapted to suit the requirements of their more developed economic partners, since the several countries had achieved very different economic levels.

Following World War II the Communist Party-states were still economically unequal; there existed and persisted a discrepancy between the development of relationships within the various Party-states and between different parts of the Communist system; there were wide opportunities for multiform ties among the Party-states which were not utilized; there were contradictions among them caused by the divergence of specific interests; there was lack of experience in the imaginative

[23] Sanakoyev, *op. cit.* (emphasis added).

[24] Editorial, "Unity of Action of the World Communist Movement," *World Marxist Review,* vol. 8, no. 4, Apr., 1965, p. 4.

[25] *Ibid.,* pp. 4–5.

shaping and evolving of multilateral economic and political ties; this was the residue of nationalistic hatred and mistrust for neighbors; and, prior to PC XX of the CPSU in 1956, there was the interference of the personality cult, which played its role in precluding the development of full, equal relations among the Party-states.

Almost with Stalin's death a search was undertaken to find more flexible and effective forms of cooperation which would conform to both the "international interests" and the "national aspirations" of the nations involved. The Council for Mutual Economic Assistance; the Warsaw Treaty Organization, within which the Soviet nuclear and missile capabilities have been of particular significance; meetings of leaders, exchange of information, and coordination of foreign policies; and cultural exchanges—all are to be viewed in this context.[26] "But because it is being carried out and tried and tested for the first time in the history of mankind," Socialist internationalism, "an exceptionally intricate undertaking," said one of its chief idealogs, requires skill, wisdom and energy to accomplish the task of strengthening the unity of the Party-state system.[27]

Progressive Nationalism and Reactionary Chauvinism

Socialist internationalism cannot develop "automatically." Socialism in the several countries may create a foundation on which Socialist relations among the Party-states can develop; but how this opportunity is used depends on the leadership in the ruling Communist Parties. The implementation of the principles of proletarian internationalism in the setting of the Communist Party-states has depended particularly on the attitude of the Party-states towards the nationalism in their midst. As Palmiro Togliatti, former Secretary General of the Italian Communist Party, put it in his political testament:

> A fact worrying us and one we do not succeed in explaining fully is the manifestation among the Socialist countries of a centrifugal tendency . . . Without doubt there is a revival of nationalism. However, we know that the national sentiment remains a permanent factor in the working class and Socialist movement for a long period, also after the conquest of power. Economic progress does not dispel this, it nurtures it. Also, in the Socialist camp *perhaps* (I underline this per-

[26] Dudinsky, *op. cit.*, p. 6; Zieleniec and Charakchiev, *op. cit.*, p. 21.

[27] B. N. Ponomaryev (Secretary of the Central Committee of the CPSU), "Proletarian Internationalism Is the Revolutionary Banner of Our Epoch," *Pravda,* Sept. 29, 1964, pp. 2–3. Also *Information Bulletin* No. 25 (Prague: World Marxist Review Publishers), Nov. 16, 1964, p. 28.

> haps because many concrete facts are unknown to us) one needs to be on one's guard against the forced exterior uniformity and one must consider that the unity one ought to establish and maintain lies in the diversity and full autonomy of the individual countries.[28]

The Soviet attitude towards the "new" nationalism is as follows: As a result of Soviet triumph in World War II, the antifascist and national-liberation struggle of a number of European and Asian countries and peoples was victorious. Not only were these peoples and countries, with Soviet aid, delivered from fascism and imperialism, respectively, but they joined the USSR as allies—and they pooled the experience of the USSR with their own for the speediest realization of socialism at the minimum cost.[29] But now the revival of nationalism in the Communist Party-states has challenged Socialist internationalism. Genuine nationalism, of course, does not contradict proletarian internationalism; for scientific socialism has found a suitable blend between the two. But patriotic affection for one's own country; legitimate feelings for national dignity, self-consciousness, and pride; and progressive nationalism of peoples in developing nations must be differentiated from that reactionary chauvinism and reactionary nationalism, which set Party-states and nations against each other. China, for example, has sought to undermine the world Communist movement united by proletarian internationalism by striving for hegemony on behalf of its own open, egotistic, bellicose nationalistic impulse. By destroying both the unity between the Communist and the national-liberation movement —and by sowing poisonous seeds of national strife among the Communist Party-states, the Chinese leaders have arrogantly been "profaning the very essence of proletarian internationalism."[30] Directing their main blow against the first Socialist country, the Chinese leaders hope that their reactionary nationalism will put an end to proletarian internationalism. "But this must not happen and will not happen. Communism will triumph over reactionary nationalism."[31]

The disunity, contradictions and centrifugal tendencies that challenge Socialist internationalism are assumed, however, to be transient phenomena. Of the three dangers to Socialist internationalism—the novelty of the transition to socialism of countries with different social, economic, cultural and historical levels and backgrounds; the cult of

[28] *The New York Times,* Sept. 5, 1964, p. 2. With an introduction by Luigi Longo, Togliatti's successor, Dudinsky, *op. cit.,* p. 5.

[29] Z. Zhivkov "People's Democracy—Tried and Tested Road to Socialism," *World Marxist Review,* vol. 8, no. 6, June 1965, p. 25.

[30] Ponomaryev, *op. cit.,* p. 34.

[31] *Ibid.,* pp. 34–35.

personality of Stalin; and the erroneous policy of China based on nationalist distortions and deviations—the third, pseudo-left, nationalistic dogmatism is depicted as the principal one. The Chinese leaders are said to counterpose their devisive nationalistic line to both Socialist and proletarian internationalism. And the following quote from Lenin is offered by Moscow, with tongue in cheek, to prove its point: "One who has adopted the standpoint of nationalism naturally arrives at the desire to erect a Chinese wall around his nationality, his national working class movement . . . unembarrassed even by the fact that by his tactics of division and dismemberment *he is reducing to nil* the great call for the rallying and unity of the proletarians of all nations, all races and all languages."[32]

For this reason—according to the Soviet position—the most compelling task for all those believing in Socialist internationalism is to assist in healing the breach and in the establishment of contacts and cooperation with the Chinese Communists. Marx and Engels held regular congresses of the International, and Lenin considered it important to hold periodic congresses of the Comintern. To strengthen both proletarian and Socialist internationalism, a new international Communist organization would perhaps be the best means of overcoming the differences. But under no condition should the present split in the movement serve as a basis for severing relations or even excommunicating anyone. In this sense, the example of the ousting of Yugoslavia is important as a guide in the present troubles:

> In the League of Communists of Yugoslavia, serious divergencies from the World Communist movement arose on a number of questions. This found concentrated expression in the Program of the League of Communists of Yugoslavia. This was noted in the Statement of the 1960 Moscow Conference, in which it was emphasized that the revisionist errors permitted by the leadership of the LCY "jeopardized the revolutionary gains won by the heroic struggle of the Yugoslav people." Every unprejudiced person who considers this position can see that the Conference, while subjecting the erroneous concepts of the LCY program to principled criticism, at the same time proceeded from an appraisal of Yugoslavia as a Socialist country. The international Communist movement has set the goal of aiding Yugoslavia and its leaders to correct the existing errors and to return to the path *of unity with the world Socialist system,* with the fraternal Parties.
>
> From this it is evident that the line of the CPSU consists not of severing Yugoslavia from the Socialist countries, and not of perpetuating the departure of the League of Communists of Yugoslavia from

[32] Lenin, *Collected Works* (Moscow [in English]), vol. VI, pp. 520–521; cited in slightly different form in Dudinsky, *op. cit.,* p. 5.

> the international Communist movement, but of helping to correct its errors and to take its place in the ranks of our movement.
>
> What would happen if each Communist Party were wilfully to excommunicate other Communist Parties from socialism, strive for their exclusion from the ranks of the Communist movement and further refuse whole nations the right to cooperate in the building of socialism?[33]

As is to be expected, the Chinese version of the issue of nationalism vs. proletarian internationalism and its consequences is somewhat different: true, the Chinese Communists support "progressive nationalism," "national independence," and "people's democracy" and oppose "reactionary nationalism," and "domestic reaction":

> If anybody, following in the footsteps of others, defends the erroneous opportunist line and policies pursued by a certain Socialist country instead of upholding the correct Marxist–Leninist line and policies which the socialist countries ought to pursue, defends the policy of split instead of upholding the policy of unity, then he is departing from Marxism-Leninism and proletarian internationalism.[34]

The nature of proletarian internationalism—say the Chinese—has changed with changed conditions. Earlier, it meant support of the USSR. Now it means the support of *all* the Communist Party-states in the camp, the fostering of their unity, *and* of "the policies which the Socialist countries *ought to pursue*":

> It is under new historical conditions that the Communist and Workers' Parties are now carrying on the task of proletarian internationalist unity and struggle. When only one Socialist country existed and when this country was faced with hostility and jeopardized by all the imperialists and reactionaries because it firmly pursued the correct Marxist-Leninist line and policies, the touchstone of proletarian internationalism for every Communist Party was whether or not it resolutely defended the only Socialist country. Now there is a Socialist camp consisting of 13 countries, Albania, Bulgaria, China, Cuba, Czechoslovakia, the German Democratic Republic, Hungary, the Democratic People's Republic of Korea, Mongolia, Poland, Rumania, the Soviet Union, the Democratic Republic of Vietnam. Under these circumstances, the touchstone of proletarian internationalism for every Communist Party is whether or not it resolutely defends the whole of the Socialist camp, whether or not it defends the unity of all the countries in the camp on the basis of Marxism-Leninism and whether

[33] "For Marxist-Leninist Unity of the Communist Movement, for Solidarity of the Countries of Socialism," *Pravda,* Feb. 10, 1963, p. 3 (emphasis added).
[34] Zieleniec and Charakchiev, *op. cit.,* p. 16.

or not it defends the Marxist-Leninist line and policies which the Socialist countries ought to pursue.[35]

The Continuing Threat of Coercion

Coercion, say the Communists, is, under given circumstances, a justifiable means to an end. Still, they would not use it if the classes departing from history would give up without the recourse to violence. But the reactionaries do not surrender; they have tried to cause troubles in several Party-states. They attempted to unleash civil war in Poland, to engineer *putsches* in Hungary and Czechoslovakia, to organize counterrevolutionary armed actions in Rumania. They failed only because the means of coercion were in the hands of the Socialist governments in these countries, and, in particular, in the hands of new Party-state security bodies, the armies and the people's militias. This preponderance of strength has limited the opportunities of the capitalists for counterrevolution and is, therefore, essential.[36]

On the other hand, coercion is inexcusable if used against fraternal Parties and states. The emergence of communism from one country had made it increasingly obvious that the traditional *modus operandi* of the Comintern was no longer suited to the needs of the Communist movement. In the past the Comintern's interference with the internal matters of Communist Parties had gone so "far as the removal and replacement of leading Party cadres and even of entire central committees, as far as the imposing from without of leaders, the suppression of distinguished leading cadres of various parties, and as far as the censure and even disowning of Communist Parties."[37]

Such coercive practices were again employed in the Cominform. Yugoslavia's Party was condemned and excluded from the Cominform, and Yugoslavia, a Communist Party-state, was expelled from the Party-states system. And the erstwhile practices of the Comintern were extended from Party to state relations, "rendering their consequences the more serious." There were "numerous cases of expulsion from the Party, arrests, trials and suppressions of many leading Party and state

[35] A letter sent on June 14, by the Central Committee of the Chinese Communist Party to the Central Committee of the Soviet Communist Party, *The New York Times,* July 5, 1963, p. 6 (emphasis added).

[36] "Statement on the Stand of the Rumanian Workers' Party Concerning the Problems of the World Communist and Working-Class Movement," *op. cit.,* pp. 48 and 49.

[37] *Ibid.*

cadres."[38] But even though the lesson of Yugoslavia had presumably been learned, the threat of coercion to be exercised by the powerful against the weak has remained. Within the 1960s the CC of the Rumanian Workers' Party has stated that it considers the sharp divergencies now prevailing in the Communist movement "of the utmost gravity," as "the danger could arise of a repetition of the methods and practices" of the past.[39] And so as reassurance that this will not occur, the Russians çite Lenin's sentiments that:

> We want a voluntary union of nations—a union which precludes any coercion of one nation by another—a union founded on complete confidence, on a clear recognition of brotherly unity, on *absolutely* voluntary consent. Such a union cannot be affected with one stroke; we have to work towards it with the greatest patience and circumspection, so as not to spoil matters and not to arouse distrust and in order that the distrust inherited from centuries of landowner and capitalist oppression, centuries of private property and the enmity caused by divisions and redivisions may have caused to wear off.[40]

The Watering Down of Proletarian Internationalism

The new inclusiveness, stratification and particularization of proletarian internationalism, while responding to new needs, also creates new problems. Proletarian internationalism stands now for the formation of a broad front of political alliance embracing four principal forces: (1) the Communist Party-states: (2) The nonruling Communist Parties; (3) the parties and organizations united in the national-liberation movement in developing nations; and (4) all peoples and organizations everywhere fighting against imperialism and for peace.[41] The line between the world Communist system—the Communist Party-states and nonruling Communist Parties—and the rest of the world is elusive and even irrelevant, for socialism "is a broad stream that attracts ever more countries and social forces."[42] United by the principles of proletarian internationalism, these countries and social forces are interrelated: the national-liberation movement would not have reached its present level were it not for the advances made by the Communist Party-states. At the same time, however, the struggle of the Communists against capitalism would have taken place in much more difficult conditions were

[38] *Ibid.*
[39] *Ibid.*
[40] Lenin, *Selected Works* (Moscow [in English]), vol. III, p. 342; cited by Dudinsky, *op. cit.*, p. 6 (emphasis added).
[41] Ponomaryev, *op. cit.*, p. 30.
[42] *Pravda,* Aug. 15, 1965, p. 3.

it not *that imperialism has been deprived of its colonial position.* The *nonruling Parties* in the capitalist countries aided by the USSR and the other Communist Party-states significantly contributed to the progress in the Party-states.[43] And the *nonruling Communist Parties* benefited greatly in their own development from the assistance rendered to them by the Communist Party-states.

In particular, the development of the national-liberation movement, "one of the most important revolutionary forces of our epoch," has depended on the unity of the Communist Party-states and the Communist Parties with the newly freed peoples. Because of their double needs —for economic development and the defense of their national independence—the young developing states are attracted to socialism. It is the duty of Communists to assist these peoples in their needs. Herein is also the meaning of present-day proletarian internationalism.[44]

The significance of modern proletarian internationalism rests then on its quadruple roles: (1) as a model of unity among the Communist Party-states; (2) as a support for national-liberation movements whose success depends upon the help of all Communists; (3) as a unifying force for all—even "the most diverse detachments" engaged in the revolutionary struggle everywhere in the world;[45] and (4) as a unifying force for all peoples of good will in their struggle against war and reaction and for peace.

Proletarian internationalism is thus expected to strengthen the world Socialist system "as the main factor in present-day revolutionary development"; to synchronize the building of socialism and communism by each Communist Party-state; to defend the unity of the international Communist movement against reactionary nationalism, factionalism and splitism; to defend and creatively develop Marxism-Leninism as the ideological foundation of the international Communist movement, and to unite all progressive forces everywhere.[46]

Now, this set of assumptions explicitly broadening proletarian internationalism has led to a deep disagreement within the Communist movement, not so much on their breadth as on the purpose, rank-ordering, and relationships within the concept. The CPSU, supported by its friends, has stipulated that all-world (all-state) Communism will be achieved *because of the great successes of the Communist Party-states.* Their economic, social, political, and scientific achievements must

[43] Editorial, "Unity of Action of the World Communist Movement," *op. cit.*, p. 4.

[44] Ponomaryev, p. 28.

[45] *Ibid.*, pp. 28–29.

[46] *Ibid.*

and will be so impressive that all mankind will be persuaded that only communism is the way of the future. Hence the *primary* purpose of proletarian internationalism must be the victory and consolidation of communism in the several Party-states; and hence the world proletariat supports all the states which construct socialism (while in turn Socialist construction in the Communist Party-states can proceed only in close association and in cooperation with the world revolutionary movement).[47]

The Chinese CP and its friends, on the other hand, maintain that the primacy belongs not to the Communist Party-states but to certain key areas in the struggle for ultimate Communist victory; namely, to the oppressed people of Asia, Africa, and Latin America. All progressive forces everywhere, including the ruling Communist Parties, have a duty which is primary and nonmutual, to support these peoples in their open, revolutionary struggle for liberation from imperialist oppression:

> The national democratic revolutionary struggles of the people in Asia, Africa and Latin America are pounding and undermining the foundations of the rule of imperialism and colonialism, old and new, and are now a mighty force in defense of peace. In a sense, therefore, the whole cause of the international proletarian revolution hinges on the outcome of the revolutionary struggles of the people of these areas whole cause of the international proletarian revolution hinges on the Therefore the anti-imperialist revolutionary struggle of the people in Asia, Africa and Latin America is definitely not merely a matter of regional significance but one of over-all importance for the whole cause of proletarian world revolution.[48]

Those who consider the significance of the national-liberation movement secondary to that of the Communist Party-state system not only "cater to the needs of imperialism" but try to create a new "theory" to justify the continued rule of "superior nations" over "inferior nations." This is not proletarian internationalism but a serious departure from it; such a theory is "fraudulent."[49]

Neither Socialist internationalism nor the Communist Party-states nor even the international Communist movement, according to the Chinese, is the principal social revolutionary force today, but rather the national-liberation movement. It leads the other forces as "the

[47] Azizian, *op. cit.*, p. 98; Korovin, *op. cit.*, p. 71; S. Sanakoyev, "The Basis of the Relations Between the Socialist Countries," *International Affairs* (Moscow), July, 1958, p. 161.

[48] June 14 letter of the Central Committee of the Chinese Communist Party to the Central Committee of the Soviet Communist Party, *The New York Times*, July 5, 1963, p. 6.

[49] *Ibid.*

storm center of world revolution dealing direct blows to imperialism." This is why the future of proletarian internationalism as a worldwide international format and model hinges on the outcome of its struggle.[50]

The Fallback to Traditional Forms

Today, the Socialist internationalist means and channels of interaction do not substantively differ from the interactional means and channels employed in the non-Communist world. In fact, the inter-Party relations among the Communist Party-states have by now been almost completely replaced by conventional interstate relations in the form of international treaties and agreements, diplomatic missions and their activities, governmental conferences, regional state organizations, political and military alliences, and trade and economic cooperation. This of course follows the development of relations among the Party-states: As the meetings and lines of communication of the CPs have been increasingly unsuccessful and therefore fewer, the states have increasingly been replacing the unfertile, rigid and constrained Party procedures with businesslike bargaining techniques. With the absence of an organization of Communist Parties, the several organizations of the states have displayed propensities toward functionalism, utility, pragmatism, and equality, and away from ideology and the simple achievement-oriented paternal hierarchy of the past.

Of course, Communist theoreticians maintain, the interstate means and channels employed by the Communist Party-states, while "in form similar" to the relations of non-Communist states, "in essence radically differ" from means of other states, since (1) "their own laws and principles operate in relations among states within the Socialist community," and (2) "these forms are used in entirely different conditions than in the old world." The *principles* are supplied by Socialist internationalism, and the *conditions* by the means and ends shared by all the Party-states operating within the Communist system: namely, common aims, common systems, a common enemy, common interests, and common accomplishments.[51]

However, as equality among the Party-states means free choice of the acceptable means of interaction,[52] it is safe to predict that increasing ideological discomforts will further emphasize the present functional and utilitarian tendencies.

[50] *Ibid.*
[51] Sanakoyev, *op. cit.,* 1965, p. 21.
[52] Dudinsky, *op. cit.,* p. 7.

In addition to these above problems—denial of simple peaceful coexistence among the Socialist states; the party-state dichotomy; sovereignty of national Communist Parties; revival of nationalism; condemnation of coercion; watering down of the proletarian internationalism concept to include even "all men of good will"; and the employment of traditional international forms—there are many other issues and concepts on which there is disagreement and which at least tangentially affect the general consensus on proletarian internationalism. These include, *among others,* the inevitability of war; the resort to armed revolution; the impact of nuclear weapons on Communist strategies; the possibility of disarmament; economic relations among Party-states; local wars (among and with developing nations); and the possibility of peaceful coexistence with non-Party states.

Events and circumstances have largely eliminated the subordination of the ruling Parties to the "victorious" CPSU. The end of rule by coercion and condemnation, initiated among the Communist Party-states by Khrushchev with his emphasis on voluntarism principally on the state level, has been carried over to the Party level and extended to the nonruling Parties as well. True, the Sino-Soviet split has affected all the Parties, and pro-Chinese factions have emerged both because of the seriousness of the conflict and the open and sustained challenge to the CPSU by the Chinese Communist Party (CCP). But the fact remains that in the process of deciding the issue for themselves, many Parties used the opportunity to assert their own growing independence of *any* other Party. Being able to select from among more than one Party gained for them the freedom to formulate their own views and policies and brought home the opportunity for perhaps influencing the movement merely by deviating from announced policies.

The results of this Soviet-initiated, though probably inevitable, process have been far-reaching. Upon the foundation of greater equality and more freedom, the Parties have displayed propensities toward greater disunity, disaffinity, and incompatibility. The state of flux which has been characteristic of the recent stage of development in the movement and the widening conflict patterns which have emerged from it, have confirmed the proposition that there is indeed an inverse relationship between the number of "equal" units within the system and the system's solidarity and cohesion. The greater the equality, the less the unity. But this decline of unity seems to be the necessary cost of the system's growth and development.

But then perhaps the dialectics of the international and national aspects of the Communist movement are such that true unity of the movement's units in the long run can be achieved only when that unity is based on independence and equality of the respective units. This is what some Communists have claimed, urging that the current stage of development, characterized by disagreements, disharmony and diversity, is indeed both unavoidable and necessary, and will lead to a new synthesis of more perfect unity.

Others disagree. The adherents of the Soviet position complain that to state that discords and splits, both without and within the Communist Party-states and Communist Parties, are necessary and unavoidable and that the dialectics of the development of the international working class movement is disunity, struggle and splits, as well as unity on a new basis, means to endow the existing Sino-Soviet discord and split with "a theoretical foundation." This is profoundly dangerous, they add. It is in fact "a call for a split."[53]

In reply, the Chinese Communists emphasize that, on the contrary,

> The leaders of the CPSU have themselves undermined the basis of the unity of the international Communist movement and created the present grave danger of a split by betraying Marxism-Leninism and proletarian internationalism and pushing their revisionist and divisive line . . . They have thus made a mess of the splendid Socialist camp . . . [and] pursued a policy of great-power chauvinism and national egoism.[54]

It was the Soviet leaders, say the Chinese, who "arbitrarily infringed upon the sovereignty of fraternal countries, interfered in their internal affairs, carried on subversive activities and tried in every way to control fraternal countries"; it was they who "openly called for the overthrow of the Party and government leaders of Albania"; it was they who "violated the Sino–Soviet Treaty of Friendship, Alliance, and Mutual Assistance"; and it was they who "provoked incidents on the Sino-Soviet border and carried out large-scale subversive activities in Sinkiang."[55]

Soft-pedaling these charges ("The interest of the world revolutionary movement now demands urgent searches for real paths toward the rapprochement of all the fraternal Parties. Attempts to discredit any of the detachments of the Communist movement, and all the more to depict them as hostile-class forces are incompatible with these interests" . . .),[56] the Soviet proponents of proletarian internationalism argue that it is the continuing struggle against imperialism and for

[53] "Statement on the Stand of the Rumanian Workers' Party," *op. cit.,* p. 50.

[54] *The New York Times,* Feb. 7, 1964, p. 6. Excerpts from an editorial in *Hung-ch'i,* published Feb. 5 by *Jen-min jih-pao* [Chinese Communist translation]. (Emphasis added.)

[55] *Ibid.*

[56] Editorial, *Pravda,* June 20, 1965, pp. 3–5.

communism which, because of its international character, is bound "inevitably" to bring about full unity among the national contingents within the Communist movement. This version, a kind of utopian proletarian internationalism synchronized with the increase of decentralized independence of members, reflects the hopes of those who, while admitting that today's concept of proletarian internationalism may be imperfect (necessarily so in order that it can cope with the many difficulties besetting the movement), predict that in the future many of these difficulties will dissolve with the disappearance of state frontiers. Nikita Khrushchev explained it in 1959 in Leipzig, as follows:

> Communist society, which will have an abundance of material and spiritual wealth, is capable of satisfying the needs of every individual as well as of every nation . . . In these conditions, the old concepts of borders as such will gradually disappear. With the victory of communism on a worldwide scale, state borders will disappear, as Marxism-Leninism teaches. In all likelihood only ethnic borders will survive for a time and even these will probably exist only as a convention. Naturally these frontiers, if they can be called frontiers at all, will have no border guards, customs officials or incidents. They will simply demarcate the historically formed location of a given people or nationality in a given territory. . . . Speaking of the future, it seems to me that the further development of the Socialist countries will in all probability proceed along the lines of the single world Socialist economic system. The economic barriers which divided our countries under capitalism will fall one after another. The common economic basis of world socialism will grow stronger, eventually making the question of borders a pointless one.[57]

With the victory of communism, borders will disappear and with them the guardians of these borders. This will mark the beginning of the end of nationalism through the fulfilment of proletarian, i.e., Communist, internationalism.

But at present, "the old conceptions of borders, formed on the basis of bourgeois legal norms, are still alive, along with other survivals of capitalism." This is why sovereign independence, respect for territorial integrity, nonintervention in domestic affairs and voluntary economic assistance on a state-to-state basis must be recognized as essential for Socialist internationalist relations among the Communist Party-states. Internationalism then denotes interstatism; and the difference between this concept and the peaceful coexistence concept is much smaller that the difference between it and the futuristic dream that "the International

[57] *Pravda,* Mar. 27, 1959, pp. 1–3; translated in *Current Digest of The Soviet Press,* vol. II, no. 13, 1959, pp. 3–7.

shall be the human race"[58] But in any case, before getting to this point, say the Moscow Marxists, all the states in the world must follow the path of the Communist Party-states via "a world-wide Commonwealth of Socialist Nations."

Proletarian internationalism, as well as socialist internationalism, has its contents and roles defined by the needs of the process of commonwealth formation and by the given reality of the world situation. If the Party-states and the other units in the movement are laying the foundation for this intermediate arrangement now, then their success depends on their ability to work together in agreement on what is to be done. If they cannot agree on the content and role of proletarian internationalism, they jeopardize the whole Communist movement.

From the foregoing it must be concluded that while proletarian internationalism may be a true "acid test" or a "test supplied by history"; a "slogan" or "a motto" ("unity, unity, and once again unity of the world Communist movement"); a "reliable tool," "an instrument," "a keystone," "a bond," and "a thesis"; and it may be a "set of principles," "an outlook" and even "a policy"; *it is not a theory.* As a generalization asserting that two or more things co-vary under specified conditions ("proletarian internationalism is a unity of all progressive forces based on their common struggle against imperialism and for peace"), it is neither precise, systematic nor verifiable. The premise of the identity of interests on a class basis no longer obtains; in fact the concept is now so broad that it has little meaning. And the subsequent limitation of the generalization by the particular exceptions designed for "the most advanced detachment" of the movement; namely, the Communist Party-states, the learning model for the future; the consequent greater concern for relations among states than among Parties; and the Chinese denial of both these latter propositions, and their disagreement on the rank-ordering of the revolutionary forces—all of these make even this limited conceptual framework questionable. The fact that some kind of broad theoretical presuppositions underlie the crude empirical search for an over-all unity and association does not bring the remote ideal any closer. The exhortative and conjectoral nature of the postulate, and the history of the theorizing on the subject, suggest that the concept has emerged not so much to analyze conditions as to create them, and to persuade all of the great value deriving from the postulate. But a

[58] G. Shanshiev, "Under the Banner of Proletarian Internationalism," *World Marxist Review,* vol. 8, no. 8, 1965, p. 60, citing R. P. Dutt, *The Internationale* (London: Terrace and Wishart, 1964).

wish for unity without providing an adequate theoretical base for it is irrelevant. This is not theory-building—it is at most a mechanistic continuation of a well-established habit.

New problems require new criteria, new ways of looking at things. Not the over-all utility but the adequacy, logic and rigor of explanation and understanding is what makes a theory. Proletarian internationalism can not be so defined.

A legitimate question in this context is whether and to what extent may the problem of theory construction be considered relevant or even necessary for the kinds of tasks facing the Communist world today: How important is it to have an adequately formulated explanation of the linkage between and among the units of the Communist movement for the current and future purposes of the movement? Though indeed intriguing and significant, this question is, however, outside the scope of this study.

The conclusion, then, is that there is no formal theory of association in the world Communist system. There is a great deal of theorizing about it, which occurs in the form of inductive reviews of *ad hoc* needs and propositions and in the making of *ad hoc* predictions for individual assumptions. This theorizing emanates from normative observations, case studies, and various nontechnical sources. Writings on the subject have often raised interesting questions but have not arrived at a theory of relations. Proletarian internationalism is *at best,* in terms of being a theory, two rival conceptual frameworks differing both in rank-ordering and in emphasis laid on particular principles; *at worst* it is an assortment of hortatory speculations—unverified, unprecise and unsystematic.

Or, to borrow language of the Communist theoreticians, they have themselves failed to develop creatively Marxist–Leninist teaching on internationalism, in keeping with the conditions of the time, the relations among Socialist countries and the conditions in the world Communist movement.

SELECTED BIBLIOGRAPHY

Barnett, A. Doak (ed.), *Communist Strategies in Asia: A Comparative Analysis of Governments and Parties* (New York: Praeger, 1963). Eight studies of communism in Asia by distinguished Western scholars. In addition to a general discussion of the relevance of the Russian and Chinese social models to Asia, three ruling (North Vietnamese, North Korean, and Mongolian) and three nonruling (Japanese, Indian, and Indonesian) parties are analyzed in detail.

Brzezinski, Zbigniew, *The Soviet Bloc: Unity and Conflict,* rev. ed. (Cambridge: Harvard University Press, 1961). A developmental analysis of political integration and conflict among the fourteen Communist Party-states, with special emphasis on Poland, by one of the ablest students of the world Communist system.

Brzezinski, Zbigniew, "The Organization of the Communist Camp," *World Politics,* vol. 13, no. 12, 1961.

Dallin, Alexander (ed.), *Diversity in International Communism: A Documentary Record, 1961–1963* (New York: Columbia, 1963). An invaluable documentary evidence, selected with wisdom and insight, of conflict in the world Communist system.

Etzioni, Amitai, "A Paradigm For the Study of Political Unification," *World Politics,* vol. 15, no. 1, 1962.

Fischer-Galati, Stephen (ed.), *Eastern Europe in the Sixties* (New York: Praeger, 1963). A comparative, cross-national and cross-cultural symposium on politics and economics in Eastern Europe by well-known students of the area.

Labedz, Leopold (ed.), *Revisionism: Essays on the History of Marxist Ideas* (New York: Praeger, 1962). A fascinating symposium on intellectual deviations from "the original Marxism" by an international set of political scientists, philosophers, historians, psychologists and sociologists.

Laquer, Walter and Leopold Labedz (eds.), *Polycentrism: The New Factor in International Communism* (New York: Praeger, 1962). Several enlightened descriptions of the consequences of political and social change in the world Communist system collected by the editors of *Survey.*

Laquer, Walter and Leopold Labedz (eds.), "The End of the Monolith: World Communism in 1962," *Foreign Affairs,* vol. 40, no. 3, Apr., 1962.

London, Kurt, "The Socialist Commonwealth: Pattern for Communist World Organization," *Orbis,* vol. 3, no. 4, 1960.

Modelski, George, *The Communist International System* (Princeton: Center of International Studies [mimeo], 1960). A path-breaking, imaginative analysis of the world Communist movement as a potential international system by one of the truly creative scholars in the field of international relations.

Nollau, Günther, *International Communism and World Revolution* (New York: Praeger, 1963). A useful historical treatment of the relations among Communist Parties. (Translated from German.)

Petersen, William (ed.), *The Realities of World Communism* (New York: Prentice-Hall, 1963). Originally a symposium by University of California scholars, this is a serious, sophisticated contribution to the study of conflict in the world Communist system.

Shoup, Paul, "Communism, Nationalism and the Growth of the Communist Community of Nations After World War II," *American Political Science Review,* vol. 56, no. 4, Dec., 1962.

Zagoria, Donald S., *The Sino-Soviet Conflict, 1956–1961* (Princeton: Princeton University Press, 1962). A detailed historical analysis, still probably the best on the market, of the origins and developments of the most important conflict in the world Communist system.

Zinner, Paul E., *International Communism: Ideology, Organization, Strategy* (New York: Praeger, 1963). A very useful historical analysis of the major intellectual and organizational problems associated with the development and growth of the world Communist system.

2

China vs. Russia

Dennis J. Doolin

THERE WAS A TIME in the mid-1950s during the soft period of Bandung and the "Hundred Flowers" when China nurtured her relations with the West and the United States in general. Chou En-lai, Premier of the People's Republic of China (PRC) even went so far on one occasion as to talk of a US–PRC "peace pact" in the Pacific.[1] But by the end of 1957 Chinese policy had returned to the hard line of the Korean War, where it remained on dead center.

What caused this hardening of Chinese policy? Why was goodwill, so carefully built, sacrificed with such apparent alacrity? Why has Mao Tse-tung wooed Pakistan, a SEATO nation, and attacked India, a nation that has literally sanctified the principle of nonalignment? Why did Chou En-lai abruptly come to demand a total US withdrawal from Asia, Africa, and Latin America as a *sine qua non* to any Sino-American detente.

The answers to these and other basic questions affecting the US, the PRC, and the USSR have their origins, among others, in two key events of 1956 and 1957: de-Stalinization and Sputnik.

Pandora's Box: Russian and Chinese Models

From the founding of the PRC on October 1, 1949, until Party Congress (PC) XX of the Communist Party of the Soviet Union (CPSU) in February, 1956, there were few signs of dissension between the two

[1] See George McT. Kahin, *The Asian-African Conference* (Ithaca: Cornell University Press, 1956), pp. 28–29.

largest Party-states. Historical roots of conflict did exist: the 1927 debacle in China; the 1947 Chinese claim that Mao Tse-tung had created an Asiatic Marxism that would be the road to revolution in colonial and "semicolonial" Asia; Soviet looting in Manchuria after World War II; Stalin's insistence (as late as 1949) that the Chinese Communists could not defeat the Kuomintang (Nationalists) in the field and, therefore, should join in a coalition government with Chiang Kai-shek; territorial questions concerning Sinkiang (Chinese Turkestan), Outer Mongolia, Port Arthur–Dairen and the Chinese Eastern Railway; the so-called "unequal treaties"; and so forth. However, the Korean War, the United Nations intervention, and the dispatch of units of the US Seventh Fleet to the Taiwan Strait, together with large-scale economic and military assistance to the Nationalist Government on Taiwan, rendered suicidal any Chinese Communist attempt to redress forcefully grievances entertained against the Soviet Union.

With Stalin's death in 1953, *the* leader was gone. Gone soon too was the leader cult that had glorified the ruthless Georgian. The new leadership, less paranoic, less powerful, realized that terror was no longer a sufficient substitute for material incentives.

Leadership embarked upon new paths—and the old and those who favored the old, the Molotovs and the Kaganoviches, had to go. To destroy them it was also necessary to destroy not only the ideology but the stature of their strongest weapon, Stalin, as well. Hence the multifaceted origins of de-Stalinization—which became a root cause of the Sino-Soviet conflict.

But de-Stalinization was only one of the sources of Russian and Chinese differences brought into play at PC XX, for it was at this Congress that three new axioms, that the Chinese ultimately came to find almost wholly unacceptable, were introduced into Holy Writ. In brief, these axioms (which have been reaffirmed by Brezhnev and Kosygin as basic tenets of Soviet policy) are:

1. Peaceful Coexistence is not a mere tactical expedient but a fundamental principle of Soviet foreign policy that will bring certain victory through peaceful competition;
2. War is not fatalistically inevitable;
3. There is an increasing possibility that a peaceful transition to socialism will be effected in certain capitalist countries.

It is generally agreed that Mao Tse-tung was unaware that de-Stalinization was to take place. However, it appears (after the fact) that Mao was, nevertheless, not immediately critical of the "revisionism" contained therein, although he did object to the exposure of Stalin as a ruthless and slightly mad tyrant. It is probable that Mao viewed de-Stalinization as an attack upon his own Olympian position in the Chinese Communist Party (CCP), for the "cult of personality" in the PRC far surpassed its earlier counterpart in the USSR, and Khrushchev was later scored for his attack on Stalin in which "he failed to consult the fraternal parties on a question of principle involving the entire Communist movement, and later attempted to impose a *fait accompli* on them."[2]

In any event, later developments indicate that neither Khrushchev nor Mao foresaw the effects of de-Stalinization. Khrushchev had intended to provide a doctrinal rationalization for a more liberal, consumer-oriented *domestic* policy, and in so doing, he overlooked two crucial factors: (1) the rationalization had to be framed in terms of universal (not just anti-Stalin, particular) constructs; and (2) the USSR was the leader of a unified world Communist movement. By downgrading Stalin, Khrushchev destroyed the myth of Soviet infallibility, and opened the way to the onrush of polycentrism.

The unforeseen (and, within the Communist movement, unsought) results of de-Stalinization quickly became apparent. The upheavals in Poland and Hungary grew directly out of the 1956 "Secret Speech."

It is possible that Khrushchev would have had to resort to force in Poland had it not been for Chinese Communist intervention. But China put her influence behind the Poles for a short time, and the crisis passed. The effect of this intervention on the Chinese view of their own role in the world Communist system cannot be overemphasized. In saving the Soviet position in Poland, China had exerted an influence where none had perhaps existed before—and, equally important, "Khrushchev felt weak enough to be thankful for this intervention."[3]

The Hungarian revolt, however, was another matter quite distinct from the Polish crisis. In Hungary, Nagy's clear intent became to take Hungary out of the bloc, and the loss of an incumbent Socialist state was as intolerable to Mao as it was to Khrushchev. This explains the apparent Chinese shift from its "soft" stand with respect to Gomulka. Thus, the Chinese were firm supporters of the Soviet use of old-fashioned terror to crush the revolt.

Yet if Khrushchev had opened a Pandora's box in his attack on

[2] Second installment of the CCP response to the CPSU "open letter" of July 14, 1963, *Jen-min jih-pao/Hung-ch'i* (*People's Daily/Red Flag*) joint article, Sept. 13, 1963. [*People's Daily* cited hereafter as *JMJP*.]

[3] Edward Crankshaw, *The New Cold War: Moscow v. Pekin* (Baltimore: Penguin Books, 1963), p. 55.

Stalin, Mao was guilty of a similar (though less irreversible) miscalculation when he launched the famous "Hundred Flowers" movement of 1956–1957. This movement (which took its name from Mao's slogan, "Let a hundred flowers bloom, let a hundred schools of thought contend") was an attempt to liberalize the intellectual climate in Communist China, thereby regaining for the CCP the active support of the non-Party intellectuals that had been lost as a result of the purges and terror of the early 1950s. His poetry notwithstanding and contrary to some portrayals and the efforts of mainland propaganda, Mao Tse-tung is not an intellectual. By mid-1956, however, with less than two years of the PRC's First Five-Year Plan to run, and with the Second Plan (1958–1962) on the drawingboard, Mao and some of his lieutenants began to doubt whether economic and agricultural problems, among others, could be solved by attacking them as if they were enemy redoubts. Experts of different (and, to Mao, alien) types were needed, not only to solve current problems, but also to train the next generation of trusted, Communist intellectuals.

Mao's famous address, "On the Correct Handling of Contradictions Among the People," delivered in February, 1957, before the Supreme State Conference, was noteworthy for the purposes of this analysis in at least two respects: (1) Stalin was criticized for his "rule of terror and liquidation of thousands of Communists";[4] and (2) Mao extended his theory of "nonantagonistic contradictions" to include such "inevitable" contradictions as those between the leaders and the led in individual countries, even after communism had been achieved. As the campaign progressed in China, non-Party intellectuals were urged to "bloom and contend," and were told that no harm would come to them even if their criticisms were patently contrary to Marxist-Leninist doctrine.[5]

During the spring of 1957, Mao pushed hard on the policy of liberation, probably further motivated by three factors: (1) the Hungarian revolt had come and gone with no similar uprising in the PRC; (2) the initial silence on the part of the non-Party intellectuals was misinterpreted as satisfaction on their part (or, at least, obedience); and (3) Mao was convinced that, even if outspoken criticism was forth-

[4] From the Polish version of Mao's speech, as reported by Sidney Gruson from Warsaw, *The New York Times,* June 13, 1957. The "official" Chinese version quite different from the original address, did not appear in *JMJP* until June 19, some eleven days after the "Hundred Flowers" were cut by Party gardeners.

[5] See, for example, the statements of Party leaders Li Wei-han and K'o Ch'ing-shih, *New China News Agency,* May 31 and June 2, 1957, respectively.

coming, the critics would still consider CCP "achievements as primary and defects as secondary."[6]

This was not the case. With renewed assurances of immunity having been offered, from early May until June 8, 1957—a period of some five weeks—Communist China resounded with violent denunciations of Mao, the CCP, Party dictatorship, and Party policy in general. Student strikes, rallies, protest marches, even suicides and riots, forced Mao to realize his "error." The movement was abruptly terminated, in fact though not in name, and the "antirightist" campaign, launched to punish the dissidents, heralded the CCP's return to a domestic hard line.

The 1956–1957 soft line at home had been accompanied by a similar lessening of tension in international affairs. Whether or not, and for how long, the PRC could (or would) have pursued a "soft" foreign policy after having reverted to the purge at home, must remain a matter for conjecture—for any possible dilemma was resolved neatly by the Sputnik, or, more exactly, by the Soviet breakthrough in rocketry. Convinced that political superiority had always resided in the Communist system, and now equally convinced that the Socialist camp possessed an *irreversible* material superiority (a claim never made by any Soviet leader), Mao attended the November, 1957, Moscow celebrations commemorating the fortieth anniversary of the Bolshevik Revolution, convinced that the "East wind" could now be made to prevail over the "West wind." Mao thus called for a hard forward strategy in order to exploit the new Soviet deterrent for his own ends, especially to consumate the Chinese revolution through the "liberation" of Taiwan.[7]

Khrushchev, however, more fully aware of Soviet limitations and of the nature of the real world, was unwilling to comply with Mao's demands, although Mao may well have returned to Peking convinced that he had succeeded in this regard. And, indeed, the oft-quoted Moscow Declaration of November, 1957, was a much more militantly

[6] A conventional Communist formula often criticized during the "Hundred Flowers" movement. See, for example, the statement of Huang Shao-hung, a prominent non-Party personage, *New China News Agency*, May 16, 1957, cited in Roderick MacFarquhar, *The Hundred Flowers Campaign and the Chinese Intellectuals* (New York: Praeger, 1960), p. 47.

[7] It is possible that Mao had mixed feelings about his Soviet counterpart by November, 1957. Khrushchev, it is true, had agreed the previous month to provide the Communist Chinese with assistance in developing a nuclear arsenal, but Mao also must have been aware that the USSR had poured approximately US $1 billion in *aid* into Eastern Europe in the aftermath of the Hungarian revolt. China's last *loan* from the Soviet Union had been negotiated in October, 1954. Was a premium being paid for rebellion rather than loyalty?

worded statement than Khrushchev's February 14 report to PC XX some 21 months earlier. The reasons for this are clear. In the aftermath of the Polish crisis, the Hungarian revolt, and the Suez fiasco, in June, 1957, Moscow hardened its attitude. However, it is crucial to note that, for all its ostensible militancy, the Moscow Declaration did not differ, insofar as fundamentals were concerned, from the February, 1956, theses. The Moscow Declaration, it is true, is offered up with a sharper sauce, but the three basic axioms remained intact. And, it must also be noted, the Chinese Communists were *co-sponsors* of the Declaration.

It is probable that this apparent absence of critical acumen on the part of the Communist Chinese was due in part to the effect of the Moscow celebrations on Mao and the rest of the CCP delegation. In less than two years, the Chinese had risen, as they saw it, to the position of co-leaders of the world Communist system. Khrushchev had attempted de-Stalinization, without prior consultation with the Chinese, and it had resulted in the Polish and Hungarian crises—from which, so the Chinese perceived, Khrushchev had been saved by the timely—indeed, invaluable—assistance of the CCP. Now (it seems likely that Mao left Moscow convinced) Khrushchev realized his "errors" and with the material superiority afforded by Sputnik, this superiority would be brought to bear against the "imperialists"—that is, the United States—in the form of a hard strategy of confrontation. The "paper tiger," unable to meet the challenge of Soviet rocketry, would be exposed. Imperialism would not submit an immediate, unconditional surrender (Lenin had taught them this), but Taiwan would be "liberated." The means were now available to complete the Chinese (as well as the world) revolution. As CCP Politburo member Ch'en Yün stated later at the Warsaw Pact meetings in May of 1958, "Why should there be any fear of imperialism when the Socialist camp has absolute superiority?"[8]

If, indeed, this approximates Mao's Moscow musings, it has since become obvious that Khrushchev did not share them. Much has been written in retrospect as to which Party was the victor during that fateful November of 1957. Most of it is academic. The problem was not even one of a communication breakdown—there was no breakdown because there was no communication. Neither side perceived the necessity of a true dialog prior to the formulation of the Declaration. The absence of such an interchange occasioned both the original misinterpretation of the other's position, and the subsequent dispute argued textually on the basis of Holy Writ as to the meaning of the Declaration itself. Put in the simplest terms, the Declaration represented a victory for neither

[8] *JMJP,* May 28, 1958.

side because neither Mao nor Khrushchev really understood the position of the other. Each side viewed the other's position as its own mirror image—each saw what it wanted to see. Both sides were therefore at fault; however, as the Soviets were merely effecting particular modifications in an extant thesis, which the Chinese would seek to extirpate, the latter were in some ways more justifiably open to later attack. This was not seen at the time—unity was strength—but it was too good to last.

With the aid of hindsight, it can be argued that 1958 will be remembered, to coin a Chinese phrase, as "the year of the split." Two events justify this appellation: (1) Mao's claim that China would beat the USSR in the race toward communism (via the "Great Leap Forward" and the people's commune movement);[9] and (2) Khrushchev's avowed intention to settle the Lebanon crisis of the summer of 1958 from what he called a position of "reason, not intimidation."[10]

In the wake of the "Hundred Flowers" disaster, CCP leaders, without the intellectuals, but armed with the "thought of Mao Tse-tung" (*Mao Tse-tung szo-hsiang*), set out to modernize China. Moreover, Party planners were going to do it literally overnight. "Twenty years in one day" was the clarion call summoning forth the explosion of energy and experimentation that swept across the Chinese mainland for over seven months during 1958.[11] Through spiritual incentive, mass application of labor, communization, and equalization of urban and rural standards of living, Mao would speedily transform China into a true Communist state. In an implicit rejection of the Soviet model, the CCP made it clear that this would not require decades of struggle and sacrifice; "even octogenarians and nonagenarians," it was stated, "will live to enjoy the benefits of communism."[12] Enthusiasm, initiative, and mass effort could work all wonders.

It was clear to the Russians that the Chinese had indeed put the cart before the horse, inasmuch as the latter were concerned (witness the communes) with problems of distribution before they had created the object of distribution. However, the Chinese, born along on a wave

[9] See Arthur A. Cohen, *The Communism of Mao Tse-tung* (Chicago: University of Chicago Press, 1964), pp. 168–169. Also Ch'en Po-ta, "Ch'üan-hsin ti she-hui, ch'üan-hsin ti jen," ("Completely New Society, Completely New Man"), *Hung-ch'i,* no. 3, July 1, 1958, p. 11.

[10] See Khrushchev's letter of July 18, 1958, to President Eisenhower; quoted in Crankshaw, *op. cit.,* p. 81.

[11] For a very informative essay on the euphoria extant in Communist China during this period, see A. V. Sherman, "The People's Commune," in *The Chinese Communes* (a special supplement published by *Soviet Survey,* London, 1959).

[12] *JMJP,* Sept. 2 and Oct. 1, 1958. See also Peking *Kung-jen jih-pao* (Daily *Worker),* Oct. 25, 1958.

of self-generated enthusiasm and statistical overestimates, had convinced themselves that they were racing toward communism. Soviet warnings went unheeded. Khrushchev later recounted that he had warned Mao the attempt would fail, but Mao was not seeking advice—"[He] was not asking me," Khrushchev recalled, "he was telling me."[13]

It was precisely during the period of the Chinese "takeoff" that the Lebanon crisis erupted in July, 1958. With the failures of the "Great Leap" and the communes, as originally envisaged, yet to come, and with Sputnik still regarded as the symbol of bloc superiority, the Chinese argued that the Russians should use force to oppose the Anglo-American landings in the Lebanon. Khrushchev, however, called for a summit meeting. The Chinese opposed this; "coddling wrong only helps the devil. The only language [the imperialists] understand is force."[14] Further, the Soviet proposal for a summit meeting included India as well as the "Big Four" (the United States, Great Britain, the Soviet Union, and France)—but not the PRC. What had happened, Mao must have wondered, to the equality of the previous November? When the United States held that the situation in Lebanon should be placed before the Security Council (which, of course, included the Republic of China as a permanent member), it is worth noting that Khrushchev nearly accepted the US proposal,[15] before hurriedly flying to Peking where he apparently had "second thoughts."

The late summer and early autumn of 1958 must have been a period of "agonizing reappraisal" for the architects of Chinese foreign and bloc policy. Faced with what the Chinese perceived to be an imperialist invasion of the Middle East (the prelude to an attack upon the Soviet Union itself?), Khrushchev reacted, they felt, like a coward. If such was the response to danger on the very periphery of the USSR, what was the likelihood of Russian power being brought to bear in support of Chinese demands in areas that, on balance, were of secondary or tertiary concern to the Soviet Union as a nation-state? And, most important, if this analysis was indeed correct, did these latter areas include the "liberation" of Taiwan? If so, then of what use to the PRC was Soviet superiority in rocketry?

The answer to these questions was forthcoming during the Quemoy-

[13] Speech of Apr. 15, 1964, quoted in Arthur A. Cohen, "Maoism," in Milorad M. Drahkovitch, ed., *Marxism in the Modern World* (Stanford: Stanford University Press, 1965), p. 178.

[14] *JMJP*, July 19, 1958. This statement appeared the day after Khrushchev's appeal for a summit meeting.

[15] *The New York Times*, July 24, 1958.

Matsu crisis of late summer and early fall, 1958. With the West pre-occupied with Middle Eastern affairs, the Communist Chinese tried to cut off the offshore islands in a calculated probe of the extent of the US commitment to aid the Nationalists in the defense of Quemoy and Matsu. It soon became clear that the United States was acting like something more than a "paper tiger." The USSR (i.e., Khrushchev) thus had a golden opportunity to dispel any doubts in Mao's mind as to Moscow's resolution by coming to China's assistance with the vaunted Soviet arsenal. The doubts, however, were not dispelled; Khrushchev's cowardice was not a possibility—it was a fact. "We have not interfered in and do not intend to interfere in the *civil war*. . . . The intention to get back Quemoy, Matsu, Taiwan, and [the] Pescadores is the internal affair of the Chinese people."[16] In a further clarification, Khrushchev added that the "USSR will come to the aid of the PRC if the latter is attacked from without."[17] The implication was clear; any attack by Nationalist forces would be an incident in the continuing civil war, and the provisions of the 1950 Sino-Soviet Treaty of Friendship, Alliance, and Mutual Assistance (by which the USSR is bound to come to the aid of the PRC if the latter is attacked by Japan "or any ally of Japan") would not obtain. The following day (October 6, 1958), Peking announced the suspension of the shelling of Quemoy and Matsu. Two weeks later, the People's Publishing House in Peking published a collection of some of Mao's more strident sayings under the title, *Imperialists and Reactionaries Are All Paper Tigers.* And so, Mao must have thought, are some "comrades."

1959: The Spirit of Camp David and No Bomb

Within a year to 18 months after the Chinese disillusionment over Quemoy–Matsu—that is, by late 1959 or early 1960—Mao Tse-tung had apparently become convinced of the necessity for Khrushchev's ouster. First of all, the Soviet leader had been proved right on the incipient failure of the "Great Leap." In August, 1959, Chou En-lai publicly refuted the earlier reports (including those on the people's commune movement) of outstanding successes.

In addition, it appeared that Khrushchev had intervened in the domestic affairs of the PRC. Later evidence established that the CCP Politburo, let alone the Central Committee, had not been unanimously

[16] See John R. Thomas, "Soviet Behavior in the Quemoy Crisis of 1958," *Orbis,* vol. VI, no. 1, *Spring,* 1962, pp. 57–58 (emphasis added).

[17] *The New York Times,* Oct. 6, 1958.

in favor of the "Great Leap Forward" and the people's commune movement.

One of those in the opposition was Marshal P'eng Te-huai, the Minister of Defense. In May, 1959, Khrushchev visited Albania, as fate would have it, at the same time as a Communist Chinese delegation, headed by P'eng. The Marshal was apparently then in the process of drafting a memorandum to the CCP Politburo stating the reasons for his opposition to the fanaticism of both the "Great Leap" and the communes. However, before presenting the memo to his colleagues in Peking, he was imprudent enough to show it to the Russian leader.[18]

It is quite possible that Khrushchev interpreted P'eng's memo as prima facie evidence of a highly placed anti-Mao Tse-tung/Liu Shao-ch'i (and, thus, pro-Soviet?) clique in the Chinese Party. In any event, when P'eng's interrogation and subsequent purge brought to light Khrushchev's "involvement" with an "anti-Party group," Mao, who had fought Stalinist intrigues in the CCP since the 1920s, had good reason to consider this as kith and kin to the earlier machinations of Stalin, especially inasmuch as in June (the month after the P'eng–Khrushchev meeting), the Soviet Union refused to honor its earlier agreement to provide the PRC with a "sample atomic bomb."

Finally, in September, 1959, occurred what *Pravda* quite correctly, though not in this context, called an "historic turningpoint," namely: Khrushchev's visit to the United States. The importance of this event to both Khrushchev *and* Mao cannot be overemphasized. No Soviet Premier had ever paid a state visit to the United States, and Khrushchev played it to the hilt from Camp David through the cornfields of Iowa and on to the Golden Gate. Praising President Eisenhower as a "man of peace," Khrushchev was on tour as a *head of state,* not as the leader of the Communist bloc. With goodwill shown by the *two* most powerful of countries, world peace seemed more secure. The "Spirit of Camp David" was indeed an intoxicating fragrance.

But not for Mao. We can only speculate, but if later developments are any criteria, Camp David must have caused shouts of rage to resound throughout the Imperial City. From the beginning, Mao's overriding ambition has been to effect the complete restoration of China's "traditional" frontiers. The Korean War had prevented this; moreover, for all the disclaimers, there were indeed "two Chinas"—and the "other" one, the Republic of (or Nationalist) China, protected by the military power of the United States, continued to hold a permanent seat on the

[18] See the analysis of David A. Charles, "The Dismissal of Marshal P'eng Te-huai," *The China Quarterly,* no. 8, Oct.–Dec., 1961.

Security Council, and continued to offer a choice of allegiance to the millions of overseas Chinese, not to mention a contrasting developmental model to the emerging nations. Nationalist China, Mao had concluded, must be destroyed. To do this, the staying power, however defined, of the United States had to be destroyed as a prior condition.

Khrushchev's definition of the 1958 crisis in the Taiwan Strait as a part of the continuing "civil war" ended Mao's hope to regain the "lost territory" (*sang ti*) by direct assault. Thus he had shifted to a strategy of *indirect* assault, as heralded by his call in the fall of 1958 for *all* peoples to band together to drive the US forces from their overseas bases. Observers have commented on Communist China's tendency to claim a stake in developments geographically far removed from what, on the surface, would appear to be areas of real Chinese concern. However, if the present analysis is correct, the Communist Chinese perceive their stake in such developments to be great indeed. According to the hard strategy in force since Sputnik (and especially since the 1958 offshore islands crisis), any and all engagements of US strength—be they in Berlin, the Congo, Cuba, Vietnam, Malaysia, or the Dominican Republic—have been viewed as small "pin pricks" that would eventually weaken the giant and bring him down. As Chou En-lai himself was to state in October of 1960, "Even if the United States does not withdraw from the Taiwan region and no breakthrough occurs there, [breakthroughs] will occur elsewhere. . . . It is only a matter of time."[19]

Yet here was Khrushchev at Camp David pushing a policy of *détente* with the United States, a policy that not only cut directly across the CCP line of open hostility to the US, but also aroused CCP suspicions that Khrushchev was going to accept the US position with regard to the status quo in the Taiwan Strait. As if to further infuriate the Chinese, only a week before Khrushchev's trip to the United States, the Soviet Government officially had adopted a position of neutrality with regard to China's serious border dispute with India,[20] a move unprecedented in Communist Party-state relations to that time.

Khrushchev himself must have realized that his recent deportment was less than exemplary in Mao's eyes; hence, the significance of his trip to Peking for the PRC's National Day celebrations immediately upon conclusion of his visit to the United States. But the Peking talks only served to exacerbate existing difficulties as the Soviet Premier suggested that, in the interests of world peace, Mao attempt to negotiate a

[19] As reported by Edgar Snow in *Look,* Jan. 31, 1961.
[20] TASS (Moscow), Sept. 9, 1959.

peaceful solution to Sino-American differences over Taiwan, a proposition literally unthinkable to Mao. Four days later, Khrushchev left the Chinese capital without signing the ritualistic joint communique that is part and parcel of any state visit to Peking. The Communist Chinese regarded Khrushchev's suggestion as tantamount to renouncing their claim to Taiwan. As the authoritative *Jen-min jih-pao* later declared, "[The PRC] has not forgotten and will not forget" this "two Chinas" plan.[21]

"Long Live Leninism"

By 1960, the convert shadowboxing of the previous two years had developed into a semipublic brawl. The volume of material pouring forth from the participants concerning the split increased, but most of it only served to reiterate positions already taken. In February, 1960, according to Peking, Khrushchev again informed the Chinese Communists that the USSR would not keep its earlier promise of October, 1957, concerning nuclear weapons. During that same month, also, the Soviet Party boss toured Southeast Asia, apparently doing nothing to further the Communist Chinese case in either Indonesia (with regard to Sukarno's treatment of overseas Chinese and the dual-nationality problem) or in India (with regard to the Sino-Indian border controversy). Peking maintained a virtual press blackout on the trip.

On April 16, in a long *Hung-ch'i* article entitled "Long Live Leninism," written by the journal's editorial board, the Communist Chinese openly challenged the Soviet leaders with regard to bloc strategy toward the West. This statement, which warrants greater analysis than is possible here, in effect accused Khrushchev of being unfit to formulate strategy for the world Communist movement. Although the Communist Chinese had implicitly attacked the Peaceful Coexistence theses of PC XX on earlier occasions, this was the first systematic attempt at refutation on the basis of uncompromising Leninist principles. Using Tito as a synonym for Khrushchev, the CCP emphasized the need for violence in the quest for power, called for unresolved support for all "wars of national liberation," and demanded that "true Marxist-Leninists" accept the fact that Peaceful Coexistence is nothing more than a *tactic* in the struggle against imperialism. Mao was not, it should be noted, calling for general war, but he was demanding a more aggressive policy against the West—and not only in areas of key Soviet concern

[21] *JMJP,* Sept. 1, 1963.

(such as Berlin) but also in the Far East, notably in the Taiwan Strait and Vietnam.[22] While Khrushchev was not attacked by name, it was quite clear whom the *Hung-ch'i* editors had in mind when they noted that "there are some . . . well-intentioned people who *want* to be Marxists, but are confused in the face of certain new historical phenomena and therefore have some erroneous ideas" [emphasis added]. Building up the fight, Soviet spokesmen countered quickly with statements concerning the destructiveness of nuclear weapons and the necessity of accepting Peaceful Coexistence as a basis of bloc policy, not merely as a tactical expedient.

It was in the wake of this exchange that there occurred one of the most serious (and perplexing) incidents in the entire course of the Sino-Soviet conflict to date: namely, the withdrawal from the PRC in July, 1960, of the Soviet advisors and technicians together with their blueprints and plans. The precise reason for this unprecedented step is not known, but the Communist Chinese reactions to the U-2 incident in May, 1960, as well as to the breakdown of the Paris summit talks, may have been factors contributing to the Soviet decision.

Mao made the most of the U-2 incident, among other things threatening Japan for allowing the United States to use Japanese bases for these planes. (This was an obvious attempt to bring Soviet pressure to bear against the Kishi Government for signing the Mutual Defense Treaty with the United States earlier in the year.) At the now-famous Bucharest Conference—the Third Congress of the Rumanian Workers' Party which occurred in June, the Communist Chinese obviously relished this evidence of what they regarded as the folly of Khrushchev's soft policies, and here not with regard to Taiwan—the U-2 brought danger to the Soviet Union itself.

At this point, it needs to be pointed out that both the Chinese and Soviet leaders were wrong in the way they viewed their counterparts. The present author is convinced that, although the *ultimate* goals professed by both the USSR and the PRC are identical, these goals are of such a long-range nature that they have little policy relevance. The Sino-Soviet dispute is a dispute over policy—policy as it affects two historically antagonistic *nation states*. Thus the Communist Chinese, if they ever expected a Soviet change of mind on the basis of textual

[22] Khrushchev, it will be recalled, had already disassociated the USSR from any Sino-Soviet Treaty obligations in the event of a showdown over Taiwan. Earlier in 1960, the USSR, as co-chairman of the International Control Commission (ICC) for Laos, had agreed to an "indefinite adjournment" of the ICC. Peking, however, had supported North Vietnamese demands for ICC resumption.

exegesis, were sadly mistaken. Conversely, if Khrushchev expected the old warrior in Peking to acknowledge that the destructive power of modern weaponry placed Taiwan permanently out of his reach, he was equally mistaken. As indicated earlier, Mao reacted to the 1958 failure to interdict Quemoy and Matsu in time-tested guerrilla fashion. "Enemy halts, we harass." Who is the enemy? The United States. And where is the enemy? Everywhere, so harass him everywhere. Support all "wars of national liberation" without reservation. Encourage terror and assassination by guerrillas in the underdeveloped areas; eliminate the thin "national bourgeois" frosting; exacerbate age-old tribal or regional hatreds; reduce areas to chaos—then the "imperialists" will have to intervene. Do this ten times, twenty times, and the United States, hopelessly overextended, will have no alternative but to come to terms.

Khrushchev gradually came to perceive the Maoist strategy, as well as the danger of this strategy for the Soviet Union, for certainly the USSR could not avoid becoming involved in the awful confrontation that would surely result. Beyond this there were two additional factors that troubled the Russians: (1) "wars of national liberation" may be fine in theory, but in practice they could have a harmful effect on the Soviet economy through the disruption of established patterns of trade; and (2) if Mao was indeed serious about installing such an openly hostile strategy as a cardinal principle of bloc policy, what would follow when Communist China acquired atomic weapons?

It was probably on the basis of such forebodings that Khrushchev summarily ordered the recall of Soviet advisors and technicians. The Communist Chinese economy was already in trouble as a result of "Great Leap" excesses compounded by natural disasters. The loss of these experts would compound existing problems and, hopefully, render still more difficult the independent Chinese development of even a fledgling nuclear capability. Atomic weapons, even in the hands of "men of reason," were awesome enough.

Communist Chinese delegate P'eng Chen[23] had argued at Bucharest that the only way to world peace was through revolution. Did Mao and the other CCP leaders actually believe this? If so, it made little difference whether the Chinese belief was based upon chauvinism, arrogance, ignorance, or a blind faith in militant Leninism. Yet as leader of the world Communist movement, Khrushchev had to counter the Chinese attack on theoretical as well as pragmatic grounds. Thus on June 21, the Soviet leader condemned Mao before the assembled delegates at Bucharest as another Stalin, "oblivious to any interests other

[23] Not to be confused with Marshal P'eng Te-huai.

than his own . . . , an ultra-Leftist, an ultradogmatist, indeed, a *left revisionist*.[24] Khrushchev further reminded his audience that "we live in a time when we have neither Marx, nor Engels, nor Lenin with us. If we act like children who, studying the alphabet, compile words from letters, we shall not go very far."[25]

On the same day as Khrushchev's Bucharest address, Mao again issued a call for the formation of a broad "United Front" against the United States, as well as declaring June 21–27 "Taiwan Liberation and Anti-US Propaganda Week." The following month, the Soviet advisors left the PRC, and from July 5 through August 26, Radio Moscow's domestic service did not carry a single commentary on Chinese developments.

The intensification of the dispute in the spring and summer of 1960 was reflected in the heated discussions at the Moscow Conference of that November. Though the Conference was attended by Party leaders from some 81 countries, Mao Tse-tung, "the greatest contemporary Marxist-Leninist" and the leading "advocate of thoroughgoing revolution,"[26] was conspicuously absent.

The December communique issued at the close of the Conference has often been labelled a compromise document. However, it did not represent a smoothing-over of differences, but rather a statement of differences with both Soviet and Chinese positions being placed in juxtaposition. In practice, each Party later cited only those passages which agreed with its own line. In addition, the bellicosity of CCP delegates Teng Hsiao-p'ing and P'eng Chen, together with the early departure for Tirana of the Albanian delegation on November 25, rendered compromise impossible. The Communist Chinese were unsuccessful in their attempts to sway even a sizeable minority of the assembled Parties to their side; Khrushchev's central thesis—victory without war—remained intact. However, this did not mean a Soviet victory. Maoist intransigence and tiny Albania's walkout indicated clearly that the time had passed when Moscow could command instant and total obedience through unilateral fiat. The Chinese action known in Communist jargon as "fractionalism," was nothing less than a declaration that Peking would work to organize a Communist movement around its own authority, a decision that would be reinforced by the events of the following October.

In October, 1961, PC XXII of the CPSU was convened in Mos-

[24] Crankshaw, *op. cit.*, p. 107 (emphasis in the original).

[25] Quoted in David Floyd, *Mao Against Khrushchev* (New York: Praeger, 1964), p. 280.

[26] *JMJP,* Oct. 6–7, 1960.

cow. Three months earlier, in the draft of the new CPSU program, Khrushchev had emphasized that communism would grow out of abundance, not vice versa. At PC XXII, the Soviet leader openly attacked Albania and ordered Stalin's body removed from its resting place alongside Lenin in the Red Square mausoleum. Chou En-lai defended Albania at the Congress, then abruptly broke off his Moscow stay and returned to Peking. The Chinese were later to cite Khrushchev's attack on a "fraternal Party" (i.e., Albania) as one of the major factors in the Sino-Soviet dispute, an act for which the Russians must apologize prior to any reconciliation.

Cuba, the Test Ban Treaty, and the Sino-Soviet Border

By mid-1962, any divergence of outlook between the PRC and the USSR had become *ipso facto* an addendum to one or more of the key issues in the controversy; the momentum of the dispute was such that even small issues were exaggerated far beyond their real importance. With each protagonist holding that *his* national interest was indeed nothing less than the interest of the *entire* "bloc," it became increasingly clear that harmony could be restored only if one side or the other recanted on all major issues: Peaceful Coexistence (especially with the United States), disarmament, nuclear weapons, and peaceful transition to socialism.

Two key events during the fall of 1962 made it clear (if there was ever any doubt) that neither Mao nor Khrushchev would consider any accommodation on these terms. These events—the Cuban missile crisis and the Sino-Indian border war—had a shattering effect on what little remained of the façade of Sino-Soviet unity. In Cuba, the Soviet Union was forced to retreat under US pressure. While the vast majority of the people of the world breathed a great sigh of relief, the Communist Chinese seized upon the backdown as a not-to-be-neglected opportunity to reduce Khrushchev's prestige. *Jen-min jih-pao* pilloried Khrushchev's acts as another "Munich," and stated that the crisis was actually the result of "carrying out an appeasement policy toward US imperialist aggression."[27] The Soviet Premier was not a fit leader, Peking implicitly declared, and Castro was assured that "the 650 million Chinese people are the *most* loyal and *most* reliable comrades-in-arms of the Cuban people."[28] According to Peking, Khrushchev was doubly guilty; he had been wrong in placing the missiles in Cuba in the first place ("adventurism") and he had been wrong in withdrawing them to avert a

[27] *JMJP,* Nov. 5, 1962.
[28] *Hung-ch'i,* Oct. 31, 1962 (emphasis added).

possible nuclear showdown ("capitulationism"). It was time for "other Parties" to "go into the front ranks of the movement,"[29] and inasmuch as the Mao Tse-tung/Liu Shao-ch'i leadership had (said Peking) never made a mistake since assuming power on the Long March in 1935,[30] it was obvious which Party the CCP had in mind.

If Mao actually entertained any real hopes of replacing Khrushchev as leader of the international Communist movement during that fateful autumn, these were doomed to failure by the Sino-Indian border war. The CPSU, together with nearly all of the Communist Parties of Eastern and Western Europe, professed the belief that the Communist Chinese action in India was further proof that Maoist "adventurism" might trigger a nuclear war. The Chinese had as their immediate aims: to teach the Indians a lesson, to destroy Indian prestige, and to boost the morale of the People's Liberation Army. It is also possible that Mao viewed the conflict as a final opportunity for Khrushchev to stand up and be counted. And stand he did, as the Soviet Union responded with military and economic aid—but to *India*—and refused to endorse the Communist Chinese proposals for negotiations.[31] At the same time, Moscow declared flatly that a Party's attitude toward Khrushchev's Cuban policy was the key to whether its leaders were for Peaceful Coexistence or for adventurism.[32]

By December, 1962, the dispute was made public in great detail. Khrushchev's speech before the Supreme Soviet on December 12 was an extremely sarcastic attack on the Maoist leadership, including charges that the Albanians "and those who push them" (i.e., the CCP) are "Trotskyites." The Communist Chinese countered with two major statements which made it clear that a split in the movement was the only alternative to a Soviet surrender. During December, the fight was also carried to the floor of Communist Party congresses in Europe—and everywhere the CCP delegates were shouted down and outvoted. The wraps were off; as one of the Italian delegates was to say, "When we mean China, we have no need to say Albania."[33]

By the beginning of 1963, the issues separating the PRC and the USSR were a matter of public record. What remained to be seen were the turn the conflict would take and the tactics each side would follow to align support.[34] However, whereas the battle hitherto had been

[29] *JMJP/Hung-ch'i* joint article, Feb. 4, 1964.
[30] *JMJP/Hung-ch'i* joint article, Sept. 13, 1963.
[31] *Pravda,* Nov. 5, 1962.
[32] *Pravda,* Nov. 18, 1962.
[33] Crankshaw, *op. cit.,* p. 146.
[34] United States Information Agency, Research and Reference Service, R–135–64, Sept. 17, 1964.

fought primarily on an ideological plane, Soviet actions during the Cuban missile crisis and the Sino-Indian border war were irrefutable proof to the Communist Chinese that their interests were being sacrified by the relatively affluent Russians on the altar of the status quo. And status quo, Mao correctly perceived, meant the continued existence of an independent Taiwan. Therefore, the CCP attempted to force the issue throughout the first six months of 1963 by means of a series of articles which first rejected a truce, then proclaimed a correct ("general") line for the entire world Communist movement, and finally agreed to bilateral talks with the CPSU in July of 1963.

However, the Maoist strategy backfired. P'eng Chen, Teng Hsiao-p'ing, and T'ao Chu—three of Mao's most militant lieutenants—were in Moscow in July, 1963, to present the CCP case when the USSR joined with the United States and the United Kingdom in signing the partial nuclear test ban treaty. The treaty, and the Soviet Union's subsequent propaganda campaign, caught the Communist Chinese off guard. Mao was outmaneuvered, for the PRC's refusal to sign the treaty more effectively exposed the chauvinistic nature of Mao's "doctrinal" argument with Khrushchev than anything the Soviet leadership could have done.[35] Mao was hard pressed to defend his position, inasmuch as CPSU ideologs effectively obscured the Chinese leader's stress on small wars ("wars of national liberation") and emphasized the Maoist stress on war *per se,* as can be seen in the following statement of the Soviet government:[36]

> This is what Mao Tse-tung actually said: "In China, construction has not gotten underway in earnest. If imperialists impose a war, we shall be prepared to terminate the construction; let us first have a trial of strength and then return to construction." It will be clear to everyone that this pronouncement has an absolutely different meaning. What does "'let us first have a trial of strength and then return to construction" mean? Is this a call to peace, to the struggle for Peaceful Coexistence? In essence, this means exactly orientation toward an armed conflict, toward a military solution of the contradictions between socialism and capitalism. And no one would succeed in depicting this orientation as a slip of the tongue.

Further, Soviet spokesmen scored heavily by condemning China for allowing nationalism (e.g., the Chinese desire for nuclear weapons) to take precedence over the struggle for world peace (e.g., the partial

[35] Arthur A. Cohen, "Maoism," *op. cit.,* p. 187.

[36] *Pravda,* Sept. 21–22, 1963. Cohen (*loc. cit.*) points out that this was the only major anti-CCP Soviet statement which was not reprinted in the Chinese press.

nuclear test ban treaty). And Mao's demand that Indian Communists support the PRC in the Sino-Indian war gave further weight to Soviet denunciations of Mao's narrow nationalism. Khrushchev's image of Mao as a fanatic xenophobe was constructed with great skill, and the Chinese rebuttals were weak in the extreme—complaints of "Khrushchev . . . playing dirty tricks with quotations."[37] Peking was clearly on the defensive as the Soviet Union stripped away the doctrinal shield concealing the real points at issue.[38] As Harry Gelman described the situation as of the summer of 1963:[39]

> Sino-Soviet relations had now reached a point where both sides were caricaturing and attacking each other's leaders by name, and where both proceeded to publish statements revealing hitherto secret aspects of their dealings with each other since the beginning of the dispute. The Soviets spoke of Mao as a senile "Trotskyite" tyrant and racist who sought world war, who had made monumental blunders in domestic policy, and whose government maintained "concentration camps" and massacred minority peoples, forcing them to seek haven in the USSR. The Chinese, in turn, characterized Khrushchev as a cowardly traitor allied with "imperialism" who was striving to restore capitalism in the Soviet Union and to undermine Marxism-Leninism throughout the world.

By the early autumn, the CPSU had apparently decided to convene an international Communist meeting at which the CCP and its allies would be charged to desist their "splitting" activities or leave the movement. However, it appears that certain key pro-Soviet Parties[40] pressured the CPSU to postpone this plan pending a reply from Peking to another call[41] for a cessation of the open polemics. The CCP refused this appeal and in early 1964 recognized a number of pro-Maoist factions which had split off from established Communist Parties as the official and legitimate Parties in the countries concerned. Furthermore, Peking announced that such recognition and support would henceforth be tendered to "revolutionary" (i.e., pro-CCP) Parties everywhere.[42] Thus, a major characteristic of the dispute beginning in early 1964 has

[37] *Hung-ch'i,* Sept. 6, 1963.

[38] Cohen, *loc. cit.*

[39] Harry Gelman, "The Sino-Soviet Conflict: A Survey," *Problems of Communism,* Mar.–Apr. 1964, vol. XIII, no. 2, pp. 14–15.

[40] See, for example, the article by Rumanian Premier I. G. Maurer in *World Marxist Review,* vol. 6, no. 11, Nov., 1963.

[41] Gelman (*op. cit.,* p. 13) points out that, according to Soviet statements, Khrushchev had asked Mao in October of 1962 to "forget the past and 'start our relations with a clean page,'" probably to ensure bloc support during the Cuban missile crisis.

[42] *JMJP/Hung-ch'i,* Feb. 4, 1964.

been the increase in Communist Chinese "splitting" activities and, concomitant with each Chinese success in this regard (for example, in Ceylon, Belgium, and Australia), a corresponding decline in Soviet influence.

As the CCP intensified its effort to split the pro-Soviet Parties, it also began to search for allies on the state level. By means of refining his 1946 idea of the "intermediate zone,"[43] Mao provided doctrinal support for enlisting any and all countries, even "imperialistic" ones such as France, as allies, provided they opposed some aspect of US policy. Being "anti-American," therefore, came to be equivalent to being "progressive," regardless of the true nature of a regime. And as the USSR refused to back certain key Maoist policies, being "progressive" increasingly included being "anti-Soviet," as well.

The tactical skill with which the CCP employed this concept of the "intermediate zone" could be seen in the Sino-Soviet territorial dispute, as it developed through the summer and early autumn of 1964.[44] In an interview with the leader of a Japanese Socialist Party mission to Peking on July 10, 1964, Mao Tse-tung criticized the Soviet Union for its "territorial ambitions" both in Asia and in Europe, stating that the CCP was prepared to "wage this war [against the CPSU] for another twenty-five years," and explicitly supporting the Japanese Socialists' demand that the USSR return the Kurile Islands to Japan. Mao concluded: "About a hundred years ago, the area to the east of [Lake] Baikal, became Russian territory, and since then Vladivostok, Khabarovsk, Kamchatka, and other areas have been Soviet territory. We have not yet presented our account for this list."[45]

Mao's position with regard to the Kuriles may well have reflected his fear of a possible Russo-Japanese accord which, given Communist China's embattled relations with both the USSR and India, would leave

[43] See "Talk with the American Correspondent Anna Louise Strong," *Selected Works of Mao Tse-tung* (Peking: Foreign Languages Press, 1961), pp. 97–101.

[44] The territorial dispute came into the open in December, 1962. In his speech to the Supreme Soviet, Khrushchev left-handedly criticized the Communist Chinese by contrasting their militant position with regard to the uban crisis with their "reasonableness" in not ridding mainland China of the "colonial cancers" of Hong Kong and Macao. This occasioned the most violent Chinese reactions in the conflict to date. On this aspect of the dispute, *see* Dennis J. Doolin, *Territorial Claims in the Sino-Soviet Conflict: Documents and Analysis* (Stanford: Stanford University Press for The Hoover Institution on War, Revolution, and Peace, 1965).

[45] *Sekai Shūhō* (Tokyo), Aug. 11, 1964. For an English translation of relevant excerpts, see Doolin, *op. cit.*, pp. 42–44.

the Chinese with no hope of a major Asian ally in any campaign against Taiwan. In any event, Mao's statement about the Kuriles was apparently secondary in his own mind to his attack in the same interview on Soviet expansionism in Europe—specifically, in Rumania, Germany, Poland, and Finland where "the Russians took everything they could."

Pravda countered on September 2, with an editorial condemning Mao's views as nothing less than a new version of the *lebensraum* theory, portraying the Chinese leader as a latter-day follower of Hitler, Tojo, and others who had advocated "an openly expansionist program with far-reaching pretensions."[46] Shortly thereafter, Khrushchev told members of a Japanese parliamentary delegation that, if the Russian tsars had been expansionists, so had the Chinese Emperors who seized Mongolia, Tibet, and Sinkiang. Elaborating on the sharp ethnic and linguistic differences of the Sinkiang indigenous population from the Chinese, Khrushchev stated that "Chinese Emperors conquered them in the past and deprived them of their independence."[47]

The Chinese Communists were infuriated by this statement. In his earlier talk with the Japanese Socialists, Mao had noted that "the Soviet Union is concentrating troops along its borders;"[48] now here was Khrushchev claiming that Sinkiang did not belong to China. On October 1, in one of the most bellicose statements in the Sino-Soviet conflict, Saifudin, alternate member of the Central Committee of the CCP and Chairman of the Sinkiang Uighur Autonomous Region, answered Khrushchev: "If the Khrushchev revisionists dare to stretch out their evils hands to invade and occupy our territory, they will certainly be repulsed. . . . Their evil hands will be cut off as relentlessly as were those of the Indian reactionaries when they invaded China."[49]

Khrushchevism Without Khrushchev

With charges and countercharges of such intensity, it is difficult to see how Khrushchev, had he remained in power, could have avoided the convocation of an international Party conference to formally excommunicate the Chinese—regardless of the boycotts and opposition that would surely have accompanied such a meeting. Even his ouster in October, 1964, only occasioned a temporary cessation of the open

[46] For an English translation of the entire editorial, see Doolin, *op. cit.*, pp. 47–57.

[47] *Ibid.*, p. 71.

[48] *Ibid.*, p. 43.

[49] Urumchi Radio, Oct. 1, 1964; translated in Doolin, *op. cit.*, pp. 75–76.

polemics. The Chinese remained inflexible, taking implicit credit for Khrushchev's dismissal and gathering strength from their successful nuclear detonation of October 16. Thus, the new Soviet leaders, Brezhnev and Kosygin, felt that they had to call for an international Party conference anyway, if only to make it clear that a world movement still existed and that the CPSU remained the leader of that movement.

The call went out on November 24, but at the same time, the new Soviet leadership was battered by a series of demands from various Parties to know why Khrushchev had been ousted. Moreover, the CPSU answers were not deemed acceptable when they were forthcoming. The difficulties confronting Brezhnev and Kosygin with these Parties was made clear in the developments at the international Communist conference which convened in Moscow on March 1, 1965.

The CPSU did get a statement out of the Conference, which, while not important for its substance, showed that some semblance of a unified, world Communist movement still existed. But the conference was hardly a Soviet victory: Rumania did not attend; the representative of the British Party arrived late; and one Italian delegate implicitly attacked both the continuation of "democratic centralism" and the suppression of fractions. The final communique stated clearly that the delegates had only "exchanged opinions."

Moreover, on March 4, during the conference, Peking made patent its opposition to its work by staging a demonstration of Chinese and Vietnamese students outside the US Embassy in Moscow—a demonstration so violent that Red Army troops were required to assist the Moscow police in dispersing the demonstrators. Shortly thereafter, the Communist Chinese attacked the new Soviet leadership for the latter's "criminal objective of Soviet-American collaboration for the domination of the world."[50]

Apart from the person of Nikita Khrushchev, it was aparent that the divisive elements in the Sino-Soviet conflict were still present. This was indicated clearly in a speech delivered on May 25, 1965, by P'eng Chen at the Aliarcham Academy of Social Sciences in Djakarta, Indonesia.[51] An analysis of P'eng's speech discloses five main points: (1) Moscow must completely capitulate to Peking; (2) the Communist bloc will be reunited only in the distant future; (3) the world is divided into two main blocs, the "revolutionary forces" of Asia, Africa, and Latin America versus the US, the USSR, and their allies; (4) the

[50] "A Great Victory for Leninism," *Hung-ch'i,* no. 4, 1965.
[51] Text in *Peking Review,* no. 24, June 11, 1965.

Chinese aim is to lead this revolutionary front rather than to repair the alliance; and (5) the Soviet leaders are no longer revolutionary—in fact, antiimperialist kings and princes are more dependable allies, since they are more revolutionary than the CPSU elite.

In mid-September, 1965, the hostilities in Vietnam and Kashmir were significant annoyances in the Sino-Soviet conflict. The Soviet leaders rebuked the Chinese for encouraging the Pakistanis; the authoritative TASS statement of September 7 criticized "outside forcess" for trying to set the Indians and Pakistanis at loggerheads and once again supported the resolutions of the UN Security Council (which Peking had denounced) calling for an end to the clashes. The Chinese viewed the conflict as an opportunity to strengthen their ties with the Pakistanis, deepen the rift in US–Pakistani relations, and further damage India's prestige. In the case of South Vietnam the strategy of the small, bleeding war applied.

Mao's belief—indeed, obsession—that US world positions can be effectively undercut by a plethora of small wars has become a key irritant in the Sino–Soviet dispute over international strategy. The Communist Chinese position on strategy has been constructed so as to enshrine Mao's military road to power as *the* road for most countries; the Vietnam war as "proof" that this plan will work; and the Soviet revolutionary experience as irrelevant in underdeveloped areas. Accordingly, Peking has stepped up its efforts to make the Chinese model for revolutionary war a law unto itself, bypassing the Soviet precedent, and increasing CCP influence among militant Communists in the world movement.

The most explicit synthesis of the idea of revolution and the Maoist concept of the small war to be made over the years by a high-ranking CCP leader appeared in Defense Minister Lin Piao's lengthy and important article in *Jen-min jih-pao* on September 3, 1965. Lin Piao indicates clearly that Mao views the protracted small war as the critical ingredient of the revolutionary process, rather than the short-duration, city-centered uprising, and that he has not changed his conviction of the 1930s—namely, that the seizure of power by war "is the central task and highest form of revolution."

The article also clearly indicates that perceptions of China's national interest, as well as the Maoist revolutionary compulsion, motivate the CCP leaders in advancing this strategy. The Chinese aparently have reached the conclusion that US pressures—i.e., containment—against the mainland can be reduced by a series of widespread attacks on, or harassments of, regimes friendly to the United States. As Lin Piao stated, "The more successful the development of a people's war[52] in a given region, the larger the number of US imperialist forces than can be pinned down and depleted there. When the US aggressors are hard pressed in one place, they have no alternative but to *loosen their grip on others* (emphasis added)."

The logic of this strategy is similar to that outlined by Chou En-lai in the fall of 1960. It cuts directly against the post-Khrushchev Soviet policy of limited US–USSR *détente* under Peaceful Coexistence. However, the increased willingness of the Brezhnev-Kosygin leadership to support *some* small wars, particularly the Vietnam war, has taken a bit of the wind from Mao's sails, and the Chinese Communist leadership has been compelled to disparage publicly Soviet military aid to Hanoi (though repeatedly raising obstacles to its transit across China), and to distort Soviet political support of the North Vietnamese. The post-Khrushchev Soviet leadership has angered and frustrated the CCP leadership by increasing its influence in Hanoi. It seems likely that a continuation of the American commitment to assist the South Vietnamese Government against the Viet Cong will refute Maoist claims with regard to the almost universal applicability of the Chinese revolutionary model, as well as further exacerbate Moscow–Peking tensions. Indeed, continued Communist Chinese intransigence may well result in that country's being declared an anathema by a majority of the European Party-states.

[52] It should be pointed out that relations between Peking and Hanoi have been less than smooth with regard to the theory of "people's war." In the fall of 1964, North Vietnamese leaders began to claim more openly than ever before that the Vietnam Workers' Party and the People's Army of Vietnam (PAVI) had created the theory and practical tactics of "people's war." The CCP implicitly rebuked the North Vietnamese leaders (for avoiding the matter of Mao Tse-tung's complete doctrine on guerrilla war) by insisting, in a *Hung-ch'i* article in late December, 1964, that "only" Mao among military strategists in various countries had formulated the doctrine of "people's war." Neither the Vietnamese Party nor the PAVI (including General Clap, author of *People's War, People's Army*) were mentioned in CCP publications as having made any contribution, and on July 15, 1963, when P'eng Chen discussed the "enrichment" of guerrilla war, he was deliberately ambiguous on the point of whether he meant the North Vietnamese or the Viet Cong in the South. Chou En-lai sustained this ambiguity in his speech of September 2, 1965. Hanoi, however, continued to insist that the North Vietnamese have "enriched Marxist–Leninist theories on revolutionary strategy and tactics as well as on military art in a people's war." (*Hhan Dan,* Aug. 19, 1965). The Chinese implicitly rebuked the North Vietnamese again in late August and early September, 1965, when they vigorously insisted that Mao's concept of "people's war" was the original creation of the Chinese leader and was the road to power for "all countries," a position which was detailed in Lin Piao's September statement.

SELECTED BIBLIOGRAPHY

Cohen, Arthur A., "Maoism," in Milorad M. Drachkovitch (ed.), *Marxism in the Modern World* (Stanford: Stanford University Press, 1965), pp. 164–190. Shows clearly how Mao Tse-tung's obsession with his own model of revolutionary take-over in many ways made the Sino-Soviet conflict inevitable.

Crankshaw, Edward, *The New Cold War: Moscow Vs. Pekin* (Baltimore: Penguin, 1963). The best short history of the conflict. Eminently readable.

Doolin, Dennis J., *Territorial Claims in the Sino-Soviet Conflict* (Stanford: Stanford University Press, 1965). An attempt to analyze and document a hitherto neglected aspect of the conflict.

Floyd, David, *Mao Against Khrushchev: A Short History of the Sino-Soviet Conflict* (New York: Praeger, 1964). A well-done analysis of the dispute through mid-1963. The 225-page chronology of documents and significant events is especially valuable.

Griffith, William E., *The Sino-Soviet Rift* (Cambridge, Mass.: The MIT Press, 1964). An excellent analysis of the conflict during 1962 and 1963, supported by lengthy documentation. Most effectively utilized in company with Zagoria (1962), see below.

Hudson, G. F., *et al., The Sino-Soviet Dispute* (New York: Praeger, 1961). Primarily a documentary volume. Still very valuable, although the analyses are understandably dated.

Kardelj, Edvard, *Socialism and War: A Survey of the Chinese Criticism of the Policy of Coexistence* (New York: McGraw-Hill, 1960). A ponderous but very effective indictment of the Communist Chinese position by the then senior Vice-President of Yugoslavia. This book has occasioned much argument throughout the Communist world.

Kuusinen, O. V., *et al., Fundamentals of Marxism-Leninism* (Moscow: Foreign Languages Publishing House, 1961). A massive, extremely significant attempt to replace Stalin's *Problems of Leninism* with a manual more in accord with the realities of the nuclear age. Should be compared and contrasted with *The Polemic on the General Line of the International Communist Movement,* see below.

London, Kurt (ed.), *Unity and Contradiction: Major Aspects of Sino-Soviet Relations* (New York: Praeger, 1962). Nineteen papers presented before a conference held in September, 1960, at Lake Kawaguchi, Japan. See especially T. H. Rigby, "The Embourgeoisement of the Soviet Union and the Proletarianization of Communist China," pp. 19–36; and Allen S. Whiting, "Conflict Resolution in the Sino-Soviet Alliance," pp. 375–391.

Lowenthal, Richard, *World Communism: The Disintegration of a Secular Faith* (New York: Oxford, 1964). A leading authority attempts to view the disintegration of world Communism as a whole. With changes of varying degree, the original versions of the chapters appeared in journals. A very provocative book.

North, Robert C., *Moscow and Chinese Communists,* 2nd ed. (Stanford: Stanford University Press, 1963). The classic account of the Communist triumph in China, first published in 1953. In the new edition, see the concluding chapter, "Conflict and Cohesion Within the Sino-Soviet Bloc," pp. 266–291.

Peking Review (1958 ff.) This authoritative Communist Chinese English-language weekly contains many major Party statements, editorials, etc. For example, the *The People's Daily-Red Flag* joint editorial (Nov. 11, 1965), "A Refutation of the So-Called 'United Action' of the New Leaders of the CPSU," appeared in *Peking Review* on the following day. A biannual subject index appears in the twenty-sixth and fifty-second issues.

The China Quarterly (1960 ff.) Published in London and edited by Roderick MacFarquhar, *The China Quarterly* is the foremost scholarly journal on Communist Chinese affairs in the English language. Several excellent articles dealing with the Sino-Soviet conflict have appeared in the *Quarterly.* Also extremely useful is the "Quarterly Chronicle and Documentation" section at the back of each issue.

The Polemic on the General Line of the International Communist Movement (Peking: Foreign Languages Press, 1965). An English translation of *Kuan-Yu Kuo-Chi Kung-Ch'an Chu-I Yun-Tung Tsung-Lu-Hsien Te Lun-Chan* (Peking: Jen-min ch'u-pan she, 1965). An indispensable volume of primary source material. Included are: the letter of the Central Committee of the CPSU to the Central Committee of the CCP of March 30, 1963; the CCP Central Committee's reply of June 14, 1963; the open letter of the CPSU Central Committee to all Party organizations of July 14, 1963; nine lengthy criticisms of the Soviet open letter by the Editorial Department of *People's Daily* and *Red Flag;* and the *Red Flag* editorial of Nov. 21, 1964, entitled "Why Khrushchev Fell."

United States Congress, House of Representatives, Subcommittee on the Far East and the Pacific of the Committee on Foreign Affairs, *Sino-Soviet Conflict: Report on Sino–Soviet Conflict and its Implications* (Washington: US Government Printing Office, 1965). Contains among other things: hearings held by the Subcommittee during March, 1965; reprints of important articles; chronologies; and the analysis and findings of the Subcommittee. Twenty-two experts of various persuasions were called to testify. An exceptional "idea book."

Zagoria, Donald S. (ed.), "Communist China and the Soviet Bloc," *Annals of the American Academy of Political and Social Science,* Sept., 1963.

Thirteen articles by specialists. Four of the articles deal with history and tradition, five with accord and conflict, and four with the implications of the conflict for third countries. An abstract precedes each contribution.

Zagoria, Donald S., *The Sino-Soviet Conflict: 1956–1961* (Princeton: Princeton University Press, 1962). A pioneering work, published at a time when some observers continued to maintain that either there was no dispute or it was only a family quarrel. Superbly researched.

3

Origins and Limits of Communist Pluralism

Pio Uliassi and Eric Willenz

THE CONTINUALLY deteriorating relationship between the Soviet Union and Communist China has provided abundant and dramatic evidence that the monolithic unity thought to be characteristic of international communism for more than a quarter of a century was, at bottom, fragile and transitory.

It is only a slight exaggeration to say that this has been a surprising discovery.[1] Ten or more years ago, only the boldest observers[2] anticipated any early and fundamental changes in the relationship of the Communist Parties to the single center of doctrinal authority and political control in Moscow, and with some justification: subordination to Moscow was actually a more distinctive characteristic of a "legitimate" Communist Party than its specific theoretical formulations; and

Note: Both authors wish to acknowledge their debt to Professor Bernard Morris of Indiana University, friend and former colleague, with whom they have often discussed the problem of authority and control in the Communist movement touched on in this paper. The first-listed author also wishes to express his appreciation to Columbia University's Research Institute on Communist Affairs, which generously provided a grant for a study of the Italian Communist Party that led him to investigate some of the broader aspects in inter-Party relations in the Communist movement.

[1] As Robert V. Daniels has pointed out, ("A symposium on polycentrism," *The New Leader,* Mar. 19, 1962, vol. XLV, no. 6, p. 6) "The basic political generalizations which people need to work with usually lag behind the flux of events. This is true of much of Western comment on the Communist movement as well as of the Communists' view of themselves."

[2] Franz Borkenau foresaw the essence of the Sino–Soviet conflict as early as 1951. In general, American academic specialists were slow to anticipate the differences and cautious in predicting its course and intensity. Specific citations perhaps would be invidious.

the doctrine of Soviet supremacy was as central to the international Communist movement as the idea of *partiinost* was, and largely remains, to the Soviet system itself. Today, however, it would take a rash prophet, indeed, to predict that the Communist movement will eventually reestablish that kind of unity that Communists and non-Communists alike once viewed as normative. The Sino–Soviet dispute has become a conflict verging on schism and both rivals have actively courted allies among Parties whose loyalties to the host Party would be, at best, limited and problematic.

The swift changes in the movement have been meticulously and, in the case of the Sino–Soviet dispute, even tediously chronicled. Textual exegesis has resulted in rough agreement among experts on the main stages of the process, but conspicuously less than full agreement on its origins and causes.[3] This is hardly surprising, since the "beginnings" of any historical phenomenon are almost always elusive and "causes" are notoriously subject to varying perceptions and interpretations. Yet if political change is to be understood at all, it is still necessary to place a particular event or process in a more general context. The thesis of this chapter (certainly not a novel one by now) is that the Sino–Soviet dispute—or conflict or schism: the terms of discussion undoubtedly reflect our assessments and expectations—is best understood as part of a more general crisis of the Communist movement, reflecting a well-advanced process of transformation and adaptation. Such fundamental changes are almost invariably painful for entrenched institutions and particularly so for a doctrinaire political movement making a fetish of unity.

In this case, the specific direction of the change is toward pluralization. However much Communists and non-Communists alike may have overstressed the monolithic character of communism in Stalin's day, most Communist Parties at the time could in fact be described essentially as instruments of Soviet policy, directed from a single center and lacking any readily perceptible margin of independence. Admittedly the description was never entirely accurate, but it contained enough truth for practical purposes.

In contrast, the movement has clearly become decentralized. Stalin's passing undoubtedly contributed to the developing crisis—authority quickly abandons a dead tyrant—and Khrushchev's "Secret Speech" in

[3] For example, compare Klaus Mehnert, *Peking and Moscow* (New York: Putnam, 1963); David Floyd, *Mao against Khrushchev* (New York: Praeger, 1964); and Edward Crankshaw, *The Cold War—Moscow vs. Pekin* (Baltimore: Penguin Books, 1963).

1956 on the sins of the late dictator accelerated the process. But the causes of the change go deeper, transcend the personal role of one man, and are to be found, to put it too simply perhaps, in the growing incompatibility between a rigidly centralized and controlled international movement and the varying environments in which the movement —or more exactly its component parts—had to operate. This is already a commonplace and exceedingly abstract observation, but useful all the same as a starting point.

The Chinese Communists have challenged, first subtly and covertly and then bluntly and openly, Soviet authority and control over the Communist movement—and with considerable effect, though the results probably have not been what they had expected or hoped for. Certainly the Chinese have not forced a reversal of Moscow's positions on the main points of controversy, or wrested control of the movement from Moscow, or created a new revolutionary international to compete with the somewhat battered old one. But they have, ironically, become involved in a virtual cold war with the Russians and they have, moreover, forced the pace of development toward a pluralistic state and Party system that bears little resemblance to the tight Communist world of only a few years ago.

One problem that arises at this point is that of explaining the long subordination of Communist Parties to the Soviet Union and then their determined rebellion against that subordination and, for that matter, against *any* central direction. One potentially valuable way to grapple with this problem, it seems to the authors, is to examine the attitudes of non-Soviet Communist elites, on the commonsense supposition that the psychological needs and the political and bureaucratic interests of these groups are important factors (1) favoring either integration or disintegration of the movement at the international level and (2) determining whatever new equilibrium may emerge from the continuing confused state of inter-Party relations.

Procrustean Politics

For a long time it was assumed, both within and outside the movement, that its "monolithic" form was an essential and permanent characteristic of communism as an international force. In retrospect, however, the long-maintained Communist unity seems a remarkable phenomenon and what needs explaining is not so much the current divisions in Communist ranks as the unique existence of an ecumenical political organization which could, despite internal tensions and changing circumstances, remain so long and so thoroughly dominated by a single power. To put it another way: Why did so many foreign Communists, most of them outside the reach of physical coercion, accept the authority and submit to the discipline of the Soviet Union? In dealing with this question, it is more useful to emphasize not the motives of Soviet leaders—whose urge to manipulate and control other Communist Parties to support their personal ambitions or the interests of the Soviet state was in a sense quite natural—but rather the seemingly unnatural acquiescence of foreign Communists to such manipulation and control.[4] Ideology alone is hardly an adequate explanation for such behavior—perhaps no explanation at all, for there is abundant evidence to indicate that a formal and codified doctrine can be a disrupting as well as a unifying element in politics—and in many instances is more likely to be the former than the latter.

Belief in the integrative function of codified political doctrine seems to be among the illusions shared by Communists and many non-Communists alike. As Daniel Bell has argued,[5] the actual content of Communist doctrine is variable and "the crucial feature of Soviet ideology is not any formal doctrine," but "the insistence on the infallibility of the interpreters"—that is, of the Party. Bell focuses on the Soviet experience, but his analysis helps to clarify the role of ideology at the international level, too. In the absence of a recognized central authority for defining the specific tenets of the creed for the Communist movement as a whole, formal doctrine is likely to prove a fragile basis for unity. Moreover, in strongly ideological movements, the very competition for authority—for the right to interpret and thus to determine the content of doctrine—becomes a source of internal conflict. Communist history itself provides ample evidence of this, particularly in its earlier period. Ideology, therefore, should be considered a unifying factor only in the special sense that Marxism-Leninism set some broad, symbolic limits within which Communists could move toward different forms and kinds of cooperation.

It seems to the authors that the early, unitary phase of international communism is fairly well explained as the result of three sets of historical circumstances. First of all, the Communist movement sprang

[4] In most Communist Parties there was—and is—a continuing turnover in membership: the disillusioned leave, but are replaced by new enthusiasts for whom the gods have yet to fail. Instability in the ranks, however, did not in the past seriously weaken the commitment of Party leaders to Moscow.

[5] Daniel Bell, "The 'End of Ideology' in the Soviet Union?" in Milorad M. Drachkovitch, ed., *Marxist Ideology in the Modern World* (Stanford: Stanford University Press, 1965), pp. 108 ff.

from a tradition of revolutionary internationalism—a tradition that was, it is important to note, essentially European. Despite the violent polemics that shook the Socialist and early Communist movements over the interpretation and application of Socialist internationalism the latter reflected some shared cultural experiences which helped the early Communists to define the categories of political discourse and the areas of political action. The universalist aspect of European Marxist socialism (and then communism by inheritance) was a compound of sentiment and doctrine: a feeling of human—or at least class—solidarity transcending national boundaries, and a conviction that the capitalist order could be overthrown only by the international cooperation of the working class. The experience of World War I demonstrated the limits of Socialist internationalism when dogma conflicted with national loyalties and with the interests of pseudorevolutionary parties that actually were better integrated in their respective domestic political systems than most of them were ready to admit. Nevertheless, the very scale of the failure represented by the inability to prevent or at least stop the war and the widespread feeling that, before and after the outbreak of hostilities, the old Socialist parties and their leaders had somehow betrayed their moral principles and political interests, prepared the ground for a more rigidly centralized movement of the left. This mood did not, of course, "determine" the unity of the emergent Communist Parties, much less their long subordination to the USSR; but it did provide an atmosphere conducive to supranational revolutionary politics, and a readiness to accept institutional arrangements purportedly designed to overcome the tendencies toward nationalist "degeneration" associated with the moderate Socialist parties and the Second International.

Still another condition for the development of a monolithic movement was set by the widespread perception, by friend and foe alike, of the Soviet Union as a "Socialist" country and thus one which merited the support and even the loyalty of the left everywhere: the "new dawn in the East" syndrome. In time, gross contradictions between old Socialist ideals and emergent Soviet realities brought more differentiated responses to the Soviet Union: ambivalence or outright hostility in democratic Socialist quarters; factional splits and individual defections in Communist ranks; and various forms of adaption even among "loyal" Party members.[6] Here the behavior of the "loyal" Communists

[6] A previously unknown work published by Bertolt Brecht in 1966 suggests how painful some Communists found it to reconcile loyalty to the Party and the demands of their own consciences. See Martin Esslin, "Brecht's 'Twists and Turns,'" *Encounter*, Aug., 1966, pp. 58–62.

is most relevant. Certainly the Communist Parties contained—and rewarded—authoritarian types. But there were other types in the Parties also—and these had to adjust, somehow, to a political movement which violated their basic values. One form of adaptation consisted of the abandonment of personal autonomy through immersion in the routine of Party life and the consequent erosion of conscience (helped by identification with a remote ideal blunting the need for moral asessment of individual acts) which gradually made cold bureaucrats out of once-ardent radicals. Another form of adjustment was more intellectual, subtle and fragile: those foreign Communists who remained aware of the vast difference between official Socialist and Communist ideals and the actual conditions of Soviet society often explained the contrast, and sometimes explained it away, by resorting to a perniciously plausible historicism which linked the evolution of the Soviet regime to the exigencies of a passing revolutionary situation and/or to the particular traditions and circumstance of Russia. However, such perceptions were held not only by "loyal" Communists, but by dissident Communists and Socialists also (as the history of the Trotskyite groups and the important, not compliant, philo-Soviet wing of Italian socialism illustrate), who used them as the basis for dissent. Thus they cannot fully account for what seems an almost docile submission to foreign control.

A third element has, therefore, to be added to explain Moscow's long ascendancy over the movement, and this is found in the turbulent history of the 1920s. The collapse of revolutionary efforts everywhere except in Russia pushed Communists, whatever their original conception of the Comintern, into submitting to Soviet leadership and eventually to Soviet control. The reaction probably was partly psychological: Communists might understandably be inclined to compensate for their own or their Party's failures by identifying with successful revolution elsewhere.[7] At a more strictly political level, also, many Communists found it expedient to remain closely associated with the Soviet Union, not only because of their universalist revolutionary goals or some mysterious loyalty to the USSR, but simply because the tie served their local and immediate power interests—a point often obscured in the past by the oversimplifying acceptance of Communist Parties as mere instruments of a foreign power. The working of the relationship was a two-way process, with foreign Communist Parties submitting to unprecedented control in order to exploit, in turn, the quasimythical appeal of the Soviet Revolution, as well as the Soviet material aid that was at

[7] See Franz Borkenau, *World Communism* (New York: Norton, 1939), especially pp. 417 ff.

times indispensable for their survival as significant political organizations.[8] Finally, narrowly personal ambitions no doubt helped to create political elites submissive to the Soviet Union. Though it would be grotesque to assume that Communist leaders who long played politics as puppets of the Soviet Union were all usually driven by selfish personal motives—the record of dedication and sacrifice is too full for that—the gradual "Bolshevization" of the Parties was certainly facilitated by the availability of men willing to sacrifice their moral convictions and their political independence in return for bureaucratic security and political success.[9]

The Winds of Change

The main point of this glance at the past has been to indicate that generally individual Communist leaders and their Parties saw submission to Moscow as serving their own purposes. When these purposes were no longer served, or no longer served satisfactorily, by the established pattern of relationships, the whole Communist system was subjected to considerable strain. Sino–Soviet relations, of course, provide an important, headline-making instance of disequilibrium in the system. But the Sino–Soviet conflict would probably not have affected the Communist movement as a whole so seriously if circumstances had not already prepared the way for drastic changes both in the internal nature of the individual Parties and in their relationship to Moscow, or indeed to any extranational center. Even before his death, Stalin

[8] A striking illustration is provided by Togliatti in a letter to Antonio Gramsci dated May 1, 1923, commenting on the positions of Amadeo Bordiga, then the Italian Party's most influential leader: "In practice, given present conditions, to do what Amadeo proposes means placing ourselves in open struggle against the Communist International, placing ourselves outside it, and finding ourselves therefore deprived of powerful material and moral support, reduced to a very small group held together almost by personal ties alone and being in a short time condemned, if not to be all dispersed, certainly to lose any real and immediate practical influence on the development of the political struggle in Italy. Are those immediate practical disadvantages compensated by the value of an absolute and intransigent affirmation of principle such as Amadeo wants to make? I confess I am still a bit perplexed in giving an answer." Palmiro Togliatti, *La formazione del gruppo dirigente del partito comunista italiano* (Rome, 1962), p. 55. (Translation by the authors.)

[9] For an impressionistic but suggestive analysis of this process, *see* Jules Monnerot, *Sociology and Psychology of Communism* (Boston: Beacon, 1960), pp. 90–99. Monnerot's main point is that the Bolshevization of the non-Russian Parties involved partly the recruitment of a new type of leaders; but the gradual adjustment of old Communists to the increasingly centralized and coercive movement was also important.

found it increasingly difficult to maintain the rigid uniformity he had imposed on the movement. Communists preserved the façade of ritual consensus and doctrinal continuity long after the conditions that had originally shaped the movement had changed drastically or disappeared altogether. And once the restraining veneer of unity was destroyed, change occurred at an accelerating rate.

Part of the change, at least, resulted from a weakening of the internationalism that had nurtured the early movement (even in the corrupted version of *proletarian* internationalism). There seem to have been two main reasons for this development. First of all, as successful Communist Parties and groups became better integrated in their domestic political systems, the traditional balance between parochial and universalistic tendencies shifted in favor of the former. This process affected both the Communist Parties in power (particularly those that had achieved power without significant Soviet aid and exercised it beyond the reach of direct Soviet control, as in Yugoslavia and China) and those Parties which, without actually attaining power, prospered by identifying themselves closely with the interests and aspirations of their domestic supporters (among others, the Italian). Also, the internationalist sentiments and ideas that once contributed to Communist unity were gradually modified by the expansion of the movement into societies that have never shared, or have shared only in part, the European universalist traditions. Indeed, it is now a commonplace that the appeal of communism in the non-Western underdeveloped countries lies largely in its exploitation of national, if not outright racist, sentiment.[10]

The weakening of working-class internationalism has been accompanied by a gradual decline in the Soviet Union's authority attributable in part to changing perceptions of the kind of social order it represented. The image of the USSR as the incarnation of the first and most powerful "Socialist" state was increasingly tarnished even in the eyes of sympathizers. Here there were processes at work which initially cast doubt on the transferability of the Soviet experience and eventually helped to "demythologize" the experience itself. Impatience with the Soviet "model" soon became evident in the newly formed Communist states of the postwar period: the Yugoslav break in 1948 was the earliest sign that, however much Communists might identify with the October Revolution and the social order that emerged from it, once

[10] William E. Griffith, "Communist Polycentrism and the Underdeveloped areas," in Kurt London, *New Nations in a Divided World* (New York: Praeger, 1963), pp. 275 ff.

in power they became unwilling or unable to accept Soviet precedents as universally applicable. A critical point in the breakdown of the pre-eminence of the Soviet experience was reached in 1955, when the incumbent Soviet leaders, anxious for a reconciliation with Yugoslavia, accepted the doctrine of "multiple ways to socialism." A second trend was equally important: by the time of Stalin's death, the Communist movement had been revitalized by a generation of younger revolutionaries less bound by traditional loyalties than their elders, and perhaps less personally compromised by the past, who were inclined to reject the automatic applicability of the Soviet system to non-Soviet settings and increasingly, though cautiously, began to cast a cold eye on the system itself. The full significance of this development did not become apparent until PC XX of the CPSU in 1956 and its accompanying denunciation of Stalin by Soviet leaders. But once the historical role of Stalin became an open intra- and inter-Party issue, it was only a matter of time before the Soviet regime, and by extension the whole of Communist history, would be subjected to increasingly critical investigation and radical reinterpretation.[11]

Again, however, the decisive factors in undermining Soviet authority and control probably were situational: the expansion of Communist power after World War II far beyond the limits of the Comintern period. Success, or unfulfilled expectations of success, bred impatience with the absolute centralization of power in Moscow. The system built by Stalin no longer served as effectively as earlier to meet the psychological, political, or even selfishly careerist needs of Communist elites. The Communist regimes of Eastern Europe clearly relied on Soviet support to help them remain in power; but in Yugoslavia, and even more in China, the local Communists could and did take pride in their own achievements. In many areas the wartime resistance activities of the Communists and the postwar successes of Communist Parties had imbued the Parties with new confidence in their own capacities.[12] Moreover, in many countries, Parties with strong domestic sources of support no longer depended exclusively on the Soviet Union for prestige and material aid. Indeed, too close identification with the Soviet Union could be a source of political embarrassment (as it was in Western

[11] The immediate public reactions and criticisms in 1956 came almost entirely from Western Communist Parties operating in democratic societies. Later, however, public controversy spread to other Parties and with it the range of matters in dispute.

[12] For an example, see Charles A. Micaud, *Communism and the French Left* (New York: Praeger, 1963), especially p. 103.

Europe)[13] rather than, or as well as, a source of strength. And elsewhere Soviet policy could be seen as cautious and conservative by Communist leaders operating in turbulent societies undergoing violent change.[14] Finally, of course, with the passage of time, new leaders pressed for recognition—younger men who had not been subjected to the Comintern experience and who had largely escaped the ruthless screening which had turned so many of their elders into a generation of eminent nonentities cast in the Stalinist mold.[15]

Even before 1956, the search for greater independence went on, and the movement had in fact become latently polycentric even before Togliatti coined the term in 1956 to describe, however ambiguously, a new system of inter-Party relations.[16] In fact, the critical responses of Togliatti and others to the de-Stalinization overtly initiated at PC XX of the CPSU demonstrate how ready the Communist movement was for changes of some sort in the established and ideologically-consecrated pattern of authority.

Khrushchev's de-Stalinization campaign showed little awareness of, and less solicitude for, the views or interests of the Communist movement as a whole. The attack on Stalin was handled from a typically Stalinist point of view as far as inter-Party relations were concerned. Khrushchev and his colleagues seemed to take it for granted that the attacks on Stalin would be supported by foreign Communists, and in view of past experience this was a perfectly normal display of arrogance. Such cavalier treatment of other Parties had not seriously or permanently undermined Soviet leadership in the past; but de-Stalinization was another matter. For one thing, it came at a time when many Communists were already restive under Soviet hegemony for reasons

[13] In Western Europe, almost every Party soon discovered that close identification with the Soviet Union, whatever its uses in the past, was becoming a net disadvantage. In Denmark and Norway, for example, the Socialist People's parties, organized by Communist dissidents, soon proved stronger than their parent bodies. It is not, of course, independence alone which probably has accounted for this, but independence plus a radical program which has still seemed to respect the democratic traditions of the two countries.

[14] In less developed countries, the view that Moscow may prefer stability and peaceful coexistence to revolution, particularly when its own direct interests are at stake, encourages sympathy towards Peking or at least ambivalence in the Sino-Soviet dispute. A good example of such conduct is witnessed in the often tense relationship between Cuba and the Soviet Union. See Theodore Draper, *Castroism, Theory and Practice* (New York: Praeger, 1965), especially pp. 45–48.

[15] Rebellion against Soviet domination, whether "leftist" or "rightist" in content, seems to be more characteristic of younger than of older Communists. In Western Europe, the "revisionists" are usually, though not always, younger men in party experience if not in age. Examples are Giorgio Amendola, Mario Alicata and Pietro Ingrao in Italy; Franz Muhri in Austria; C. H. Hermansson

already noted. For another, it threatened directly and dramatically the most basic dogmas and myths of the movement. As a result, the internal discipline of many Parties was undermined. Communists everywhere suffered the embarrassment of trying to maintain a semblance of ideological continuity and political consistency while adapting to new and profoundly disturbing revelations and circumstances. Far from least, many older Communist leaders were themselves compromised by their past loyalties to a man who was now being publicly vilified by his former associates.

The events of 1956—PC XX, the crisis in Poland, the rebellion in Hungary, and the reactions of the Soviet and other Communist Parties to these developments—made it clear that the authority of Moscow was no longer sufficient to maintain stable international relations among Communist states and Parties. During the year, the Chinese took an unprecedentedly active part in Western Communist affairs and for some time seemed anxious to maintain a centrally directed international movement, although significantly one that would follow the doctrinal and political lines *they* believed to be "correct." But quite soon the Chinese began to exploit the crisis of authority, exacerbated it, and even claimed the mantle of authority for themselves as the most authentic vanguard of proletarian revolution—only to discover, eventually, that the Soviets' losses were not necessarily their gains.

Moscow and Peking

The crisis in the international Communist movement, then, should be seen as a complex development whose root causes do not stem from

---

in Sweden; Ele Alenius in Finland (although Alenius, leader of the Communist-dominated Finnish People's Democratic League and now a member of the Cabinet, is not formally a Communist). Even when the top leadership has not changed, younger people have often been vocal critics of past and present policy, as illustrated by the French Party's experience with its rebellious student wing. The splinter pro-Chinese groups in Western Europe, again with some exceptions (especially in Belgium), also tend to be dominated by younger men.

Elsewhere the picture is less clear. Data on age group conflicts, if any, in Latin American Parties are too sketchy to permit generalizations. In New Zealand and Australia, where the revolt against Moscow has taken an extreme leftist direction, the pro-Peking groups of V. G. Wilcox in New Zealand and E. F. Hill in Australia appear to consist largely of younger men, though the leaders themselves are long-established Party people. In the Near East, opposition to Khalid Bakdash, leader of the Syrian Communists and perhaps the most prestigious Communist in the Arab world, seemingly comes from younger Communists. (These are mere impressions of "generational conflict" in the Communist Parties. There is no systematic study of the subject for the movement as a whole.)

[16] Palmiro Togliatti, "Nove Domande sullo Stalinismo," in *Nuovi Argomenti,* no. 20, May–June, 1956, pp. 136–139.

the Sino–Soviet dispute—although they are powerfully reinforced by it because the very stature of the two contenders gives the conflict an epochal quality and because their respective positions, however distorted by polemical crudities, touch on genuine doctrinal and political issues facing Communist Parties everywhere. The occasional tendency to regard Communist China as a principal cause rather than as an important catalyst of the post-Stalinist evolution of the Communist movement can lead to overly simple pictures of inter-Party relations and consequently of the ordering of Parties behind the Soviet Union and Communist China. The labelling of Parties as "pro-Moscow" or "pro-Chinese" has only limited usefulness and it can even mislead by implying a clear bipolarity which is hardly justified by the facts.

As has often been noted, the Sino–Soviet controversy has encouraged a crystallization, not so much of views perhaps as of styles or moods or attitudes—in which the Russians and Chinese are, respectively, dubbed "revisionists" and "dogmatist-sectarians." The labels at best suggest general inclinations toward moderation or militancy. Beyond that, they are more usefully to be regarded as polemical weapons rather than as descriptive terms with precise and verifiable empirical referents. In the current controversy, individuals, factions, and Parties can usually be identified as leaning toward varying degrees of moderation or militancy and thereby have either more or less sympathy for the Soviet Union or China. Nevertheless, on the host of issues agitating the movement, ranging from domestic matters to questions of inter-Party relations to problems of world affairs and the proper role of the Communist movement in them—the Parties do not cluster into two well-defined blocs characterized by internal ideological and political consistency, although there are marked regional differences in the responses of Parties to the issues and to the prime contenders.

Both Peking and Moscow have been actively seeking allies and supporters for their respective causes in the other Communist Parties—and both have found them. Their competitive efforts, however, have helped to raise the bargaining power of the national Communist Parties, especially the more important ones. Moreover, the struggle for adherents has given all Parties—despite residual loyalties to Moscow and a nostalgic desire for unity—an opportunity, on a variety of issues, to take positions which are not quasiautomatic responses to external directives but rather reflect, far more than in the past, the specific circumstances of their own political situations and, increasingly, the dominant values of their national political cultures. Some are definitely inclined toward Peking; a much larger number toward Moscow; but in almost all cases commitment to one side or the other is neither uncritical nor complete[17] nor, evidently, necessarily permanent.[18]

Although the Soviet and Chinese search for allies can be viewed in diplomatic terms, the nature of the two rivals carries their competitive bids for the support of other Communist states and Parties beyond the traditional limits of big-power politics. Certainly both Moscow and Peking are anxious to extend their influence and power and to find support for the specific policies each considers to be in its own national interest, assuming for the moment that national interest can somehow be separated from the presuppositions or ideologies that help to define it. It is even likely that the search for allies is motivated partly by the desire for consensual validation—the symbolic approval of others which, for governments as for individuals, provides reassurance that beliefs, politics, or acts are, somehow, "right." But the rivalry is also ideological in the purest sense: though the doctrinal formulations propounded in Moscow and Peking largely reflect the different traditions and circumstances of the two countries, both Soviet and Chinese Communists are inclined to claim universal validity for their particular interpretations of Marxism–Leninism and to buttress their claims with evangelical efforts which have often annoyed and/or worried other Parties.[19] The search for allies or supporters or clients, then, is part of a power-ideology struggle which admits of little room for the compromises of pragmatic politics.

World Communist history since 1956 can be seen as a process of gradual disintegration, with the Chinese striving to win supporters and establish their hegemony over the movement, the Russians defending their positions, and the other Parties, or most of them, pleading for solidarity while resisting the creation of central institutions that would

[17] The sympathies of most Parties for the Soviet Union certainly have not prevented them from opposing the USSR on specific issues. This is especially true of the West European Parties, which, despite their pro-Soviet stance in the conflict with China, have, for example, criticized Soviet explanations of the Stalinist regime; commented on the inadequacies of institutional reforms carried out by Khrushchev; openly showed their displeasure at the manner of Khrushchev's removal; attacked Soviet cultural policy in general and specifically disapproved of the 1966 trial of the two writers, Sinyavsky and Daniel; and resisted Soviet efforts to convene an international conference of Communist Parties.

[18] The instability of alignments is illustrated by the ruling parties of Cuba, North Vietnam, and North Korea and by the Communist Party of Japan, all of which shifted in 1965–1966 from markedly pro-Chinese positions to more neutral or pro-Soviet ones. The Communist Party of Australia, which favored Peking in the early and less public phases of the dispute, returned to the Soviet fold in 1961.

[19] Charges and countercharges about interference in the internal affairs of other Parties are common themes in the dispute. Examples: the alleged Soviet

limit their freedom of action. The main phases in the process are fairly clear: for a few years, Sino–Soviet differences were aired behind closed doors—witness the major confrontations between the Soviet and Chinese representatives at the Rumanian Workers' Party Congress in mid-1960 and at the Conference of the Eighty-one Parties later that year, neither of which was officially publicized until more than a year later, when the French, Italian and Belgian Parties all released comments and documents on the full conference. Once the dispute broke into the public arena, it was carried out, for some time, largely although not entirely with proxy targets—Yugoslavia for the Russians and Albania for the Chinese—not only because these "stand-ins" were vulnerable in their own right but also, probably, because both the chief contestants were reluctant to press for a showdown for which the other Communist Parties, apart from a few top leaders who were privy to the details of the conflict, were still psychologically and politically unprepared. By the end of 1962, however, these indirections and restraints were abandoned for direct and increasingly bitter public controversy symbolically opened when Giancarlo Pajetta, at the Italian Party Congress in December, attacked the Chinese openly: "When we mean China we have no need to say Albania." The attack on the Chinese was continued at the East German Party Congress in January, 1963, and led to increasingly vitriolic polemics in the follow months.

In challenging the Russians, the Chinese moved along several lines. One part of their offensive consisted of a global propaganda campaign which began with the systematic distribution of official documents and polemical literature and became especially intense in late 1962 and 1963 with the proliferation of pro-Chinese factionalist groups and pub-

---

circular letter addressed to Communist Parties before PC XXIII of the CPSU (April–May, 1966) claimed that "the Chinese leadership increasingly intensifies subversive activities against the Soviet state and social order" and that "direct appeals are being made to engage in political action against the CPSU Central Committee and the Soviet Union." The Chinese, in turn, in their letter rejecting Moscow's invitation to PC XXIII, accused the Russians of sending "an anti-Chinese letter to other Parties, instigating them to join you in opposing China." See excerpts from the alleged Russian letter and the text of the Chinese note in *The New York Times,* Mar. 24, 1966.

The Japanese Communists have accused, at different times, both Moscow and Peking of interfering in their affairs. In mid-1965, the Japanese Party paper attacked Soviet leaders for having "carried on and intensified their divisive activities" in the Japanese Party and its affiliated organizations. More recently, the Japanese rebuked the Chinese by castigating those people in their own ranks who "share a blind adherence to the standpoints and opinions of the Parties of foreign countries, bringing them into our country mechanically." See *Akahata,* June 22, 1965, Oct. 6, 1965, and May 11, 1966.

lications throughout the world, many of them, undoubtedly, not only inspired but supported financially, as well, by Peking. At the same time, the Chinese carried their attack to various national congresses; challenged Soviet domination of, or even participation in, international front organizations and conferences; and set up rival organizations which excluded the Russians. Factionalism moved rapidly towards actual schism as, in the summer and fall of 1963, the Chinese openly encouraged the formation of secessionist Parties in those areas where pro-Chinese factions had failed to win control of existing Party organizations. In fact, it became abundantly clear during 1963 that the Chinese Communists, in their "shameless claim to hegemony" as the Russians later put it, were quite willing to encourage organizational splits as acts of purification and to justify them as the inevitable historical response to "revisionism" in the movement.[20]

In the meantime, the Russians were by no means passive, although they did, in general, try to play down differences between themselves and Peking until 1960; and again, after the fall of Khrushchev, they sought to moderate the tone if not the substance of the controversy. Because the Soviet Union has been identified with the status quo which the Chinese have been trying to change, the Russians have been forced, for the most part, to play a defensive role. In doing so, however, they have had some inestimable advantages over their rivals. The vast majority of non-Asian Parties, it soon became evident, did not find the arguments of the Chinese very persuasive or their policies very congenial, and the fanatical excesses of the Chinese eventually alienated even some of their early sympathizers. In addition, despite the erosion of their authority, the Russians still enjoyed a traditional prestige which helped to insure them of the support in their anti-Chinese stand even of some foreign Communists who were otherwise inclined to be critical of Soviet activities. In a variety of forums, the Russians justified their specific policies; accused their antagonists of "dogmatism" and worse; and decried the "divisive" tactics of the Chinese and their allegedly disreputable sympathizers. They also counterattacked by encouraging factionalism in some of those Parties under the control of pro-Chinese leaders—most visibly in Japan. More important, after some hesitation, Khrushchev tried to convene a full international Communist conference with the evident intention of isolating the Chinese and, perhaps, also enabling the Soviet leaders to consolidate the ranks of their

[20] See Kevin Devlin, "Schism and Secession," in Leopold Labedz, *International Communism after Khrushchev* (Cambridge, Mass.: The MIT Press, 1965), pp. 29–49.

own somewhat undisciplined sympathizers. From the Russian point of view, it turned out to be a serious misstep, although Krushchev's successors eventually managed to retreat from the ill-starred venture with reasonably good grace.

The Conciliar Movement

When both the Soviet Union and China discovered that they could not impose their will on the movement through persuasion, cajolery, or threats, they were compelled to pay increasing attention to the wishes and needs of other Parties in an effort to reach some minimal consensus that might pass as unity. For a time it seemed possible that if the movement could no longer be "papal" it might still be "conciliar," or perhaps might combine the two forms in a compromise reminiscent of the early Comintern, creating a genuinely multinational system in which every Party would be bound by majority decisions.[21]

But such was not to be the case. While the Russians have been increasingly willing to tolerate a considerable measure of doctrinal and political variety in their former subordinates, the Chinese have demanded rigid ideological conformity based on a single doctrinal authority, a view which has made it difficult, if not impossible, to develop a looser, pluralistic form of worldwide Communist unity.[22] As a result the Russians and Chinese have increasingly disagreed on three main issues: (1) *On the principles for reaching decisions.* The Chinese preferred unanimity; the Russians (with most Parties still on their side on most issues) eventually opted for majority decisions that would be binding on the entire movement. (2) *On problems of membership in the movement and representation.* The early controversy over the Communist "legitimacy" of Yugoslavia and Albania was vastly complicated by the proliferation of dissident groups, which the Chinese wanted represented at all-Party conferences and the Russians did not. (3) *Timing.* Chinese demands after 1960 for a new all-Party conference were, at first, ignored by the Russians: and then, when the Russians came out in favor of convening a preparatory meeting for such a conference, the Chinese—aware of their minority status—denounced it as a unilateral act designed to split the movement.

[21] See Peter Wiles, as quoted in Walter Laqueur, "The Schism," in Walter Laqueur and Leopold Labedz (eds.), *Polycentrism* (New York: Praeger, 1962), p. 4.

[22] See Richard Lowenthal, "The Prospects for Pluralistic Communism," in Milorad M. Drachkovitch (ed.), *Marxism in the Modern World* (Stanford: Stanford University Press, 1965), pp. 227–230.

The global Communist meeting—of the Eighty-one Parties held in Moscow in the Fall of 1960—showed the limitations of conciliar decision making, under the existing circumstances. Although the Sino–Soviet dispute dominated the gathering, the traditional Communist distaste for any public controversy was still strong enough to prevent an open break. Yet in retrospect the outward display of harmony (which some Communists later correctly dubbed "artificial unity") concealed serious private disagreements that were even more serious than most observers guessed at the time. The intransigence of both sides was publicly masked by a unanimously adopted declaration which tried to be all things to all Communists and predictably led to further arguments over interpretation and implementation.

But both sides evidently left the November meeting fully resolved to rally their forces, maneuver and prepare for a new confrontation, which came less than a year later at PC XXII of the CPSU. At the Congress a new relationship in the Communist movement was clearly delineated. For one thing, the open Soviet attack on Albanian leaders, though it scandalized even some Communists who agreed with its substance, established a precedent of public disagreement that was soon followed by others. Then the Chinese ostentatiously walked out in protest. Some other delegates deviated from the Soviet position at least to the extent of avoiding any reference to Albania. Observers were thus confronted with the then unusual spectacle of open dissent in the Communist movement although they were far from being fully able to assess its pervasiveness or its ramifications. If the Eighty-one Party Conference in 1960 may be regarded as the last formal act of unity in the Communist movement, then PC XXII of the CPSU is to be seen as the beginning of a new chapter in inter-Party relations. Henceforth, the alignment of Parties in the growing Sino–Soviet dispute would come to assume considerable importance.

As already noted, the Soviets were anxious to avoid a new conference after the meeting of the Eighty-one Parties in 1960, and particularly after the repeated clashes which occurred between Chinese and Soviet delegatcs at other meetings throughout 1962. Khrushchev evidently felt that the conflict with China could be contained through private talks, or at least, was better kept under wraps, but when this proved impossible, he called for a preparatory session of 26 Parties to lay the groundwork for a full world conference of Communist Parties—only to run into opposition not only from the Chinese and their friends, but also, and more significantly, from Communist Parties which sided with the Soviets on most of the substantive issues in dispute. The latter could not be persuaded to support a global conference which would formalize a split in the movement and define a new orthodoxy which might eventually limit their own autonomy, although some did attend a kind of rump meeting held in Moscow in March, 1965, after Khrushchev had been ousted, but this was little more than a face-saving ceremony.[23]

The key point of this post-Khrushchev "preparatory" meeting was that its composition, attendance, and results reflected the choice of neither Moscow's nor Peking's position. The Chinese could not prevent the meeting from taking place, although they refused to attend, as did the Communist Parties of North Korea, North Vietnam, Japan, Indonesia, Albania and Rumania. Soviet leaders did persuade 18 Parties to participate, but had to be satisfied with a pale final communique which practically buried plans for the full conference. The equalization process in the movement, with its corollary of bargaining, had reached a new high. Clearly the other parties were inclined to defend and even to widen their independence against future attacks by either of the two foremost Communist powers.

Allies, Sympathizers, and Neutrals

It is ironic but hardly surprising that the competition between the Soviet Union and China for hegemony over the Communist movement has created something that neither had probably anticipated: an entirely new system of relations between themselves and among Communist powers and Parties generally.

There are about one hundred Communist Parties, including splinter organizations of some importance, and the Russians are far ahead of the Chinese in winning support, or at least a measure of sympathy, among those Parties. Moreover, the Russians seem to be gaining as a result of

[23] The conciliar formula may prove somewhat more useful for coodinating Communist policies on a regional rather than on a world-wide basis, although the results thus far are indifferent.

Outside the Soviet bloc, several regional gatherings have been held in the past few years. In November, 1964, Latin American Communists met in Havana; detailed information on the proceedings is not available, but there is little evidence of Communist consensus on regional problems. In December of that year, Arab Parties met and generally agreed with the Soviet-supported policy of cooperation with non-Communist radical forces and regimes. [See *Al-Akhbar,* Beirut Dec. 20, 1964.] West European Communists have met twice in recent years: in Brussels (June, 1965) and in Vienna (May, 1966). But the Swedish Party carried its autonomy to the point of boycotting the Brussels meeting on the ground that it could only be bound by decisions taken by its own organs; and the Dutch, although present at the meeting, refused to sign the final resolution because they disagreed with it. The British and Dutch Communists did not attend the Vienna conclave, apparently for similar reasons.

Chinese excesses and blunders.[24] The dispute has also resulted in the breakdown of the disciplined obedience once thought so characteristic of Communist Parties and so evident in their readiness to submit to Moscow's directives. This has been replaced by assertiveness and an inclination to take advantage of Moscow's weakened position in the movement to establish reciprocity of support or even detachment in some cases. A kind of mutuality also marks the relationship of some Parties and splinter groups to Peking, which—whatever its appeal to various elements—cannot rely on conventional authority in dealing with foreign Communists and must, at least outside the Asian sphere, try to win and hold supporters largely on the basis of symbolic identifications which have yet, as of this writing, to be firmly institutionalized.

The Russians have been quite successful in winning support for their cause among ruling Parties, but the price they have had to pay has included the virtual abandonment of their claim to hegemony; an increasing respect for the national interests and sensibilities of the former satellite countries; and an air of relative reasonableness in dealing with Peking's provocations. Of the dozen smaller ruling Communist Parties, seven are more or less pro-Soviet (Bulgaria, Czechoslovakia, East Germany, Hungary, Poland, Yugoslavia, and Outer Mongolia);[25] three incline toward the Chinese (Albania, North Korea, and North Vietnam —although the latter two are visibly, especially North Korea, edging toward less committed ground[26]); the remaining two (Rumania and

[24] See US Department of State, *World Strength of the Communist Party Organizations,* Eighteenth Annual Report, Jan., 1966.

[25] The East European Communist regimes, with the exception of Albania, are understandably anxious to maintain good relations with the Soviet Union while at the same time seeking a more equitable status (witness developments in the Council for Mutual Economic Assistance and in the Warsaw Pact) and a considerable measure of internal autonomy. East European nationalism represents both an assertion of sovereignty vis-à-vis the Soviet Union and Communist accommodation to the local culture, the latter exemplified by Nicolae Ceausescu's claim that the Communists are "the continuers of the best traditions of the Rumanian people."

Outer Mongolia is a traditional area of confrontation between the Soviet Union and China. The Mongolian regime, which appears to be firmly pro-Soviet, expelled thousands of Chinese workers in 1964 and accused China of interfering in its internal affairs—evidence that there may be some pro-Chinese sentiment in the country and its Party.

[26] Geographic proximity and economic and military ties obviously go far to explain North Korean and North Vietnamese inclinations toward China. Since the fall of Khrushchev, however, Chinese bungling, plus the Soviet Union's more active involvement in the Far East, have reduced Peking's influence. Significantly, both North Korea and North Vietnam sent delegations to PC XXIII of the CPSU.

Cuba) may perhaps be considered neutral, although Rumanian–Chinese relations cooled perceptibly during 1966–1967 and Cuban—Chinese relations deteriorated seriously.[27] In these alignments doctrinal sympathies, though they no doubt play a part, are far less important than pragmatic calculations of the kind that traditionally underlie state systems.

Most of the Communist Parties out of power have been inclined to support the Soviet Union. Among these, Soviet leaders have found their strongest and most important allies in Western Europe. However, the Sino-Soviet dispute has encouraged a kind of national communism which by now seems irreversible, although European Communists still pretend, and no doubt many feel, an allegiance to the movement as a whole—although an allegiance based on tolerance for considerable diversity among the Parties. The result has been a seeming paradox, with West European Parties that have moved farthest on the revisionist road strongly opposing the formal ostracism of Communist Parties which are worlds removed from them ideologically and politically.[28]

European Communists have not responded uniformly to the dispute and to the opportunities provided by it, but the majority of them have concluded that change or decay are the choices they face.[29] And they are moving, although at different rates, to refurbish their ideological wardrobes and to modify their strategies in efforts to end their virtual

[27] Rumania and Cuba are special cases. Rumania's neutrality reflects a regime which is increasingly pragmatic and inward-looking. (It is amusing to note that only a few years ago some Western experts considered Rumania singularly unfertile soil for an autonomist national communism—a reminder that in politics explanations after the event are easier, and safer, than predictions.) Cuba's neutrality seems to be largely an expression of frustration resulting from efforts to reconcile sympathy for the radical postures of Peking and material dependence on Moscow.

[28] Among Western Communists, the French for a long time favored a showdown international conference with the Chinese and were strongly seconded in this by the exiled Spanish Communists, both arguing that if the proposed conference indeed led to a split, it would merely recognize what already existed. The Italians, Australians, Belgians, British and Dutch, though all inclined to favor the Soviets on the main substantive issues, opposed such a conference. Their case was put most clearly in Palmiro Togliatti's Yalta memorandum, published soon after his death. Togliatti, while arguing that unity of the whole movement was essential, was clearly more concerned with the independence of its parts and opposed any semblance of a new centralized international organization and a "declared break" within the movement which might lead to a new and troublesome Chinese-led "international." For the text of Togliatti's memorandum, see *Rinascita* (Rome), Sept. 5, 1964.

[29] For more on the development of West European Communism, see Chapter 10.

political isolation and governmental impotence. The Italians and Scandinavians have set the pace, with the French, Austrians, British and others trailing more or less enthusiastically. In recent years, it has become clear that the real battle within West European communism is not between the pro-Soviet and pro-Chinese factions but between those who insist on merely keeping pace with Soviet developments and the more adventurous and usually younger Communists determined to shake their own Parties from foreign tutelage and their long dogmatic slumbers. For their part, the pro-Chinese groups in the Western movement are a motley collection of strident gadflies who evidently consider themselves the conscience of a still long-distant revolution.

In Africa, where Communist Parties are few, weak and mostly illegal[30] the Sino-Soviet dispute has had only a limited impact at the Party level. The Communist Parties proper, most of which began as branches of Parties in the "mother countries," have been overwhelmingly pro-Soviet, though not particularly vociferous about it; but pro-Chinese groups have appeared in a few areas, notably in Cameroon, Senegal, and South Africa. The dispute has been far more evident in the African policies of the USSR and China. The ostensibly common interest of the two Communist great powers in furthering good relations with "progressive" forces has not prevented the development of marked differences in strategy and competition for influence. In general, the Russians, skeptical of the immediate prospects for African communism, have tended to work through established nationalist regimes and leaders, as indicated, for example, by the large number of African non-Communist delegation invited to PC XXIII of the CPSU.[31] The Chinese are more inclined to support dissident elements and to incite them to subversion and rebellion. Both countries have suffered serious setbacks

[30] Of the 37 independent African states, only eight have known organized Communist Parties: Algeria, Malagasy Republic, Morocco, Nigeria, Senegal, South Africa, Sudan and Tunisia. Only the Malagasy Party operates legally but it is weak and ineffectual. In colonial Africa, there is only one legal Communist Party, the Communist Party of Lesotho (Basutoland), which apparently is dominated by exiled members of the South African Communist Party. Individuals and groups with ostensibly "Marxist–Leninist" orientations are of course found throughout the continent.

[31] At PC XXII of the CPSU in 1961, the (non-Communist) ruling parties of Ghana, Guinea, and Mali sent representatives. At PC XXIII in 1966, at least nine African non-Communist delegations were present representing the United Arab Republic, Tanzania and Zanzibar, Mali, Guinea, Congo (Brazzaville), Nigeria, Senegal, Angola and Algeria. At the opening session, the Algerian FLN delegation walked out in protest over the simultaneous presence of Algerian Communists.

in their policies.[32] Competition for influence over the miniscule Communist Parties and conflicts over general strategy have emerged with particular bitterness in fronts and in such international groups as the Afro–Asian Solidarity Organization. The situation in the Near East is similar in many ways to that in Africa.[33]

Latin America provides a more complicated situation. There the established Communist Parties, which remain firmly loyal to the Soviet Union, have had to contend with pressures from internal dissidents emboldened by the Sino–Soviet dispute and from the "Jacobin Left" (non-Communist groups exemplified by early Castroism, whose inclinations toward violence are encouraged and at times supported by the Cubans and the Chinese). The Communist Parties have no impressive revolutionary tradition, but have, rather, with few exceptions, historically followed cautious and even opportunistic policies of accommodation with forces and regimes at all points of the political spectrum. The "Jacobin Left" or Castroites, apparently driven as much by violent nationalism as by any variant of Marxist ideology, have been emotionally attracted to the Chinese in recent years, but can hardly be considered a disciplined and stable part of Peking's following. For their part, the Chinese have encouraged the Castroites and attempted to split the Communist Parties—in the latter case with little success.[34] Both the Russians and the Chinese face serious problems in Latin America. The

[32] Some examples: The Niger government has accused the Chinese of aiding exiled groups that organized an assassination attempt on President Hamani Diori in April, 1965. Burundi, the Central African Republic, and Dahomey all expelled Chinese diplomatic missions in 1965 and early 1966. The Kenya government expelled some Russian, Chinese and Czech diplomats in early 1966 after indicating that foreign Communists were providing political and financial aid to leftist dissidents in the Kenya African National Union (KANU). The overthrow of Ghana's Kwame Nkrumah in February, 1966 was certainly the severest blow of all, and it was followed by a mass exodus of hundred of Russian and Chinese Communist advisors, technicians and diplomats.

[33] In Near Eastern countries, the Communist Parties are for the most part illegal or weak, and are all pro-Soviet, although scattered pro-Chinese groups exist and are encouraged and probably aided materially by the Chinese Communist Embassy in Damascus. In the Arab countries, particularly, Sino-Soviet competition is expressed largely, as in Africa, in the rival wooing of radical "anti-imperialist" governments, despite their persecution or repression of local Communists. Local Communists, in turn, are on the whole more inclined to work through or with other radical nationalist groups than to launch a direct attack on them or on the established regimes.

[34] The three-fold division of the extreme left sketched here is elaborated by Ernst Halperin, "Latin Amrica," in Leopold Labedz, *International Communism after Khrushchev, op. cit.,* pp. 154–157, and in Halperin's *Nationalism and Communism in Chile* (Cambridge: Mass.: The MIT Press, 1965), *passim.*

USSR, intent on maintaining friendly relations with some regimes (for example, the Christian Democratic government in Chile), must at the same time retain its commitments to local Communist Parties (on the whole a prudent lot), and also preserve its revolutionary image.[35] The Chinese have succeeded in drawing off fringe groups from the Communist Parties and encouraging insurrection, but have not been able to bring substantial radical forces under their control;[36] nor have they demonstrated that political violence has much chance of success in the area at present.[37] The existing divisions on the left have made Latin American Communists far less anxious than some of their colleagues elsewhere about the local consequences of a complete break in the world movement; for example, at the PC XXIII of the CPSU an Argentine delegate called for an international Communist conference "even without the participation of those Parties which for any reason do not wish to attend"—a thinly disguised call for a complete break with Peking.

[35] The Soviet Union's difficulties in reconciling the strategy of Peaceful Coexistence, backing for local Communist Parties, and at least theoretical support for insurrectionary actions were dramatized by the Tri-Continent Conference held in Havana from January 3 to 15, 1966. One conference resolution called for "economic, financial, and material aid of all kinds, including arms and munitions, to the authentic representatives of the countries which fight with arms in their hands, so that they may liberate their country and consolidate peace in the world." The Russians, whose support of extremist positions at the Havana meeting was no doubt partly motivated by the desire to validate revolutionary credentials constantly questioned by the Cubans and the Chinese, were embarrassed by strong Latin American official reactions to the conference. For example, on February 2, the Council of the Organization of American States condemned the Soviet delegation's endorsement of the Havana resolutions as a form of intervention.

[36] The major Chinese success in penetrating the old Communist Parties has been in Brazil, where a dissident Party was organized in 1962 in opposition to the pro-Soviet parent group. Castro's regime, once so friendly to China, moved closer to the Soviet Union in early 1966. See Daniel Tretiak, "Cuba and the Soviet Union: The Growing Accommodation," RAND Corporation, Memorandum RM-4935-PR, July, 1966. Elsewhere, the extreme left is usually so fragmented that it is difficult to identify all the forces in play, and particularly difficult to distinguish Castroite groups from those more directly inspired, guided, or aided by the Chinese.

[37] Despite the calls for greater militancy at the Havana Tri-Continent Conference, there was a marked decrease in guerrilla activity in Latin America in 1966. In Venezuela, most Communist leaders apparently concluded that continued armed rebellion was pointless in the immediate future. In Columbia, also, Communist-led insurgent bands virtually ceased operating in early 1966 and Party leaders explained that although guerrilla warfare was one means of fighting the government, it was not then the "principal form." In Peru, guerrillas led by the Castroite Movement of the Revolutionary Left (MIR) seem to have been effectively repressed by government forces. Nevertheless, both the Chinese and the Cubans continued to encourage armed violence as a "reliable method of struggle" in Latin America and to castigate those who thought otherwise.

Asia had been the one area in the world where the Chinese had been conspicuously successful in winning the support of other Communist Parties, and until 1966 there was good reason to see "a new Peking-led Communist coalition—all the Parties in southeast Asia, the Korean and the Japanese, and sizable portions of the divided Indian and Ceylonese Parties—which will loom large for at least the next decade and probably more."[38] During 1966, however, the West wind began to prevail over the East wind, and Asian Communism and the prestige and influence of Peking both suffered serious setbacks. Rightly or wrongly, Chinese radicalism was linked with the attempted coup in Indonesia, in late 1965, which led to the virtual destruction of the pro-Chinese Communist Party there, once the largest and one of the most powerful non-ruling Parties. A few months later, the ruling Parties of North Korea and Vietnam began to turn away from Peking and toward Moscow again, and the Japanese Party soon joined them in what was at least a more neutral or independent role in the conflict.[39] Even India's Communists, divided since 1964 into right and left factions, showed signs of resolving some of their differences along lines acceptable to Soviet leaders.[40] The messianic extravagances of the Chinese, the sobering effects of the Indonesian Communist disaster, and the more positive involvement of the USSR in Asian affairs have all probably contributed to the gradual alienation of some of China's former friends.

In this maze of relationships in the Communist movement, the

[38] Donald S. Zagoria, "Communism in Asia," *Commentary,* Feb. 15, 1965, p. 53.

[39] Early in 1966, the Japanese Communists sent delegations led by Secretary General Kenji Miyamoto to Peking, Hanoi, and Pyenyang in an apparent effort to moderate the Sino-Soviet dispute. Although the Japanese rejected an invitation to PC XXIII of the CPSU, thus seeming to differentiate themselves from the North Koreans and the North Vietnamese, the Party soon began to strike a more neutral tone in public statements, which suggested that top leaders had come to regard continued close identification with Peking as no less threatening to Communist prospects in Japan than close association with Moscow. "In order to overcome . . . modern revisionism, which is the principal danger for the international movement," said a typical editorial in the Party daily, "it also becomes necessary to fight correctly against doctrinairism and sectarianism." *Akahata,* May 11, 1966.

[40] The Communist Party of India, the largest competitor of the dominant Indian National Congress split in 1964, mainly over questions of domestic tactics, but the two wings are clearly generally oriented toward Moscow (right) and Peking (left), respectively. Following the split, the leftists gained over the rightists in electoral strength and apparently in prestige. Partly at the urging of Moscow, the two wings of the Party began to reappraise their policies. The rightists, shaken by the erosion of their position, and some leftists, who apparently are having difficulties with their own extremists, seemed inclined to consider some sort of covergence, if not full reunification.

following may be said to generally hold: "alignment" has come to reflect positions consonant with the specific and immediate interests of a Party and no longer implies subordination or even commitment to "international solidarity" (despite the conventional rhetoric of Party gatherings); alliances or sympathies are subject to fairly rapid shifts; many Parties are inclined to remain neutral and to cultivate their own domestic gardens. It is, in fact, precisely because the Russians have come to recognize and to tolerate a degree of heterogeneity among the Parties that would have been unthinkable only a few years ago that the former have been able to gather around themselves a loose association of Parties which still constitutes a movement of sorts, and one better adapted than the Chinese alternative to what Brezhnev has called, somewhat stiffly, "life in all its complexity and variety."

How Much Unity in Diversity?

Unity, or the lack of it, in the Communist movement can be measured in different dimensions, each of which provides a somewhat different conclusion. Despite the Sino-Soviet breach and the progressive differentiation of Parties, there will continue to be some cohesion in the foreseeable future. Most Parties consider and are likely to go on considering themselves part of a community of sorts, no matter how bitter their internal controversies. But this subjective sense of community is, paradoxically, being weakened by contradictory tendencies. Some Communists, those closest in spirit to the Chinese, accuse their more moderate comrades of a heresy which shades into infidelity—a view which inevitably tends to fragment the movement. On the other hand, the more moderate Communists are unmistakably moving toward an accommodation with non-Communists in their immediate environment. In Latin America, Africa and the Near East, Communists already tend to support or blend with non-Communists who share the same, or similar, goals. And how long can the West European Communists, for example, maintain the fiction that they have more in common with the Communists of Asia, Africa or Latin America than with the more progressive political forces in their own countries or in Western societies generally? There is, it seems, an irrepressible trend toward autonomy and toward a gradual loss of whatever was once distinctive about the movement and the Parties within it.

Despite this, however, it is still the case that most Parties remain responsive to Moscow's wishes, almost as a kind of reflex action, but also out of coldly rational calculation, and continued loyalty is made easier, as noted, by Moscow's increased tolerance for diversity. The

Parties are bound in any case to bear for a while some imprint of the past, no matter how "free" they may seem. Many old Party leaders still have emotional attachments to the Soviet Union strengthened by intellectual rigidities which retard ideological and political renovation and by a commitment to their own past which, if abandoned too rapidly, could ruin personal reputations and further undermine internal discipline in many Parties. Apart from such emotional, ideological, and prudential constraints imposed by history, a considerable part of Moscow's remaining appeal to the majority of Communist Parties apparently results from genuine if qualified agreement on many current international issues. In the final analysis, Moscow's "revisionism," however exaggerated by Peking and however inadequate and contradictory it may seem to the more restless European Communists, still makes more sense to most Communists than the shrill extremism of the Chinese. And another point in Moscow's favor cannot be overlooked: the USSR's political and economic power gives it means beyond anything the Chinese can yet muster in the game of winning friends and influencing people, as the Cuban and even the North Vietnamese cases, among others, testify.

The role of China as leader of a Communist bloc is bound to be different from that of the Soviet Union, but in the scramble for allies the Chinese have their own set of advantages, although they have been remarkably heavy-handed and unsuccessful in exploiting them. Not the least of these, perhaps, is China's symbolic value to Communists who resent, however tardily, past Soviet domination of the movement. (By the same token, however, Communists who welcome China's attack on Soviet authority and control are wary of submitting to a new power center in Peking.) The Chinese also exert a powerful emotional and perhaps even an ideological appeal to many Communists in the former colonies and/or underdeveloped countries who, dissatisfied with the status quo and despairing of moderate means for a basic transformation of society, respond to Chinese militancy. The latter are inclined to grasp at doctrinal formulations which make the underdeveloped areas and their agrarian masses the decisive revolutionary forces in the world struggle against capitalism and imperialism—thus relegating the Western industrial workers and their Parties to a secondary historical role, in an almost perfect reversal of classic Leninist doctrine. And, at least in Asia, the Chinese are able to count on the common strategic interest that they share with both the ruling and the nonruling parties in eliminating or weakening the Western, and especially American, presence in the area.

The lines of battle between the Soviet and Chinese Communists have now been drawn, but it seems unlikely that many of those involved welcomed the erosion of central authority and the gradual fragmentation of the international movement. The record, in fact, shows that most Parties have been reluctant to acknowledge that Moscow and Peking were engaged in a serious quarrel, which at the same time reflected and accentuated centrifugal tendencies long latent in the movement. Most Communists simply are not temperamentally prepared to admit that "proletarian internationalism" can be anything but monolithic in its political manifestation. Nor is it easy for them to concede that international communism in its "classic" form was perhaps a transient historical phenomenon. Moreover, many national Party leaders probably have feared, quite presciently, that differences among Parties would, sooner or later, affect the internal cohesion of the national Parties; that the erosion of Moscow's authority, combined with the public airing of differences between Moscow and Peking, would encourage factionalism as the domestic counterpart of polycentrism, especially within the nonruling Parties, which could not invoke state power to enforce internal discipline. There is evidence also that some of the smaller Parties regarded a unified international movement as an important element of support for their hopes of ultimate success. All this suggests that in the midst of a period of polycentric tendencies, many Communists sincerely, though for widely different reasons, yearn for the form and perhaps some of the substance of the old unity. It seems a vain longing, however.

In a schematic way, Communists can now perhaps be placed in three categories in terms of their attitudes toward unity or disunity. At one extreme stand the Chinese and their ardent, numerically diminishing sympathizers, who presumably quarreled with the Russians originally, certainly not with the intention of disrupting the movement but rather with the hope or even expectation of imposing on it a different and "correct" line. Only gradually, and perhaps reluctantly, did the Chinese move toward factionalism and schism, covering their moves with a theoretical justification paralleling Lenin's own rationale for the clean break he made with the parties of International II.

At the other extreme, the Italians, with their polycentrism, postulated an entirely different conception of unity—a "return" to equality among Parties and a search for consensual politics based on the inevitable diversification of Communist Parties.

Actually, neither the Chinese appeal to a unity immanent in history nor the Italian advocacy of a polycentrism that echoes Western pluralist theories of politics promises real unity for the movement, if the developments of the past few years are any indication. It would appear that for the time being most Communist Parties are content to ignore theoretical subtleties and to drift toward autonomy while maintaining residual attachments to an international movement which is increasingly difficult to define either in organizational, ideological, or programmatic terms.

SELECTED BIBLIOGRAPHY

Borkenau, Franz, *World Communism* (New York: Norton, 1939; reissued at Ann Arbor: University of Michigan Press, 1962). An old standby. Still popular and useful despite the revelations of a quarter of a century.

Brzezinski, Zbigniew K., *The Soviet Bloc: Unity and Conflict,* revised (New York: Praeger, 1961). An analysis of developments to early 1961.

Dallin, Alexander with Jonathan Harris and Grey Hodnett, *Diversity in International Communism—A Documentary Record, 1961–1963* (New York: Columbia University Press, 1963). A valuable sourcebook.

Degras, Jane (ed.), *The Communist International, 1919–1943,* 3 vols. (London and New York: Oxford University Press for the Royal Institute of International Affairs, 1956–1965). Comprehensive. Knowledgeably selected and edited.

Drachkovitch, Milorad M. (ed.), *Marxism and the Modern World* (Stanford: Stanford University Press, 1965). Interpretive essays on the current varieties of communism by some of the best-known names in the field. Papers on the occasion of the 100th anniversary of the publication of the formation of the first International.

Griffith, William E. (ed.), *Communism in Europe,* 2 vols. (Cambridge, Mass.: The MIT Press, 1965, 1966). These volumes contain excellent monographs on individual Communist Parties in Europe.

Labedz, Leopold, *International Communism after Khrushchev* (Cambridge, Mass.: The MIT Press, 1965). Originally appeared as a special issue of *Survey.* It covers the movement on a regional and country basis.

Landauer, Carl A., *European Socialism,* 2 vols. (Berkeley and Los Angeles: University of California Press, 1959). The complex history of the international movement. Volume II contains a succinct review of post-World War I Socialist moods and developments leading to the founding of International III (pp. 790 ff.).

Laqueur, Walter and Leopold Labedz (eds.), *Polycentrism* (New York: Praeger, 1962). Also originally a special issue of *Survey.* Gives a treatment similar to that of the later *International Communism after Khrushchev.*

Monnerot, Jules, *Sociology and Psychology of Communism* (Boston: Beacon, 1960). A Frenchman's impressionistic but perceptive view of the social-psychological aspects of commitment to communism.

Morris, Bernard S., *International Communism and American Policy* (New

York: Atherton, 1966). Part I deals historically and analytically with the problem of authority and control in the Communist movement.

Russian Institute of Columbia University (ed.), *The Anti-Stalin Campaign and International Communism* (New York: Columbia University Press, 1956). Documents illustrating the responses of the major Western Communist and pro-Communist Parties to the secret Khrushchev report of February, 1956.

US Department of State, *World Strength of the Communist Party Organizations.* (Washington, D.C.: Department of State, annual publication). This annual survey prepared by the Bureau of Intelligence and Research of the Department of State is a useful quick reference source giving basic information on all parties.

Zagoria, Donald S., *The Sino-Soviet Conflict, 1956–1961* (Princeton: Princeton University Press, 1962). The best-known work on the Sino-Soviet rift.

4

Soviet Communism

Dan N. Jacobs

ON MARCH 5, 1953, Stalin died.

He left behind a society of great physical capacity but soulless and intimidated, formed of unequal and intermingled parts of Russian tradition, of pseudo-Marxist theory, of the institutionalized pragmatism that was called forth for the sake of keeping the latter alive in the face of the frequent hostility of the former, and of the preferences and predilections of the now-expired Man of Steel.

In one sense, Stalin's death left Russia rudderless in a fashion that may have been true of no other previous modern society, for no other society had been dominated for so long by one man with such coercive resources at his disposal.

In the West, and in much of the Communist world, there is little argument that by 1953 the USSR had "outgrown" Stalin and that his continued domination had stunted the multilateral development of the Soviet economy and people. The Stalinist path, which gave scant consideration to Marxist goals but had been laid out to build and maintain power, even under Stalin was less and less viable—and for his successors it was gutted with potholes. A gigantic overhaul of the system under Stalin had to be undertaken. This is what the Soviet Union and much of the Communist world has been involved in doing since 1953—and in particular since 1956.

Already in 1954 aberrations in Stalinism, some greater harbingers than others, had begun to appear. None of these, however, did by any means prepare the world, Communist and otherwise, for the thunderbolt-like repudiation of Stalin that was to be delivered by Khrushchev in

February, 1956. The Communist world would never be the same. For hours, before thousands of the leading members of the Russian Party Khrushchev carried out radical surgery on international communism, possibly[1] believing all the while that the operation he was performing was no more serious than a tonsilectomy. As it turned out the patient would not die, and certain of his parts would be, arguably at least, as strong as—if not stronger than—ever. But the whole body of international communism would never again coordinate as before.

The Stalin strategy was that of the forced march and of pushing ahead in prescribed areas, not always regardless of the cost, but always willing to pay whatever price was necessary to maintain control and to build up heavy industry and the defenses of the country. Stalin's methods were not oblivious to the use of the carrot as well as the stick. He had developed a spectrum of positive incentives, but these were of limited attraction and narrow range. Always much stronger were the coercive forces—the dread labor laws, the secret police, the slave labor camps. Towards the end of his life Stalin indicated less and less concern with attracting men to achieve and produce and depended increasingly upon the deadening spectres of fear, force and habit.

The Problems of Stalin's Heirs

For the men who came after Stalin, there remained the concern for the continued development of the national economy that had become the principal justification of the system. But these leaders were primarily concerned with maintaining a power, as they felt, not so surely held as it had been by Stalin, and, on the part of the individual contestants, with gaining that power for themselves. Whether popular support was required for the achievement of the latter two goals in the totalitarian society that existed in Russia in the mid-1950s is questionable. Were the people not too cowed to be politically significant? Could not the battle have been waged entirely at the top without involving the masses? Such a course, perhaps, was an unlikely one for ambitious and desperate men groping for backing from whatever source. In any event it was not followed—and a searching after popular support, largely

[1] Our knowledge of the details of Soviet political manipulation, to say nothing of the psychological state of the actors, is so incomplete that the writer on Soviet subjects is forced to resort again and again to such linguistically unsatisfactory expressions as "it would seem," "it would appear," "possible," probably," and so forth, in order to warn the reader.

through the distribution of what was hopefully to be regarded as material largess, commenced.

It seems likely that Soviet leadership did permit itself at times to think in terms of concern for the masses, of bringing terror and privation to an end, of at long last achieving some of the goals of the revolution in the form of a higher standard of living—for the sake of the masses. But the leaders were dominated by other, power considerations. The guiding principle remained, as in Stalin's day, to give as little as possible, to take as much as possible. This was the way in which Stalin had acted and he had achieved great successes. It was part of the Soviet way and not to be casually dropped. Only gradually did the thinking of the leading group—and by no means all of it—come to the conclusion that to get more, more was going to have to be given. Though perhaps not acknowledged, in the following terms, the realization dawned that if men are kept at starvation levels, under slave conditions, they would produce only as do men under such conditions. The incentives of terror, having been all but exhausted, could not elicit greater productivity. As much as could be done with negative sanctions had been done, and still Soviet productivity was inferior to that of the West. Slowly it was perceived that the worker had to be given positive, material incentives to make him produce at a higher level. And so, while additional consumer production still was presented as a benefit bestowed by a kindly parent upon his doting children, given purely out of love, increasingly the purpose of the "concessions" was not the purchase of acquiescence or of support, but of involving the physical and mental energies of the masses in the continued growth of the Soviet machine. Nevertheless, in the dozen years following Stalin's death despite mushrooming demand, consumer industry failed to take precedence over heavy industry. Soviet industrial goals remained primarily in the area of expanding capital facilities, as they had been in Stalin's day.[2]

Soviet leadership justifiably took pride in the gigantic complex of heavy industry that it had forced into existence; but its creation was now three decades and more old. It was no longer possible, as it had been to a considerable degree during the years when the Soviet economy

[2] When it comes to the matter of the forces that have brought about change in the Soviet Union since 1953 and 1956, the need to satisfy the unleashed economic demands is of paramount importance, but it is difficult to unravel it in a cause-and-effect relationship from such other important and intertwined non-domestic factors as the effectiveness of the United States containment policy which disappointed expectations of forcing expansion and focused attention inward, and the breakdown of the monolith.

was being "founded," to neglect technological advancement and obsolescence, except at tremendous cost.[3] Morevover, the system had gotten to the point where the annual percentage rate of growth, a principal Soviet index of success, was steadily falling—and by the early 1960s alarmingly.

The problems of industry increasingly involved Khrushchev's attention after he had survived the attempts to squeeze him out in 1957 and, as he thought, had taken care of other pressing matters. The difficulty with the Soviet industrial economy at the time, as Khrushchev saw it, was that it was too highly centralized. The center ordered excessively dictatorially—and, being the center, it could not clearly see the individual trees in distant forests. Khrushchev had inherited the Leninist confidence in organization. Given the infallibility of the system, there was no problem that proper organization in the hands of the "right" men could not solve. If there is too much centralization, then decentralize. If decentralization doesn't work, then recentralize, but not all the way, at least not at first. Experiment. It is only necessary to find the correct formula and the proper personnel—and everything will fall into place. Given the problem as he saw it, Khrushchev decided to decentralize, spooning out varying dosages of local authority; but it was not long before the Soviet press began running complaints of "localism," that respective *sovnarkhozi* (councils of national economy into which the USSR had been divided) were not giving sufficient attention to the needs of other regions as called for in the plan but were producing primarily in response to local demands. Then Moscow began playing the numbers game in the continuing attempt to raise production. In some areas at some times the number of *sovnarkhozi* was increased; in others they were amalgamated, and in October, 1965, they were eliminated. Officials were quickly shuffled in and out of important positions. Men hidden in Siberian obscurity one day, were rushed to the top on the next on the basis of some success, and then, failing to universalize their local triumph, booted back to the sticks again. Moscow was in the continuing bureaucratic dilemma, traditional in Russia, but not in Russia alone, of wanting the benefits of greater local autonomy but being unwilling to pay the price of the consequent reduction in centralized control. Khrushchev in the late 1950s and early 1960s continued to seek the achievement of a bureaucratic apparatus that

[3] The Soviet system stuck with outmoded equipment and technique long beyond the point of diminishing returns. The argument was that change was expensive. Even if existing machinery and methods were less efficient than more modern replacements, total production would be enhanced by continuing to follow the tried-and-true, rather than scrapping it and innovating.

would permit effective local authority without diminishing his own national control. And he sought this ideal marriage through continued tinkering with the apparatus, the result of which was to be mounting confusion in the Soviet economy.

In the backing and filing of decentralization and recentralization, the changing role assigned to the formal planning apparatus of the USSR further complicated a job already made almost impossibly difficult by the growth of the Soviet economy. To plan, which meant making choices, and to coordinate plans for the tens of thousands of factories and the millions of different items now produced—and each year the number of both grew—became a horrendous task, even though only a fraction of one percent of the total number of different items produced was specifically planned for by the central planning apparatus. Increasingly, Soviet planners experimented with the use of complex mathematical formulas (even dragging up the disavowed work of their own mathematicians who had for decades received respectful attention in the United States) and of computers in order to assist in making choices.

But the problem of the planners persisted and in the area of consumer production its existence became most evident. In the early 1960s, Soviet industry had begun to produce consumer goods in greater quantity, but not always what the public demanded. A few years earlier, whatever appeared was snapped up. This was no longer the case, and the system was, for the first time, face to face with consumer resistance. Tens of thousands of pairs of shoes, of suits and dresses, of toilet articles, unsalable at the prices asked (later at any price), piled up in warehouses. Some of these items could be unloaded by shipping them to the hinterlands. But these measures provided little relief since factory directors still received numerous production targets to fulfill, calling, among other things, for the production of a set number of pairs of, for example, ladies' shoes. The factory director had no responsibility for the saleability of his output, only the meeting of assigned production targets, including volume. Therefore, he produced the same styles, or scarcely changed ones, that he had turned out for years to the satisfaction of the authorities—and in increasing quantity. But the women of Russia's cities, growing more style-conscious, did not want the same design of shoe they had seen on the counters of the local *univermag* for the past decade. And so the surpluses began to pile up.

On September 9, 1962, a now-famous article appeared in *Pravda* over the name of Yevsei Liberman, a business economist at Kharkov University, who, among other things, suggested that plants should be geared to produce for consumer preference and that this should be enforced by having production success based, in part, not on the number of pairs of shoes produced, but on the number actually sold at the retail level. A factory that did not produce saleable merchandise, no matter what the quantity of its production, would no longer receive the all-important bonus. The Liberman proposal, though mild in comparison with others subsequently offered, was nevertheless for its time a radical one because of the elements which it included of consumer preference and increased discretion to be permitted the factory director as to number of workers, wage rates, production techniques employed. Khrushchev allowed the debate, officially ignited by the article, to continue until his own increasingly desperate situation led to the damping of the speedy development that seemed in the offing. Nevertheless, experimentation was carried out under Khrushchev and, within ten days after his political demise, his successors ordered a kind of consumer preference into effect in one-third of the shoe, textile and garment factories in the USSR and instructed that further experiments be carried out, particularly in the matter of increased managerial discretion at the plant level, in other branches of industry. The plenum of the Central Committee, meeting in October of 1965, extended the principle of increased managerial discretion throughout Soviet industry, but by no means without reservation and controls.

The struggle between the demand of an authority constantly wary of losing its power, to maintain control—and the necessity for the development of local initiative if more efficient, effective and greater production was to be achieved, was apparent in the Soviet economy in both industry and agriculture. Agriculture had been, was and is likely to remain the Soviet Union's greatest continuing economic problem. The success of leadership in substantial measure was judged by what it had done to improve the situation in that branch of the economy which employed almost half of the available manpower, yet consistently failed to satisfy more than, sometimes even, minimal food and raw material requirements. In the middle of an average summer in the mid-1960s, the largest government market in the center of Moscow could still offer only onions, radishes, cucumbers, stunted cabbage, a few Bulgarian apricots and some lemons, selling at twenty-five to thirty-five cents apiece. The easy abundance of St. Denis, Les Halles, or the fruit and vegetable section of an American supermarket seemed as elusive to the Soviets as ever.

The farms remained the great backwater of Russia. On many of them, life was endured at substantially the same level as before the

Revolution. Those who could benefit from their education left for the city, where comfort, adventure and opportunity for advancement beckoned. The farther away from Moscow, the smaller the village, the less the old order had changed.[4]

Between 1953 and 1957, steps had been taken to improve the agricultural situation, hopefully to involve the peasant in the work of the collective area and to expand production of grain. Restrictions on private plots were reduced; so were taxes; procurement prices were raised. It was during this same period that the virgin soil and corn-planting campaigns were inaugurated. Through these and other means, the good fortune of sufficient rainfall at the proper time and other favorable factors, Soviet agricultural output grew encouragingly—to such a degree that Khrushchev evidently concluded that Soviet agriculture had been righted and that it would henceforth continue to increase through its own momentum, with relatively little immediate attention and further investment being required. He considered that the political levers represented by the Machine Tractor Stations could be safely removed and that funds could be derived from the collectives through forced payment for the MTS machinery and be used for a variety of purposes. But then came the crop failures of the late 1950s and Khrushchev was forced to be concerned with agriculture once again. Additional investment in equipment and fertilizer, higher prices to the collective and the proferring of other incentives seemed called for. But Khrushchev had committed Russia's resources elsewhere; it would have been difficult to make the required adjustments, even if Khrushchev had been so minded. He tried to brazen things through. Here, as in industry, he seemingly operated on the hypothesis that success was only a matter of finding good men and "correct" solutions. There was nothing fundamentally wrong. He tried to prevail by badgering, shaming and pressuring farm administrators. In 1961, still seeking a "cheap" solution, he ordered the elimination of the fallow areas of the collective farms (previously left untilled each year to permit the land to replenish itself) with such determination that, as he later admitted, the farmers become afraid to grow grasses at all, no matter how badly needed. The elimination of the fallow in certain places and under certain circumstances was a constructive measure, as were the bulk of the reforms put into effect under Khrushchev, but not in every place and under all conditions,

[4] The Soviets, in permitting the publication of Feodor Abramov's *One Day in the 'New Life'* (New York: Grove Press, 1963) as well as other works on farm themes by such authors as Solzhenitsyn and Stadniuk, testified to the corruptness and hopelessness of rural life and to the falseness of the Socialist realist picture they themselves had given of it in the past.

as Khrushchev, conditioned by Soviet campaign psychosis, seemed to insist. Then, success still eluding him, Khrushchev reverted to the use of the organizational solution, deciding that the agricultural problem was to be overcome by the increased attentiveness of local officials. For example, the Party secretary in a given area, responsible for both industry and agriculture, could not possibly pay sufficient attention to both. Therefore at the *guberniya* level and at all levels below, in both the government and the Party, the apparatus was split, requiring in many instances a doubling of the number of officials. To fulfill the need for personnel, men were sent out from the cities, but they knew little of agriculture. The result of the reforms was confusion and consternation. In addition, in terms of weather, 1962–1963 was a bad time. Production fell. Then, realizing that the organizational solution had failed, Khrushchev unveiled in the fall of 1963 his designs for the large-scale production of inorganic fertilizers, as part of the new campaign for the chemicalization of Soviet industry. But by now Khrushchev's time was running out. His bets had not paid off. The last reluctantly adopted solution had no time to pluck his already burning chestnuts from the fire.

Khrushchev's successors, almost immediately following their successful coup, and apparently recognizing that the continuing low level of material incentives played a significant role in farm difficulties, attempted to inveigle the peasants with the same sort of *enrichez-vous* warblings that had last been directed at them by Bukharin and Stalin almost four decades before. Encouragement was to be given to the intensive tilling of the peasant plots and the increase of personally held livestock. Within two months Khrushchev's dual system in Party and government organization was ordered abandoned. And within six months the state procurement system for grain and livestock was radically reorganized, raising the prices offered on obligatory procurements, lowering the amount that had to be delivered, offering still higher prices for additional production and permitting the farms themselves to determine what they would raise over and beyond the obligatory requirements. These were radical concessions, and together with the increased production of inorganic fertilizer that had been instituted by Khrushchev, and other incentives offered, including a guaranteed minimum collective farm wage and old-age benefits, would have been expected to result in a raising of Soviet farm output. They did not—at least immediately—as 1965 witnessed another disappointment in grain crops. This first great post-Khrushchev domestic failure heightened the force of such previously raised questions as to whether the new incentives were enough to raise the lethargy of the peasant working on the collective acreage, whether the Soviet power could keep hands off long enough to give the reforms an opportunity to succeed, and, granting affirmative answers to these, whether the measures already taken could overcome the short growing season and the lack of rainfall, which plague almost all of agricultural Russia, and the mounting distaste for rural life.

Contemporary Soviet Society

If the pressures that were brought to bear upon the Soviet leadership were, in the areas of economic demands, more or less society-wide, there were other more concentrated domestic pressures, as well, emanating from a variety of sources; one such being the military. In Stalin's later years the military was as much as, if not more than, any other part of the population subject to the whims of Stalin and Beria. The heroes of the military had been cut down to size after World War II by such patent ingratitudes as the assignment to oblivion of the wartime stalwart Marshal Zhukov. But what most rankled was Stalin's decimation of their ranks on the eve of World War II, when a large percentage of the officers of the rank of colonel and above fell in the purges.[5] Thus had perished Tukhashevsky, Blucher and hundreds of others of the military leaders who emerged from the Civil War. The military claim against Beria, for his role in the purge of the armed forces, as well as for the formidable personal military force he had assembled, was a deeply felt one. There was undoubted military support for his forced removal.

The early post-Stalin leadership in its immediate drive to cement national "unity," recognized that the support of the military was essential. As one of its first acts, the reconstituted Presidium recalled Marshal Zhukov and brought him into their own ranks. It was later Khrushchev who recruited Zhukov to his personal colors in the battle with what he later dubbed the "anti-Party" group. In the life-and-death struggle which Khrushchev waged against Molotov, Kaganovich and company in June, 1957, it was Zhukov who was one of his most steadfast allies.[6]

Yet Khrushchev, as had Stalin a decade earlier, apparently felt

[5] According to Herbert Dinerstein and Roman Kolkowicz, who have investigated the matter meticulously, while there is agreement among researchers that a very high proportion of the officers of the Red Army of the rank of colonel and above perished in the purges of the 1930s, there are only guesses as to whether the exact figure would be at or near the 65, 70, 75, or other percent, given by various Western authors.

[6] Zhukov supposedly made airplanes available so that members of the Central Committee favorable to Khrushchev could be flown from distant points.

threatened by the independent-minded, outspoken Zhukov, and soon thereafter sent Zhukov back to the same limbo from which he had emerged four years earlier. Khrushchev could not, however, have so acted and maintained his position in the fall of 1957 had he not had the compliance of the military.

Following 1957, however, Khrushchev repeatedly antagonized the marshals and generals by his willingness to sacrifice some military priorities in favor of increased consumer production, by the reduction of the armed forces, by his handling of the Cuban situation, by his virtual exclusion of the military from policy formulation, and, what is often overlooked as a principal element in the shaping of the coup against him, by his speech of September 19, 1964, questioning the value of tank forces for modern combat.[7] Within a month after Khrushchev expressed such doubts, seemingly foreshadowing further curtailment, he was in retirement. In 1957, he had had the support of the military, or a power-wielding part of it—and had survived the attempts to unseat him. Yet, in 1964, he no longer had that support—and he fell, not for that reason alone surely, but its significance is not to be overlooked, particularly in light of the post-Khrushchev bows made by his successors in the direction of conventional military forces.

The technologists make up another "interest group"—one that many specialists on the USSR at one time saw as a threat to Party control. When Saburov and Pervukhin were taken into the Presidium, it was seen by many as a concession to the technologists; and when they were removed, it was stated that the immediate threat, at least from the technologists, was over. Yet, it was overlooked that the technologists did not constitute a group apart like the military; they had no organizational, let alone physical force of their own. In the majority of instances they had achieved their high positions in management at least partly, usually mostly, through active Party work—Pervukhin and Saburov, in particular, being more Party than managerial. Finally, the Party had no intention of being eased out of its leading role. Certainly the Party had to consider the needs and problems of the technologists, but in more than one vital area their demands were not of one voice, as the varying generations and types of specialists pursued their own mutually antithetic aims and ambitions.

"Intelligentsia" is one of the very few concept words to come into English from the Russian. In the Soviet Union it is loosely applied to everyone who has completed higher education, regardless of specializa-

[7] Pravda, Sept. 22, 1964, p. 1; translated in *Current Digest of the Soviet Press* (hereafter cited as CDSP), vol. XVI, no. 38, p. 9.

tion and interest. It would be incorrect to state that the intelligentsia in this broad sense had as a group brought special pressures to bear upon the regime. However, pressures of a sort were applied by at least two segments of the Russian intelligentsia: the scientific intelligentsia and the "creative" intelligentsia.

The scientific intelligentsia has become probably the most prestigeous group within Russian society. Because of the high regard and need for its achievements, it is given greater freedom than perhaps any other segment of that society, though not because the government wants to trust it, but only because it feels it must. Its members have access to Western publications, largely without restriction or question, apparently even in areas beyond their particular specialization. They attend foreign congresses, sometimes without being accompanied by police agents. They spend extended periods abroad on special projects in the developing countries. They write letters abroad and receive mail from abroad without the concern felt by the average Soviet citizen. In general, they are more hospitable and frank than other echelons of the Soviet populace. They even induced the authorities to eliminate, for the most part at least, the limiting Stalinist remnants in the field of biology.[8] Nevertheless while its own sphere of freedom has been broadened, undoubtedly in response to pressures its members applied, there has been little indication of any conscious effort to have those freedoms extended beyond its own circle, nor of any realization that those freedoms could be assured for themselves only as they were circularized, nor, as far as can be determined, even any widespread discussion of such matters.

The broadening of freedom for Russia's scientific intelligentsia was carried out rather quietly, but the creative intelligentsia has had to be far more sensationally and openly involved as it struggled to bring an end to the strictures of "Socialist realism." Even during the most leaden days of Stalinist power there were those who wrote or painted for their "desk drawers," as the expression had it. Some manuscripts, particularly of poems, might be hand-copied or mimeographed, and then distributed to followers who would pass them around and often memorize them. But what was published, and exhibited, reflected solely

[8] Trofim A. Lysenko was a favorite of Stalin's because of his apparent success as a horticulturist and his theory that changes accomplished in a single generation could be genetically passed on to the next, thus giving hope for the speedy accomplishment of the "new Soviet man." Khrushchev kept Lysenko around because of his announced agricultural successes and allowed his quack biological theories to continue to call the tune for the field, despite increasing criticism. The post-Khrushchev era finally seemed to cement Lysenko's doom, though his cult sank slowly, and it must be remembered that he had bounced back before.

the requirements of Socialist realism, which embodied the prejudices of Stalin and his doyens. Those who could not comply with these had at the least to find some other way of making a living.

The leadership, eager after February, 1956, to prove itself unlike Stalin, was willing to permit some leeway in straying from the Socialist realist straight-and-narrow. But how much could it permit? How far could criticism be permitted to go? Would not any loosening at all threaten the entire fabric? Once the unraveling began, could it be stopped? By the first quarter of 1957, conservative forces began to make their regrouping felt, and thus 1956's short-lived "thaw"[9] came to an end. Despite this, the fabric could indeed not be retightened; the persistent claims to be heard would not be put down. Moreover, the brief period of the thaw not only broke the Stalin-cast spell of acceptance, but opened the way for new authors and painters to dare to create the previously all but unthinkable, and thus increased the pressure for a renewed thaw.

Under Khrushchev,[10] permissiveness for the writer and artist would have its more expansive and its less expansive moments, sometimes being buffeted by the winds of political combat storming in other seas, sometimes seeming to be affected more or less according to the personal prejudices, and pleasures, or immediate dispepsia of Khrushchev. At times there were honors for the new school of Soviet *scritori* and *artiste,* who were almost all Party members, undoubtedly loyal to the regime, not necessarily even in essence devoted to the concept of art for art's sake, but determined to experiment, to say what they had to say, and perhaps to return in their own way to the humanism that was part of the Russian intellectual tradition. At other times,[11] they were scolded—by Khrushchev wondering out loud whether a painting at an exhibition had not been daubed on with the tail of a jackass[12]—or worse. They

[9] The period took its name from Ilya Ehrenburg's significant but shallow book of the time that bore that title.

[10] A great deal has sometimes been made of the alleged antiintellectuality of Khrushchev. Whether it is true or not—and it probably was—it should be observed that politicians and political leaders in general, are not usually distinguished by their affinity for intellectuals and the interests of intellectuals. Such a proclivity on the part of the leaders of Khruschev's generation with their personal histories is scarcely to be expected.

[11] March 7, 1963, saw the height of Khrushchev's final major attack on the intellectuals. Following Khrushchev's lead, Ilyichev, *agitprop* chief, publicly and at length, castigated the "new school" before a session of the Congress of Russian writers (*Pravda,* Mar. 9, 1963 p. 2—CDSP, vol. XV, no. 10, pp. 3–6). But within two months it was apparent that the strictures that he had set down at that time were being publicly broken.

[12] *Pravda,* Dec. 2, 1962, p. 1—CDSP, vol. XIV, no. 48, p. 20.

were shipped off to do penance in Siberia—or Cuba. Some of the "worst" offenders, usually the least popular or the most untractable, were sent to "rest" homes, though it was not always clear that this is not where they should have been. But without exception those sent into exile came back and, with few exceptions, began to be published again.

Out of their struggle to be permitted to write and paint as they saw fit, to be published and exhibited, out of the restrictions and punishments they suffered, and the successes they met artistically and in that struggle, and out of their survival the young artists of Russia developed a confidence that the authorities could not easily intimidate.

It was true that, here as elsewhere, if the Kremlin wanted to crack down with all the force at its disposal, it could. Considering that the poets, for example, were once more among the heroes of Soviet youth, that ten thousand young people filled Dynamo stadium to hear Yevtushenko recite "Stalin's Heirs," and that the hall of the Sovietskaya Theater was packed on Sunday mornings and at other times to hear Voznesensky read his works, the price would be costly. Still, silence, if not acquiesence, could be enforced.

But here, too, Soviet leadership has been caught: it is not eager to restrict. Remembering the old, it does not want a new Stalinism; but it also does not want to lose its control. It seeks the "new Soviet man," who will do the "right" thing because he can conceive of doing no other, who will be thoroughly and completely Sovietized, always in agreement with the Party line but filled with initiative and energy. Yet, despite official assertion to the contrary, he is not on the horizon, and so here, as in industry and agriculture, every step into the future seems beset by a threat to that which the Soviet leadership values most highly and feels that it must keep in its own hands, undiminished, namely, power.

It seems clear that among much of the creative intelligentsia—and even among those with an understanding of *raison d'état*—there has been a drive for wider permissiveness, but that these goals are prime objectives of other echelons of society is, at best, dubious. It is true that there is, among certain strata of the urban youth, sympathy for the contemporary writer. Whether this is so because it is the vogue or because poets have for a century and more been Russian heroes, or because of the struggle the intelligentsia have waged—and to what extent the youth identify with the struggle, understand it, particularly in its political implications, and are willing to become involved in it —all of this can only be conjectured. It is true that the Russian people have a considerable curiosity, even more, a deep emotional involvement, in what transpired during the Stalin regime, particularly in the days of World War II. For example, in mid-1965 copies of Marshal Sheremenko's newly-published book *V Nachala Voina* (*At the Beginning of the War*), advertised as "what Stalin did after the German attack," were literally torn from the hands of Moscow street hawkers by eager purchasers. On the other hand, there has been little evidence of such curiosity about more recent events, for example, Khrushchev's removal and the reasons for it. In part this was undoubtedly because there was official "permission" to conjecture about Stalin's regime, within limits—and no such "permission" about Khrushchev. Even so, in the present context, this does not seem sufficient to account for the abundant lack of expressed interest in domestic contemporary politics. Many would attribute this to what is so generally termed "alienation," to which one is tempted to add and ask: when were the Russian people, pre-Soviet or Soviet, not alienated from their government?

There has been no evidence of an increased willingness on the part of authority to permit, leave alone encourage, public discussion of such vital questions as how the "errors" of the Stalin era occurred and why the Soviet people, including those near Stalin, acquiesced in them for so long, an understanding of which is vital for the development of any kind of democracy in the Soviet Union. Nor has there been much evidence of a popular demand to discuss such questions. It would seem more than mildly arguable that to a high degree the Russian people, including their intellectual leaders, have been conditioned, not only over the past decades but over centuries, simply not to permit themselves to think in terms involving the chief authority—and not to be unhappy about it—since it is after all not their "business."

There are those observers of the Soviet scene who assert that as the industrialization of Soviet society proceeds and it becomes more sophisticated, the pressures for the meaningful democratization of the system will increase. But this is a hope, rather than a conclusion based on previous experience. There is no evidence that where democracy has not previously existed industrialization and sophistication will give it birth. On the contrary, the antidemocratic tendencies of modern industrial life may be pointed to with much greater justification. Soviet leadership has, indeed, throughout its first five decades continued to speak of the increasing democratization of Soviet life, but in Soviet practice democratization has meant heightened public participation in terms of numbers of bodies but scarcely in terms of influence or power. The comrades' courts and the *druzhiny* (people's volunteers), the circulation of offices and the increased emphasis on popular decision making at the lower governmental levels, have done relatively little to lessen the central control of the Kremlin. They have, in many instances, only been new vehicles for registering the latest whim of authority. Here, a elsewhere, the Party has seemed to seek local initiative (read, "active cooperation") but with no thought in mind of lessening its own control.

There seems to be little reason now to stray from the conclusions of the Air Force-Harvard study, completed in the early 1950s and based on interviews with those who had left or been taken from the USSR a decade or more before, that the average Russian citizen had no objections to having power completely in the hands of the center (a center about which he expresses little curiosity), indeed preferred it, *as long as the center was doing a good job.*

For the time being, what the Soviet citizen seems to want of his government is that it feed, house and clothe him better than it has done in the past. He is willing to work very hard to achieve these goals, but he anticipates their realization. What he would do if put off indefinitely would be to reduce the level of his effort, perhaps, if excessively provoked, to strike, as happened on a few occasions in the early 1960s—though seemingly only spontaneously and then against "misguided" local authority, never against the center. Going beyond this, if it would occur to him to do so, he would be faced with overwhelming force in the hands of an effective bureaucratic apparatus that has in the past given every indication of the will to defend itself and is firmly opposed to any kind of organization that it itself does not sponsor. The creation and utilization of any such organizations for antiregime purposes would appear impossible except in a situation that has deteriorated far beyond any presently forseeable. The transfer of purpose of existing organizations seems more likely, but again there is no evidence that this is taking place.

For now, Ivan Ivanovich appears to be generally satisfied with the growing material benefits that are accruing to him. Perhaps at some later date he will begin to become concerned about other issues, such as greater popular political control of the center, but there has been little pressure for this in the past and little indication of it in the present.

Nevertheless, it must be recognized that the Kremlin by no means has the authority today that it enjoyed in Stalin's time. Increasingly it must pay attention to the requirements of the masses to maintain their continuing level of cooperation and in the hope of heightening it. It cannot disregard them. In this sense, the central power has been diminished. But that such a development has yet led to an accretion of manipulable political power by the masses there is no evidence.

The Soviet man as he exists today bears little relation to the aspiration that Marx had for the man of the Communist stage. Once the working population was adequately fed, clothed and housed, a new type of individual, less self-centered, less petty, less mean was to develop. There would be no reason for the accumulation of personal possessions since all would have enough; man would be motivated to produce by factors other than acquisitive, and the remnants of differences between groups based on national background, experiences, education, types of labor performed and so forth would disappear. Crime itself, which was a function of deprivation would also disappear. A well-fed, clad and housed man would have no reason to become drunk or to engage in street brawls, or beat his wife—let alone to cheat, rob or murder.

But in the Soviet Union of the 1960s, there was no evidence that crime had disappeared. The Soviet press repeatedly urged the police to develop new techniques of discovering malfactors. Speculation and pilfering remained a major concern. The persistance of drunkenness as a major problem could be witnesses around the clock in the streets of any city or town in the USSR. And rowdiness and hooliganism gave public concern, though they did not appear to be as widespread as in the large cities of the United States.

Still the Soviets persisted in lauding the "new Soviet man," of the desired type who had, according to almost daily press reference, either already had been formed or was in the process of rapid development. While it was true that drunkenness and rowdiness and speculation were not the most prevailing characteristics of contemporary Soviet man, it was equally true that the past decade had in general witnessed the emergence of an individual quite different from the Marxist ideal. The run of successful Soviet citizens had become possession-oriented,[13] responsive principally to personal incentives, with increasingly less concern for equality and more for the good life, including the bourgeois graces. The reasons that the ideal new Soviet man has not developed can be argued at length: such a man is an impossibility; the Soviet system has not yet developed the proper atmosphere for the creation of such a man; the remnants of capitalist society remain infectious;

[13] The story, perhaps apocryphal, is told of the noted Soviet musician, a frequent performer abroad, who receives payment for his foreign concerts in electric appliances. His four-room apartment is reportedly piled to the ceiling with refrigerators, washers and dryers, electric irons, blenders and so forth.

circumstances have forced the system in practice, willingly or unwillingly, consciously or unconsciously, to appeal to the base element in man, and so forth—some of these arguments being offered by those inside the system, some by those outside; but, regardless of the reason or reasons, the "new Soviet man" has not yet infested society.

In contemporary Soviet society, higher education has become the most important requisite for success. Entrance to the universities and institutions is normally on the basis of academic achievement; and in the USSR, as elsewhere, those who come from families that have achieved, have a better opportunity for high performance than those born into working-class or agricultural families. Whether or not Khrushchev recognized the decisiveness of this factor, he did recognize the mounting social differentiations within society and acted to correct the trend by manipulating the entrance requirements to institutions of higher learning, though at the time his action was probably primarily motivated by another factor: the immediate need to infuse large numbers of additional laborers into the industrial force.

In 1958, Khrushchev introduced a major educational reform, stressing shop training virtually at every educational level and making it impossible for the majority of college-minded students to continue their studies full-time after the completion of middle school without an interval spent at full-time industrial or agricultural labor.

This was, in a sense, a highly idealistic effort on Khrushchev's part: to arrest the increasing class distinctions within the USSR, to reduce the differences between mental and physical labor, insuring, if not that all physical laborers could perform mental tasks, at least that all mental laborers could and did perform physical work. Moreover, the new reform gave certain advantages to the sons and daughters of workers and peasants seeking admission to higher education.

It stands to reason that not everyone was happy with the reform. The educators privately, some not so privately, lamented the turning away from the academic program that had become the hallmark of Soviet education under Stalin. Standards suffered.[14] Students disliked the interruption of their education; and parents, particularly "middle class" parents, concerned for their children's future, were distressed. Getting into Soviet institutions of higher learning, always a tense affair for students and parents alike, became even more so. Sometimes students would go to the outlying republics believing they had a better chance to be admitted to a Kazakhi or Uzbeki school, inferior though the education received might be. Sometimes bribes were paid to insure

[14] *Izvestia,* Aug. 3, 1961, p. 4; CDSP, vol. XIII, no. 31, pp. 11 and 24.

admissions,[15] or "ringers" hired to take examinations.[16] Moreover, the time spent in the factory and shop while in school proved to be largely a waste. Most of the students were sent to nearby shops which had no facilities for training them, did not want to use the funds and personnel to set up such facilities and regarded the students as a nuisance. Thus, for the most part, students would often spend two or three days a week sitting around, generally loafing and eventually going off to the movies.[17]

The reform was extensively modified in early 1965, in part to eliminate an unpopular instrument, in part because it had proved ineffective as an educational device, in part because it had already achieved its immediate objectives of increasing the labor force during a critical period. It had apparently achieved little as a piece of social engineering—and it must be asked (as some non-Soviet Communist leaders have done) if, given the mounting stress in Russia on incentives and achievement, there is much possibility for reducing the considerable class differentiation within the Soviet system, and, given the present crop of Soviet leaders, most of them "bourgeois" to the core, if such considerations hold any high priority of concern for them.

The Dilemmas of Power

What *did* above all else concern Soviet leadership, as has been emphasized here, was the matter of power: maintaining the power of the Party, maintaining the power of the center over the Party, both in undiminished form; *and* the struggle for personal power which the individual members of the leadership wage in their own behalf. For the most part, too, leadership had to concentrate on all of these interests simultaneously, during a period when the realistic possibility for the wide-ranging use of the power at its disposal was becoming increasingly restricted.

However, leadership gave clear indication that it had no intention of surrendering any controls that were not literally grasped from it, sometimes even when it could see the need for such surrenders.[18]

[15] *Izvestia,* Sept. 28, 1963, p. 4—CDSP, vol. XV, no. 39, pp. 29–30.

[16] *Sel'skaya Zhizn,* Aug. 6, 1962, p. 4—CDSP, vol. XIV, no. 35, pp. 29–30.

[17] *Komsomolskaya Pravda,* Mar. 7, 1961, p. 2—CDSP, vol. XVII, no. 10, pp. 5–6.

[18] E.g., in Criminal Law. It was argued by the judicialists, and evidently agreed to by the central power in the 1958 Codes of Criminal Law and Procedures that the law needed to be regularized, not be subject to short-term whims. Yet authority could not refrain from *ex post facto* changing of the law to meet ticklish social problems. Such continued official meddling with the law should be

Khrushchev did not bow in the direction that Yugoslavia had, towards the withering away of the Party, but, on the contrary, announced its "eternalization."[19] The Party, he declared, would always be needed to perform the tasks of organization and direction. Communist society required that these functions be performed—and the Party had performed them in the past and would perform them in the future. The notion of anarchy implicit in Marx was even more firmly disavowed by Khrushchev and his successors than by their predecessors.

Thus, though the totality of control, the ability to pull the strings of power to the same extent that Stalin had been able to so do, may have been slipping away from the Party leaders, they clearly indicated that they had no intention of surrendering the game. Where centralized control *could* prevail, they *would* continue to prevail.

In the post-Khrushchev period authority claimed that it was now definitely fixed upon the path of collective leadership, but it had made this claim before, only to see it fall before the onslaught of ambition and perhaps the temperament and requirements of Russia. It was possible that the job of ruling Russia had become so complex and/or the force of those contending for the top authority so balanced with the times and events producing no single leader able to gain control in his own right, that leadership, more or less collective (for some leaders are by their nature always more "collective" than others), would continue indefinitely. Again, however, there was nothing to indicate that this had become an ironclad law—or even that it was particularly likely.

Within the Soviet system, theory has rarely for long, if ever, stood in the way of political realities.[20] Under those circumstances when theory has opposed what necessity seems to dictate, theory has given way, although usually refusing to recognize the contradictory character of the situation that confronts it and so it has remained "unviolated" in its own eyes. Theory thus tends to be preserved, and classical statements or misstatements maintained, whether used as guides to action or not. Even so, when circumstances require, new theoretical "contributions" may be forthcoming, but they are always presented as having authorization in, and being perpetuators of, the Leninist heritage,

---

viewed not only in the context of restraint vs. lack of restraint, but also as the absence of respect for the *law* which in practice is seen more often as a threat to "justice" being done than as a protection for the individual.

[19] Program of the CPSU, in D. N. Jacobs (ed.), *The New Communist Manifesto,* 3rd ed. (New York: Harper & Row, 1965), p. 38.

[20] As a contemporary commentator on Soviet law puts it: "Theory goes more or less its own way, state and law go theirs." Ivo Lapenna, *State and Law: Soviet and Yugoslav Theory* (New Haven: Yale University Press, 1964), p. 1.

and Lenin wrote so voluminously[21] and changed his position so frequently to meet changing situations, that support for almost any stand may be found in his works.

By and large, the leaders of the 1950s and 1960s were not primarily men of theory any more than their predecessors had been. They knew their theory, more or less, but it colored their thinking, less and less; they were practical men, involved in the day-to-day task of running a country, getting and staying in power, and they increasingly had gained knowledge of the outside world as it actually existed. Yet Soviet tradition had it that Communist leaders were men of theory, who were expected to prove their fitness to wear the mantle of Marx-Lenin by saying something "in theory." Often such latter statements consisted largely of assessing how close the world currently was to the fulfillment of the Marxist-Leninist prophecy of capitalist catastrophe.

But sometimes, however such changes have been disguised, leadership statements have provided ideological justification for major policy changes. Certainly, de-Stalinization involved a theoretical change, a whole series of them—with ramifications far beyond the ideological—wiping out, as it did, the authority of one of the Bolshevik greats, though Stalin's *pronunciamentos* generally remained largely unviolated, perhaps to be cited as justification in some future reinterpretation.

Both domestic and international pressures made it necessary for Khrushchev to provide a support for his decision to avoid Russian involvement in nuclear war at almost any cost. Khrushchev insisted that nuclear war was too horrible to be allowed to happen; that in such a war even the victor would be a loser; that communism did not require wars to prevail, but that it would be achieved through the superior attractivenes of the life it provided for its followers. Khrushchev's corollary reinterpretation of "Peaceful Coexistence" was, of course, a change from Stalin's position, implied and stated, that communism could not advance significantly without armed conflict—and was seen as a direct threat by the Chinese, who were in no position to have the meager economic benefits that they had secured for their people serve as a beacon light for the world. But once having made his pitch for the pied-piperish attractions of Soviet plenty, Khrushchev had to demonstrate that such plenty existed. This, as well as his native enthusiasm and optimism and his recently reinforced self-confidence, accounted for what seemed to be the euphoria and the perpetual-motion-machine approach that characterized the middle Khrushchev period in particular.

[21] The most recent addition of his complete works in Russian covers 55 volumes.

In late 1959, Khrushchev announced that the USSR had moved one step closer to communism on its own territory, had progressed to a new stage, designated as the "state of all the people," which was beyond the dictatorship of the proletariat and beyond socialism, "a higher state of the building of communism." And in 1961, Khrushchev announced in the new Party program that within two decades the foundation of communism in the Soviet Union would be "in the main" achieved—and then indeed the peoples of the world would flock to communism.[22]

No Soviet leader would admit that he has introduced changes into Marxism-Leninism; this would be tantamount to the admission of heresy in altering Holy Writ. He has interpreted "in light of the present world situation," but nothing more. Yet whether leadership acknowledged "change" or not, and sometimes reluctantly it did, change there was—and in the Soviet Union in the 1950s and 1960s leadership had been its vehicle if not its perpetrator.

The question that remains is: what does that change mean for the future of the Soviet Union and of its citizenry?

"Quo Vadis?"

Change implies transition from something to something else. What Russia was after the death of Stalin seems clear enough. The outlines of what she is to become, even in the almost immediate future are not so discernible. That Russia's industrial growth will continue, despite the setbacks of the early 1960s there seems no doubt. The problems that need to be overcome are seemingly not insuperable, given the determination and willingness to bend before necessity that is characteristic of Soviet leadership. If major war is averted—and there is certainly little will to the contrary in the Soviet Union—it is to be expected that consumer goods production will continue to grow, perhaps even at a greater rate than heretofore, as pressures to which insecure leaders may succumb build up.

The picture for Soviet agriculture is less bright. It still remains to be seen to what extent increased incentives and investment will increase Soviet food production. They should, even at the levels introduced during the year following Khrushchev's fall, prove sufficient to evoke production necessary to meet the basic requirements of the country and

[22] There were other important changes in theory, too, during these years: the concession that there was more than a single "path to socialism" and the concomitant reform of relations with other Communist Parties and states, but these belong to the area of foreign relations and are covered elsewhere.

to guarantee in normal years that minimal reserves are accumulated. But the production of foodstuffs in sufficient quantity to provide the country with the widely varied and bulging larder to which the regime says it aspires seems beyond the short-term capacities of Soviet agriculture. Utilization of rapidly emerging agricultural techniques may eventually permit these greater goals to be achieved, but the adverse climatic conditions of the USSR remain seemingly as a permanent hinderance.

As for the people of the USSR, the acquisitive impulse, so long pent up, now voluntarily or involuntarily encouraged by the system, will continue to develop. There will be complaints both at home and from foreign Communist Parties about the escalating "bourgeoisation" of Soviet life, but, given peace, it seems unlikely that such tendencies will be soon or easily contained.

What is perhaps most difficult to anticipate is the Soviet political future. In general, the changes that have taken place in Soviet society since 1953 have been least decisive here, for power still lies heavy in the hands of the Party. While that power has been met by other forces within the society—and authority has had to recognize those forces, and has on occasion bowed before them—it has been authority's decision as to whether they were to be assuaged or not. That decision could at any time be recalled, and sometimes has been. Moreover, those other "forces" have no formal organization or even very tangible existence. To a great degree, they are characterized by passivity. There is connected with them the image that, if something is not done to relieve the pressure emanating from them, there may be adverse results, for example, in the form of lower production, but scarcely on an "organized" basis. But thus far, at least, despite the stubborn fight that some of the creative intelligentsia have more or less victoriously waged to paint and write more or less as they want, there is no evidence of any realization by these forces of the existence of a power that is potentially theirs; there is no evidence of any widely-held demands for political freedom. It may be that the demand for artistic freedom will bring in its wake a demand for political freedom. It may be that once the cravings of the masses for clothing and shelter have been at least partially satisfied that a strong political appetite will develop. But thus far it has not.

As for the contention that democracy will follow in Russia in the wake of industrialization and urbanization, it must be remembered that where democracy has developed, it has been democracy that came first and then industrialization. Democracy did not develop out of an industrial environment. While democracy may have blossomed in an industrial environment, though often, and perhaps increasingly, in spite of it, its origins were in a feudal past, which was gradually passing to capitalism, never touching Russia. Russia's preindustrial tradition was overwhelmingly one of *samoderzhavie,* autocracy—and its modern governments have been in that tradition.

The ultimate demand and responsibility for democracy resides within the people. They must want it, demand it, and somehow develop the habit of expecting it. Thus far there is no evidence of any such demand, let alone habit, developing among the Russian people. They demand of their government chiefly success in meeting their material and a few of their esthetic requirements. Beyond this, what leadership wants to do in the area of politics, seems to be its own business, which the public is willing to leave undisturbed. This is the bent of Russian and Soviet tradition and little has occurred since the mid-1950s, or for the three decades before, to upset it. Perhaps a developing sophistication and/or a regime that cannot or will not satisfy nonpolitical demands will lead to a more widely developed political interest and an understanding leading to action that in a people's state—or any other kind —the satisfaction of popular demands is dependent upon the positive as well as negative pressures that the people can mobilize to express their determination for the fulfillment of those demands—and not upon the gratuitous bequests of others. To say that such a development *will* occur would be unwise. To say that it will *not* occur, would be less unwise, but still not certain.

Postscript

The years 1966 and early 1967 witnessed developments in the Soviet Union that were more portentious in their ultimate implications than in the immediate effect which they had upon the life of the nation. Though the leadership, operating in the general context of a struggle for power, remained conservative,[23] abjuring adventures, and many top *apparatchiki* would have preferred to proceed even more slowly, there was at least an apparent continuing commitment to change in the economic sphere.

The number of factories and enterprises operating under the profit system was increased, and other managerial reforms were widely implemented. The planners and reformers, "conservatives" and "liberals,"

[23] The USSR was referred to as one of the "great conservative powers" of the world in *The New York Times* editorial, Apr. 11, 1966, p. 34.

"Stalinists" and "anti-Stalinists" finally come to grips with the price problem and reached a tentative compromise whereby significant numbers of wholesale prices would more accurately reflect costs but would still, in the final analysis, be set by the regime, not the market. Output of consumer goods such as refrigerators, washers, television sets went up 13 percent or more in 1966 over 1965 levels.[24] And in the former year a contract was signed to produce Fiat passenger autos in the USSR with production to reach 2,000 cars per day by 1970. Still, heavy industry continued to move ahead more rapidly than did the consumer sector of the economy.[25]

Official figures indicated that the decelerating trend of previous years in the increase in industrial production had been reversed in 1965 and 1966. In general it appeared that the various measures adopted by Soviet leadership to increase industrial output were being successful; however, published comments in the Soviet press made it apparent that there was serious opposition to many of the innovations. There were allusions to a new *Oblomovshchina*.[26] There was a scoring of the "conservatism" and "petty tutelage" of those who tried to evade the spirit of reform and continued to use "old methods of leadership, condemned by life."[27] The press referred to "inertia," "apathy," and "distrust," towards the "new" methods. But whatever the terms used, the meaning was the same: opposition to change. It seemed clear that such opposition was being overcome, but it was apparently widespread and existed in high circles.

In agriculture, reform was extended to the sovkhoz, where bonuses were to be distributed to the workers out of profits. On the kolkhoz individual cash incomes were up greatly. Through the establishment of country stores, traveling state merchandise caravans and the like, there were attempts to draw off the new purchasing power. However, peasant goods demands remained unsatisfied and there was a clear threat of "inflation" in the countryside.

Among consumers, interest in acquisition was hardly diminished by the increased amount of production reaching the market. The bourgeoisation of Soviet society, though sometimes complained about as at the Komsomol Congress in May, 1966, continued unabated. There was obvious interest in such matters as "Well, does it really matter how you

[24] *Pravda,* Jan. 29, 1967, p. 2.
[25] *Pravda,* Jan. 29, 1967, pp. 1–2.
[26] Great promises, but nonfulfillment, resulting from apathy. From Goncharov's XIXc fictional hero, Oblomov.
[27] *Pravda,* Sept. 28, 1966, p. 2.

use your knife?",[28] as well as "litter-bugging," proper conduct towards the ladies, and so forth.

If one was seeking sensational developments in the Soviet Union, they were most nearly to be found among the intelligentsia. The Sinyavsky–Daniel trial received worldwide attention, but even it represented a moderating development in the Soviet context. The defendants in the trial were allowed to plead their case at length. There was no evidence of physical coercion. Their sentences, by prior Soviet standards, were mild. There continued to be a struggle between writers and bureaucrats over the writer's duties and obligations to the "system" and to "truth." The all-union Writers' Congress was postponed repeatedly due to this issue. Sometimes the regime cracked down when it decided that a writer or painter or sculptor had gone "too far." But there was little pattern in such "crackdowns"; and what was not permitted last month might be permitted next month. Sometimes the regime attempted to take a "neutral" stand as it did in lambasting both the "liberal" journal *Novy Mir* and its conservative opponent *Oktyabr*.[29]

Though opposition was still considerable, progress in the direction of permitted self-expression continued to be made—but slowly and with a clear uncertainty on the part of the intelligentsia as to how far they really ought to go and with no definite regime policy as to how far to permit them to go. Here as elsewhere, the transitional nature of Russian life persisted.

There were a few indications of willingness on the part of individuals to stick their necks out in the cause of freedom: some fifty youths demonstrated in front of the Pushkin statue on Gorky Ulitsa for the repeal of Article 70 that permits sentences of up to ten years for the dissemination of "anti-Soviet" propaganda. Sixty-three Soviet writers signed and sent abroad for publication a protest against the Sinyavsky–Daniel trial. Alexander Tvardovsky, the poet and editor, sought to "correct" Leninist mythology.[30] The fact that such risks, greater in the first case involving relatively low-status individuals than in the last two, were taken, is undoubtedly significant for the development of a potential for greater freedom. But that there were apparently rather few such instances is also noteworthy.

[28] The answer, "Yes, it does matter. . . . You should not, for instance, eat with your knife instead of the fork, if for no other reason than that you may accidentally cut your lips." *Izvestia,* Oct. 9, 1966, p. 2—CDSP, vol. XVIII, no. 41, p. 22.

[29] *Pravda,* Jan. 27, 1967, pp. 2–3.

[30] *Izvestia,* Apr. 11, 1967, p. 4—CDSP, vol. XIX, no. 15, p. 34.

The great majority of Russians seemed to be satisfied, for the time being, to indulge their craving for acquisition. The regime, still concentrating on domestic problems, seemed intent on not interrupting that attention.[31] Its concern was with the here and the now—and not the long range consequences of its actions. Whether other kinds of demands can permanently be averted in this manner is discussed in some detail at the end of this volume, but, in any event, the regime was making the attempt to deflect them for the present.

While the pressures that continued to play upon the regime from the various interests of Soviet society gained effectiveness, among other things from the continuing struggle to inherit Khrushchev's mantle, there was no indication that the Party intended to lay down what it conceived to be its leading role. On the contrary, it both declared and acted out its intention to continue calling the plays, but its aggressiveness had strong defensive overtones and had to be seen in the context of the power contest.

July, 1967

SELECTED BIBLIOGRAPHY

Billington, James H., *The Icon and the Axe* (New York: Knopf, 1966). An outstanding work on Russian culture. Exceptionally well-written.

Brzezinski, Zbigniew, and Huntington, Samuel P., *Political Power: USA–USSR* (New York: Viking, 1964). A sometimes rewarding, often disappointing pilot comparative study of the Soviet and American systems.

Campbell, Robert W., *Soviet Economic Power,* 2nd ed. (Boston: Houghton Mifflin, 1966). An excellent brief and readable account of the operation of the Soviet economy.

Ehrenburg, Ilya, *Men, Years—Life,* 6 vols. (London: MacGibbon and Kee, 1961–1966). The latter-day effort to rewrite his own history, by one of Russia's most honored writers. First appeared in *Novy Mir.*

Fainsod, Merle, *How the Soviets Are Ruled,* rev. ed. (Cambridge, Mass.: Harvard University Press, 1963). The best extended treatment on the subject.

Feifer, George, *Justice in Moscow* (New York: Simon & Schuster, 1964) Mr. Feifer does the study many Soviet specialists thought about and projected: of Soviet justice in practice as witnessed over a period of months in courts of original jurisdiction. Valuable in spite of the axes the author seems to grind at times.

Fischer, George, *Science and Politics: The New Sociology in the Soviet Union* (Ithaca, N.Y.: Center for International Studies, Cornell University, 1964). A beginning.

Gorbatov, General A. V., *Years Off My Life,* trans. by Gordon Clough and

[31] See Brezhnev's report to PC XXIII, *Pravda,* Mar. 30, 1966, pp. 2–9.

Anthony Cash (New York: Norton, 1965). Memoirs of a Russian general imprisoned in the purges. A little book, often pathetic in its *naiveté* and faith. But noteworthy in indicating prevailing attitudes in some circles. First appeared in *Novy Mir*.

Hayward, Max (ed.), *On Trial: The Soviet State versus "Abram Tertz" and "Nikolai Arzhak"* (New York: Harper & Row, 1966). Report and analysis of the Sinyavsky–Daniel proceedings. Helpful in gauging how far Soviet permissiveness has moved since Stalin.

Hazard, John N., *The Soviet System of Government,* 3rd rev. ed. (Chicago: University of Chicago Press, 1964). The best short treatment of the subject.

Johnson, Priscilla, and Leopold Labedz (eds.), *Khrushchev and the Arts—The Politics of Soviet Culture, 1962–1964* (Cambridge, Mass.: The MIT Press, 1965). Selections from Soviet writers as well as a skilled analysis of the interaction of arts and politics in the turbulent give-and-take of the later-Khrushchev period.

Morton, Henry W. and Peter H. Juviler (eds.), *Soviet Policy Making* (New York: Praeger, 1966). A collection of case studies; those of Maurice Friedberg and Juviler deserve particular attention. Morton's introduction is noteworthy for its attempts to put the cases in a contemporary political science framework.

Lowenthal, Richard, *World Communism: The Disintegration of a Secular Faith* (New York.: Oxford, 1964). Translation of *Chruschtschow und der Weltkommunismus* (Stuttgart: 1963) Often lucid and compelling essays by one of the sharpest Soviet specialists. The Soviet Union plus.

Meyer, Alfred G., *The Soviet Political System* (New York: Random House, 1965). A broad analysis of Soviet politics by one of the most respected American scholars. Heavy on interpretation.

Mihajlov, Mihajlo, *Moscow Summer* (New York: Farrar, Straus and Giroux, 1965). Things done and people met and impressions gained while on a Yugoslav government grant in Moscow, 1964. The authors' anti-Soviet sentiments, expressed here, got him in trouble at home. The anti-Communist sentiments he made known later got him into still bigger trouble.

Parry, Albert, *The New Class Divided: Science and Technology versus Communism* (New York: Macmillan, 1966). Parry is a proponent here of the interest group thesis of Soviet society.

Ploss, Sidney I., *Conflict and Decision-making in Soviet Russia: A Case Study of Agricultural Policy 1953–1963* (Princeton: Princeton University Press, 1965). Controversial and labored, but valuable study with far-reaching implications in an area where much information is lacking and much work remains to be done.

"The Soviet Union Since Khrushchev—New Trends and Old Problems," *Proceedings of the Academy of Political Science,* vol. XXVIII, no. 1, Apr. 1965.

Swearer, Howard R., with Myron Rush, *The Politics of Succession in the USSR* (Boston: Little, Brown, 1964). Quotations and comments on a much commented-on yet still inadequately understood topic.

Tucker, Robert, *The Soviet Political Mind* (New York: Praeger, 1963). A group of essays, most of which have appeared elsewhere previously. Noteworthy particularly because of Professor Tucker's psychological insights.

Ulam, Adam B., *The New Face of Soviet Totaliarianism* (Cambridge, Mass.: Harvard University Press, 1963). A readable analysis.

Periodicals

Current Digest of the Soviet Press (New York: Joint Committee on Slavic Studies, American Council of Learned Societies and the Social Science Research Council). Translations from the most significant Soviet newspapers and periodicals. A weekly. The indispensible tool of the Soviet specialist.

Novy Mir (Moscow). Russian periodical in which most of the most controversial literature of the post-Stalin period appeared. Long under the direction of A. Tvardovsky.

Problems of Communism (Washington: United States Information Agency). Uneven government publication, available in wide variety of languages. Often first in print with more-extensive-than-newspaper analysis of new development. Sometimes very good indeed.

Survey (London). Excellent English quarterly on Communist affairs. Some special numbers, such as "The State of Soviet Science," are frequently reprinted in book form.

5

Chinese Communism

James R. Townsend

THE YEARS 1956 and 1957 were as critical in Communist China as elsewhere in the Socialist world. China had no real equivalent to the Twentieth Party Congress (PC XX of the CPSU) or to the events in Warsaw or Budapest, yet its leaders experienced during these years a period of sustained indecision and reappraisal that resulted in the "Great Leap Forward" and set the Chinese Communist Party (CCP) onto a collision course with the Soviet Union. Events in Europe had a great influence on the decisions that were to be made in China, but it was China's domestic situation that defined the basic problems and alternatives that emerged at this time. A general estimate of where China and the CCP stood in 1956 is essential, therefore, to an understanding of the development of Chinese communism since 1956.

The CCP came to power in 1949 as the ultimate leader of a century-long struggle to restore unified, independent and effective government to China. It came to power, too, with an explicit commitment to establish a Socialist system, but its Socialist goals contributed relatively little to its emergence as a contender for political power or to its final victory. The decisive factor in Communist victory over the Kuomintang (KMT) was the disciplined effectiveness of the Chinese Red Army, combined with widespread faith in the Party's ability to pursue a nationalistic and broadly progressive program. The Red Army won the battles, while popular sympathies increasingly shifted to acceptance of CCP leadership or, at least, to nonsupport of the thoroughly discredited KMT. The groundwork for this situation had been laid during the war with Japan (1937–1945). The Japanese invasion forced a KMT retreat from large areas of North and East China. The Communists, a small group of harassed and isolated revolutionaries who had relocated to Northwest China in 1935 after several years of unsuccessful rebellion against the KMT in the southern mountains, seized the opportunity to solidify their base areas and to assume leadership of guerilla activities against the Japanese. Under the nationalistic banner of resistance to foreign invasion, Communist strength increased enormously. By April, 1945, Mao Tse-Tung claimed that the Party had 1,210,000 members, that it governed areas with a total population of 95,500,000 and that its armed forces consisted of 910,000 regular troops plus a 2,200,000-member militia.[1] Moderate economic policies and tolerance of non-Party groups, coupled with impressive organizational skills and efforts, further strengthened the CCP's image as an effective national leader. When the postwar struggle with the KMT ensued, the Communists proved that their troops were better disciplined and their supporters more determined than those of their opponents. For the large uncommitted segments of the Chinese population, the CCP seemed to be the better alternative for bringing about the national unity, independence and reform that had for decades been the major demands of the Chinese revolution.

The policies pursued by the CCP in the first few years after the establishment of the Chinese People's Republic in October 1949 largely reflected the circumstances that brought it to power. Socialist goals were held in abeyance (though not concealed), while the Party moved vigorously toward economic reconstruction, political consolidation and social reform. By the end of 1952, agricultural and industrial production had recovered from the disruptions of the 1940s, in many cases exceeding the peak levels of pre-1949 years; the hyperinflation which had been a major reason for popular loss of confidence in the KMT was checked.[2] Politically, under Mao's slogan of a "people's democratic dictatorship," the Communists continued to cooperate with and seek support from as wide a spectrum of the Chinese people as possible, even though they made no secret of their leadership within the "United Front" and relentlessly suppressed all active opposition. Strenuous organizational efforts among workers, peasants, women, and youth brought the overwhelming majority of the population into Party-controlled organizations that propagated and mobilized support for central directives. Administrative authority was extended down to the lowest level of

[1] Mao Tse-tung, *Selected Works* (New York: International Publishers, 1956), vol. IV, p. 242.

[2] W. W. Rostow *et al., The Prospects for Communist China* (New York: Wiley, and the Technology Press, 1954), pp. 237–41, 243–45.

Chinese society and made more prominent by the creation of popular consultative bodies at each level in the hierarchy. The reform aspects of Communist rule were equally evident in a massive campaign for land redistribution and in a variety of measures to improve the status of women and eliminate prostitution, corruption, and crime.

It is difficult to evaluate the effects of these early efforts by the CCP. By and large, the Party was successful in restoring political unity and economic stability to the Chinese mainland and in breaking down the old socioeconomic patterns that had been the source of much popular misery and discontent in modern China. Much of its success was due to the fact that pressures for change had been accumulating for so long and that previous political movements had popularized many of the objectives now pursued by the Communists. But it was the discipline and vigor of the CCP, and its ability to organize support for its programs, that enabled it to translate objectives into reality. The Party's approach in this period drew heavily on its wartime experience. Tasks of reconstruction were cast in terms of a national struggle which demanded extraordinary individual effort and sacrifice; patriotic enthusiasm and organized effort were to compensate for deficiencies in equipment, matériel and manpower. Chinese involvement in the Korean War from late 1950 through 1953, though a hindrance to economic stabilization, was critically important for sustaining the nationalistic fervor and unity that the Party desired.

Reconstruction was not without its difficulties, however. The urgency of the period, combined with the fanaticism and/or inexperience of some cadres, produced strain and uncertainty. Change was sweeping and unpredictable; political judgments came arbitrarily, directly from the new leaders, rather than from legal or institutionalized sources; CCP appeals for support and trust were mixed with suspicion and harassment of those who did not cooperate fully with the new regime. In some cases, production and unity suffered as a result. Behind this situation was the CCP's intent to use reconstruction as a basis for Socialist construction more than as an end in itself. Economic reconstruction was to lead directly to Socialist industrialization; political unification and centralization was to ensure the effectiveness of Party controls throughout society; social reform was to transform the nonproductive and apolitical into active participants in Socialist construction. Thus, even while the CCP was effectively handling the problems of reconstruction by drawing on long-frustrated popular energies, it was preparing for a "transition to socialism" which would create new problems and new frustrations.

Although the CCP announced at the end of 1952 that reconstruction had ended and the First Five-Year Plan (FFYP) would begin in 1953, there was in fact no sharp transition from "reconstruction" to socialist construction. The FFYP itself was not drafted until February, 1955, and not made public until July, 1955, two and a half years after the Plan was said to have begun.[3] The establishment of a new constitution and a permanent state structure, signifying the consolidation of Party controls and confidence in the political reliability of the administrative apparatus, did not occur until September, 1954. On the other hand, some preparations for the transition to socialism clearly antedated 1953. The first attack on private enterprise came in 1952, in a campaign that was ostensibly aimed at corruption and crime among businessmen but which had the effect of drastically curtailing the independence and economic resources of private enterprises. Discussion about the collectivization of agriculture began as early as 1951, although collectivization was to proceed very slowly until late 1955. Evidence of the ideological demands of the transition period appeared in the Party's attempts at "thought reform" of the intellectuals in 1951–1952. In short, Party statements notwithstanding, reconstruction blended into Socialist construction with little change in either the CCP's demand for national struggle or in the sense of urgency and strain that the struggle produced. A period of reflection, and possibly relaxation, came only in 1956–1957 as the Communist leaders began to assess the results of the FFYP and to consider how the second plan would proceed.

The general situation in China at the beginning of 1956 was probably more favorable, from the leadership's point of view, than at any time since 1949. The danger of counterrevolution seemed past and the Party appeared united again after the purge of the "anti-Party bloc" of Kao Kang and Jao Shu-shih in 1954. Socialization of non-agricultural enterprises was virtually complete and, after several years of disappointing experimentation, the collectivization of agriculture was advancing rapidly after a crucial late-1955 decision to push ahead on this front. The FFYP was already showing signs of fulfilling its major objectives in rapid development of heavy industry. Internationally, Chinese prestige was rising as a result of successful reconstruction at home and China's ability to fight the United States to a stalemate in Korea. The Korean Armistice of 1953 and Chou En-lai's "Peaceful Coexistence"

[3] Li Fu-ch'un, "Report on the First Five-Year Plan for Development of the National Economy of the People's Republic of China," in *Communist China 1955–1959: Policy Documents with Analysis* (Cambridge: Harvard University Press, 1962), pp. 43–45.

foreign policy, typified in his moderate diplomacy at the Bandung Conference in 1955, added to the impression that China was entering a period of tranquil domestic development. There were, to be sure, some very real problems of which the Party was fully aware: Agricultural production, which was to bear most of the cost of industrialization, was not keeping pace; the heavy industrial emphasis of the FFYP was leading to shortages of consumer goods and tendencies toward excessive centralization and bureaucratization; the intellectuals, on whom China's future progress depended so heavily, were neither as numerous nor as politically reliable as the CCP would have liked. Nevertheless, these did not appear to be insurmountable problems. In agriculture, for example, the pace of collectivization, was carried out with little opposition, exceeding the most optimistic hopes, and the 1955 harvest was the best in several years. The Chinese leaders entered 1956 prepared to make corrections and adjustments, but confident that none of their major goals or assumptions would be relinquished in the process. However, as the Chinese "thaw" progressed, it was complicated by outside events, confidence was to give way to concern and indecision, and utlimately to a conviction that drastic efforts were necessary to keep China on the preferred path of Socialist construction.

The "Hundred Flowers" are Weeded Out

Although signs of moderation were evident before 1956, particularly in foreign policy, the first important statement on the Chinese leadership's reassessment of Socialist construction was Chou En-lai's speech on the intellectuals before a special conference in January, 1956.[4] Chou promised the intellectuals better working conditions, better treatment by cadres and better utilization of their talents, and also acknowledged that only 40 percent of them actively supported the CCP and its Socialist program. However, the Premier was neither making major concessions to the intellectuals nor admitting serious Party weaknesses. His primary point was that the future of Socialist construction in China required fuller development and better utilization of China's own intellectual resources; neither Soviet assistance nor unskilled enthusiasm could substitute indefinitely for inadequacy in this realm. Chou confidently predicted that the necessary increase in intellectual investment in development could be coupled with ideological "remolding" that would transform the great majority of intellectuals

[4] Chou En-lai, *Report on the Question of the Intellectuals* (Peking: Foreign Languages Press, 1956).

into "progressives" who could actively support Socialist construction. In effect, therefore, his analysis reflected the optimistic premise that the FFYP was a success which could be further enhanced by exploiting an as yet insufficiently utilized resource. Nevertheless, Chou had opened the door for reassessment, and two important developments in subsequent months were to alter considerably the optimism of early 1956.

One of these developments was a growing realization that the rapid completion of agricultural collectivization during 1956 was not going to solve the problem of agricultural production. In fact, the 1956 harvest was a poor one, which necessarily raised serious questions about China's ability to continue its development of heavy industry through reliance on surpluses from agriculture.[5] Consequently, the FFYP came under closer and closer scrutiny as the year progressed. The other development was the emergence of a slight but perceptible uneasiness about the CCP's relations with the population of whom it had demanded, and was continuing to demand, so much effort and obedience. Khrushchev's denunciation of Stalin in February, 1956, undoubtedly contributed to this concern. In an April 5 editorial in *Jen-min jih-pao,* commenting on Khrushchev's exposures, the Chinese leadership observed that "*every* (Communist) leader must be prudent and modest, keep close to the masses, consult them on all matters, investigate and study the actual situation again and again, and constantly engage in criticism and self-criticism." Stalin's mistakes, said the editorial, stemmed precisely from his failure to do these things.[6] The CCP could find ample material for self-criticism in its own earlier practice of "commandism" and in the growing popular restiveness over collectivization and shortages of consumer goods. The intellectuals were the first beneficiaries of the Party's reappraisal of its forced march to Socialist industrialization. By May, the slogan of "let a hundred flowers blossom, a hundred schools of thought contend," reflected a significant change in the position taken in Chou En-lai's earlier statements, by encouraging greater freedom in literature, art and academic study, with a hint that freer discussion in political matters might also be tolerated.[7]

The Eighth Congress (PC VIII) of the CCP, held in September, 1956, brought into the open the Party's new awareness of the funda-

[5] See the discussion in Li Choh-Ming, *Economic Development of Communist China* (Berkeley: University of California Press, 1959), pp. 219–220.

[6] *The Historical Experience of the Dictatorship of the Proletariat* (Peking: Foreign Languages Press, 1959). pp. 5–6 (emphasis added).

[7] See Lu Ting-yi, "*Let Flowers of Many Kinds Blossom, Diverse Schools of Thought Contend!*" (Peking: Foreign Languages Press, 1957).

mental problems and choices that it faced.[8] Since the Congress considered these questions with surprising frankness, and thereby delineated the alternative courses of action that were to be debated during the next year and a half, it will be useful here to summarize the Party's predicament. Throughout the greater part of its history, the CCP had relied on relatively close and personal contacts with the people to mobilize them for social action. This pattern, which reflected the decentralized prosecution of revolutionary war from scattered rural bases, produced and sanctified the "mass line" as the most characteristic feature of CCP ideology and behavior. The mass line, with its emphasis on mass movements and direct Party exhortation and leadership to elicit the greatest possible popular efforts, had been applied during the reconstruction period and had carried over into the start of Socialist construction. However, the initiation of the FFYP brought pressures for bureaucratization, centralization, urbanization and specialization that were in some ways antithetical to the mass-line style; conversely, the continuing use of the mass line was in some ways antithetical to the stability that seemed most appropriate for a period of sustained economic development. The crux of the problem was that the Chinese leaders had adopted a Soviet pattern of development without fully understanding how it would work in the Chinese context. By the time of PC VIII, they had recognized that it was not working to their fullest satisfaction.

It is imperative to remember that the Chinese leadership was not willing in 1956 to downgrade its goal of rapid industrialization. In spite of certain defects, the FFYP was producing notable advances in transforming China into a world power. What the Party sought was adjustments in its approach to this task. At the risk of oversimplification, the difficulties of choosing the proper adjustments may be demonstrated by dividing the general proposals voiced at PC VIII into economic and political categories. The leadership saw the main economic problem as excessive centralization and bureaucratization, coupled with weaknesses in the nonindustrial sectors. The heavy industrial focus that had encouraged these defects was defended, but there were repeated references to waste and bottlenecks in the FFYP, to the desirability of decentralization and more flexible planning, and to the need for achieving "over-all balance" by greater attention to agriculture, handicrafts, local industry and educational and cultural advances. Nevertheless, although the proposals for the Second Five-Year Plan (1958–1962) that were presented

[8] For documentation on PC VIII, *see Eighth National Congress of the Communist Party of China,* 3 vols. (Peking: Foreign Languages Press, 1956).

to the Congress specified some increase in agricultural investment, they maintained the primacy of industrial development, calling for a faster rate of increase in capital goods industry than in consumer goods industry and for a greater share of national income to be devoted to accumulation (as opposed to consumption) than in the FFYP. "Balance" was to be achieved by attacks on waste and inefficiency, by increasing labor productivity in the weak sectors of the economy and by administrative decentralization. Diligence, economy, and more effective leadership, rather than significant alterations in investment priorities, were the corrective devices favored. Decentralization and greater reliance on human efforts, both of which implied greater responsibility on the part of Party leadership at the local level, were later to be key elements in the "Great Leap Foward." Thus, the Congress pointed toward some of the practices of the "Great Leap," even though it advanced them much less directly and extravagantly than in the later period.

On the political side, PC VIII directed its most significant criticism toward manifestations of excessive Party control and rigidity. No doubt with Stalin's example in mind, CCP leaders announced that, while mass movements and sweeping decrees had been necessary during the establishment and construction of the new regime, the period of revolutionary "storm and stress" had given way to a new situation calling for more moderate and regularized political action. Specifically, speakers at the Congress admitted miscarriages of justice in the early campaigns, complained about "formalism" and lack of democracy in the people's congress, called for codification and closer observance of the laws, and repeated the newly announced policy of greater toleration of non-Communist personnel and opinions. As in the economic sphere, the CCP was relatively objective in noting where the problems lay. What it did not seem to recognize, however, was that there was a possible contradiction between the respective solutions that it advocated for its economic and political difficulties. How was the Chinese leadership to proceed with the institutionalization and stabilization of a political system in which popular demands would be given freer expression and in which Party control would be less arbitrary when it was, for economic reasons, simultaneously encouraging greater popular efforts and austerity, involving more tinkering with the location of decision-making power and a greater concentration of responsibility in local Party committees? The CCP resolved this dilemma in the "Great Leap," but only after more than a year of debate and an abortive experiment with political liberalization in the "Hundred Flowers" campaign of 1957.

As the preceding discussion has indicated, the "Hundred Flowers" policy was an understandable product of the Chinese political and economic scene and was not dependent for its basic justification on developments elsewhere in the Socialist camp. The *timing* of the dramatic episode in the spring of 1957 must, however, be related to the profoundly disturbing events that transpired in Europe in October–November, 1956. This is not to say that fear of outbursts comparable to those in Poland and Hungary forced the CCP to make political concessions, but rather that these events drove the Chinese leaders to a decision on whether or not their views on "liberalization" were correct.[9] There was a brief period during the winter of 1956–1957 when the Party, dismayed by the rise of "revisionism" and "counterrevolution" in Europe, backed off from its plans to encourage freer discussion of its failings. But on February 27, 1957, Mao delivered his famous speech on "contradictions" to the Supreme State Conference, signalling his intention to proceed with the policy that had been taking shape during the previous year. Fundamental to Mao's decision was his conviction that "contradictions" in China were "nonantagonistic" (existing among people who basically supported socialism) and hence were amenable to solution by open discussion; the idea that these contradictions might turn out to be "antagonistic," as in Hungary, was rejected.

The rectification campaign itself, designed to execute the "Hundred Flowers" policy, began at the end of April. It was technically a drive to correct "bureaucratism, subjectivism and sectarianism" at the upper levels of Party and government; but since the basic aim was reconciliation of conflicts between the regime and the people, the scope of the movement was quite broad. In fact, the CCP explicitly *encouraged* popular criticism of a general nature and even organized discussion meetings for this purpose. For approximately six weeks, the intellectuals, and to a lesser extent other strata of Chinese society, openly expressed their discontent with various aspects of Communist rule.[10] By early June, however, the movement had apparently gotten out of hand. Not only was some criticism far too pointed from the CCP's point of view, but a number of unruly demonstrations had broken out and, perhaps most important of all, there were signs of a developing anti-Party movement among the students. Debate was abruptly shut off and

[9] For a succinct discussion of various theories about the motivation of the "Hundred Flowers" campaign, see Edward Friedman, "The Revolution in Hungary and the Hundred Flowers Period in China," *The Journal of Asian Studies,* vol. 25, no. 1, Nov., 1965, pp. 119–122.

[10] See Roderick MacFarquhar, *The Hundred Flowers Campaign and the Chinese Intellectuals* (New York: Praeger, 1960) for documentation and discussion of the campaign.

the most severe critics were denounced as "rightists" and compelled to acknowledge their errors. An "antirightist" campaign followed during the summer of 1957, eradicating all signs of the liberalization except the "Hundred Flowers" slogan itself which was retained as hollow testimony to the hopes that had fostered the episode.

The "Hundred Flowers" was one of the most significant periods in the history of the CCP, for it decisively demonstrated the incompatibility between "proletarian dictatorship" and some of the Party's more democratic and populistic ideals. In theory, according even to the tougher revised version of Mao's speech on contradictions that was released in June, 1957, critical discussion was beneficial and necessary so long as it supported socialism and Communist leadership; without it, nonantagonistic contradictions among the people could not be resolved. While much of what was said in the spring of 1957 challenged neither socialism nor Party leadership as such, focusing instead on specific mistakes and Party monopolization of positions, it was still found to be unacceptable. Mao's statements and the implications of mass-line theory notwithstanding, there was henceforth to be no encouragement of criticism of the Party except as a device to expose and "correct" the critics.

The "Hundred Flowers" was equally important in terms of the debate over what general policy should be followed in future Socialist construction. As noted, PC VIII had posed two possible courses of action that were in part contradictory. One of these had argued for political stabilization and institutionalization and had provided much of the rationale for a relaxation of Party controls, but in the aftermath of the "Hundred Flowers" it ceased to be a meaningful alternative. References to the need for political regularity, codification of laws, greater tolerance of non-Party personnel and so forth, faded away. They were replaced by the assertion that reconstruction of the system was basically completed and that what remained (and the experiences of the spring "flowering" was offered as proof) was the ideological reconstruction of the Chinese citizen. Accordingly, starting in the late summer of 1957, the CCP revived the rectification campaign but now transformed it into a nationwide "Socialist education" movement that had as its goal the indoctrination of all Chinese with "correct" Socialist ideology. This movement lasted until the summer of 1958 and was to provide the ideological base for communication of the "Great Leap" philosophy to the population at large. It also brought the CCP's political outlook into closer harmony with some of the economic remedies proposed at PC VIII, clearing the way for the emergence of the "Great Leap" in the winter of 1957–1958.

While the debate over political liberalization resolved itself into a new drive for political and ideological uniformity, the debate over the economy had continued. PC VIII had soberly spotted the main economic deficiencies of the FFYP, but had stopped short of advocating a period of economic stabilization, or even retrenchment, which some high-ranking officials apparently believed was necessary. The undesirable consequences of the rapid pace of development in 1955–1956 were sufficiently clear to bring a modest cutback in goals and investment in 1957. There was uncertainty, too, about the agricultural cooperatives which had been so hastily established in 1955–1956. The Party expressed great concern during 1957 about consolidating the cooperatives, which in some cases were starting to disintegrate, and as late as September, 1957, the official line was to retain them in their existing form or even reduce them in size. However, for several reasons, a cautious and conservative approach to economic development failed to materialize. For one thing, the results of the "Hundred Flowers" experiment were inimical to the very idea of relaxation. Pleas of technicians and professionals for greater independence from Party controls had been interpreted as political opposition and evidence of political unreliability; rightly or wrongly the CCP leadership associated arguments for "rational" economic adjustments with the sort of "rightist" or "revisionist" thinking that had blossomed among the intellectuals and it became much more suspicious of proposals for economic moderation.

Moreover, we must recall that the CCP's deliberations at PC VIII had shown a preference for a decentralized economic system relying on local Party leadership and human effort as opposed to the more centralized and bureaucratized Soviet model used in the FFYP. Political liberalization and a willingness to consider other forms of economic adjustment temporarily obscured this preference, but with the return of Party-defined orthodoxy in the summer of 1957 it emerged as the dominant CCP response to the economic debate of 1956–1957. There was nothing inherently radical in this preferred alternative, at least in the relatively moderate context in which it was initially suggested, as it was in keeping with the CCP's traditional political style and was manifestly an attempt to capitalize on China's vast pool of unskilled manpower. What made it so radical as the cornerstone of the "Great Leap" was the apparent fanaticism with which it was pursued. Fanaticism is never easy to explain, but it is possible to point out some of the influences that contributed to the Chinese leaders' new surge of aggressive optimism in late 1957.

The greatest influence on the Chinese leaders' change of mood was probably the new strength and apparent unity of the Socialist camp. In retrospect, it is evident that the progress of events in 1957 did little to avert the approaching schism between the two great Communist powers. Nevertheless, there was every reason for the Chinese to believe, in 1957, that their position had improved substantially as a result of three developments. First, Khrushchev had succeeded in June in consolidating his position within the CPSU, thereby bringing firm leadership to the Soviet Union for the first time since Stalin's death; the advantages of decisive leadership in Moscow outweighed the political implications of Khrushchev's victory, implications which were by no means obvious in 1957. Second, the Moscow Conference in November, 1957, was seen as evidence of a restoration of some degree of Socialist solidarity and of the failure of "counterrevolution" in Eastern Europe. Mao Tse-tung was dissatisfied with many points in the Moscow Declaration, particularly those pertaining to the role of war in Communist revolutions and international politics, but he had secured in the Declaration the statement that "revisionism" (or "right-wing opportunism") was the "main danger at present," a statement that reflected on the one hand, Chinese hostility toward Yugoslavia, and, on the other, political trends within China itself. Finally, Soviet space achievements in October and November were taken as confirmation of the growing technological power of the Soviet Union. The Chinese may have read more into the first sputniks than did the Russians, but 1957 was a year in which the Russians were extremely vocal in their claims about outstripping the United States in the future. The then current recession in the United States and Western Europe, of which the Chinese were well aware, added to the conviction that the Socialist systems were demonstrating their superiority over capitalism and that the tide of the international power struggle was running in their direction—a situation neatly summarized in Mao's phrase, "the East wind prevails over the West wind." In sum, there was an atmosphere of contagious optimism in the Socialist camp in 1957 and the Chinese, having recently defeated their domestic critics and prepared the way for a new upsurge, were intoxicated by it.[11]

To summarize to this point: The Chinese Communists recognized early in 1956 that the hectic pace of reconstruction, early industrialization, and collectivization had created both political and economic tensions. They began to correct these tensions from a position of confidence but were thrown into confusion and uncertainty by upheavals in

[11] For summary and analysis of all of these aspects of the "favorable" Chinese situation at the end of 1957, see Chou En-lai's report on the international situation to the National People's Congress in February, 1958; text in *Communist China 1955–1959, op. cit.*, pp. 401–410.

the Communist world and even more disturbing trends at home. At PC VIII, the Party tentatively decided on a policy of modest political liberalization, coupled with a relatively open debate on economic problems. However, the CPC's preferred response to economic difficulties was to bring backward sectors of the economy up to standard by administrative changes and intensified effort rather than to modify the goal of rapid industrialization. Political liberalization prolonged the debate and uncertainty but ended in the summer of 1957 with a decisive reaction that cleared the way for a new national effort at industrialization along the lines tentatively suggested at PC VIII. The "antirightist" struggle in China and favorable international developments imparted to the new policy a mood of aggressive optimism that made the ensuing "Great Leap" a very distinctive and even revolutionary phenomenon. The "Great Leap" as such emerged slowly, however. The basic decisions on decentralization and nationwide rectification were made at a CCP Central Committee meeting in September, 1957, and implemented during the following months. Nevertheless, resistance within the Party persisted for some time and it was not until the summer of 1958 that the full implications of the new policy became evident.

From "Leap" to Leap

In his report to the Second Session of PC VIII in May, 1958, Liu Shao-ch'i gave the first definitive description of the "Great Leap."[12] Liu emphasized four themes, which taken together constitute a summary exposition of the CCP stance during the "Great Leap." First, he gave full expression to the grandiose optimism that had developed within the Chinese leadership since the fall of 1957. He acknowledged that "the sky was overcast" in 1956, but insisted that both China and the Socialist camp as a whole could now look forward to great prospects and successes. The rectification campaign, now drawing to a close, had thoroughly united the Chinese people on the basis of correct Socialist ideology, said Liu, and had broken the barriers between cadres and masses that had caused so much tension in the preceding years. It is "always the newcomers who outstrip the old," he asserted, and China, specifically, would overtake and surpass Great Britain in fifteen years.

Another powerful theme in Liu's report was the apotheosis of the mass line, the claim that human effort can accomplish seemingly im-

[12] Liu Shao-ch'i, "Report on the Work of the Central Committee . . . ," in *Second Session of the Eighth National Congress of the Communist Party of China* (Peking: Foreign Languages Press, 1958).

possible tasks: "It is man that counts; the subjective initiative of the masses is a mighty driving force." This rendition of the mass line was close to a direct reversal of the Marxist dogma that productive relations determine political consciousness; Liu argued to the contrary that ideological and political work, said to be the "soul and guide" of all work, could instill Socialist consciousness which would in turn bring about great changes in production. A corollary to this theme was the glorification of manual labor, the insistence that cadres and intellectuals be "sent down" (*hsia fang*) to engage in productive labor at lower levels and thereby build their working-class character. Implicit in the practice of *hsia fang* and the mass line generally was the idea that specialized skills and professional knowledge are secondary in importance to the "correct" political point of view and consciousness.

A third theme in the "Great Leap" philosophy was the assertion that great advances could take place simultaneously on all fronts—in all sectors of the economy as well as in political, ideological and cultural matters. Liu cited output statistics for the first four months of 1958 to indicate that such "leaps" had already begun. The slogan of "exerting utmost efforts to achieve greater, faster, better, and more economical results" was indicative of the mood, and also of the extent to which the hopes for simultaneous advance relied on the mass-line assumption that China could do anything that was humanly possible, regardless of material weaknesses and the restraints of economic laws. To those who questioned the substance of this belief, Liu simply said that fears of "imbalance" were groundless or inconsequential. On the key point of how agriculture was to keep pace, he stated that local effort and initiative would do the job without any diversion of state investment from industry.

The last theme cast a somewhat different light on the "Great Leap," being, as it was, an admission of the serious opposition encountered by the new policy. Liu traced resistance by "some comrades" back to 1955–1956, when they had opposed what was termed the "reckless advance" of those years. And, although he claimed that the September, 1957, meeting of the Central Committee had affirmed the "Great Leap" program, he made many references to "rightists" who had, subsequently been expelled from the Party and to the existence of continuing doubts about China's ability to achieve "greater, faster, better, and more economical results." Clearly, the "Great Leap" did not have total support even within the CCP, and this explains both its prolonged emergence and some of the eventual difficulties in its implementation.

The above constitutes not only an overview of the "Great Leap" period itself, but also a rough description of the dominant political trend in China down to the immediate past. That is, even when the Chinese leaders backed off from the line established in 1957–1958, they did so reluctantly, without conceding any permanent shift in their basic outlook. Nevertheless, the changes that took place after 1958 are of considerable importance and fall readily into three stages: The "Great Leap" of 1958–1960; the retrenchment of 1961–1962; and the political consolidation and renewed efforts of 1963–1965.

The major changes that occurred during 1958–1960 derived directly from the themes expressed in Liu's report. A massive labor mobilization was one of the most important developments. Beginning in the winter of 1957–1958, rural cadres organized peasants into large groups, sometimes exceeding the manpower of individual cooperatives, for work on flood control and water conservation projects. In the spring, the campaign moved into the cities, encouraging large numbers of people to join the rural labor force and organizing nonworking people, such as housewives, for productive activity in "street factories," service and welfare functions, and handicraft shops. Similar practices continued throughout the "Great Leap" in a frantic effort to extract the maximum amount of productive effort from the Chinese population. Hours were long, work groups were large and special care was devoted to bringing previously uninvolved people into the labor force. Especially in the countryside, cadres promoted labor intensive projects (deep plowing, close planting and the primitive "backyard steel furnaces" that flourished briefly in 1958 are examples) that were designed to fulfill Liu's claim that rural production could be significantly raised without major infusions of capital.

Along with labor mobilization came a series of mass movements focused on ideological indoctrination and stimulation of productive effort. The main purpose of these movements was to provide ideological commitment, excitement, exhortation and group competition which, in the absence of immediate material gains, had to serve as the incentive for sustained sacrifice and hard work. Lectures, rallies, discussions, political study, criticism and self-criticism, and emulation campaigns—in short, the major techniques of the mass movement—became nearly universal and perpetual features of Chinese life. Virtually no task or occupation was too complex or sophisticated for the application of these techniques. Ideologically inspired enthusiasm and faith was to compensate for and overcome the absence of sufficient material and intellectual resources.

Institutional and administrative changes, of which the formation of the people's communes is the best example, were equally significant aspects of the "Great Leap." The decentralization decrees of late 1957 transferred large numbers of enterprises from central control to the control of local authorities in hopes of encouraging greater initiative and flexibility in enterprise operation without giving up over-all central leadership. As the "Great Leap" developed, there was also an amalgamation of basic-level units into larger units, with the result that the communes and other local governments became the key operational locus of the period. The amalgamation of basic-level administrative units was actually a long-term trend in Communist China. The number of *hsiang* (a township or cluster of villages), the lowest level of administration in the countryside, had been reduced from about 220,000 in 1951 to about 80,000 in early 1958, with similar reductions in the number of urban administrative districts. This increase in size of basic level units was supposed to improve efficiency, reduce the number of administrative personnel and maintain governmental direction over production units which were expanding in size. With the labor mobilization of early 1958, many cooperatives began to merge into even larger production units and a further reduction in the number of *hsiang* ensued. The process reached its climax in the late summer of 1958 with the formation of the people's communes, which were to combine in a single unit both the lowest level of governmental administration (that is, the commune replaced the *hsiang*) and the management of rural production. By the start of 1959, virtually the entire rural population had been organized into about 24,000 communes, indicating a truly significant administrative shift from early 1951. A campaign to establish urban communes was also beginning to unfold.

The implications of this change were varied and profound. From a long-range point of view, the Chinese leadership apparently regarded the communes as a shortcut to communism by virtue of the enforced collective living and production they entailed. More immediately, the communes were to serve as the primary vehicle for the "simultaneous advance on all fronts" pledged by the "Great Leap" policy. As units which were large enough to take in a variety of agricultural, industrial, cultural and social activities, and yet small enough to encourage flexible operation, they were to break down old economic and social barriers and establish new self-sufficient centers that would promote locally planned growth throughout China; they were, in brief, to be the institutional agents of forced economic and political modernization.[13] By the same token, however, they also involved great disruptions of

[13] For a penetrating analysis of some of the economic implications of commune formation, as well as many of the other points discussed in this section, see G. William Skinner, "Marketing and Social Structure in Rural China," *The Journal of Asian Studies,* vol. 24, no. 3, May ,1965, pp. 365–399.

existing institutional patterns and large-scale transfers of administrative personnel. Among other things, institutional disruption was largely responsible for a rapid decline in the importance of basic-level elections and people's congresses, in spite of the fact that much concern about the vitality of both had been expressed in 1956–1957.

A final important change of the period was a generally increased emphasis on the role of Party leadership and an increased concentration of power in the local Party committees. Resting as it did on ideological incentive and political conformity, the "Great Leap" demanded close controls and supervision by the CCP; the "Hundred Flowers" experiment had, in any case, noticeably increased Party suspicion of and toughness toward non-Party personnel, particularly the intellectuals. Furthermore, decentralization naturally favored local Party organizations because they held an even greater monopoly of positions and skills at the local level than at the national level. The Chinese leaders made no attempt to conceal this development but rather broadcast it under the slogan "politics takes command," a phrase which simply meant that political personnel and criteria (i.e., Party members and objectives) were to determine courses of action in all areas of life. CCP directives made it clear that Party members were to hold all key positions and that Party committees were to be consulted about decisions at all levels of organization.

It is common to speak of the "Great Leap" as a failure, and so it was in terms of its high hopes, but it nonetheless scored some positive achievements. There was a bumper crop in 1958, and the massive labor efforts of these years produced significant advances in rural construction and, at least at first, in industrial output, although precisely how much is uncertain because of unreliable statistical reporting from 1958 on. The encouragement of rural industry also imparted a certain amount of technical knowledge and skills to the countryside, even though it was ultimately unsuccessful in terms of output goals. On the other hand, the "Great Leap" policy did end in a severe economic crisis with accompanying popular discontent—and must be judged accordingly. The CCP initially claimed that inclement weather was responsible for the "three bad years" of 1959–1961, but ultimately it conceded that the policy had contributed to the disaster. Bad weather did have an adverse effect on the 1959 harvest, which was far below that of 1958, but the all-around deterioration that followed reflected fundamental Party errors as well.[14] The decline in agricultural produc-

[14] See Alexander Eckstein, "On the Economic Crisis in Communist China," *Foreign Affairs,* vol. 42, no. 4, July, 1964, pp. 655–668, for a summary of problems in this period.

tion continued in 1960, leading to shortages in investment funds and raw materials that caused a slowdown in industry. By 1961, the Chinese economy was stagnating, demonstrating that human effort alone was not sufficient to overcome China's economic situation. Many other related difficulties also began to appear. Poor harvests led to food shortages which lowered both physical and mental work capacity, thereby reinforcing downward production trends. Transfer of basic-level personnel brought inexperienced men to cadre status and disrupted the cohesion and efficiency of work groups. Distrust or disregard of specialists resulted in frequent errors in attempted technological innovations. Ideological indoctrination could awaken progressively less enthusiasm and cut further into the already scant leisure time of the labor force. There were still other difficulties which were consequent to the political mood of the times; for example, planning and accurate statistics were virtually forgotten, although the leadership did not deliberately encourage this, and many communes were unwisely formed by overenthusiastic or ambitious cadres in spite of cautioning statements from the central authorities. The deepening rift with the Soviet Union and the departure of Soviet technicians in 1960 also added to the bleakness of the situation. By the winter of 1960–1961, the CCP faced not only an economic crisis, but also a serious loss of popular confidence, a deterioration of political authority at the basic level and a renewal of opposition within the Party to the "Great Leap." The result was the retrenchment of 1961–1962.

The leadership actually began to backtrack from some of the extreme features of the "Great Leap" soon after the policy was inaugurated. Some of the more communistic aspects of commune life and the worst abuses of working conditions were checked by the Central Committee as early as December, 1958. The same meeting called for a period of "consolidation" of the rural communes, observed that there should be no rush to set up urban communes (in fact, they were never widely established although there was much experimentation with them) and generally argued the need for a good measure of caution and realism in pursuing the "Great Leap." The basic policy remained, however, and was reaffirmed in the face of "rightists" attacks in another Central Committee meeting in August, 1959. The first authoritative evidence of the abandonment of the "Great Leap" in fact (though not in name) came from the Ninth Plenum of the CCP Central Committee in January, 1961.[15] The Central Committee (CC) admitted the

[15] For the text of the Ninth Plenum's communique, see *Peking Review,* vol. IV, no. 4, Jan. 27, 1961, pp. 5–7.

seriousness of the economic situation and emphasized the importance of "taking agriculture as the foundation," a slogan which meant that strengthening agricultural production was to receive top priority while industrial investment would be reduced. Concern for quality, variety and "consolidation" replaced the earlier emphasis on rapid growth in output. The Party also acknowledged the necessity of increasing the supply of consumer goods and improving market conditions. In the political realm, the Ninth Plenum tacitly admitted that significant numbers of both Party and non-Party people were dissatisfied, lacking in ideological consciousness, or were even in some way obstructing Party policies. A Party rectification campaign to improve work and weed out "bad elements" had already started and was to continue during 1961.

The CCP remained on the defensive throughout 1961 and most of 1962, making a series of concessions and admissions that stripped the "Great Leap" policy of much of its meaning. A much more sober view of the peasants' capacity for political and economic change emerged, as the Party reminded itself of the continuing weight of "thousands of years of feudalism" on popular attitudes; Socialist consciousness could not, after all, be instilled overnight, but would require years of political education and some substantial gains in living standards, as well. Accordingly, the indoctrination campaigns slacked off, with warnings to cadres not to let political activities interfere with working hours or reasonable amounts of rest and leisure for the workers. The "red and expert" slogan, which had reflected the Party's mistrust of specialists and its efforts to build a group of ideologically reliable intellectuals, also came in for revision. "Experts" were told that they ought to engage in political study, but that they should not sacrifice their technical training for this purpose and that their expertise was socially useful even if they were not "red."

There were other changes of more economic substance. In addition to the new concentration on agricultural development, there was a partial return to more centralized planning in recognition of the lack of coordination that had developed under the "Great Leap" policy (as critics had predicted in 1957–1958). The greatest changes took place in the rural communes, however. Commune members received small private plots which they were free to use as they wished; and a system of limited free markets was allowed for the exchange of produce raised on these plots. Moreover, fundamental alterations in commune structure were made. The communes had settled, after the consolidation of the winter of 1958–1959, into a relatively uniform pattern of "three level management." Each commune was divided into production brigades, which were equivalent to the former cooperatives and were usually based on the village, and each brigade was divided into production teams of 20–40 households each. Initially, the commune level itself was the critical unit with control of production and distribution within the commune. By 1961, the brigade had assumed these functions, with the commune level relegated to over-all administration and management of the larger commune enterprises. During 1961–1962, control shifted downward again to the production team, which became virtually independent with respect to agricultural production and distribution. At the same time, many communes were subdivided so that the total number increased from 24,000 to about 75,000. Thus, by the end of 1962, the commune structure remained but had become quite similar to the rural administrative structure that existed in 1957–1958 at the start of the "Great Leap"; production management, moreover, had returned to a relatively small rural unit (the production team normally consists of a small village or a section of a village), a situation approximating that existing in the early 1950s during the early stages of cooperativization. These structural changes brought with them a return of many rural cadres to the units in which they had worked before commune formation; presumably, these cadres included men who commanded the loyalties of villagers, possibly on kinship grounds.[16]

Retrenchment was relatively successful in initiating economic recovery and averting the threatened collapse of Party authority at the basic level. It was a very painful process, however, for the Chinese leaders who had to sacrifice so much of their program. Whatever the rate of recovery might be, it was clear to all that the leadership had erred, that the Party's claim to unfailingly superior judgment and knowledge had been opened to question. The Party, too, now had reason to doubt the power of mass action and its own ability to transform China into a Socialist society in a short period of time. The question that arose, therefore, was whether retrenchment was to be a tactical maneuver of short duration or whether it was to be the beginning of a fundamental change in the character of Chinese communism. The answer, soon forthcoming, was that it was a tactical maneuver to be followed by a resumption of revolutionary advance, albeit with some important qualifications.

In September 1962, the Tenth Plenum of the CC gave the first indication that retrenchment had ended and a new offensive was be-

[16] See John Wilson Lewis, "The Leadership Doctrine of the Chinese Communist Party: The Lesson of the People's Commune," *Asian Survey,* vol. 3, no. 10, Oct. 1963, pp. 457–464.

ginning.[17] The CC ignored many of the concessions made to redress the errors of the "Great Leap" and focused instead on the task of overcoming all obstacles to the building of a collective economy and Socialist society; it forecast, in no uncertain terms, the renewal of class struggle and ideological indoctrination. Two years later, in December, 1964, Chou En-lai confirmed that this had indeed been the sense of the Tenth Plenum when he told the National People's Congress that the Plenum had launched a counterattack in order to check the "evil winds and noxious influences" that were then advocating further extensions of private plots, free markets and independent enterprises and a general policy of "liberalization."[18] The mass movements of 1963–1965 bore out the assertion that the Tenth Plenum consciously rejected a policy of continued retrenchment or further liberalization. "Socialist education" and the "cultivation of revolutionary successors" were massive campaigns introduced to indoctrinate the population in the revolutionary traditions of the CCP, the Chinese brand of Socialist orthodoxy and the necessity of unrelenting class struggle at home and abroad. Two other major movements, "Learn from Lei Feng" and "Learn from the People's Liberation Army," put forward, as models for popular emulation, the activist, disciplined, self-sacrificing and politically conscious unit or individual that would demonstrate the superiority of human over material factors. The CCP also reaffirmed its faith in the mass line in countless statements and acted on it most dramatically by abolishing rank insignia and differential titles of address in the army in 1965. A general tone of antiprofessionalism prevailed, not only in the military but in other realms as well. The practice of *hsia fang* compelled intellectuals and bureaucrats to engage in periods of manual labor, while large numbers of students were sent on graduation to long-term or permanent assignments at physical labor in the countryside.

Mindful of the excesses and resentment that the above practices produced during the "Great Leap," the CCP concurrently embarked on a program of political consolidation. Purges of deviants from the Party's line in its debate with the CPSU revealed a determination to maintain ideological conformity. The "Socialist education" campaign in the countryside became a vehicle for attacking "bad" cadres and "capitalist" influences that had appeared during retrenchment; peasants' associations, which had been the primary rural organizations during

[17] For the text of the Tenth Plenum's communique, see *Peking Review,* vol. V, no. 39, Sept. 28, 1962.

[18] "Premier Chou En-lai Reports on the Work of the Government," *Peking Review,* vol. VIII, no. 1, Jan. 1, 1965, pp. 12–13.

civil war and land reform, were revived to bolster these attacks. The CCP also began early in 1964 to establish "political departments," modelled on the political departments in the army, in various state agencies. These departments were responsible for promoting and supervising political work within their units, and were gradually extended into more and more ministries and governmental units. Insistence on the "primacy of politics" in all types of work was perhaps the chief characteristic of the CCP's attempt to ensure tight Party control over resumed advance.

In spite of many similarities, however, the 1963–1965 line differed significantly from that of 1958–1960. Most importantly, the Chinese leadership retained, though reluctantly, many of the economic adjustments of the retrenchment period. Private plots, rural markets and production team independence remained, in spite of continued Party insistence that the communes and a thoroughly collectivized economy were the path of the future. Remaining, too, was the slogan of "agriculture as the foundation" in continuing recognition of the realities of Chinese developmental problems. In further contrast to the "Great Leap," the Party began to focus its plans for most rapid development on key areas possessing generally favorable resources rather than calling for simultaneous advances on all fronts. The revival of the mass line was also subject to qualifications, as the CCP was clearly more respectful of the expertise of technicians and more concerned about providing adequate rest and leisure for workers than it had been in 1958–1960. A good illustration of the injection of caution into the mass-line style of thought appeared in Chou's December, 1964, report to the National People's Congress.

> We must promote both the revolutionary spirit of daring to think, daring to speak and daring to act *and a scientific and realistic approach.* On the one hand, there must be great enthusiasm in work and, on the other, *labour must be alternated with rest.* Innovations must be *put on trial* before they are *gradually* introduced.[19]

In sum, the consolidation and renewed efforts of 1963–1965 were close to the "Great Leap" in language, and to some extent in practice, but a note of patience, caution and calculation had replaced the unrestrained enthusiasm of the earlier period.

Prognosis

During 1965, the CPC began to talk about a new "upsurge" that would lead into the Third Five Year-Plan for 1966–1970. Details on the next Plan had not been announced by the end of 1965, but general

[19] *Ibid.,* p. 11 (emphasis added).

statements indicated that it would follow the pattern that emerged in 1963–1965. Thus, in its editorial of October 1, 1965, celebrating the sixteenth anniversary of the founding of the People's Republic, *Jen-min jih-pao* claimed that the Socialist revolution was developing in greater depth and that the "all-around upsurge" in agriculture and industry was more substantial than ever before.[20] *Jen-min jih-pao* emphasized that China's "new stage of advance" in the Third Five-Year plan would rely on its "two biggest assets"—the thought of Mao Tse-tung and the strength of China's 650 million people. Universal Socialist education (with "no mood of relaxation whatsoever"), the primacy of politics, struggle with enemies at home and abroad, the further revolutionization of all organizations and undertakings, hard work, diligence and thrift were the dominant themes in the editorial. However, there were also significant cautionary reminders that Socialist construction would be a long-term task and that "while paying attention to what is necessary, it is even more important . . . to pay attention to what is possible, thus ensuring that the high tide of production and construction advances in a steady and healthy way."

There are many reasons for believing that the present stance of Chinese communism will endure for some time to come. For one thing, the cautious "upsurge" that emerged from the difficulties of 1959–1961 has proven to be moderately successful. Although the Communist regime has not released a reliable set of statistics since the start of the "Great Leap," most estimates agree that recovery to 1957 levels was generally achieved in 1963–1964 and that 1965 output was approaching or reaching new peaks in most major agricultural and industrial items.[21] Although the growth rate is undeniably low, the current realistic approach of the CCP will probably find it acceptable, and certainly preferable to the risk of another economic crisis. Moreover, the present policy is generally in tune with the established, and now perhaps fixed, style of the aging leadership. The commitment of Mao and his colleagues to the primacy of politics and the decisive importance of the human factor, and to long-range faith in the Socialist future of the Chinese Revolution, is probably unshakeable. We must remember, too, that Mao's immediate successors will not be radically different in experience or outlook; a new "post-revolutionary" generation will not approach the top for another decade or two. Finally, the international situation will probably continue to encourage the political mood that now prevails in China. The rift with the Soviet Union has been a critically

[20] For the text of the editorial, see *Peking Review,* vol. VIII, no. 40, Oct. 1, 1956, pp. 8–11.

[21] For some recent estimates of Chinese production levels, see *Current Scene,* vol. 3, no. 17, April 15, 1965, and vol. 3, no. 32, Dec. 1, 1965.

important factor in maintaining the CCP's suspicion of domestic heterodoxy and its determination to resist any political or economic concessions that might smack of "revisionism." The withdrawal of Soviet economic assistance, coupled with the threat of an expanded war in Asia, enforces economic caution, while China's joint confrontation with the Soviet Union and the United States provides opposition against whom the revolutionary struggle so constantly stressed by the CCP may be waged. Thus, there are several factors in addition to the will and control of the Chinese leadership that favor the continuance of the present stance.

However, the CCP's attempt to attain economic development via revolutionary struggle and sacrifice will produce serious tension in Chinese society. There is, first of all, no assurance that China can maintain even the slow rate of growth that has now been reestablished. With a steadily growing population and a sluggish agricultural foundation, a series of bad harvests might again hurl the regime into a crisis that would force wide-ranging political and economic changes. It seems almost certain that China cannot develop exclusively by its own efforts, in spite of all of its talk about "self-reliance," and it has already turned to non-Communist countries for imports of grain and industrial equipment. China need not sacrifice its Socialist system for such trade, but its ideological militancy may become embarrassing if its dependence on ideologically despised sources of supply increases. The preservation of the mass line is another source of tension. As China develops, demands for regularization of life and tendencies toward bureaucratization and specialization will become more persistent, as they did in 1956–1957. The point at which these pressures will become serious cannot be predicted, but they will no doubt make it increasingly difficult for the CCP to persist in its mass line style of work. Intellectuals and students, especially, will become more critical of the old revolutionary mythology and more resentful of limitations on the use of their abilities. Ultimately, of course, the CCP must also face up to the succession problem—not simply the question of who will succeed Mao but the question of whether or not the truly new generation of leaders that must arise will throw over the old tradition and establish a new style more appropriate to the times.

Postscript

Since the foregoing analysis was undertaken, a massive campaign known as the "Great Proletarian Cultural Revolution" has engulfed China. The ideological content of this campaign is similar to that of the major movements of 1963–1965; it is ostensibly aimed at eliminating all traces of bourgeois and "revisionist" thought in China, and ensuring the permanent dominance of the Maoist line within the Chinese leadership. The "Cultural Revolution" has gone beyond previous campaigns in several important ways, however. First, it has attacked not only the vague specter of revisionism, but also a large number of specific individuals, some of them of the highest rank. Second, it has produced a new mass organization of young students—the Red Guards—which has served as a militant and sometimes violent action corps for carrying the "Cultural Revolution" to the people. Third, it has zeroed in on propaganda and educational institutions, forcing the suspension of several publications and the postponement for at least one school year of normal educational operations. These developments, taken together give current Chinese politics a greater degree of tension, uncertainty and disorder than at any time since the early years of Communist rule.

It would be premature to conclude that these events mark the beginning of a new, long-range political line in China. The elevation of Marshall Lin Piao to the position of Mao's likely successor and the purge of several high-ranking figures certainly suggest a new lineup in CCP leadership; there have been hints, too, of a resurrection of the "Great Leap Forward." However, the current campaign has thus far stopped short of major new proposals in either the political or economic realms. Details on the Third Five-Year Plan have still not been released. Moreover, the Party has tried, albeit rather belatedly, to restrain those actions of the Red Guards which have interfered with the economy. The directors of the "Cultural Revolution" have used it as a vehicle for eliminating their rivals and trying to implant a uniform acceptance of Maoist orthodoxy, without committing themselves to major policy initiatives. Whether or not they attain their objectives, and what they will do with their power if they can maintain it, remains to be seen.

Nevertheless, caution in predicting the outcome of the "Cultural Revolution" ought not to obscure its profound significance. Perhaps the most important aspect of the campaign is simply the fact that it was believed to be necessary, and that implementation of it has led to such virulent attacks and counterattacks. It is now evident that the attempt to perpetuate Mao's revolutionary style has met resistance from a variety of sources. The resistance goes back at least to 1959 and has come from prominent members of the Party bureaucracy as well as the usual scapegoats among the technicians and intellectuals. The severity of the campaign against these "revisionists" may be partly explained in terms of intra-Party power struggles and the Sino–Soviet conflict. But it also reflects real and growing tension between those who retain their literal faith in Mao's doctrine and those who believe their personal and national interests are best served by a new approach to China's problems. A Chinese Khrushchev may still be far away, if indeed he ever arrives, but some of the general pressures that guided Khrushchev's actions are beginning to appear in China.

November, 1966

SELECTED BIBLIOGRAPHY

Barnett, A. Doak, *Communist China in Perspective* (New York: Praeger, 1962). A brief but perceptive discussion of the historical background to Chinese communism, the main objectives of the CCP and the problems it faces in the future.

Brandt, Conrad, Benjamin Schwartz, and John K. Fairbank, *A Documentary History of Chinese Communism.* (Cambridge: Harvard University Press, 1952). Selected documents of the Communist movement, in English translation, from its origin to 1950. The editors provide critical analysis of the selections and a chronology of the movement.

Ch'en, Jerome, *Mao and the Chinese Revolution* (London: Oxford, 1965). A historical narrative of Mao's life and times from childhood to 1949. Synthesizes all of what is currently known about Mao's life and much of what is known about the history of the CCP.

The China Quarterly, The most useful journal for the student of Communist China. Detailed and scholarly articles about the mainland regime, with book reviews and a quarterly "chronicle and documentation" in each issue.

Clubb, O. Edmund, *Twentieth-Century China* (New York: Columbia University Press, 1964). A political history of China from 1900 to the present. Packed with details on the political and military events of the period, but also useful for broader perspectives on modern China.

Communist China 1955–1959: Policy Documents with Analysis, with a foreword by Robert R. Bowie and John K. Fairbank (Cambridge: Harvard University Press, 1962). A nearly indispensable guide to the years indicated, containing all of the key documents in translation and providing a forty-page summary and analysis of the period.

Fairbank, John King, *The United States and China,* rev. ed. (Cambridge: Harvard University Press, 1958). A concise history of modern China with a thorough discussion of the premodern tradition. The best introduction to the subject.

Hughes, T. J. and D. E. T. Luard, *The Economic Development of Commu-*

nist China, 1949–1960, rev. ed. (London: Oxford, 1961). A brief, relatively nontechnical survey of the subject, also useful as a general introduction to Communist China.

Johnson, Chalmers A., *Peasant Nationalism and Communist Power* (Stanford: Stanford University Press, 1962). A study of the rise of CCP power during 1937–1945, emphasizing the nationalist sources of the Party's growth.

Lewis, John Wilson, *Leadership in Communist China* (Ithaca: Cornell University Press, 1963). A theoretically oriented study of the CCP's leadership techniques which also provides a great deal of information about Party organization and structure.

Li Choh-ming (ed.), *Industrial Development in Communist China* (New York: Praeger, 1964). A collection of articles from *The China Quarterly* dealing with a variety of topics relating to economic development. Particularly useful for analysis of the post-1958 period, for which little hard data is available.

Lifton, Robert Jay, *Thought Reform and the Psychology of Totalism* (New York: Norton, 1961). A study of "brainwashing" in China, based on interviews with Chinese and Westerners who experienced thought reform. Suggestive analysis of the techniques and effects of Communist persuasion.

Liu Ta-Chung and Kung-Chia Yeh, *The Economy of the Chinese Mainland: National Income and Economic Development, 1933–1959* (Princeton: Princeton University Press, 1965). The most thorough study of the subject to date.

MacFarquhar, Roderick, *The Hundred Flowers Campaign and the Chinese Intellectuals* (New York: Praeger, 1960). Useful collection of excerpts from statements made during the Hundred Flowers' campaign of 1957, accompanied by analysis and background information.

Mao Tse-tung, *Selected Works,* 4 vols. (New York: International Publishers, 1956). This edition of Mao's works covers only the first three of the four-volume Chinese edition. Volume IV of the Chinese edition is available in English translation from the Foreign Languages Press (Peking).

Schram, Stuart R., *The Political Thought of Mao Tse-tung* (New York: Praeger, 1963). Consists mainly of excerpts from Mao's writings topically arranged and includes many rare or difficult to locate selections. A lengthy introduction offers a provocative interpretation of Mao's political theory.

Schurman, Franz, *Ideology and Organization in Communist China* (Berkeley and Los Angeles: University of California Press, 1966). The most ambitious and penetrating analysis of the Chinese Communist system.

Schwartz, Benjamin I., *Chinese Communism and the Rise of Mao* (Cambridge: Harvard University Press, 1958). A pioneering study of the origins of the "Maoist" strategy in the Chinese Communist movement up to 1935. Deals mainly with ideological shifts but also useful as a political history of the Party.

Snow, Edgar, *The Other Side of the River: Red China Today* (New York: Random House, 1961). A rambling but comprehensive account of a famous journalist's 1960 visit to China. Includes a great deal of background information on Chinese communism and offers a generally favorable view of the mainland situation.

Tsou, Tang, *America's Failure in China, 1941–1950* (Chicago: University of Chicago Press, 1963). The most thorough study of Sino–American relations during this critical period. Also sheds light on KMT-CCP relations during the civil war.

Walker, Kenneth R., *Planning in Chinese Agriculture: Socialisation and the Private Sector, 1956–1962* (Chicago: Aldine, 1965). A brief but valuable study which emphasizes CCP policy toward the private sector of agriculture and offers important information on the agricultural effects of the "Great Leap Forward."

Yang, C. K., *A Chinese Village in Early Communist Transition* (Cambridge, Mass.: The MIT Press, 1959). Based on field research in a village near Canton during the years immediately before and after Communist takeover. Informative descriptions of pre-Communist village structure and of CCP policies at the village level.

6

Communism in Eastern Europe

Andrew Gyorgy

THE YEAR 1956 was a climactic one in the history of Eastern Europe. Its two great popular rebellions, Poznan–Warsaw in Poland and Budapest in Hungary, marked the end of one major chapter in postwar Soviet–satellite relations, and the beginning of a new one—filled with the groping for new directions, particularly in political action and ideology. After years of depressing silence, so singularly characteristic of Stalin's monolithic rule, a variety of new and hopeful sounds began to emanate from the Balkan–Danubian area. 1956 produced not only political convulsions, but also gave indication that the Curtain was not "Iron" any longer. Multiple changes in leadership, cautiously disguised anti-Soviet policies and, above all, the quickening rate of exchanges of people, ideas, books and a proliferation of travel opportunities contributed to a gradual change in the ideological and intellectual atmosphere. The post-Stalinist "New Course" yielded to a post-1956 "Newest New Course."

The important years since 1956, are best described as *postheroic* and nonrevolutionary. Gone were the feverish convolutions attendant upon the crises in East Berlin, Poznan and Budapest. The magic moments for popular uprisings passed by, and the recurrence appeared most unlikely. Rather it seemed likely that future changes in Soviet–Eastern European relationships would occur through quieter processes of gradual

Note: The author of this chapter is indebted to Professor Kurt L. London, Director of the Institute for Sino-Soviet Studies of The George Washington University. The Institute's hospitality, extended to the author in the summer of 1965, greatly facilitated the preparation and writing of this chapter.

transformation or erosion, rather than by violent and revolutionary means. In the decade after 1956, both leaders and followers had time to simmer down and to step back to view their relative positions and relationships with a long-term perspective and in the light of the possible.

In the aftermath of 1956, three major factors emerged with force and clarity on the Eastern European political stage. Not necessarily in order of importance, these were (1) the revolution of rising expectations; (2) the increasing lack of interest in Marxist–Leninist ideology; and (3) a multicolored, truly *polycentric* pattern, dividing the once-monolithic camp of the former "Soviet satellites" into several different groups each having its own shade of "new" communism. While the first of these three factors has been of global significance, with the world's exploding population everywhere insisting on better living standards and a happier "way of life," the latter two have had more restricted, regional implications. They were applicable primarily to the Eastern European political scene and created local problems and "variations on the theme" which served to make the formulation of general principles, encompassing the area's one hundred million people, increasingly difficult, if not downright impossible.

The Revolution of Rising Expectations

Eastern European societies are by and large split into two distinct and often distant groups: (a) the Communists—the elite and inner-core or activist Party members—and (b) the broad groups of the public-at-large which have been described as "apolitical and sometimes crassly materialist . . . less and less concerned with aspirations that are clearly beyond attainment."[1]

"Catching up with the West" has always been an urgent and appealing world Communist slogan. Interestingly enough (and as far as Communist ideology is concerned, disappointingly enough) individual Iron Curtain countries seem to be disinterested in the catching-up process simply in terms of over-all production of the East vs. the West. Instead, the rapidly rising expectations of the masses project the catching-up campaign onto a different level: The people in general want to "catch up" with the West in terms of a better way of life, a higher standard of living, more consumer goods—regardless of whether the distinctly materialistic values which these connote fit into a properly Marxist–Leninist atmosphere or not.

[1] Robert Bass, "The Post-Stalin Era in Eastern Europe," *Problems of Communism,* vol. XII, no. 2, Mar.–Apr., 1963, p. 76.

Two major factors contributed in the post-1956 decade to the emergence of this all-pervasive spirit of materialism: The end of the Stalinist police state with the attendant weakening of terror and repression; and the rapidly mushrooming new opportunities for trade, travel, cultural exchange with Western European countries, which opened new and more abundant economic vistas for the tired and goods-hungry peoples of Eastern Europe.

The two factors usually operated in close interrelationship. In ideologically "tough" situations, where even years after Stalin's death at least a "Stalinoid" atmosphere persisted and where only few and limited breaks occurred in the cultural and commercial Iron Curtain, there were few open indications of "rising expectations." This was the situation in East Germany, Bulgaria, Albania and Czechoslovakia for years after 1953 and even 1956. But, where Stalinist terror yielded to a Khrushchev-encouraged aura of political relaxation and "goulash communism" and where thousands of citizens could apply with impunity for exit visas and be granted them (in Poland and Hungary, particularly), material demands and expectations increased demonstrably almost overnight. Indeed, from an Eastern European perspective, it is now clear that Nikita Khrushchev's loudly proclaimed Soviet Communist Party Program goals, set with such abandon and exuberance for achievement by 1970 and 1980, had a much more exhilerating effect among the former satellite peoples than among the Soviet citizenry. Thus, by arousing dormant materialistic instincts and turning people away from the austerity of the Communist belief system, the former Soviet leader may have done Soviet communism's cause a distinct disservice. And by loosening Eastern European and Soviet bonds, he weakened his country's once formidable *colonial* position in the Balkan–Danubian area.

Ideological Fatigue and Indifference

It is a fact of political life in Eastern Europe that after more than two decades of Communist rule a large number of Party people have acquired a vested interest in the maintenance and perpetuation of the governmental system. Nevertheless, this Communist core is often a surprisingly small one, and the moment one steps beyond the small, magic circle of the "New Class," the truly devoted *apparatchiki,* one encounters a society composed of nonpolitical persons who will cooperate passively with the ruling elite, but are essentially indifferent to, and tired of, the all-enveloping, ceaseless Communist propaganda. The ideological shock that set in after the great popular rebellions of the 1956 period later yielded to a sense of political fatigue and frustration. "I won't openly oppose you, but please leave me alone!" became the in-effect attitude of the "man in the street" in the satellite countries.

The members of the citizenry of the bloc express their sense of negativism to the regime's political blandishments in differing degrees, ranging from the opportunistic repetition of Communist slogans and formal observance of rules and regulations (These are the "bread-and-butter" or, more properly, "margarine" Communists.) through a position of cautious neutrality (passive cooperation) all the way to outright indifference. The common denominator that unites all those who are not *apparatchik*-oriented is a generally characteristic *apolitical* attitude which should be understood in terms of the original Greek semantics where "a-" signifies "totally devoid of." The ideological fatigue of the peoples of Eastern Europe can be compared to building a wall around one's own individuality and closing-off the external political world. In a sense this is a form of that "inner emigration" that gripped many non-Nazi Germans during the critical early years of the Third Reich.

This qualified pattern of "ideological alienation" actually has been encouraged by such internally insecure and politically hesitant regimes as Kadar's in Hungary and Gomulka's in Poland. Both governments for years engaged in a frantic, often unsuccessful, search for respectability and popular acceptance and, with this in mind tried to deemphasize ideological factors that separated them from the masses. "Those who are not against us, are with us!" proclaimed Janos Kadar in 1961 in an unusually conciliatory mood. In addition, both the Hungarian and Polish regimes have attempted to bolster the technical, less political, areas of their administration by appointing and promoting non-Communist but technically qualified experts, to important positions. While this "non-Communists are welcome" approach may have strengthened the over-all performance of the governments in question, it has definitely contributed to the continuing erosion of ideology and of that moral fervor which has traditionally characterized Communist leaders. The stress on the technical and nonpolitical aspects of everyday life has thus produced a *non*ideological atmosphere in Eastern Europe which borders on the *anti*ideological.

The Polycentric Pattern of Communism

The deeply founded and increasingly obvious polycentricity of the Eastern European Communist Parties must be stressed as one of the foremost characteristics of the regional political landscape. In the following passage, Donald Zagoria forcefully points to this phenomenon of the once-satellite world of Eastern European communism:

> Belgrade and Warsaw have tried to pull Soviet policy toward moderation, while Peking, Pankow, and Tirana have sought more or less consistently in recent years to pull it in the other direction. Because such differences in perspective are intimately bound up with each Party's sense of its own security and best interests, *they are not likely to disappear.*[2]

Polycentrism in this context can best be understood as the composite effect of three closely related causes: (1) the impact of de-Stalinization, (2) the rapid emergence of China on the world Communist scene, and (3) the broadening scope of the Sino–Soviet dispute.

This "cluster" of closely related developments led to the splitting of Eastern European Communist Parties into three distinct groups: (1) Parties openly, secretly, or semisecretly espousing the "Chinese line" —Albania *in toto;* certain East German, Bulgarian and Czech Communists occasionally and quietly taking an anti-Soviet line on key issues; (2) Parties pursuing the "Soviet line"—Hungary and Poland *in toto*—officially East Germany, Bulgaria and Czechoslovakia—and Yugoslavia on major, across-the-board foreign policy issues affecting the Communist camp and the course of European and world communism in general; and (3) a selectively *polycentric* line seeking a skillful "centrist" position between Russia and China—pursued by Rumania which, however, leans toward the Soviet position on essential foreign policy and regional economic questions.

The crucial ideological issues involved in the extension of polycentrism, are not numerous—or of primary significance. However, the stands taken in the following five problem areas are significant for determining where a country stands on the Soviet-Chinese spectrum:

1. On the current Soviet leadership, formerly the person of party boss Nikita Khrushchev—the Soviet line is *for,* the Chinese line violently *opposed.*
2. On de-Stalinization—the Soviet line is for, in a restrained manner, while the Chinese line is against, without reservations or restraints.
3. On Peaceful Coexistence—the Soviet line for, the Chinese line violently against, but with qualification that both groups are *for* national liberation movements and *for* "national revolutions," with

[2] Donald S. Zagoria, *The Sino-Soviet Conflict, 1956–1961* (Princeton: Princeton University Press, 1962), p. 387 (emphasis added).

the pro-Chinese endorsing these enthusiastically and the pro-Soviets supporting only those which seem to carry minimal risks for them and maximum embarassment for the West, particularly the United States.[3]

4. On attitudes toward the West—the Chinese line is viciously anti-Western, the Soviet and "independent" line is uneven in its orientation, although generally the latter two are all for trade and improvement of cultural relations, but anti-NATO and anti-American on the Vietnam issue.
5. On internal "relaxation of tensions"—the Soviet line is for, while the Chinese line is definitely against, demanding a mass mobilization of the citizens and "eternal vigilance" at home and abroad.[4]

It would seem that polycentrism is likely to breed more polycentrism causing new and widening old splits in the body politic of Eastern Europe. It contributed directly to the deterioration of the Soviet Union's once dominant colonial position in the area. It is significant both as a current trend and as a portent of future developments.

Major Political Changes in Eastern Europe Since 1956

In appraising the complicated political scenery of the Danubian–Balkan area it is useful to employ a kind of historically oriented double-entry system, juxtaposing politicoeconomic factors favoring and opposing cohesion. The former grouping catalogs the forces which have operated in a *centripetal* direction, binding the individual Eastern European nations to the USSR and, on the whole, strengthening the newly won and established colonial position of Soviet Russia. The latter category has obviously exerted *centrifugal* tendencies which have weakened and in the long run undermined the once-monopolistic status of the Soviet Union. As a broad generalization it can be suggested that for a 12-year period (1944–1956) in the post-World War II era the cohesive factors considerably outweighed the divisive forces to the extent of seeming to almost completely hide the latter. Commencing

[3] On Vietnam, Cuba and Algeria there was general agreement among Eastern European Communist Parties, although, understandably, more violent anti-Americanism and demands for the support of revolutionary activity were expressed by the "Chinese-line" advocates.

[4] Judging from Ulbricht's, Novotny's and Zhivkov's behavior, the "subtle" Chinese line advocates would just as soon return to a Stalin-type domestic social and economic pattern. But their inclinations are complicated and largely frustrated by popular demands for a better life and internal ideological relaxation. Hence the domestic headaches and crises which have marked the "evolution" of East Germany, Czechoslovakia and Bulgaria.

with the climactic events of 1956, however, the areas of disruption became more evident, to a degree that for several of the East-Central European nations, the decade beginning with 1956 marked the end of an era of abject and total dependence on the USSR and ushered in the era of the "new communisms."

Keeping this approximate time frame in mind and using the useful distinction of Professor Kurt L. London who has concluded that following the 1956 upheavals the Soviet Union took essentially two types of measures to stabilize the East European bloc: "institutional and 'diplomatic' or persuasive,"[5] we turn to a consideration of the centripetal forces linking the Soviet Union to its once-satellite partners in Eastern Europe.

The most basic and frequently overlooked fact of life militating in favor of closer USSR–Eastern European relations has been the time element. Well over two decades of "colonial rule" have left an indelible impact on these societies, influencing, in particular, the life and educational pursuits of their younger generations. Another two decades of Soviet Communist domination, despite the gradual loosening of the colonial bonds, would make it most difficult to shake off the impact of cultural Russification and a Communist political ideology.

Another area in which each passing year makes the possibility of removing Soviet influence more remote is that of the exploitation of local strategic resources. These include the uranium of the easily accessible Ore Mountains (on the Czechoslovakian-East German border), Hungarian bauxite, Polish iron and coal, control over 1500 miles and more of the Danube River, an immensely important means of inland navigation with political and military overtones, the industrial capacities of such technologically advanced societies as East Germany, Poland and Czechoslovakia, as well as the agricultural resources of Hungary, Rumania and—to a lesser extent—Bulgaria.

The USSR profited directly and often immediately from the satellite economies where the advanced skills, the higher technological level of knowledge and expertise of individual peoples or groups could be exploited without intermediaries. It further attempted to maximize the benefits to it by promoting regionwide integration through the establishment of a network of complex economic arrangements. Founded in 1949 (and mislabeled at the time in the West as the "Molotov Plan"), the Council of Mutual Economic Assistance (CEMA, also

[5] Kurt L. London, "Soviet Strengths and Weaknesses" in D. M. Abshire and R. V. Allen (eds.), *National Security: Political, Military, and Economic Strategies in the Decade Ahead* (New York: Praeger, 1963), p. 59.

known more popularily as Comecon) tried to organize the economies of the Eastern European countries into a cohesive and self-sufficient bloc. Since 1955, in particular, Comecon's frantic activities have increasingly reflected the double intention of the Soviet leadership: (a) to tie Eastern Europe firmly to the USSR by the skillful exploitation of economic resources and the encouragement of a division of labor among the individual bloc countries; and (b) to keep the satellite economies in fair-to-prosperous shape, seeking the passive cooperation of their peoples and hopefully preventing a recurrence of the revolutionary blow-ups of the 1953–1956 period. Comecon, as Kurt London has observed, has played an eminently political role in Soviet–bloc relations, significantly promoting unity, particularly beginning with the early 1960s.[6]

In the troubled "Cold War" world the cohesive force provided by a military integration factor, namely, the Warsaw Treaty Organization (WTO) or Warsaw Pact has been considerable. Like Comecon, founded in 1949 and goaded into greater activity after 1955, WTO has attempted through a multilateral military design to maintain the Soviet Union's postwar strategic "safety zone" in Eastern Europe. The idea behind WTO is neither new nor complex but the latter-day Communist version of the traditional nineteenth-century Western "sphere of influence" notion. WTO can be considered the Stalinist revival and expression of the old Tsarist ambition to secure the western flanks of Russia, by developing its own imperial *cordon sanitaire*.

Seen in the above context, the Soviet's current military "safety zone" in the Danubian–Balkan area here under consideration seems to serve a double function: (a) in a negative sense, it denies the use and control of the region to all non-Communist forces; (b) in a positive sense, it incorporates the region into the Warsaw Pact's aggressive blueprints, which include the launching of offensives from Eastern European bases, the planting of weapons and food caches in strategic points, the control of satellite airfields and the deployment of highly trained and battle-ready Soviet divisions in such key countries as East Germany and Hungary.[7] The geostrategic picture emerging from this pattern of Soviet military planning points to the intended possible use of Eastern Europe as a conventional battleground of sorts.

[6] Kurt L. London, *ibid.*, p. 60.

[7] For about ten years after the end of World War II Red Army troops were stationed in almost all of the Eastern European countries. In 1955, the troops were withdrawn from Rumania, Poland and Bulgaria; Soviet forces remained in East Germany and Hungary, though there were at times rumors of their imminent withdrawal.

The Soviet Union's military emphasis is clearly on the centrally located clearing house status of East Germany. The 22 Soviet divisions, comprising 420,000 Russian troops, stationed in the DDR also serve to express, indirectly at least, the Soviet military planners' distrust of satellite troops which, despite the manifold Warsaw Treaty Organization bonds, have been considered unreliable and probably expendable. In case of direct, "hot-war" type of engagements in the area, the military establishments of the individual People's Republics are likely to be used sparingly with the following restricted alternatives available: (a) they will be completely ignored by the Soviet military leadership; (b) they will be used sparingly in small units for localized "guerrilla war" purposes, etc.; or (c) they will be promptly disarmed as not only unreliable, but as actually or potentially subversive—especially in a situation which would go counter to the nationalistic expectations of, say, Polish or Hungarian troops.

Despite Soviet reservations, the newly developed People's (or National) Armies have been kept well-armed and battle-ready. Bolstered by Soviet officers in most of the high-ranking positions, they must, all caveats to the contrary, be considered important cohesive forces; the Warsaw Pact operates as a tightly knit institutional bond between the USSR and its former satellites in Eastern Europe.

Beyond the economic and military forces working for cohesion, there loom basic political and governmental factors moving in the same direction. It has often been noted that the national CPs almost slavishly imitate the structure of the CPSU, with fundamental parallelities of administrative procedures and personnel policies. During the Stalinist period of total, monolithic control (1944–1953), the USSR succeeded first in transplanting and then in proliferating Soviet Russian governmental, bureaucratic, policing, and economic patterns of operation in a wholesale manner, throughout Eastern Europe. Thus, the local replicas of the mother "body politic" reflected and still reflect many similarities and instinctive duplications of the Soviet original.

Another factor working for cohesion has been the relationship of the satellite and Muscovite leadership. During the critical "takeover" years of 1944–1948, it was Soviet direction and violent Stalinist impulse that cleared the way for the *institutional* establishment of communism in this area. Stalin's carefully planned "revolutions from above" systematically and ruthlessly destroyed the major, native political forces, such as those made up of members of the liberal middle-class or of various peasant groups, which could have offered resistance to communism. The first institutional contacts between the Soviet leaders and the newly established satellites were the series of National Democratic Fronts, Fatherland Fronts, and People's Fronts which also served as useful shields for the still anemic, local Communist Parties. In later years when Communist hierarchies were already clearly and openly in power, local leadership still needed or thought it needed the Kremlin's support. In any event, it had the Moscow habit, which was strengthened during the periodic summonses to appear before the international Communist "Holy of Holies." Soviet impulses, radiating from Moscow, moving through Soviet-oriented leaders and Soviet-designed institutions, were promptly translated into local action by the Warsaw, Budapest, Bucharest or Sofia exponents of Stalinism.

When Stalin lashed out at the so-called *national* communism of Tito, native "Titoists" were arrested, persecuted and often executed throughout Eastern Europe. When Stalin's fury turned against the cosmopolitan *international*-style Communists (the so-called "Muscovites"), then a long list of Paukers, Slanskys, and Clementises were quickly silenced, when not liquidated.

Nor did the death of Stalin interrupt the style. After March 5, 1953, local Stalins suddenly faded away throughout Eastern Europe, and the hour struck for "collective leadership" there, as in Moscow. When, in turn, the "collective leaders" began to wither away in the USSR, yielding their places to Nikita Khrushchev, a corresponding narrowing of the spectrum occurred in satellite regimes. One-man leadership, or at most, dual government once more raised its head from Czechoslovakia to Bulgaria and the "cult of the individual" returned to Eastern Europe despite the conflicting, and sometimes disturbing, background cacophony of de-Stalinization. By the time of Khrushchev's political demise in October, 1964, the Soviet impulses seemingly, at least, temporarily had lost their vigor for whatever reasons. Occasionally, there were instances of tactical "splittism" separating the Prime Minister's job from that of the more powerful First Secretary.[8] Generally speaking, however, the Khrushchev pattern still persisted in Eastern Europe with a combination of the "cult of personality" and of restricted, only semitotalitarian powers reposed in one man, an arrangement that could be characterized as a Stalinoid, pseudototalitarian type of Communist dictatorship.

Extending beyond the formal institutional umbrella coupling the Soviet and East European leadership elites, there is the more tenuous

[8] To illustrate this point, in July, 1965, Janos Kadar relinquished the office of Prime Minister of the Hungarian government to Gyula Kallai. This move did not, however, undermine Kadar's "strong man" position.

and intangible link that exists between the rank-and-file of the respective Communist Parties. This involves membership-at-large which provides protected positions on the home front, and affords political and cultural connections with "good Communists" everywhere. Since in a Communist society the Communist Party is the central organization, its members must be made secure economically and otherwise. A 1965 Radio Free Europe analysis rightly stressed that no Communist regime "can permit wholesale attack on devoted Party members by those whose Party zeal and loyalty are, at the least, open to question, for this would ultimately mean undermining the authority of the Party itself."[9]

This same informal defensive alliance that binds members of the same Party also prevails between the *good* Russian Marxist and the *good* satellite Marxist. Occasionally a major crisis reveals the depth of this area of "persuasive cohesion." In the spring of 1965, a conspiracy was unmasked in Bulgaria involving several high-ranking officials, leading to the arrest of several and the suicide of at lease one. Party First Secretary Todor Zhivkov, mentioning the "plot" for the first time in public, gave full expression to Soviet–Bulgarian cohesion when stating that:

> "In the West the reactionaries are now screaming that some plot has been discovered in our country which was aimed at separating us from the Soviet Union, and I do not know what other nonsense. . . . *There is no force on earth which could separate the Bulgarian People's Republic from the Soviet Union.* We have been and will continue to be with the Soviet Union in life and death."[10]

Intra-Party links have been strengthened over the years in a variety of ways. While the basic motivation has been that of Russifying the satellite nations, particularly in the Stalin era, in later years such policies have become less obvious and less effective. In historic terms, the following Soviet weapons in the area of propaganda have been most useful in Eastern Europe: (a) the compulsory teaching of Russian language and literature from grade school all the way to the doctoral level; (b) a broad-based and exceedingly comprehensive cultural exchange program saturating the satellite countries with an endless flow of "cultural" missions ranging from school teachers through agricultural experts, but also including opera singers and ballet dancers. Local universities have been utilized in this program, as well as a veritable

[9] Herbert Reed, "The Conflict of Generations in Eastern Europe Today," *Research Department Bulletin, Radio Free Europe,* Mar. 12, 1965, p. 7.

[10] "Situation Report on Bulgaria," *Research Department Bulletin, Radio Free Europe,* Apr. 29, 1965, pp. 1–2. The last sentence of the quote presents a gloomy prophecy and expectation (emphasis added).

across-the-board network of Soviet Friendship Societies, institutes, and scientific academies, operating both as instruments of the "Russification" drive, as well as the sources of an endless stream of propaganda in Russian and in the local language; (c) a conscious and systematic play on the Eastern European peoples' fear of West Germany, picturing, by way of dramatic contrast, the USSR as the model of a peace-loving nation of "friendship and socialism." In recent years this fear of a belligerent, "revanchist" Germany has been enlarged to include a hatred of NATO, of the American presence in Europe, and—in general—of an alleged Western predisposition to engage in war mongering and "adventurist" military policies.[11] At any rate, the USSR has made full use of Czech and Polish, in particular, fear and hatred of the "Teutonic conqueror"; (d) the impact of the transplanting of Soviet Russian institutions that resulted in the molding of a daily life of remarkable similarity throughout the satellite world.

Opposed to the forces linking the Soviet Union and the countries of Eastern Europe together there is a cluster of "divisive" forces negatively influencing Soviet–Eastern European relations and, on the whole, working against the Soviet Union's national interests in this area. These "negative" factors tend to weaken and undermine the once-unassailable and monopolistic "control position" of the USSR, ending, to a great degree, the imperial dreams and designs which were part of the baggage of the Stalin era.

There would appear to be three major sets of divisive factors: (a) the inadequacy of Eastern European Communist leadership; (b) the increasing impact of nationalism; and (c) the diminution and decentralization of police terror and violence. The operational result of these forces has been that previously mentioned ideological "erosion," which has generally weakened the hold of Marxism–Leninism on the political landscape of Eastern Europe.

The inadequacy of its political elite groups has been a enduring characteristic of Balkan–Danubian communism. The Eastern European Party leaders have repeatedly displayed a susceptibility to a variety of corruptions, a failing that has played a significant role in the high early postwar expectations of the long-suffering peoples of Eastern Europe. Perhaps it is difficult to believe from the distant perspective of the 1960s, but in 1945 and 1946 even in the newly returning Communist leaders (who had spent the war years in Moscow receiving Comintern-style, postgraduate Marxist–Leninist training) they found promise for a "brave new world" of economic and political improvements.

[11] One aspect of this hate campaign has been the massive anti-United States effort in connection with Vietnam.

The hopes were short-lived, however. The weary and war-torn masses soon understood the meaning of the old folk saying that the next round will be even worse than the last one.[12]

Such leaders came to the fore as Walter Ulbricht in East Germany and Ana Pauker in Rumania, who represented not only the most brutal Stalinism in action, but also projected crassest materialism onto the political stage of Eastern Europe. These were Communists who extravagently enjoyed the benefits and privileges of high rank in captive societies whose citizens were living on the verge of starvation and destitution. They exploited the possibilities that their positions offered for luxurious living to the full, apparently disregarding the fact that their people considered them to be the agents of a foreign conqueror. They seemed to be content to be unpopular, to govern in the teeth, so to speak, of public opinion, with a minimum consensus of their subjects. While Walter Ulbricht became the towering monument to such massive unpopularity, there have been Ulbricht-style leaders in Bulgaria (Vulko Chervenkov, Anton Yugav, etc.) and elsewhere, as well.

The aura of materialism which pervaded the people's elite in the 1940s and 1950s had by the mid-1960s spread throughout the masses, bringing not only feelings of ideological apathy and indifference, but also a general sense of venality. *Blat* (the Communist version of payoff, blackmail and bribe) became epidemic throughout the region, accompanied by the oft-articulated battle cry: "Let's work against the State!—Who cares if *they* ('the authorities') are gypped." Reduced effort, tremendous absenteeism, and the embezzlement of public funds became rampant. There was created a pattern of dishonesty in daily life that further added to the sense of alienation.

Although such creeping corruption is a complete denial in practice of the basic tenets of Marxism–Leninism, the Communist regimes accepted it with uncomfortable silence, not daring to upset the uneasy political truce. This has been particularly obvious in Kadar's Hungary and in Gomulka's Poland where the regimes have literally attempted to buy at least the passive cooperation of a large sector of their reluctant populations. Over the years such "tolerance" has enlarged the circle of those who do not have a vested interest in the maintenance and even perpetuation of the Communist system. Yet it may be observed that a temporary truce is not necessarily permanent peace, and the seeming acceptance of a status quo does not necessarily guarantee long-term political and social stability.

[12] The expressive German original is: *"Selten konnt was besseres nach"* ("Seldom does anything better follow").

The impact of nationalism has been historically an all-pervasive force on the Eastern European political stage. In recent years a significant renaissance of anti-Russian, and frequently of anti-Communist, nationalism has occurred principally in two important spheres: Political and cultural. As Hugh Seton-Watson has pointed out,[13] these two aspects of nationalism have asserted themselves in the Balkan–Danubian area through the related instrumentalities of the state, religion, and language.

The "state" concept has had a strong tradition in this area. It has too many and too vital national roots to be suppressed lastingly by Russian-dominated communism. Ruling classes created the "state" and in turn the "state" produced the "nation" idea, whether in its primary political manifestations, or in its more recent, economic form.[14] The nation concept in Eastern Europe has seemed bound eventually to turn against Russian control and shake off its latter-day pattern of imperial domination.

It is the context of the "state" and "nation" that religion and language emerge as significant divisive forces, with respect to the Soviet Union. Religion has decisively shaped the peculiar national identity of each country. It has a disruptive impact whenever the national group had been a submerged minority ruled by a different religion. Thus Protestants, Roman Catholics and Orthodox lived close by one another —and often in conflict with one another. This "religious Balkanization" with its centuries of inbreeding has since World War II been complicated by the impact of communism, Sovietization and Russian Orthodox predominance. Each major religion was forced to assume a posture of its own vis-à-vis Soviet communism. The broad spectrum of behavior patterns have ranged from the unyielding resistance of Cardinals Stepinac, Mindszenty, and Wyszinski (respectively in Yugoslavia, Hungary, and Poland); through the generally determined and skillful opposition of the Jews (though their position was complicated by pressures

[13] Hugh Seton-Watson, in a lecture at Harvard University, Russian Research Center, 1965.

[14] This brief chapter cannot offer a detailed analysis of the many manifestations of contemporary *economic* nationalism on the Eastern European political scene. Concentrating on the Rumanian case-study, Victor Meier suggests that in countries like Rumania industrial progress was "inaugurated against the will of the Soviets, and every new modern factory in the country is, in the eyes of most Rumanians, a sort of bulwark or fortress against that foreign power which, on the pretext of pursuing an international division of labor, *wanted to keep Rumania in the condition of a supplier of agrarian products or, at least, of some oil.* Victor Meier, "Rumania's Way," *Swiss Review of World Affairs,* vol. XV, no. 4, July, 1965, p. 9 (emphasis added).

seeking to make possible the mass-exodus of remaining Jewish groups to Israel); to the "mixed" adjustment of Protestantism which displayed a willingness to seek accommodation with communism in such countries as Hungary but which opposed it vigorously in East Germany where both Lutheran and Calvinist ministers have resisted the Ulbricht regime in the face of a nearly hopeless local situation; all the way to various *national* Orthodox churches (Rumania, Bulgaria) which have cooperated abjectly with their Communist governments as religious servants of a secular master. As the Communists themselves have recognized, nationally oriented churches have not been able to offer the resistance to communism that the internationally organized religious institutions were capable of providing. Although religious instruction is now either suppressed or minimized in these countries (with the possible exception of Poland) on the national level, the international churches have stubbornly held out against the ideological onslaught of Marxism-Leninism. Hence their significance as divisive and/or disruptive elements in the life of Eastern Europe.

The linguistic factor closely parallels the religious one as Greeks, Bosnians, Croats, Bulgars, Magyars *and Russians* today increasingly oppose each other on a linguistic basis in the Balkan-Danubian area. This linguistic differentiation, in turn, contributes to the strengthening of a Polish, Hungarian, or Rumanian national identity.

In recent years the Soviet drive toward Russification has been effectively decelerated with the minimizing of Russian language instruction, the closing of Russian language schools and institutes and the downgrading of Soviet Friendship and Cultural Societies. Restrictions have even been imposed upon the broad field of Soviet-sponsored cultural exchange programs. This de-Russification process has been most vigorously conducted in the non-Slavic linguistic-cultural areas, such as Hungary and Rumania. On the other hand, Bulgaria—Slavic and pro-Russian—has continued its deference to Russian cultural values—with Czechoslovakia and Poland occupying in-between positions.

Undoubtedly the gradual diminution and decentralization of the terror-and-repression aspects of life under Eastern Europe's Communist regimes has contributed to the strengthening of centrifugal political tendencies. In this context the "New Course" following Stalin's death in March, 1953, brought about major and qualitative changes. But a decade would pass before a more relaxed ideological environment and social atmosphere would begin to appear.[15]

[15] Albania and, to a less degree, East Germany (the DDR) must be excepted from this generalization.

One evidence of this "return to normalcy" is to be seen in the increased emphasis on "Socialist legality." While it would be an exaggeration to talk in terms of the actual observance of civil (human) rights, legal and court procedures have been far more carefully and meticulously handled than under Stalinism or in the immediate post-Stalinist (1953–1965) period. Various people's courts, youth movement (Komsomol) courts and the such have come to interpret "Socialist law" in a less arbitrary and infuriating manner. Within narrowly prescribed political limits, the practical application of legal principles has improved to the point where it can stand open scrutiny. By Western standards, however, there is still an immense and often incomprehensible dichotomy in the ex-satellite states between the theory of jurisprudence and its daily, administrative interpretation.[16]

While *basic* patterns of coercion and potential for violence may not have altered since 1956, the *visual* differences between the old, Stalinist police state era and the post-Khrushchev period became immense. The all-pervasive secret police apparatus was deemphasized and, following the Soviet pattern, reorganized, broken up into several administrative subgroupings and deprived of its more obvious repressive functions. Vigilance largely replaced open terror and brutal repression as the method of police surveillance, and incarceration in comparatively mild city jails gradually replaced the previous techniques of mass arrest and concentration and slave labor camp treatment. The attempt has been made (especially in Poland and Hungary) to transform the image of the secret police from that of an organ of open persecution and brutality to that of an agency of prevention and "persuasive coercion" —occasionally referred to as "coercion with sugar coating." Each of the people's democracies has desperately tried to conceal, and even eliminate, the old manipulators of the purges and the handlers of the guillotine, emphasizing that the executioner's place has now been taken by friends and helpers of the populace. "Prevention instead of repression" has become the watchword. Under this "social prophylaxis," police and security organs are primarily to be called upon to render

[16] Western observers were shocked by the treatment of Professor Mihajlo Mihajlov, the young Yugoslav scholar who was jailed by his government in the spring of 1965 because he wrote critically of the Soviet Union, and thus violated a section (presumably Art. 175) of Yugoslavia's press law. Mihajlov was fired by his university and refused a passport which he had requested in order to visit American universities. His two law suits, charging that his constitutional rights were violated, were summarily dismissed and he was kept in prison. For the best treatment of the Mihajlov case, see "Moscow, Summer, 1964," *The New Leader,* vol. XLVIII, no. 7, Mar. 29, 1965. Also, "Yugoslav Critic of Soviet Presses Suits Over Rights," *The New York Times,* Aug. 9, 1965, p. 8.

"cooperation" and "assistance" to the various comrades' courts. A police machinery "capable of coercing"—but rarely actually doing it—is to have replaced the bloody, unmitigated and direct terror characteristic of the Stalinist system.[17] Thus decentralized *potential* terror has gradually replaced direct mass application of violence; other forms of economic, political and moral action have been substituted for it.

In this same general area, theory and practice concerning purges has also changed—in keeping with the changing patterns in the USSR. Just as Lenin and Stalin purged—so did Khrushchev and his Eastern European contemporaries—though almost with "disinclination" and without the genocidal overtones of the Stalin era. They did make use of such techniques as: (a) demotion to lower-ranking positions, (b) firing and removal to geographically remote areas, (c) transfer from Party service either to an innocuous government job or to a diplomatic assignment—preferably to a "friendly, Socialist" government within the bloc, or (d) temporary house arrest.

While the pattern may have involved greater violence in such countries as the DDR, Albania and Bulgaria (where one high official was reportedly forced to commit suicide in connection with an antigovernment conspiracy in the spring of 1965), the mass purges, the dreadful "voluntary confessions" and the farcical, but also frightening show trials of the 1940s and 1950s were conspicuously missing from the Eastern European political landscape of the early and mid-1960s.

Prospects for Eastern Europe

Since the profound crises of 1956, the Eastern European area has been largely quiescent. As Paul Zinner observed some years ago, it is not "a focal point of popular unrest and strife between subjugated peoples and their political masters. Nor is it a locus of ideological and power struggles . . . Attention has shifted elsewhere in the Communist bloc, to the adjustment of relations between Communist China and Russia, and outside the bloc, to the rekindling of East-West frictions."[18]

[17] In this connection it is worth noting that the Eastern European regimes have discovered and employed methods of "brain-washing," imitating their Soviet and Chinese counterparts. Until October, 1964, Nikita Khrushchev's remarks, made in May 1959, to a group of Soviet administrators and writers, were widely quoted in the Eastern European press: *"You must wash the brains of people* with your works, do not just clutter up their minds!" (Emphasis added.)

[18] Paul Zinner, paper delivered before the American Political Science Association, New York, Sept., 1960.

Clearly, the Soviet Union's Eastern European ex-satellites as well as Tito's Yugoslavia are caught in the midst of today's two gigantic power struggles: The Sino–Soviet dispute, and the Soviet–American competition. Despite their own quiescent attitudes, they are, nevertheless embroiled in a truly "double-pincer" type world political situation. In view of this position, their obvious and justifiable fear is that they will become the atomic battlefields of the near future, trapped—as so often in the past—in their hopeless buffer position between the camps of struggling giants. It is because of their experiences in the past and their hopes for the future that Khrushchev's "Peaceful Coexistence" theory elicited immediate endorsement and genuine approval on the part of the peoples of the Danubian–Balkan region. Khrushchev's thesis was overwhelmingly preferred to the bloodthirsty Maoist assumption that almost all forms of war are both inevitable and desirable. After the Hitler–Stalin eras and the destruction in the Hungarian November revolt, emotions of vengeance and mass violence have been drained, being replaced by suspicion, fear, and the deep-seated desire to be left alone. To this extent then Eastern Europeans fervently hoped that the Soviet-promulgated doctrines of "Peaceful Coexistence" would prove to be ideologically durable and applicable in practice, in short, that it would be more than a purely tactical device of international communism, and would eventually blossom into an enduring strategic theory. "We must accept it," they have stressed, because most of the other alternatives are "too dreadful to contemplate." Khrushchev's political demise in October, 1964, did not affect the fervent popular hope for the continuation of Peaceful Coexistence as a *permanent* Communist foreign policy line.

The developing attitudes of Eastern Europeans that have been cited here include increasing indifference to ideology and growing trends in the direction of economic unreliability and political instability (as far as the USSR is concerned). The first of these "mood patterns" is well articulated by Victor Meier whose comment on Rumania is again applicable to the entire geopolitical region:

> Hardly anyone . . . is interested in thinking very much about questions of Marxist–Leninist ideology. There is no "revisionism," but neither is there any notable official contribution to the enrichment of Marxist theory.[19]

The other two related attitudes presage a growing spirit of defiance and independence among the area's future ruling elites. It seems likely that Gomulka's, Tito's and Kadar's heirs will be much more difficult to

[19] Victor Meier, *op. cit.*, p. 11.

control and keep in line ideologically than the current crop of aging Muscovites and run-down ex-Stalinists. Indications are clear that the once-ambitious integration and annexation plans of the USSR will be increasingly frustrated, contradicted and deflated by future home-grown leaderships in the Danubian–Balkan region. Polycentrism will further accelerate no-longer-so-latent nationalistic tendencies and speed up changes in the USSR, in its former satellites and in its increasingly complex relations with them. The current search for autonomy in all likelihood will continue unabated; and the Eastern European peoples will be able to shore up their national positions vis-à-vis the declining usable power and hegemony of the Soviet Union with growing effectiveness.

However, to balance the picture, it is necessary to indicate that outer limits to such centrifugal polycentrism remain clear and observable in Eastern Europe. The goals of the USSR have an aspect of permanence and constancy with respect to the ex-satellites; while operational techniques and concrete policies may change and fluctuate, these changes—to use Marxist categories—are bound to be of more quantitative than qualitative proportions. There are set and tangible boundaries beyond which the existing and future leaderships of East-Central Europe's Communist societies will not be permitted to move. The ex-satellites remain within the Soviet Union's lines of primary concern—and while internally they may be granted wide latitudes and it may even be expected that Moscow will tolerate considerable erosions in the power of local Communists, it will not permit them to abandon their membership in the bloc anymore than it was willing to see happen in 1956.

Postscript

It is a difficult task to survey the various facets of the turbulent Eastern European political scene as it has evolved in the second half of the 1960s. We shall first consider here some of the major domestic issues which have affected the eight governments of the region, and then turn to the rapidly changing problem areas of foreign policy—both in European and world politics.

Shifting Trends in Domestic Issues

Placed in an "order-of-importance" ranking, three issues have emerged on the domestic scene of the Soviet Union's Eastern European ex-satellites. The first of these can be labelled the problem of *generational change* involving a serious and increasingly ominous confrontation between the aging generation of leaders originally imposed by Joseph Stalin, and a much younger age group of leadership aspirants. The latter represent a different pattern of communism and work toward changing goals in today's political setting. We witness here the development of a "communication gap" between the revolutionary generation of Stalinist stalwarts and a distinctly nonrevolutionary and more technically oriented, ideologically more neutral group of the subelites. Even if a direct confrontation will prove to be incompatible with the rigid framework of modern communism, the generational change (or the struggle to effect such a change) is bound to contribute to the further growth of a spirit of mass alienation widely observable in most Eastern European societies. Such alienation takes several obvious and concrete forms: it involves a sharp dichotomy between *"them"* (a distant, alien, unfriendly regime, an *apparat* of Party and government) and *"us"* (the defenseless, innocent and well-meaning citizen), pitting two conflicting sets of interests against one another and urging people toward an economic and moral exploitation of state and nation.

More specifically, stealing, even looting of state property, juvenile delinquency, widespread drunkenness, a high degree of absenteeism as well as loafing at work or damaging government equipment are among the sociologically more evident symptoms of economic alienation. Popular impatience and frustration with lagging economic outputs as compared to the glittering promises of the regimes' five- and seven-year plans have greatly jeopardized the political standing, prestige and domestic accomplishments of such inefficiently struggling Communist hierarchies as those of Poland and Hungary.

In effect, this complex of popular feelings expresses itself eventually in a more or less violently anti-Soviet form of economic nationalism which had always lain dormant below the surface of Balkan politics. In recent years this phenomenon has been exacerbated not only by the mistakes, wrong policies and economic misallocations of the home-front but also by the welter of contradictory and often irrational Soviet directives (*ukazes*) which had emanated from Moscow under Khrushchev's temperamental and unpredictable leadership. Soviet economic setbacks, particularly during the 1961–1965 period, also contributed to the proliferation of economic complaints and suspicions on the part of ex-satellite societies. The widening impact of the Sino–Soviet dispute further undermined popular confidence in the once-monolithic leadership of the USSR.

Economic nationalism, currently one of the most powerful motivating phenomena in Eastern Europe,[20] is the result of two factors working in close combination:

1. Certain specifically local circumstances (dissatisfaction with their own and Soviet leaders, and so forth, mentioned above), triggering fundamental and long-term popular complaints.

2. A set of globally existing conditions, namely the sweep of a worldwide "revolution of rising expectations" which has emerged in Eastern Europe in recent years in a vigorous fashion similar to that of Africa, the Middle East, and Latin America. While the Eastern European variant is generically similar to such economic waves of revolutions everywhere else, it has certain special and distinctive features of its own since it is, after all, an economic revolt under the umbrella of Communist ideology. By definition communism and genuine popular mass aspirations conflict rather than coincide in purpose or ultimate fulfilment.[21]

Last, but certainly not least, we must stress the myriad psychological implications of a widespread popular feeling of ideological "fatigue" or "erosion" which has strikingly emerged throughout this region in recent years. People are desperately tired of Marxism–Leninism and genuinely sick of the incessant din of daily propaganda surrounding Communist doctrinal pontifications. The rejection of ideology cannot be frank and open: its results resemble rather that sentiment of "internal emigration" which had characterized certain anti-Nazi German intellectuals in the early Hitler period. It is well-articulated in an article in *Neues Deutschland* by a leading East German poet, Paul Wiens, who is also chairman of the Berlin chapter of the DDR's "Writers' League,":

> This does not mean, however, that I would like to end every poem with the formulation: "Besides, I approve of our society!" *Tenaciously repeated declarations of creed and love,* even if expressed in imaginative variations, *soon get on everyone's nerves.*[22]

[20] This pattern of nationalism has inevitably produced economic changes in Eastern Europe. "The Year of Economic Reform" throughout Communist Europe was 1965; it is ably analyzed by Gregory Grossman in his "Economic Reforms: A Balance Sheet," *Problems of Communism,* Nov.–Dec., 1966, pp. 43–55.

[21] This brief summary cannot encompass all the variations on the theme of Eastern European nationalism. Of the noneconomic patterns, we must forcefully distinguish between religious and political nationalisms which have also been age-old characteristics of the Balkan–Danubian scene, but have come into their own again only recently—with a weakening of the fabric of an alien-imposed ideological system. In effect, there seems to be a direct correlation between the deterioration of a central, controlling authority and the slow re-emergence of native political forces and endemic socioeconomic drives.

[22] See *Neues Deutschland,* Sept. 18, 1966, as analyzed by Dorothy Miller, "The First Annual Conference of the East German Writers' League," *Research Department Bulletin, Radio Free Europe,* Nov. 9, 1966, pp. 2–3 (emphasis added).

These reactions are not confined to the urban white-collar intelligentsia, but are symptomatic also of the more youthful next generation and of such other significant categories as the skilled industrial workers and the rising group of non-Communist technocrats who have come to occupy important positions in economic life. Silence, boredom, apathy, indifference and attitudes of remoteness from the torturous daily battles of ideological—or partisan—politics are some of the emotional variations on this popular theme.

Changing Problems in Foreign Policy

In this context the continuing impact of the Sino–Soviet dispute and a relatively new East–West dialogue are among the fundamental forces shaping the current Eastern European political scene.

During the first five-to-six years of its emergence into the open, the disruptive conflict between the two Communist giants has had a threefold political influence on the states of Eastern Europe. Specifically, it presented these countries with the following alternatives:

1. To support Communist China unequivocally to the point of precipitating an open break with the USSR. This dubious choice was made only by Albania which severed relations with the Soviet Union in the 1960–1961 period;

2. To gain an area of political maneuvers and material advantages by playing off one of the major ideological antagonists against the other. Attempted in a modest way by several of the Eastern European countries, this alternative was exploited only by Rumania which has played the bribery-bargaining-exploitation game with acrobatic skill and great national satisfaction.

3. Meanwhile, the majority of Eastern Europe's ex-satellites chose the course of pledging complete loyalty to the USSR in the hope of gaining sizeable political rewards and economic concessions thereby. Although Bulgaria has been the most loyal to the Soviet Union, Hungary, East Germany, Poland and Czechoslovakia have certainly echoed this policy in its military, economic and diplomatic aspects, insisting in turn on a "most favored satellite" treatment from the Muscovite leadership. By now all of these countries, except Albania, have either directly or indirectly profited from the Communist camp's internecine power struggle.

Finally, certain new East–West stirrings must be recorded in the expectation that a massive *rapprochement* between the two may alter the future course of European and world politics. Theoretically the lines of approach were generously drawn in President Johnson's New York speech of October 7, 1966, which stressed a theme of flexibility in Western approaches to the Communist East and talked specifically in terms of "bridge building" and "peaceful engagement." In actual practice, however, both the German Federal Republic and France took much fuller advantage of the increasingly liberalized atmosphere of Eastern Europe. In trade policies, cultural exchange and even in formal diplomatic relations Chancellor Kiesinger's coalition government, and in commercial and political matters General de Gaulle's Fifth Republic successfully undertook the widening of existing bridges as well as the vigorous construction of new ones. These bold and important Western initiatives not only helped to weaken Moscow's control over the once-homogeneous Communist nations of Eastern Europe, but also tended to accelerate the latent mellowing processes and polycentric trends typical of the new European communisms everywhere.

March, 1967

SELECTED BIBLIOGRAPHY

Bartsch, Gunter, "Die Kommunisten und das Generationsproblem," *Osteuropa,* vol. XIV, no. 5, May, 1964, pp. 329–340. An interesting and useful summary.

Bromke, Adam (ed.), *The Communist States At the Crossroads: Between Moscow and Peking* (New York: Praeger, 1965). A carefully edited, but somewhat uneven symposium examining several aspects of the Sino–Soviet dispute. The best contributions deal with Poland, Hungary, and Czechoslovakia.

Brzezinski, Zbigniew, *Alternative to Partition: For a Broader Conception of America's Role in Europe* (New York: McGraw-Hill for the Council on Foreign Relations, 1965). An able theoretical analysis stressing not only an "East Europe in Disarray," but also the various alternatives available to American foreign policy.

Current History, "East Europe in Flux," special issue, Mar., 1965.

Dulles, E. L. and R. D. Crane (eds.), *Detente, Cold War Strategies in Transition* (New York: Praeger for the Center for Strategic Studies, George-

Note: In an attempt to keep this Bibliography both up to date as well as selective, only the most recent additions to a rapidly mushrooming Eastern European political literature were cited here. The author assumes that students will be aware of an consult such permanent classics in this field as Brzezinski's *The Soviet Bloc: Unity and Conflict* (Cambridge: Harvard University Press, 1960) and F. A. Vali's *Rift and Revolt in Hungary* (Cambridge: Harvard University Press, 1961). The polycentric nature of contemporary communism also dictates the addition of works with a broad perspective of world communism, *including* the recent evolution of the ex-satellties (*see* London, Lowenthal, Wolfe, etc.).

town University, 1965). A broad-based and interesting symposium illuminating many facets of the contemporary Eastern European scene. Particularly relevent are contributions by Klaus Mehnert ("Political Evolution in the Communist World") and E. L. Dulles ("Berlin—Barometer of Tension").

Fischer-Galati, Stephen (ed.), *Eastern Europe in the Sixties* (New York: Praeger, 1963). Disregarding the country-by-country approach and concentrating instead on a topical outline, this book deals with social, economic and political projections for the 1960s. Useful background reading.

Gyorgy, Andrew, *Communism in Perspective* (Boston: Allyn and Bacon, 1964). An introductory survey of the broad and general field of communism. Chapters 4, 6, and 11 offer materials relevant to the current political scene in Eastern Europe.

Jacobs, Dan N. (ed.), *The New Communist Manifesto, and Related Documents* (New York: Harper Torchbooks, 3rd ed., rev. 1965). A collection of documents, with particular relevance to Eastern Europe in sections dealing with E. Kardelj's *Socialism and War* as well as with an edited version of the CPSU letter of July 14, 1963.

Kousoulas, George D., *Revolution and Defeat: The Story of the Greek Communist Party* (London: Oxford, 1965). A fascinating and microscopic survey of the ups and downs of Greek communism. Many facets of this case study bear direct relevance to Eastern Europe, but particularly chapters 13, 14, 16, and 18. A well-written and painstaking study.

London, Kurt L., "Soviet Strengths and Weaknesses," in D. M. Abshire and R. V. Allen (eds.), *National Security: Political, Military, and Economic Strategies in the Decade Ahead* (New York: Praeger, 1963). A careful survey of Soviet politics and society with numerous useful cross-references to current Eastern European politics.

Lowenthal, Richard, "The Prospects for Pluralistic Communism," *Dissent,* Winter 1965. A brilliant, incisive study by one of the foremost students of contemporary world communism.

Problems of Communism, "New Winds in Eastern Europe, vol. XIII, no. 3, May–June, 1964, pp. 4–34.

Problems of Communism, "The Iron Curtain today," vol. XIII, no. 6, Nov.–Dec., 1964, pp. 3–31.

Problems of Communism, "Ten Years After Stalin," vol. XII, no. 2, Mar.–Apr., 1963, pp. 1–104.

Rush, Myron, *Political Succession in the USSR* (New York: Columbia University Press, 1965). An able review of the Soviet's major succession crises. In view of the similarity of succession problems in Eastern Europe, chapters IV, VII, and IX are of particular significance for the better understanding of Communist politics in the Danubian–Balkan area.

Stern, Carola, *Ulbricht: A Political Biography* (New York: Praeger, 1965). A lively and well-translated biography by one of the foremost students of East German communism. As a revealing portrait of a Stalinist *apparatchik,* it is invaluable for a further understanding of the Rakosis, Paukers and Gottwalds of the 1944–1956 period.

Wolfe, Bertram D., *Marxism: One Hundred Years in the Life of a Doctrine* (New York: Dial, 1965). A spectacular review of the major aspects of Marxism after one hundred years of practice. For students of Eastern Europe, Parts V ("The Flaw in the Foundation") and VI ("Problems of Utopia") are the most noteworthy. A brilliantly written study.

7

Communism in Latin America

Federico G. Gil

HISTORICAL conditions have countenanced the ascent of the Communist movement in Latin America. This region is the scene of two simultaneous revolutions—an *industrial* and a *social*—which have brought widespread hostility to traditional conditions and archaic structures and the demand for a rapidly rising standard of living. The growing impatience of the peoples of Latin America with the traditional order has been amply exploited by the Communists.

Among the social and economic characteristics of Latin America are: the predominantly agricultural nature of its economies; semi-feudal land holding patterns and class differences sharply defined by racial distinctions; obsolete methods of exploitation of land and labor; and an exceedingly low income of the rural workers, many of whom live at subsistence level. The postwar population explosion, which has given the region the highest birth rate in the world, has demanded a huge expansion of the economy merely to maintain the present living standards. In recent years, thousands of rural workers have fled to the cities causing a spectacular increase in the urban population. The rural worker's flight to urban industry, although it often has not brought him any substantial improvement in his lot, has nevertheless given him new social and economic freedom, liberating him from bondage to the landholding class. His increased independence and his feeling of unrest when transplanted to the cities, among other things, have been important to the development of the Communist movement; for the Latin American social revolution is basically an *urban* phenomenon.

The social revolution in Latin America has had four basic components: nationalism, economic development, change in the social structure, and political democracy. The social segments most active in this revolution have been the working class—both white collar and manual—and the emerging industrial and commercial middle class. As a distinguished student of Latin American communism has pointed out, the Communists have tried with relative success to use each and all of the ingredients of the social revolution in furthering their own movement![1] Then, in the middle 1950s, a new element was added when the Soviet Union launched its economic offensive among the underdeveloped nations, and the Communists were able to present the socialist camp as an alternate source of technical assistance.

Latin American nationalism is essentially antiimperialism. Its manifestations are chiefly directed against the United States—originally against that nation's interference in the internal affairs of the Latin American countries (particularly of those in the Caribbean region) and later, against the economic subordination resulting from United States ownership of key elements in the Latin American economies and the influence of foreign private business interests.

Aware of the dangers of narrowly based economies, and eager to diversify their economic activities and to develop manufacturing industries, the Latin American countries, particularly after World War II, engaged in an almost obsessive drive for economic development, which turned government into an active participant in the economic process. One important consequence of this development was the strengthening of the political role of the urban against the rural elements.

Demands for restructuring of society manifested themselves principally in two forms: the cry for drastic changes in the landholding system and the move to organize the urban worker. The development of trade union movements and the introduction of extensive social-labor legislation became an integral part of the transformation of society. Although the rural worker has as yet benefitted little if at all from this legislation and has scarcely been unionized, it is likely that pressure from this sector will constantly increase. In any case, agrarian reform has at least drawn the rural masses into the political and economic life of the nation. The growth of a strong middle class in some countries has also had profound effect on the social and political structures. Its rise has been phenomenal in countries such as Mexico, Chile, Argentina, and Uruguay. In others, it is still slowly emerging and, consequently, the shift in class relations has yet to occur.

[1] Robert J. Alexander, *Communism in Latin America* (New Brunswick, N.J.: Rutgers University Press, 1957) pp. 6–11.

Lastly, the struggle for political democracy is an important element in the Latin American social revolution. The masses, with profound effect in every country of Latin America, are demanding a greater share in the political process and effective safeguards of their political freedoms. On the other hand, it is obvious, however, that there is a significant danger that social and political ferment may be diverted into totalitarian channels. And here it is noteworthy that the Communists have systematically endeavored to capture the leadership of every dissident sociopolitical group.

The Latin American Communists have consistently sought to utilize all the basic components of the social revolution and have often managed successfully to identify themselves with the movement for reform. They have portrayed themselves as the only authentic nationalists. They have embraced anti-imperialism and have deliberately resuscitated the half-buried ghost of anti-Yankeeism; they have been ardent defenders of industrialization while spreading the notion that the United States has deliberately frustrated Latin American economic development. The Communist argument that in a world dominated by two superpowers, it is not in the best interest of Latin America to identify itself exclusively with one of these nations and to deny itself access to the experience of the other simply because it has a different political system, is powerfully appealing to many Latin Americans. The Communists have also been in the first ranks of those seeking to change the traditional social organization. They have assumed leadership of trade union movements; they have repeatedly appealed to suppressed racial groups; they have agitated for agrarian reform. The Communists have also attempted to depict themselves as supporters of the principles of political democracy and civil freedoms. In short, at every point they have aimed at establishing an identification with the sweeping tide of the Latin American social revolution.

Although the overriding concern of most Latin Americans for rapid development and change was certainly not caused by Communist stimulation, the Communists have been able, nevertheless, to associate themselves in the popular mind with this almost universal sentiment. Yet their successes have been limited, due at least in part to the fact that they have had to compete with some indigenous reform movements which, at least in some countries, have been able to direct revolutionary ferment in a democratic direction. The attraction of these competing mass movements, which give forceful and dramatic presentation to national and socioeconomic problems, is that they seek to lead the masses into change without sacrificing in the process the personal freedoms which are treasured by the highly individualistic peoples of Hispanic America.

Thus, in Mexico, for example, the Revolution of 1910 has continued to undercut the appeal of communism to the Mexican masses. Communist attempts over more than three decades to attract followers have been ineffective. The Mexican national character with its characteristically all-virulent nationalism has refused to tolerate outside interference in its revolution. The attempts to unify the three Communist Parties in Mexico, a score of front groups, and numerous infiltrated cells in non-Communist organizations have only led to further bickering and frustration.[2] With the exception of Cuba, the non-Communist parties of Latin America have, so far, been able to retain the support of the majority of the electorate. They can be expected to continue, however, to receive this support only as long as they can satisfy—or provide the hope that they will be able to satisfy—the expectations of the great mass of Latin Americans.

The Development of Latin American Communism

As in the case of the international Communist movement, Latin American communism has also passed through a series of distinct stages. Professor Robert J. Alexander divides the historical development of the Communist movement before 1956 into seven periods, and suggests that Latin American communism has experienced each of these phases.[3] The first period extended from the founding of the Comintern to Lenin's death in 1924. The second, covering the events from the death of Lenin to approximately 1929, included the establishment of collectivization and industrialization in the Soviet Union. The third phase which extended to 1935, the year in which the Seventh and last Congress of the Comintern was held, was noted for the self-imposed isolation of the Communists from other movements. It was succeeded by the period of the Popular Front which ended with the signing of the Nazi-Soviet agreement and the outbreak of World War II. The Stalin-Hitler Pact era was of brief duration, terminating with the German invasion of the USSR. This next period was marked by collaboration with any groups which could assist in the struggle against the Nazis and continued until

[2] For an analysis of the Communist lack of success in Mexico, see Karl M. Schmitt, *Communism in Mexico: A Study of Political Frustration* (Austin: University of Texas Press, 1965).

[3] Robert J. Alexander, *op. cit.*, pp. 18–19. For a detailed country-by-country account of the rise of Communist Parties, see Rollie E. Poppino, *International Communism in Latin America* (New York: The Free Press, 1964) pp. 55–95.

shortly after the end of the war. It in turn was succceded by the seventh, the "Cold War," period characterized by hostility toward the United States and the West. Following Stalin's death still another, the eighth period, emerged, the beginning of which was signalled by Nikita Khrushchev's "Secret Speech" to PC XX of the CPSU.

In the beginning phase, the Communist International attracted attention in Latin America from among such diverse groups as anarchists, Socialists, the syndicalists, the military leaders of the Mexican Revolution and middle-class revolutionaries. However, the Comintern's famous "Twenty-one Points" (to which any party wishing to adhere to the International had to agree) and the early decision to permit affiliation by political parties had a dampening effect. In Chile and Uruguay, for example, the Socialists decided to accept the "Twenty-one Points," but in Argentina, they refused, and in several countries the anarcho-syndicalists decided to join a new anarcho-syndicalist trade union organization called the International Working Men's Association.

During the second period of Comintern history, intense internal struggles developed among Latin American Communist groups, as in other parts of the world. These differences arose essentially from personal rivalries among leaders. The struggles often merged with the great battle then taking place within the CPSU, Latin American leaders taking the side of one Russian faction or the other. However, in this connection, it is significant that there were no cases in which a strong dissident Party emerged. Efforts to develop Trotskyism in Chile and Cuba were short-lived, and the Right Opposition led in Russia by Bukharin was also of little or no import in Latin America. It should be noted that the Titoist current in the 1940s also failed to score any success on the Latin American scene. No Titoist party was organized and not a single important Latin American Communist leader sided with the Yugoslav chieftain.

The third period, that of extreme Communist isolation from other political groups, appeared clearly in the Latin American movement. Perhaps, as Alexander suggests, although this is debatable, the Latin American tradition of political violence made the extremism of the third period more acceptable there than it was in countries with stabler political systems, such as the United States and Great Britain.[4] Whatever the reasons, the fact is that during this period, the Latin American Communists remained completely isolated, by choice, from all other radical and working-class parties. In Chile, for example, the Communists even opposed the short lived "Socialist Republic" of June, 1932.

In contrast, the "Popular Front" period witnessed many collabora-

[4] Robert J. Alexander, *op. cit.*, p. 22.

tionist activities by Communists all over the hemisphere. In Chile, Mexico, Brazil, and elsewhere they were actively seeking alliances with groups representative of the reformist, moderate left. Often, as was the case in Cuba and Brazil, the Communists also made alliances with dictators (Fulgencio Batista and Getulio Vargas). Such alliances with dictatorial regimes were often profitable for the Communists because they thus gained a measure of freedom for their activities in the trade union movement in exchange for supporting the dictator. The opportunism of the Latin American Communist Parties at the time was indeed extraordinary. Frequently they intentionally split into two apparently opposed factions, one of which joined the dictatorial government while the other allied itself with the opposition. Once the political scene changed, however, the two factions invariably reunited.

Through the policy of collaboration, the Communist Parties in Latin America acquired political significance for the first time and began to enlist substantial following from among the workers and intellectuals. This period of flourishing activity came to an abrupt end when the Latin American Communist leadership was forced to support the Soviet–German Pact, therefore becoming political untouchables once again. However, their isolation was brief, and, with the entry of the Soviet Union into the War, the period of greatest Communist prosperity began.

Elsewhere, the Communists in Latin America worked with democratic groups of the most diverse coloration, even with Catholics, and also resumed the previously fruitful policy of alliance with dictators, in Ecuador, Nicaragua, Cuba, Brazil and the Dominican Republic. Their efforts to penetrate the trade union movement were notably successful, their influence among the workers becoming greater than ever before. In 1944, the Communists constituted the majority of the Executive Committee of the Confederation of Workers of Latin America. There were Communists elected to the national legislature in some ten Latin American countries; in Cuba, Chile, and Ecuador they were appointed to cabinet positions and participated in the formulation of government policies. A great asset of the Latin American Communists during this period was the new respect for the USSR that developed as a consequence of the heroic resistance of the Soviet people during World War II.

The end of World War II and the advent of the Cold War brought about a changed political climate in Latin America, as well. Communism shifted to the advocacy of nationalism and violent hostility toward the United States. Successive governments in the Latin American countries tightened up in face of actual and threatened Communist advances. In public opinion, in the political arena and the trade union movement, the Communists lost much of the ground which they had gained during World War II. Their only notable success in the first decade of the postwar period was in Guatemala, where, with the advent of a major social revolution which they succeeded in having identified with themselves, they gained by 1953 an influential voice in the circles of the revolutionary government. Their influence, however, was temporary, ending with the downfall of the Arbenz regime the following year.

Two observations must be noted at this point. The first is that, throughout its history, the Latin American Communist movement has followed the general pattern established by the international Communist movement. Generally speaking, the Latin American Communists have been an integral part of the international movement and they have always mirrored with exceptional fidelity the changes in ideology, the internal dissensions, and the shifting strategy and tactics which have characterized that movement. However, it must also be pointed out that often these Parties have been allowed much greater maneuverability by the international Communist leadership than their European counterparts. The reasoning behind such freedom of movement was obviously a lack of concern for Latin America on the part of the Soviet Union, particularly during the "socialism in a single country" period. Also Latin American Communists were not seriously expected to seize power, since their continent was so conspicuously under the preponderant power and influence of the United States.

A second reflection is that Latin America communism, having always depended for its mass support, at least until recent years, on the urban industrial proletariat, has followed the Western European pattern of development rather than the Asiatic one. Although the Latin American Communists have been consistent champions of agrarian reform, the practices of using rural guerilla armies and recruiting membership among the peasants were not utilized by their movement until after the triumph of the Cuban Revolution of Fidel Castro. Communism's basic support has been consistently concentrated throughout the years among the urban workers and the intellectual middle class. The doctrinal point that "objective conditions" were not yet ripe for revolution has hitherto enabled the Latin American Communists to follow more moderate policies in matters of collaboration and infiltration. As is often said, in practice, although perhaps not in theory, Latin American Communists are less sectarian than their counterparts in most other areas of the world.

Despite the fact that, generally speaking, Latin American communism has mirrored developments in the international movement, the repercussions in Latin America to the momentous events which shook international communism in 1956 were few and not highly significant. When PC XX determined the downgrading of Stalin and the cult of personality and repealed the two fundamental Leninist doctrines of the inevitability of war and violent revolution, replacing them with the "Peaceful Coexistence" (known in Latin America as the "Peaceful Road") policy, Latin American Party reactions were slow in coming and, when manifested, took the form of rather mild and cautious criticisms of the Stalin era. Although rumors of impending purges in some of the Parties were not lacking, none materialized; there were no cases of soul-searching or deep internecine crisis such as beset some of the European Communist Parties. More than one Latin American Communist Party had been practicing the policy of the "Peaceful Road" for many years already.

The impact of PC XX can perhaps be best illustrated by describing the way Mexican and Chilean Communists reacted to events. In Mexico, the local Communists gave no public indication of their reaction for almost two months, although the matter was widely discussed in Party circles. Silence was broken by a series of articles on the Congress published in the local Communist press. Many of the articles were translations of items taken from Soviet bloc publications. It was not until June, 1956, that the Mexican Communist Party (PCM) Central Committee went into session to draw up a formal Party resolution on the February events, and it was not until the following month that the resolution was published. In essence, the document stated that both Stalin and the PCM had committed errors in propagating the cult of the personality and promised changes in the PCM. The other Mexican Communist faction, the Socialist People's Party (PPS.),[5] reacted in identical fashion. After a silence of several months its leader, Vicente Lombardo Toledano, spoke of the wisdom of collective leadership, the necessity of averting war and the possibility of achieving socialism by various roads. In short, Mexican Communists accepted without question or opposition the findings of the Congress and the interpretation of them by their Party leaders who, obviously, tried in every case to identify their ideas and actions with those of the CPSU.[6]

[5] In 1948, Vicente Lombardo Toledano, the influential labor leader, was expelled from the PCM subsequent to his proposal that a new party of the left be formed under the auspices of the Federation of Mexican Workers (CTM). The same year he formed the People's Party (Partido Popular—PP). In 1960, Lombardo announced a reorientation of the PP toward Marxism–Leninism and a change in the name to the Socialist People's Party (PPS). A splinter group of the PCM led to the merging of the POCM with Lombardo's PPS in June of 1963.

[6] Karl M. Schmitt, *op. cit.*, pp. 207–210.

The case of Chile was somewhat similar. It appears that first the Chilean Party leadership failed to grasp the importance of the new Soviet doctrine of the "Peaceful Road," and almost dismissed it as a continuation of what their own Party had practiced in Chile for over twenty years. In fact, they maintained that the possibility of peaceful revolutionary transition in their own country had been planted more by changes in the world situation and by Chilean conditions and national characteristics than by PC XX.[7] For the next four years, the actions of PC XX were given, if any, only scanty attention; it was not until *1960, a much more important year than 1956 for Latin American communism,* that the doctrine of the "Peaceful Road" turned into a vital issue for the Chilean Communists[8] when the Sino–Soviet conflict became a subject of official debate in the Communist world.

The Cuban Revolution and the Communists

By this time, however, another momentous event had taken place. The Castro Revolution, in Cuba, a country whose alliance with and economic subordination to the United States had long been taken for granted in Latin America, as elsewhere, broke the traditional framework in which United States and Latin American foreign policies were formulated and shaped.

As far as international politics are concerned, the impact of the Cuban Revolution was twofold. First, Cuba's incorporation into the Soviet bloc shattered the traditional pattern of power relationships and introduced the balance-of-power system into the Western Hemisphere. This system had been traditionally excluded from the continent by three factors: (1) the Monroe Doctrine that prevented the intervention of non-American powers in hemispheric affairs; (2) the development of inter-American regional systems based on the rule of internal law and on the principle of the juridical equality of nations; and (3) the great power advantage which the United States held over her weaker Latin American neighbors. This traditional pattern of relationships was broken when Cuba sought and received help from the Soviet Union. A second effect of the Cuban Revolution was the fact that a small country, traditionally dependent on its northern neighbor, had successfully challenged the influence, the might, and the prestige of the preponderant power of

[7] *El Partido Comunista de Chile y el Movimiento Comunista Internacional: Documentos e Informes Emanados de Plenos y Congresos del Partido Comunista de Chile* (Santiago, Chile: Empresa Horizonte, 1964) p. 14.

[8] Ernst Halperin, *Nationalism and Communism in Chile* (Cambridge, Mass.: The MIT Press, 1965) pp. 59–62.

the Western Hemisphere.[9] The problem created by the countervailing force of Cuba's increasingly radical path against the "Peaceful Road" policy soon became crucial for all the Communist Parties of Latin America.

Dismissed at first by the Communists as a "putschist" and a bourgeois adventurer, Castro, as a result of his amazing victory, became a popular hero throughout Latin America. Soon he was to claim for himself the leadership of the Latin American Social Revolution and call for the conversion of the Andes into another Sierra Maestra.

By its association with the Cuban Revolution, a communism "that had become stale and bogged down in humdrum trade union activities and sterile drawing room debate has been rejuvenated by the influx of thousands of enthusiastic new activists."[10] Nevertheless, the relationship has been an inexhaustible source of problems and dilemmas for the Latin American Communists.

Before examining those aspects which have been detrimental to the Communist cause, it is necessary to explain certain peculiarities of the Cuban phenomenon. Although the Cuban Revolution could be classified as "Leninist" in type, its uniqueness has been noted by students of revolutions. Leninist revolutions occur when Communist Parties are able to exploit popular discontent caused by economic inequities. Some conditions such as the predominance of agrarian workers, archaic social structures, a weak and ineffective middle class, disillusionment with representative democracy, disruption caused by an incipient industrialization, and so forth, must be present to cause an upheaval from which the Communists can profit. A keen analyst of the Cuban Revolution has shown that this concept was not applicable to Cuba.[11] Although certainly poor, Cuba enjoyed a higher standard of living than most of the Latin American countries. Social and economic inequalities were also less pronounced than in most countries in the region, and the agricultural system, though it was based on monoculture and dominated by the sugar cane industry and latifundia, was not feudal. The middle sectors were numerous in Cuban society and were steadily increasing. Representative democracy was popular and highly valued. In addition, the Cuban Communist Party never constituted more than a small minority (10

[9] Federico G. Gil, "Latin America: Social Revolution and U.S. Foreign Policy" in Marian D. Irish (ed.), *World Pressures on American Foreign Policy* (Englewood Cliffs, N.J.: Prentice-Hall, 1964) p. 149.

[10] Ernst Halperin, "Castroism: Challenge to the Latin American Communists," *Problems of Communism,* vol. XII, no. 5, Sept.–Oct., 1963, p. 10.

[11] Boris Goldenberg, "The Cuban Revolution: An Analysis," *Problems of Communism,* vol. XII, no. 5, Sept—Oct., 1963.

percent of the vote in free elections) of the population, and had always accommodated itself to the prevailing political system.

In 1959, the Communist leadership on the island described the Castro movement as a "progressive, democratic, antiimperialist revolution led by the petite bourgeoisie," that is to say, as a fundamentally bourgeois nationalistic revolution. This Communist assertion would be difficult to demonstrate, for most observers agree that, given the peculiar conditions of Cuba, there was no basic conflict between a landed oligarchy and the bourgeois capitalists—both groups being mixed and intimately related to each other. The bourgeoisie needed no revolution to come to power. Similarly, there was no fundamental conflict between imperialistic interests and the Cuban bourgeoisie.

The argument used by those who maintain that the Cuban Revolution was a peasant or a proletarian revolution does not withstand serious examination either. The peasants formed only a small minority of the total population and peasant unrest characteristic of the Mexican and the Bolivian Revolutions was practically nonexistent. As far as the proletariat was concerned, the workers as a whole, were fairly content with their economic lot, and they were perhaps the most passive segment of the population during the struggle against dictator Batista. The Marxist interpretation advanced by others, according to which the Cuban Revolution, in its initial phase, was essentially a "popular" revolution, to be equated with the Paris Commune of 1871, is not convincing either, since relatively speaking there was little active participation by the masses in the Cuban upheaval.[12]

Much more convincing than the above explanation is the one given by Goldenberg, who suggests that, if one searches for a social basis for the revolution it can only be found among the large conglomeration of rootless persons in Cuban society—unemployed or underemployed, undisciplined—who had never been able to develop a common consciousness or to form a common political organization. According to him, these are the people who gave something like a social basis to the Cuban Revolution as a whole.[13] Analyzing further the Cuban phenomenon, Goldenberg sees three chief characteristics which distinctively mark its uniqueness: (1) it was initiated and led, not by Communists, but by a charismatic leader; (2) it passed through a "humanist phase" during which the mass of the underprivileged were the recipients of immediate benefits; (3) its transition from the democratic to the totalitarian phase

[12] Jacques Arnault, "Cuba et le Marxisme," *La Nouvelle Critique* (Paris), special issue, 1962, pp. 53–54.

[13] Boris Goldenberg, *op. cit.*, p. 5.

was a continuous, peaceful one, and its leadership remained unchanged. This last peculiarity meant that the revolution, insofar as it was violent (during the armed struggle stage) was not Socialist, and insofar as it was Socialist (in the second stage) was not violent.[14] The change of the democratic into the Socialist revolution was essentially the outcome of the interaction between the personal decisions of the "Maximum Leader" and their consequences.

The Cuban Revolution will always be incomprehensible to those who fail to understand that it is essentially one man's revolution, that every facet of the revolutionary process in Cuba bears the indelible imprint of Fidel Castro's personality. A cunning politician with the true leader's gift for manipulating men, bred by a continent only superficially touched by modern ideologies, Castro was not a Communist, but "a man possesed by the idea of 'justice' and by the notion that his is the instrument chosen to bring it about."[15] At first, he was without an ideology or even a clear program for Cuba, but he eventually came to the conclusion that nothing less than a complete and drastic revolutionary restructuring of the social order would suffice. His ideas developed with the change of circumstances. As more social reforms were promulgated, new and increased resistance to the revolutionary regime developed, and this resistance in turn imposed new decisions which in time rendered any form of capitalism or any system that combined a mixed economy and relations with the United States out of the question. Inexorably, these decisions forced Castro, domestically, to seek support from the Communists, a docile minority with a clear program to offer, and externally, drove him to increasing dependence on the Soviet Union. Castro's identification with the Soviet bloc was determined by the above circumstances and by shrewd opportunism; it was not dictated by ideological considerations.

Actually, Castro's doctrine of absolute justice is difficult to reconcile with the tenets of orthodox Marxism, which argue that communism will rise not because it is just, but because it is the highest stage in the process of socioeconomic development. As if this was not a rich enough source of ideological friction, there was added an even more serious heresy: the doctrine, contributed by "Ché" Guevara to Cuban revolutionary ideology, which maintained that guerrilla warfare waged in the countryside primarily with peasant support was the main instrument of social revolution in Latin America. Guevara's theory clearly was

[14] *Ibid.*, pp. 5–7.

[15] Ernst Halperin, *"Castroism: Challenge to the Latin American Communists,"* p. 10.

counter to the Moscow version of orthodox Marxism–Leninism which holds that the urban proletariat is the main revolutionary force and that the revolution cannot take place until this class has rallied to the Communist banner and become the spearhead of the struggle. Another heretical aspect of Guevara's doctrine denied the need to wait for a "revolutionary situation." According to Guevara, such conditions can be created by guerrilla wars. Thus, the Soviet ideological monopoly was boldly, if unconsciously, challenged by the Cuban revolutionaries. According to the new Castroite doctrine, "it is not necessary to wait until all conditions for making revolution exist; the insurrection can create them."[16]

Acceptance of such a doctrine by the Latin American Communists would have meant a complete change in their traditional policies and tactics. As has been seen, the principle that conditions for revolution were not ripe in Latin America, has hitherto served as a justification for the pursuance of moderate policies of accommodation and acceptance of the prevailing rules of the political game. If the Latin American Communists were to accept the Castroite thesis and resort to violent guerrilla tactics, they would stand in danger of losing the advantages gained through collaboration with other political groups, including the security of their position as members of a legal party.[17] Without even openly expressing disapproval, the Latin American Communist leadership chose, with one exception (in Venezuela), to reject the strategy advocated by the Cuban leaders, and to continue the traditional "soft" policy of infiltration. This did not mean, however, that there were not groups in almost every country of Latin America, either outside or within the Communist Party, which ardently advocated Guevara's thesis. They did exist, even though they were denounced by the Party leadership as "adventurers" and "dogmatists."

To continue with the problems created for Latin American Communism by Castro's triumph, that victory ultimately led to serious rifts between the new Castroite elements and the old-guard leaders. No one can doubt, that in Cuba at least, Fidel Castro had remained in undisputed control, first of the new United Party of the Socialist Revolution (PURS, Partido Único de la Revolución Socialista), and later, of the new Communist Party of Cuba. Castro let the old-guard Communists build the skeleton of the new ruling Party and then assumed command himself, disbanding the old Communist organization (Partido Socialista Popular),

[16] Ernesto Guevara, *La Guerra de Guerrillas* (Havana: Ediciones Minfar, 1960) p. 15.

[17] *Ibid.*, pp. 11–13.

disputing its leadership and relegating the old guard Communists to insignificant or secondary positions in the power structure. Not more than half the eighty thousand members of the new PCC, if that many, can be regarded as disciplined Communists.

Elsewhere in Latin America, Castroite nationalists seem to have gained control of the Communist Party itself, while in Venezuela and other countries, an open rift or at least strained relationships were created between the "orthodox" Communists and the Castroites. Beginning in 1960, numerous "fidelista" groups appeared in almost every Latin American country, many of them as leftist wings of the established nationalist-democratic mass parties. Among the most significant were, in Venezuela, the MIR (Movimiento de Izquierda Revolutionaria) and a faction of URD (Democratic Republican Union), and in Peru, a segment of the *apristas* (Alianza Popular Revolucionaria Americana—APRA) which called itself *APRA Rebelde.* In Colombia, a group of dissident members of the Liberal Party formed a Castroite organization; in northeastern Brazil there were Julião's Peasant Leagues; in Chile a powerful faction of the Socialist Party joined in; and in Argentina a left wing of the Peronista movement.

All of these groups were distinguishable by their avowed acceptance of a Marxist–Leninist ideology and their admiration for the Cuban pattern of revolution and socialism. Yet it would be a grievous mistake to consider them simply as adherents to the Communist Party line, or as coparticipants in a vast international Communist plot, because the differences between them and the regular Communists were significant indeed. These groups without exception have maintained an independent position in world affairs and have subordinated themselves to the dictates of neither Moscow or Peking. They have been pro-Soviet or pro-Chinese only to the extent that they have considered it in the best interests of their respective causes to affiliate with the Soviet Union or Communist China. They do not accept the Russian formula of "Peaceful Coexistence," since this policy would necessarily imply reconciliation and adjustment of differences with the United States, which is an abhorrent thought to Latin American extreme nationalists. Their Marxism–Leninism is a peculiar variation, actually having little ideological substance. Rather simplistic in approach, their affinity with the standard Soviet ideology is reduced to acceptance of Marx's concept of capitalist exploitation and of Lenin's theory of imperialism as the final stage of capitalism.[18]

The purpose of the Castroite groups has been to generate and direct

[18] Ernst Halperin, *Nationalism and Communism in Chile, op. cit.,* pp. 10–12.

popular sympathy for the Cuban regime as well as, in some instances, to seek the overthrow of their own governments. In achieving these ends, the Castroites abroad have often received the assistance of the Cuban government. Such assistance has generally taken the form of training facilities and arms furnished to revolutionary bands such as those active in parts of Central America, Venezuela, Colombia, Ecuador, and Peru. However, the failure of these attempts has led the Castro regime to alter its tactics somewhat and to declare that revolution was not exportable, although all the while continuing to provide at least moral support to potential revolutionaries in nearly all of Latin America.

The irony of Castro's espousal of revolution is, as suggested above, that his Cuba is actually a good example not of the violent achievement, but rather of the "peaceful transition" to socialism advocated by Moscow. As one writer has stated, "neither Castro's acquiescence in the Communist takeover of his revolution nor his nonconversion to communism after he had come to power can alter the fact that the transition from non-Communist rule in Cuba was accomplished without major violence."[19]

The Impact of the Sino-Soviet Dispute

The disagreement between the Moscow-brand Communists and the Castroites as to the proper means of bringing revolution to the Latin Americas has been further complicated by the Sino–Soviet dispute. Among the Latin American Communist Parties, the dispute has centered about the same precise point: namely, the methods that should be used by the Latin American Communists to effect the desired social revolution and to impose communism. The Soviet Union, although recognizing that violent revolutions may be inevitable in certain situations, has maintained that the revolutionary objectives may be achieved at less cost and risks if other tactics are employed. However, the policy of "Peaceful Coexistence," has not precluded the Soviet Union from carrying out its own clandestine campaign to supplement the subversive activities conducted by "local" revolutionaries. For its part, Communist China has declared that violence is the most effective, immediate procedure to effect the Communist revolution, and criticizes the policy of "Peaceful Coexistence" on two chief grounds: (1) that "Soviet flexibility" will, in the long run, deprive the Communist movement of the trust and determination needed for an effective revolutionary work; and (2) that the Soviet policy means dangerous and erratic oscillations between risky maneuvers

[19] Rollie Poppino, *op. cit.*, p. 189.

and shameful withdrawals when confronted by the determination of the West.[20] The key to the Chinese formula is armed struggle against imperialism and the integration of an effective united front of the working classes with the peasants and eventually with the petite bourgeoisie and the national bourgeoisie. The Cuban Revolution has served the Chinese well by lending credence to their assertion that violence is the only practical route to power; it has cast doubt on the validity of the Russian doctrine of the "Peaceful Road" for Latin America. In the eyes of the Chinese, Castro's success has proved beyond question that their own experience in seizing power is the appropriate strategy for all revolutionaries in underdeveloped areas, although the similarities between the two revolutions was almost coincidental.

The Chinese position coincides with that of the Castroites—particularly the most extreme ones—on three basic points: rejection of Soviet moves to lessen tensions with the United States; insistence on violent revolutionary struggle as the only realistic way of promoting revolutions anywhere and everywhere; rejection of the Soviet evolutionary formula as a mere excuse to avoid revolutionary action.

In 1960 the Latin American Communists were called upon to give full adherence to the Soviet Union in its feud with the Chinese Communists and to express their support of the Cuban Revolution. In June, delegations from several Latin American Parties attended the Rumanian Party Congress, which served Khrushchev as a forum for presentation of the Russian view; and, in August, fourteen Latin American Party delegations attended the Eighth Congress of the Cuban Party in Havana. The solidarity of the Latin American Parties was further evidenced by the attendance of Communists from all twenty republics at the November Moscow meeting of the eighty-one Communist and Workers' Parties which considered the Sino–Soviet rift. The Latin American leaders were counselled by the Russian and East Europeans to avoid a dogmatic approach to the strategy of revolution and to adopt the road best suited for each country.[21] *Without exception,* Latin American leaders attending the Moscow meeting reaffirmed their loyalty to the Soviet Union, although there was some reluctance and discontent among younger members in a few Parties.

PC XXII of the CPSU in October, 1961, again brought to the fore the Sino–Soviet conflict. Khruschev's open attack on Albania, and thus

[20] Organization of American States, *Report to the Special Consultative Committee on Security,* (Washington, D.C.: OEA/Ser., L/X/II, 7, 11 Dec., 1964) pp. 31–33.

[21] Rollie Poppino, *op. cit.,* pp. 169–170.

on the Chinese position, further deepened the rupture between the two Communist powers and caused almost as much commotion in the Communist camp as PC XX. On this occasion, however, the Soviet leadership, its prestige enhanced by Russian successes in the development of its military strength and in the exploration of space, as well as by other factors, was able and prepared to exercise greater authority than the year before. In addition, survival of the Castro regime in Cuba, seemed to prove particularly to the Latin American Party stalwarts that the Soviet Union was capable of and willing to protect other Communist governments that might emerge in that area.

The reorientation of Soviet foreign policy which followed the October, 1962 missile crisis in Cuba had far-reaching effects upon the thinking of the Latin American Communist Parties. It was clear now that the United States was determined not to allow further expansion of Soviet power in the Western Hemisphere; thus the establishment of another Communist regime in Latin America seemed highly improbable. The main effect of the new Soviet policy to reduce world tension was a renewed emphasis on the part of the Latin American Parties on the traditional policy of tactical alliances with non-Communist groups to pursue limited aims. But an additional effect of the Caribbean crisis was the recurrence of the Peaceful Road controversy within the Party: Could the revolution ever come to power in Latin America by following the Soviet way?

The Cuban crisis further increased the conflict between the Soviet Union and China, as the latter accused the former of timidity, cowardice, and appeasement. This deterioration of relations was brought sharply into focus by open confrontations between Chinese and Soviets at Party congresses in Bulgaria, Hungary, Czechoslovakia, and Italy during November and December, 1962, as well as by the increased Chinese propaganda campaign against the USSR.

Although it is difficult to measure precisely the extent to which Peking's "hard" attitude has gained support among Latin American Communists, it is fairly clear that the Chinese have attracted sufficient following among the most militant members to pose a considerable challenge to continued Soviet predominance. Most of the Party members sympathetic to Peking are young and, by and large, the present Communist leadership in most of the Latin American countries is old and will surely be renovated within the next few years. When this change in the top leadership occurs, it is possible that some of the new leaders may come from among these militant "Pekinese."

Meanwhile, the Chinese Communists have been intensifying their operations in Latin America. Their activities have consisted chiefly of agitation aimed at weakening Moscow's authority within the Communist Parties and other leftist circles. This political and subversive campaign increased noticeably after 1963, when the Chinese publicly declared that Latin America was one of the regions in the world where political Parties that truly represent the proletariat will necessarily arise and those with pro-Chinese sympathies were urged to seize the leadership of their respective Parties. Parallel with this activity, financial support has been given to the Peking adherents and an intensive campaign, of a "cultural" nature, has been aimed at the Communist and intellectual youth. In addition, in 1963–1964, the Chinese initiated serious efforts to increase trade with various Latin American countries, organizing trade fairs and appointing commercial representatives.

The extent to which the Chinese Communists may have succeeded in splintering the Latin American Communist movement is suggested by the table on p. 202.

As seen in the table, internal divisions have taken place in four important countries: Brazil, Bolivia, Chile, and Mexico. In Venezuela the ideological position of the Front of National Liberation (FLN) is not clear although it has utilized the guerrilla tactics and terrorist activities which are part of the strategy advocated by Peking. Peru, Chile, and Brazil all highlight in different ways the difficulties confronted by the pro-Soviet leaders in their ideological struggle with the Peking Communists. In each case it has become increasingly apparent that results of the Soviet's "Peaceful Road" policy are not particularly encouraging. Recent electoral defeats in Chile, inability to influence the adoption of acceptable land reforms in Peru, and a vigorous anti-Communist campaign of governments controlled by the military in Ecuador, Honduras, and Brazil are all viewed by many Communists, including some who still see themselves in Moscow's camp, as a vindication of the "Chinese Way" and a condemnation of the "evolutionist" Soviet line. As far as Cuba is concerned, Castro had been able to maintain an equivocal neutrality *vis-à-vis* the Sino–Soviet conflict until late 1964,[22] when Soviet–Cuban relations reached their low point because of delays in renewing the trade and financial agreements. In November of 1964, a conference of some twenty-two Communist Parties from Latin America, marked a temporary end to the frictions between Castro and the traditional Latin American Commu-

[22] Pablo Piacentini, "China or Russia," *Atlas,* vol. 9, no. 4, Apr., 1965, pp. 208–211. For the events leading up to the open Chinese–Cuban differences, see *The New York Times,* Apr. 27, 1965; Nov. 14, 1965; Jan. 3, 1966; Jan. 9, 1966; Feb. 7, 1966; and Feb. 14, 1966. Also, D. Bruce Jackson, "Whose men in Havana?" *Problems of Communism,* vol. XV, no. 3, May–June, 1966, pp. 1–10.

Country	*Membership*	*Legal Status*	*Position on Sino-Soviet Dispute*
Argentina	45,000	Proscribed, 1959	Pro-Soviet
Bolivia	6,500 (3 parties)	Legal	2 Pro-Soviet 1 Pro-Chinese
Brazil	31,000 (3 parties)	Proscribed, 1947	Open split
Chile	25,000	Legal	Pro-Soviet (Chinese group)
Colombia	11,000	Legal	Pro-Soviet
Costa Rica	300	Proscribed, 1948	Pro-Soviet
Cuba		In power	Equivocal
Dominican Republic	Unknown		Pro-Soviet
Ecuador	2,500	Proscribed, 1963	Internal factions
El Salvador	500	Proscribed, 1956, 1963	Pro-Soviet
Guatemala	1,300	Proscribed, 1956, 1963	Pro-Soviet
Haiti	Unknown	Proscribed, 1957	Pro-Soviet
Honduras	2,400 (2 parties)	Proscribed, 1957	Pro-Soviet
Mexico	50,000 (4 parties)	Legal	Open split
Nicaragua	250	Proscribed, 1945	Pro-Soviet
Panama	400	Proscribed, 1953	Pro-Soviet
Paraguay	3,500	Proscribed, 1936	Open split
Peru	8,500	Proscribed, 1948	Apparently pro-Chinese
Uruguay	10,000	Legal	Pro-Soviet
Venezuela	30,000	"Suspended," 1962	No stand taken

SOURCE: United States Information Agency compilation, cited in Larry Larson, "*Informal Access/Penetration: The Chinese Communists in Latin America*" (unpublished paper, University of North Carolina, Chapel Hill, N.C., 1965).

nist leaders. This conference set the stage for a series of Cuban moves pleasing to Moscow, ranging from the disappearance of "Ché" Guevara to the eventual open rift with China. In March of 1965, Castro denounced the Sino-Soviet rift as detrimental to the small Communist countries. In late 1965, the fading of Chinese–Cuban relations became clear after Guevara's departure.

At the Tricontinental Solidarity Conference held January 3–15, 1966, at Havana, Castro announced a planned cutback in Chinese trade with Cuba. The indications were that China was punishing the Castro regime for its pro-Soviet line-up. The economic and political pressure of the Soviet Union seemed to have convinced Castro that instant revolution was dangerous to push in Latin America. Castro explained that the Chinese move was politically motivated—the Chinese had accused the Cuban Government of trying to improve U.S.–Cuban relations referring specifically to the recent U.S.–Cuban agreement over refugees (November 6, 1965).

Castro's regime took a closer step to an official break with the Chinese in February, 1966. He berated China for its betrayal of the Cuban people's faith; and he further related the late 1965 activities of the Chinese in their attempts to spread anti-Soviet propaganda through Cuban military officers. Most observers agree, however, that in spite of the growing rift over the cutback in Chinese commerce, Castro did not intend to take sides in Sino–Soviet ideological differences. Although Cuba is now more economically dependent upon the USSR, he still advocates the unique character of Cuba's Marxism–Leninism, and it would also appear that both the Chinese and the Russians, after having exhausted all their pressures on Havana have come to accept its neutral stance.

Even in countries where the split within the Communist ranks was not serious, as in Argentina, the Party leadership considered it wise to take a number of measures to neutralize the activities of dissident sections. The expulsion of several members, adopted by the Party Central Committee, was accompanied by decisions authorizing the Party youth organization to conduct an ideological discussion on basic problems existing in the leadership of world communism, and permitting the temporary use of violence on *particular occasions*. In Bolivia, although there is a strong current in favor of violent action, only a few small groups are openly pro-Chinese. However, the Trotskyite Revolutionary Workers' Party (POR) favors the Chinese position, and a few youth groups which are also considered Communist, although they are not formally part of the Communist apparatus, strongly support a violent strategy for gaining power.

In Brazil, the chief dissident Communist faction has founded a separate organization headed by several top leaders who were expelled from the regular Party for having challenged the leadership of the well-known Latin American Communist chieftain, Luis Carlos Prestes. The new Party has about 1,000 members and is stronger than the regular organization in the states of São Paulo, Rio Grande do Sul and Guanabara. It has declared its adherence to the Chinese Communist position, and its leaders have officially been recognized by Peking as *the* Marxist leaders in Brazil. In spite of Prestes' efforts toward reconciliation, the dissident group has continued its efforts to undermine the regular Party's position and, with Cuban and Chinese support, has been promoting guerrilla attacks and agitation among the urban masses.[23]

In Colombia, a strong pro-Chinese current began to develop within the Party youth organization in 1961. The result was a split among the officers, but the Russian Communist position prevailed, and after the expulsion of four youth leaders, the Party reaffirmed its loyalty to Moscow. In Chile, the Communist Party has categorically adopted the Moscow line, but the debate on the Sino–Soviet conflict and its implications has been carried out more exhaustively perhaps than in any other Latin American country. This is understandable since the Chilean Party is by far the strongest and most influential of the Latin American Communist Parties. In addition the Chilean Party has a strong antagonist in the Socialist Party of Chile, representing the extreme nationalist trend and counting among its ranks a strong pro-Peking group.

Ecuador furnishes a good example of profound dissension between the "gradualists" and the group favoring the violent Chinese tactics—a condition further aggravated by some personal and regional rivalries among Party leaders. Both groups maintain that they constitute *the* Communist Party, and each has expelled the other. In Peru the pro-Chinese group has caused a serious split in the Party. Although it is difficult to estimate the numerical strength of the rival factions, it appears that the pro-Peking faction dominates almost all the regional organization of the Party, and is followed by the Communist youth group, while the old guard in the principal urban areas remains loyal to Moscow.

Within the Communist Party of Venezuela—the only Party in Latin America that has refused to take a stand in the Sino–Soviet dispute and that follows closely in the path of Cuba's course—there exist three divergent currents. One group favors the "soft line," and is anxious to remove the Party from the armed struggle. A second

[23] OEA/Ser., L/X/II, 7, *op. cit.*, pp. 41–44.

group—apparently the dominant one—advocates the Guevara thesis of the use of active guerrilla fighting and urban terrorism with the intention of creating a revolutionary situation. This group is strongly supported by the Castro regime. The third group, closer to the Chinese views, argues that armed conflict may be suspended but not repudiated, and advocates continuous efforts to strengthen the movement among the farmers and laborers. Despite the existence of these three divergent positions within the Venezuelan Party, there has been no open split, nor any expulsion of members.[24]

From the above it seems that the following may be concluded: First, the majority of the Latin American Communist Parties have chosen to remain in the Soviet fold; and that in only a few cases have pro-Chinese elements tried to seize the leadership of the local Communist movement, with limited success. Secondly, the Chinese doctrine that existing regimes can only be overthrown through violent revolutionary struggle has been much more readily accepted by youth groups and intellectuals than by the old guard, who make up the bulk of the Party membership. Thirdly, splintering and damage to unity within the Communist movement has been most evident when top Party leaders have taken sides in the dispute, as in Brazil, Ecuador and Peru. Finally, although it is difficult to discern a clear pattern in the appearance of pro-Chinese sentiment, Chinese efforts in Latin America are directed toward the goals of discrediting and eliminating the pro-Soviet leaders of the Communist movement and of securing complete domination of the Party apparatus for themselves. Presumably, this is considered an essential for obtaining support for the Chinese position in the international movement.

Summary and Prospects

It has been indicated in this chapter that the Latin American Communists have concentrated their efforts on the industrial proletariat and especially on the trade union movement. Two serious disadvantages for the Communist cause have been the inherent difficulties in organizing the Latin American working class as a whole, and the fact that those elements which can be organized, with some exceptions, are not imbued with any particular revolutionary fervor. These factors have, in part, led the Communists to consider that conditions in Latin America are not ripe for revolution, the masses not yet being convinced of its necessity, and that the Party's task, therefore, is one of long and patient

[24] *Ibid.*, pp. 57–60.

labors of propaganda and organization. This negative view of revolutionary potential has been cited as the reason for opposing immediate action and as the justification for collaboration with non-Communist groups and dictators alike. The gift for political opportunism and their ability to exploit the often wildly contradictory currents in the Latin American political milieu, explain to a large extent the rapid expansion of the Communist Parties in recent decades. Indeed, the accusation against the Communists, often made by other extreme left groups, that they are not authentic revolutionaries, absurd as it may appear at first sight, is nevertheless, well founded. There is no revolutionary tradition in the Latin American Communist movement, and few other political groups can exhibit a record freer of political violence and insurrection. From this point of view, one may even conclude that they represent, as a matter of fact, the most conservative sector of the Latin American left. Lacking the ruthless determination to seize power, they have always been content to play, to a far greater extent than Communist Parties in the rest of the world, the normal game of give and take in Latin America politics in return for small benefits.[25]

Collaboration has been facilitated by Communist emphasis on qualities that enable them to secure cooperation or at least tolerance from a wide spectrum of the Latin American peoples. Many of the non-Communist reformist parties have spoken the same political language as the Communists and have often been more like than unlike them in their approach to immediate political problems. The relatively small numerical strength of the Communist Parties has made it easy for non-Communist groups to tolerate their activities and to even accept them as political allies. The latter often seek the Communists for their organizational skills and their effective and well financed propaganda apparatus. As allies, they are usually able, prompt to deliver on commitments and they generally keep their word. Moreover, their relative numerical insignificance makes it a rather simple matter for politicians to shake them off when they cease to be useful. Thus, the majority of Latin American Communist Parties are more often well-organized, smoothly operated machines run by professional politicians, who are highly skilled at political dealings, than militant revolutionary organizations committed to the introduction of drastic political changes.

Furthermore, the Latin American Communist movement has always had another important characteristic. Although purporting to be the standard bearer of the cause of the working classes, communism's strongest appeal has been to the intellectuals. The Party's top leader-

[25] Ernst Halperin, *op. cit.,* pp. 12–19.

ship, as well as the greatest number of its sympathizers, has, almost without exception, been recruited among the intellectuals, who traditionally have played influential roles in Latin American politics.

The Cuban Revolution and the emergence of China as a major Communist power, while creating new opportunities for the Latin American Communist movement, have also beset it with problems. As long as the Soviet Union maintains its predominant position in the Communist world, there seems to be little chance that Latin American communism will move significantly to the Chinese position. Nevertheless, as long as Castro remains what is regarded as a successful example of Marxism–Leninism in the hemisphere, those Parties which advocate violent means can expect support from Cuba. Thus, the Castro regime —"the monument to Soviet presence in the Western Hemisphere"— contributes to keeping alive and giving fire to the echoes of the Sino–Soviet dispute within Latin American ranks.[26]

As for the future, it should be remembered that, despite the Sino–Soviet ideological rift—whose principle implications for revolutionary activity would probably have been argued out on the Latin American political scene even had there been no Sino–Soviet dispute— Latin American Communists are only divided among themselves on the question of tactics, and not in the analysis of the factors conducive to political change. It can be predicted that political opportunism and tactical flexibility will continue to characterize Communist political action, while the appeal of communism will remain strong among opinion leaders and a large part of the masses, as popular demands for social and political reform increase. It can also be ventured that, in view of the experience in Cuba, the Communists will seek to collaborate closely with, and if possible convert, any charismatic figure who may rise in Latin America, hoping to ride to power on the wave of a dynamic, nationalist revolutionary movement. Their hopes further lie in the development of a fortuitous coincidence of national and international circumstances that would create a situation in which they might come to power.

SELECTED BIBLIOGRAPHY

Alba, Víctor, *Historia del Communismo en América Latina* (Mexico City: Ediciones Occidentales, 1954). A brief history of the Latin American Communist Parties and their relations with the international movement.

Alexander, Robert J., *Communism in Latin America* (New Brunswick, N.J.:

[26] Rollie Poppino, *op. cit.*, p. 189.

Rutgers University Press, 1960). An authoritative and comprehensive history of the Latin American Communist movement with emphasis on its role in the labor movement.

Allen, Robert Loring, *Soviet Influence in Latin America: The Role of Economic Relations* (Washington, D.C.: Public Affairs Press, 1959). A detailed and useful account of the Soviet economic drive in Latin America.

Dillon, Dorothy, *International Communism and Latin America: Perspectives and Prospects* (Gainesville, Fla.: Latin American Monograph No. 19, School of Inter-American Studies, University of Florida Press, 1962). A brief survey of Soviet political, economic, and cultural relations with Latin America.

Draper, Theodore, *Castroism: Theory and Practice* (New York: Praeger, 1965). A fine analysis of the nature of Castroism and its relationship to the Communist movement within a historical framework.

Draper, Theodore, *Castro's Revolution: Myths and Realities* (New York: Praeger, 1962). A most searching and objective analysis of the Communist ascent to power in Cuba.

Goldenberg, Boris, *The Cuban Revolution and Latin America* (New York: Praeger, 1965). A keen analysis of the nature of Castro's revolution and its unique features.

Guevara, Ernesto "Ché." *Guerrilla Warfare* (New York: Monthly Review Press, 1961). The well-known book in which the ideologist of the Castro movement expounds his thesis of the violent road to power and guerrilla warfare as the main instrument to revolution in Latin America.

Halperin, Ernst, *Castro and Latin American Communism* (Cambridge, Mass.: The MIT Press, 1963). One of a useful series of reports prepared by the International Communism Project, Center for International Studies, Massachusetts Institute of Technology.

Halperin, Ernst *Nationalism and Communism in Chile* (Cambridge, Mass.: The MIT Press, 1965). A valuable analysis of the interactions among the three leftist parties of Chile and an appraisal of the crucial presidential election of 1964 in that country.

James, Daniel, *Red Design for the Americas: Guatemalan Prelude* (New York: Day, 1954). A detailed treatment of the Guatemalan Communist bid for power.

Poppino, Rollie E., *International Communism in Latin America: A History of the Movement, 1917–1963* (New York: The Free Press, 1964). A thorough and authoritative treatise focused on the origins of the various Communist Parties, their leadership, organization and operational methods, with an analysis of important factors in the Communist political expansion in Latin America.

Ravines, Eudocio, *The Yenan Way* (New York: Scribner, 1951). A study of the "Popular Front" technique with much detail on the origins of the

Peruvian Communist movement and on the activities of various Latin American Parties in the Comintern.

Roca, Blas [Calderío, Francisco], *The Cuban Revolution* (New York: New Century Publishers, 1961). An authoritative Communist interpretation of the Cuban Revolution written by a prominent Cuban Party leader.

Schmitt, Karl M., *Communism in Mexico: A Study in Political Frustration* (Austin: University of Texas Press, 1965). A solid treatment of the history of communism in Mexico.

Schneider, Ronald, *Communism in Guatemala,* 1944–1954 (New York: Praeger, 1958). A detailed analysis of the methods and techniques employed by the Communists in their nearly successful attempt to seize power in the Central American republic.

Suárez, Andrés, *Cuba: Castroism and Communism, 1959–1966* (Cambridge, Mass.: The MIT Press, 1967). An excellent analysis of Cuba's position *vis-à-vis* the Soviet Union and China and of Castro's dilemma in the Sino-Soviet schism.

8

Communism in Subsaharan Africa

D. C. Beller and M. Rejai

THIS CHAPTER focuses on three main aspects of communism in sub-Saharan Africa: (1) pre-1956 Communist political activity in colonial Africa; (2) post-1956 developments, including interstate relations and Communist rivalry for position and influence; and (3) the ideological context of African politics in relation to the Communist doctrine.

African Colonies and Communism

Marx had little to say about Africa. Although he was concerned to a certain extent with Asian countries, primarily, of course, Marx developed his ideas in a context of, and for application to, modernized, industrialized—and hence, Western—societies. When Marx wrote, indeed, the massive European colonization of Africa had not yet taken place: the "scramble for Africa" was a phenomenon of the 1880s and 1890s. It should not be forgotten, then, that applications of Communist ideology to Africa are fundamentally post-Marxian.

Lenin preoccupied himself with Africa only little more than Marx, though he was immensely interested in colonialism and the countries of "the East."[1] It was Lenin who extended the basis of Marx's prole-

[1] "The East" referred in a general way to Asia and came to include, vaguely, Africa. It is clear, however, that when Lenin (and others) made references to specific countries of "the East," it was primarily to China and India, and secondarily to the Levant, that they referred, but not to Africa.

tarian revolution to nonproletarian classes, especially the peasantry, to make communism more appropriate to Russia; he afterwards defined imperialism as an extension of capitalism, thus making of antiimperialistic movements a "progressive" force in the Communist view.

When Lenin called a meeting in Moscow to establish a Communist International in 1919, all the countries of the West had their own long-established traditions of organized working-class movements—with parties and groups of a variety of Marxist and other persuasions. Asian countries, by contrast, had only small numbers and occasional groups of Marxist-oriented intellectuals, but no large parties; and African territories had had virtually no contact with communism at all. Invitations to the First Congress of the Comintern were sent to Parties in Western countries only; at the meetings, only Western delegates participated. The Bolsheviks had no contact with Africa, and, indeed, knew little about it.

The First Comintern Congress did little more than establish the machinery to enable the organization to exist. It was at the Second Congress (July–August, 1920) that delegates adopted several "theses" on substantive issues of policy for the spreading of the world proletarian revolution. One of the major issues was labelled the "National and Colonial Questions," and it was on this topic that the Communists sought to define their position toward the Asian and African areas—though, it should be noted, there were, as at the First Congress, no African delegations present. The context had been set that anticolonial nationalist movements were "progressive," even though their leaders were "bourgeois." What remained at issue was the tactical question of whether and to what extent the Communists should cooperate with such movements, or compete against them. Lenin's position, which prevailed over the more "left" view of the Indian Communist, M. N. Roy, was that Communists should be flexible and opportunistic, and cooperate with nationalists wherever they could.

At no time after the Second Congress did the Lenin Comintern devote as much attention to the colonial areas, although, from the Third Congress on, there was representation from the small South African Communist Party at the Congress meetings. Soviet leaders were faced increasingly with the fact that their expectations of imminent revolution in Europe had not materialized. In the Comintern, attention was turned from the engineering of agitation and revolution to the building up of Comintern organization, with rigidly disciplined Parties dependent on the Comintern's Moscow headquarters. The Fourth Congress (1922) adopted the "United Front" policy—in effect a logical extension of Lenin's earlier practice of cooperation with nationalists.[2]

In Africa, the only significant development of a Communist organization during the time of the Lenin Comintern was the Communist Party of South Africa. South Afrcia had been in political turmoil since the turn of the century, having gone through war, the creation of the Union, and the beginnings of industrialization. A myriad of political organizations had sprung up, the two most important Africans' groups being the African National Congress (ANC) in 1912 and the Industrial and Commercial Union (ICU) in 1919. Within the white community a national South African Labor Party was formed in 1909; it led to the founding of an International Socialist League, which in turn became the Communist Party of South Africa in 1921 and affiliated with the Comitern.

Racial segregation, *de facto* and *de jure,* was a phenomenon centuries old in South Africa. The newly formed Communist Party was almost entirely a whites' organization at the outset; however, a minority in the party, led by one Sidney Bunting, favored inclusion of the native Africans. Bunting launched a campaign to enlist African support for communism; as he succeeded, increasingly, white members dropped out. When the crisis came to a head in 1924, the Bunting group successfully challenged the Party leadership. In the years that followed, Bunting and his associates retained a position of unqualified opposition to racial injustice, for which they earned the respect of South African liberals and opponents of *apartheid.* By the 1930s, the Party was attracting an increasing number of Africans, including prominent leaders, intellectuals, and trade union organizers. Gradually, it became a predominantly African organization, although its leadership remained disproportionately white.

The Communists, following Comintern policy, sought closer association and "cooperation" with the ANC and ICU, encouraging radical leaders of those organizations to join, or at least support, the Communist Party. One of the activists in this campaign was James Gumede, who, along with some colleagues, became prominent in both organizations. The activity of the Communists was not unknown to the nationalist leaders, however, and eventually the ICU expelled the Gumede group from membership. This event caused serious disruption within the ICU,

[2] The "United Front" policy was designed largely with European politics in mind, though not exclusively so. Its major application in the non-Western world was the alliance between the Chinese Communist Party and the Kuomintang, which ended with disastrous results for the Communists. With the single exception of South Africa, the policy had little meaning anywhere on the African continent, because of the virtual absence of indigenous Communist organizations.

and soon thereafter, that powerful organization, which at its zenith claimed a membership of a quarter million, split into several factions. Afterwards, nationalists bitterly criticized the Communists for causing dissension and fragmentation in valued nationalist organizations.

Gumede fared better in the ANC, winning election as its fourth President-General in 1926. Not long after, Gumede and some others were sent on an extended tour of the Soviet Union. Gumede returned to South Africa full of enthusiasm for the USSR.

Throughout Gumede's presidency of the ANC, and beginning even before that, the ANC had been suffering a general decline. With the ICU fragmented, and the ANC in decline, the Communists seized upon the opportunity to fill the gap with a new African organization of their own creation. They founded the League of African Rights, with Gumede at its head and other sympathetic leaders in key posts. Though known to be a "front" organization, the African response was favorable, and the League's prospects seemed bright. This was on the eve of the Sixth Congress of the Comintern.

Stalin clearly made his influence felt in the latter 1920s; as his position became more secure, the direction of his policies became more evident. At the Sixth Congress of the Comintern, held from July to September, 1928, with Stalin the undisputed leader, new theoretical positions and policies were set forth. The Congress adopted a "Program" of the Communist International, in which a very revealing section, devoted to the "principal types" of revolution, divided up the non-Communist world into four categories, and gave examples of each. The four types, and examples, were: (1) "countries of highly-developed capitalism (United States of America, Germany, Great Britain, etc.)"; (2) "countries with a medium development of capitalism (Spain, Portugal, Poland, Hungary, the Balkan countries, etc.)"; (3) "colonial and semicolonial countries (China, India, etc.) and dependent countries (Argentina, Brazil, etc.)"; and (4) "still more backward countries (as in some parts of Africa)."[3] Elaborate policies were enunciated for each of the types except the fourth, which was dealt with only generally and superficially. This suggests a great deal, at least of the thinking of Stalin and his contemporaries (or rather, the lack of thinking), about the place of Africa in the Communist view of the world.

The Sixth Congress did not abolish the "United Front," but made

[3] *The Program of the Communist International* (New York: Workers' Library Publishers, 1929), pp. 39–41. Judging from the occasions on which the Comintern at this time made specific references to individual African territories by name, it seems fair to conclude that by "some parts of Africa" was meant all of Africa except the countries of North Africa and the Union of South Africa.

a change which amounted almost to its abolition: Communists were thenceforth to seek the "United Front from below," and eschew the "United Front from above." The new policy, made obligatory on all Parties, called for a breaking off of all cooperative efforts with non-Communist organizations.

The Comintern Congress did not meet again for seven years. The Seventh Congress (1935), which was the last, reflected a shift away from international concerns and toward developments within the Soviet Union—a result of Stalin's policy of "socialism in a single country." To the extent to which international events were taken into account, the Congress revealed a deep concern with the rise of the fascist and Nazi movements. Antifascism largely replaced the earlier concern with antiimperialism; great emphasis was placed on antifascist coalitions, now called "Popular Fronts." By the time of the Second World War, the "Popular Front" policy, demanding Communist cooperation with all anti-fascist "democratic" movements, finally led Stalin to dissolve the Comintern (1943) as a conciliatory move toward his Western allies. Colonial agitation, which could only be interpreted by the allies as intervention in their dependencies, became an all but forgotten thing.

As a result of the policies of the Stalin Comintern, the South African Communist Party was directed in 1929 to abolish at once its newly formed League of African Rights. Instead of championing the causes of the established African nationalist groups, the Party was ordered to campaign among Africans for a "Native African Republic" within the Union—something repugnant to the African intelligentsia.[4] The old-time Party leadership was sufficiently outraged to contemplate disregarding the order. Shortly thereafter, however, the League was disbanded, and a group of Communists was sent out from Britain to take over the Party. Bunting and his supporters were purged from their positions, and soon after from membership in the Party itself. This had the effect of causing the disaffection of many Africans who had been attracted to the Bunting group.

[4] It should be noted in this connection that at about the same time, the Communist Party of the United States had been directed to cease supporting American Negro organizations, to agitate against the then-popular Garvey Movement, and to offer, in contrast to the "Back to Africa" policy of the Garveyites, a policy aimed at creating a "Black Belt State" in the American South. At the same time, provision was made for having selected American Negro Communists trained and equipped in the Soviet Union and sent to Africa as Comintern agents. Thus, it is difficult to ignore the possibility that consistency with this policy constituted a stronger reason for the Comintern decision on South Africa than did any considerations of actual conditions there.

The difficulties caused by the Stalin Comintern in the 1930s produced yet another development: the South African equivalent of Trotskyism. Never fully organized, these ultraleft purists were a varied collection of radicals, with a disproportionately large number of "Coloureds."[5] Various Trotskyite organizations maintained a sporadic existence and press output—frequently with intense ideological wranglings—from the 1930s until the end of World War II. They never amounted to any significant political element from the point of view of threat to the established regime, but they were occasional thorns in the side of nationalist and labor organizations, and especially of the Communist Party.

After 1930 the Communist Party went into decline, despite some individual successes in local areas. Nationalist organizations and groups began working to discredit and weaken the Communists; the government stepped up its drive to quash them; and Gumede was defeated for reelection as ANC president. These difficulties reduced the Party to a small core of ideologues with little left of their former ties with the masses.

World War II contributed further to the Party's attrition. After the Seventh Comintern Congress, the South African Party dutifully campaigned for "Popular Front" opposition to Hitler, and then, with the signing of the Stalin–Hitler pact, it switched its "line" to opposition to the war in Europe. This was more attractive to Africans, who were reluctant to fight for their government under conditions of rigid racial discrimination. But when, in 1941, Russia was attacked by Germany, the "line" switched again, and the Communists called for energetic prosecution of the war, resulting in a new round of Communist losses, in membership and sympathy, of Africans.

The conditions worsened after the war and popular demonstrations and outbreaks grew in scope. The Communist Party was rarely a leader in these affairs, but it did try to get in on all moves against oppression. In 1946 there was a massive strike of African mine workers, in which illegal and Communist-affiliated African trade unions played a prominent role. Following the brutal smashing of the strike by the police, the leaders of the Communist Party, the ANC, and other groups were arrested and their homes raided. The entire Communist Party Executive Committee was accused of treason, but these charges were eventually dropped. In 1948, the Afrikaner National Party led

[5] South African usage—and law—divides the population into four racial groups: Europeans (whites), "Natives" or "Bantu" (Africans), "Asians" (mostly people of Indian descent) and "Coloured" (people of racially mixed descent).

by D. F. Malan—long the most extreme of the racist parties of South Africa—won national elections. The policy of *apartheid* began receiving expression in national law.

Malan's victory might have served to unify all opposition groups. But the ANC, though always willing to accept "cooperation" from the Communists, steadfastly refused "unity" with them. The nationalist view has been summed up by an ANC historian, paraphrasing from a statement of the ANC's Youth League:

> [The Youth League's bulletin, *African Lodestar,* in 1949] declared that since the workers were Africans and were oppressed primarily because they were African and only secondarily because they were workers, "it is clear that the exotic plant of communism cannot flourish on African soil."[6]

In 1950 the Malan government passed the Suppression of Communism Act. Aimed at quelling *all* protest, this law marked a new development in autocratic rule by allowing the government to persecute real as well as "statutory" Communists. Under this Act, anyone *defined* as a Communist by the government could be held or imprisoned without the rights and liberties guaranteed to the citizens of the country. The Communist Party disbanded and went underground; since then, the South African Communists have lived a shadowy existence outside the law. Many of the radicals in the African nationalist organizations (themselves since outlawed) have kept up contact with Communists. Though still active, the Party has not enjoyed significant rejuvenation in the post-1956 era.

During the 1930s and 1940s, the only other significant Communist contacts with Africans took place between some Western European Communist Parties and a small number of young Africans who had managed to make their way abroad, mostly for higher education. This included such important future leaders as Jomo Kenyatta, Nnamdi Azikiwe, Kwame Nkrumah, and many others. Especially in the early 1930s, before the Comintern shift toward antifascism, Africans were frequently attracted by the anticolonial content of the Communist doctrine. The existence of a tiny colony of expatriot black intellectuals in London had in fact began earlier, particularly with youths coming from British colonies in the West Indies. This elite group experimented with various ideologies, sought in various ways to germinate pressure on the colonial ministries for reform, and helped found such important

[6] Mary Benson, *The African Patriots* (London: Faber and Faber, 1963), p. 163.

organizations as the West African Students Union (WASU) and the international Pan-African Congresses.

From time to time these groups were accused by conservative elements in the Western press and elsewhere of being Communists and "agencies of Moscow"; from the other side, the Communist Parties of the West occasionally accused the African groups of "petit-bourgeois nationalism."[7] On other occasions, the Communist Parties tried the "front" organization tactic (e.g., the League Against Imperialism in 1927) for improving relations with African elites. These techniques never had much success. In fact, the African groups were never Communist, and most of their members tended to be skeptical of all ideologies. Individuals did drift in and out of personal commitment to Marxist doctrines in greater or lesser degree, but few were ever thoroughgoing Communists for very long. Communist effectiveness suffered further as the Comintern shifted in policy before and during the war. In 1935, many Africans were disillusioned at the news that the Soviet Union had sold oil to Mussolini when he was invading Ethiopia; then came the policy of switches of the Stalin–Hitler pact and the war.

In the French colonies limited domestic politics (within the structure of the Empire) had been allowed. Senegal had representation in the French Assembly in the Third Republic. A Socialist Party had by the 1930s become the strongest party in the Senegalese capital, but it was always more a branch of the metropolitan French Socialist Party than a native Senegalese party, and it was always anticommunist. The French Communist Party was able in the early 1940s to establish Communist Study Groups in the cities of French West Africa, which attracted young intellectuals and introduced them to Marxism–Leninism. After the Second World War, the Fourth Republic provided for African representation in the French Assembly from all the colonies, bringing nearly 100 African deputies to the French capital. As a result, the formation of political groups among Africans abroad began as a federative effort. In 1946 a group of these Africans in France formed an interterritorial party, the Rassemblement Democratique Africaine (RDA). The new party formed a tactical alliance with the French Communist Party.

From the African leaders' point of view, this relationship was pri-

[7] For their part, the nationalists often criticized the Communists (and Socialists) for inattention to the problems of the colonies, and at times, not only inattention, but equivocation on anticolonialism. Communist Parties of Western Europe did sometimes equivocate, and were on occasion chastised by the Comintern for it.

marily useful for political maneuvering in the Assembly, and for access to well-developed political party organization techniques. From the Communists' point of view, the relationship was useful as a vehicle for extending their influence into the colonies. RDA sections were established as territorial parties in most of the individual colonies, and they grew rapidly. As the colonial administration stepped up its persecution, the RDA leadership determined to break with the Communists. RDA President Houphouet-Boigny effected the break in 1950. The RDA was never allowed to become a Communist organization; while a few individuals in it were persuaded to embrace the Communist doctrine, and while many of the younger members of the party received their political education from Marxist texts in the RDA, the party was always a nationalist organization. Several of the leading parties in French-speaking Africa today are descendents of old RDA sections.

During and after World War II, when the USSR emerged as a major world power, Soviet leadership was able to approach its foreign policy with a much-enlarged perspective. The emergence of "people's democracies" in Eastern Europe meant that, for the first time, the Soviet Union was not alone as a Communist state in a hostile world; now there was a "Communist Camp." The revolution in China in 1949 added greatly to this new self-image. In this context, Stalin was able rapidly to return to the "hard" lines of the prewar period. Revolutionary agitation and open violence replaced "Popular Fronts," alliances, etc., as tactics in non-Communist countries; cooperative relationships between Communist Parties and other groups were ended. Armed insurrection by Communist groups broke out on a major scale in several Asian countries. A successor to the Comintern was formed—the Communist Information Bureau (Cominform)—in 1947, and it duly adopted the new policy, summed up in the "two-camp" thesis.

With respect to Africa, where indigenous Communist Party strength was virtually nil, the Communists could do little more than spurn the anticolonial nationalist movements (for which they already had limited precedent), and this they did vehemently. The vilification of African nationalist leaders produced a Communist literature that has since become embarrassing to Soviet leadership. In this period, when nationalist movements were generating real political power for the first time in African colonies, the Communists accused African leaders of

[8] Perhaps most symbolic of this attitude was the depicting of the man then leading the world's major anticolonialist movement, Mahatma Ghandi, as an enemy of his people, guilty of "social treason." African nationalist leaders were later to be called "African Ghandis."

being "lackeys," "puppets," "lickspittles," and "shields" for imperialism. Bourgeois nationalists, the communists insisted, were not to be trusted; they were the betrayers of the public interest.[8]

African Independence and Communism

Throughout the 1940s and 1950s, major changes were taking place in colonial Africa. To the complete imperception of the Soviet leaders, the "bourgeois" nationalists in the colonies were mounting a vigorous offensive against colonial rule. Leaders of these nationalist movements, virtually all of them "modernized" elites, and many of them having familiarity since their student days with Marxist ideology, and with past Comintern policies as well, were appearing as successful revolutionaries, and without any significant help from the Communists. Soviet leadership was still not at a point of recognizing that despite some three decades of concern with world revolution, they knew, in effect, practically nothing about Africa and had no real "Africa policy."[9] The Chinese Communist regime made the recognition before the Russians that nationalist leaders were revolutionaries, and of value to communism; apparently also, the Chinese contributed to a similar (and belated) recognition by the Soviet Union, which was in danger of being bypassed by some of the most far-reaching changes in Africa. Not until the mid-1950s, for the most part, did the Soviet leadership begin to react. The change, when it came, was dramatically indicated at Party Congress XX (PC XX) of the CPSU in 1956. Much had happened in Africa in the meantime.

The first African colony to attain independent statehood was Ghana, in 1957; the following year Guinea became independent when a popular vote rejected the French Constitution's provision for association with the French "Community." By the end of 1960, seventeen additional African colonies had become independent states, and more had been committed by the colonial regimes to independence. These successes were, however, products of nationalist activity in most cases already several decades old, so that it was much earlier than 1957 that political victories were being won by the nationalist leaders.

By 1956, a number of things had occured to induce a change in Soviet policy from the "hard" line of the "two-camp" thesis. There had been a glimmer of recognition among some Soviet academics as early as 1949 that realities in Africa bore little relation to Soviet pro-

[9] It should be kept in mind, however, that the Western countries, including especially the United States, were hardly in a better position in this regard.

nouncements about Africa; slowly and cautiously, scholars like Ivan Potekhin—later Director of the Soviet Africa Institute—began to move Soviet thinking about Africa out of the rigid Stalinist mold. Asian countries won independence in the late 1940s and early 1950s; at about the same time reforms had begun in parts of West Africa. China, having been propelled into international prominence by the Korean War, set out to make friends and allies of nationalist leaders in Asia and Africa. In 1955 the famous Bandung Conference had been held, demonstrating the scope and significance of nationalism in the non-Western world. Another major factor, of course, was Stalin's death in 1953.

At PC XX of the CPSU, a number of significant changes were introduced in Soviet policy and attitude towards colonial countries. Once again the terms "unity" and "United Front" were heard. Khrushchev buried the "two-camp" thesis by declaring an "extensive zone of peace," which incorporated the anticolonialist sector of the world. The way was then paved for cooperation with African nationalists, soon to be heads of independent states, and no longer illegal conspirators hostile to established political authority. African independence tended to forestall antigovernment activity by the Communists, at least openly, since the latter desired to keep favor with the nationalist leaders. Increasingly after 1956, Soviet activity was to be on the level of interstate relations. The "Communist Camp," the new line averred, desired to consolidate the independence of Asian and African states by means of improved political and economic relations, and thus free them from the pressures of Western imperialism.

By the early 1960s, Soviet thinking tended to identify, within this context, a number of "progressive" African states, including Ghana, Guinea, and Mali. The select status of this group of states was symbolized by their participation, as "fraternal parties," in PC XXII of the CPSU, in October 1961.

Since the mid-1950s, the USSR evidently has established a policy of moving quickly to establish relations with the newly independent states. In 1957, the Soviet government named Professor Potekhin the head of a delegation to Ghanaian independence ceremonies. On this, his first trip to Africa, Potekhin stayed in Accra several weeks; following his visit, Soviet writing on Africa reflected a renewed effort to achieve a modicum of realism in understanding political events on the continent.

For Ghana, Potekhin's visit paved the way for the establishment of diplomatic relations, and for trade agreements soon thereafter. In

1961, a Soviet aid agreement was concluded, which included major projects on Ghana's massive Volta River development scheme, including a hydroelectric plant.[10] The political approach toward Ghana (as toward the other African countries) has been exclusively to curry favor with the leader and his followers, and to avoid all independent Communist activity that might be regarded by the government as subversive. Potekhin is reported to have advised a group of young Ghanaian Communist radicals not to operate independently, but to work within existing organizations. Reports from time to time indicated that some of the advisers to Nkrumah, particularly the younger, were more or less orthodox Marxist–Leninists. Although there was a certain latitude for such leftists to congregate in subsidiary organizations within Nkrumah's Convention People's Party (CPP), there never was any effort to form an independent Communist Party or group, which would involve direct or implicit competition with the CPP. The Soviets were quite willing to proceed indirectly, through gaining influence with Nkrumah and his lieutenants in the party. It was in neighboring Guinea that the Soviets tried a more direct approach.

In 1958, Guinea was the only French African colony whose people voted against the French Community as proposed in DeGaulle's Fifth Republic Constitution. Guinea became an independent state as a result of the vote, but the country was put into economic straits as a consequence of the precipitous withdrawal of the French administration and French trade, and the failure of any other states friendly to France to take up Guinean exports. The Soviet Union stepped in immediately to conclude trade agreements and grant loans, followed up by generous promises of further loans. A Guinean government delegation travelled to Moscow in the summer of 1959, and negotiated a Soviet loan of some 140 million rubles. Within months, however, Guinean officials were complaining about the slow and inadequate manner in which the Soviet government fulfilled its promises. Touré himself visited Moscow in November of 1959, at which time Khrushchev agreed to deliver the loan, on the condition that Soviet experts go to Guinea to oversee the utilization of the credits.

Thus in early 1960 a large number of Soviet officials arrived in Guinea and began insinuating themselves in the economic and political structure of the country. Other delegations came from Soviet satellite

[10] The financing on the central project of the Volta hydroelectric project—the dam—came from Western (chiefly American) sources. The Ghanian press, however, lauded Soviet assistance, while deprecating or only grudgingly acknowledging the Western contributions.

countries, and from China, under similar arrangements. Although the individual national contingents appear to have operated separately more than jointly, from this large body of Communist advisers and experts, a massive propaganda effort began to spread throughout Guinea.

In September 1960, Touré made a second visit to Moscow. Guinean foreign policy, in a state of flux at this time, began to resemble, from the Western standpoint, that of a Communist-bloc state. By 1961, Guinea had become quite dependent economically upon the Soviet Union; the Soviets had begun referring to it as a "people's democracy." Nevertheless, Soviet fulfillment of its economic pledges continued to be grudging and laggard. Supplies and foodstuffs were frequently late or never arrived at all; sometimes shipments of spoiled goods were delivered. Construction projects were not finished, or when finished broke down; some projects were postponed repeatedly and in the end were never begun. Machinery and equipment did not arrive, or were of the wrong kind.

In 1961, even before completing the delivery of its promised aid, the Soviet government began pressing for the first repayment—at a time when Guinea was hard pressed financially. As propaganda and infiltration mounted, matters became extremely grave for the Touré government. An antigovernment plot was discovered, which ultimately disclosed undeniable Soviet involvement, and antigovernment demonstrations by youths broke out into the streets. The government acted swiftly: schools were closed, numerous arrests were made and trials held. In December 1961, the Guinea government stated that it had discovered a "Communist-inspired conspiracy" and demanded the immediate recall of the Soviet Ambassador. Many of the experts were hustled out of the country. Moscow sent its chief troubleshooter, Anastas Mikoyan, to renegotiate the entire Soviet–Guinea relationship.

During this crisis, only Soviet relations in Guinea suffered; Guinea's relations with East European states and with China were not seriously affected. For its part, the Soviet Union's praise of Ghana and President Nkrumah increased notably right after the crisis in Guinea. Frequent references to Ghana's "efforts" and "progress" in "building socialism" indicated a Soviet reconcentration on that country. And indeed, down through 1965, the Nkrumah regime appeared to be moving closer to some Communist practices. Although the "leftward drift" of Ghanaian policies was not, strictly speaking, "Communist," it did entail such features of Soviet totalitarianism as the increasing suppression of all political opposition and the development around Nkrumah of a "personality cult." In addition, Communist ideological inroads, especially from 1964 on, were in small increments becoming apparent. There was a noticeable increase in the use of orthodox Marxist–Leninist phraseology in the CPP press—such as the tendency to replace former usages of "African socialism" with "scientific socialism" and to refer to "class struggle" in Africa. Government control of the economy grew, and a form of "state farm" became part of the government's agricultural policy. Soviet officials in Ghana gradually had substantial portions of the press put at their disposal.

At about the same time similar developments were taking place in the Republic of Mali. Malian policies, like Guinean and Ghanian policies, began to take a pro-Soviet posture; of the three countries' delegations to PC XXII of the CPSU, Mali's representative gave the most fiery speech, incorporating not only the usual attacks upon capitalism but lavish praise for communism.

The other states of Africa were in less prestigious categories in the Soviet view, although some of them (including Ethiopia, Nigeria and Somalia) were offered large loans. Occasionally, local Communist organizations were initiated, such as the one in Nigeria, but these have remained very small, and without overt Soviet support. By the early 1960s, a new force affecting the interests of both the Soviet Union and the African states was beginning to make its presence felt: the Chinese People's Republic had reached Africa.

The Chinese revolution, Mao Tse-tung and his colleagues have argued, is of special significance for all the "oppressed peoples" of the "backward" nations; it is a model to be followed in all colonial countries. The basic notion, of course, is that Mao Tse-tung's formulation of Marxism–Leninism represents a transformation of a set of essentially European ideas into non-Europeans forms. The shortest formulation of this proposition is probably Chen Po-Ta's assertion that "The theory of Mao Tse-tung is a development of Marxism–Leninism in the East."[11]

Since 1949 the Chinese Communists have been using this claim as a basis for a special appeal to Asians and Africans. Of late, this argument has been reinforced by a racial appeal, a development which came into sharp focus during Peking's running battle with Moscow. Russians, like the imperialists, the Chinese argument goes, are "whites," while Chinese and Africans are colored "brother races."

In 1955 China acquired a new image as one of the major participants of the Bandung Conference, as a result of which (at least in part) Peking and Cairo established diplomatic relations a year later.

[11] Che'n Po-ta, *Mao Tse-tung on the Chinese Revolution* (Peking: Foreign Languages Press, 1953), p. 86.

This was a major step in China's arrival upon the international scene. In 1957 the Afro-Asian Solidarity Organization (of which China is a member) established its permanent Secretariat in Cairo, thus bringing Peking into sustained contact with representatives of African states. China established relations with the Sudan in 1958, with Guinea in 1959, and with Mali in 1960. Touré's visit to Peking in 1960 was the first in a long series of visits to the Chinese capital by non-Communist heads of state. On Touré's visit, China signed her first "treaty of friendship" with an African country, accompanied by a large loan, interest-free. In 1961 a similar treaty was signed with Ghana, also accompanied by an interest-free loan.[12]

At about this time, Chinese and Soviet policies were coming into open conflict in Africa. One chief issue was the question of negotiating a settlement of the Algerian War: the Soviets tended to favor it, the Chinese to oppose it. Another issue was whether to support the Cameroun government of President Ahidjo or the rebel forces of Felix Moumie's Union des Populations Camerounaise (UPC). Leftist and militant, the UPC had vigorously opposed the Ahidjo regime since Cameroun's independence in January, 1960. Moumie had made no secret of his Communist affiliations, begun in his students days through the RDA. The Soviet Union had been supporting the UPC for some time prior to independence, but after 1960, and with an interest shown by the Ahidjo government in normalizing relations between the two countries, the USSR ceased to support UPC revolt; it sought instead to use its influence in the UPC to effect a reconciliation with government forces. In the spring and summer of 1960, the Chinese Communists stepped in to replace the Soviets as supporters and financers of militant revolt. Moumie and other UPC officials paid several visits to China. The Chinese provided for a large "Camerounian" contingent in their program of education for African students in China. Camerounian students were endorsed by the UPC, in contrast to other African students who came through their respective governments.

Moumie died mysteriously at the end of 1960. Thereafter, following a period of widespread fighting in the country, the Ahidjo government was increasingly successful in confining and localizing the rebel contingent, and in winning reconciliation with some dissident officers of the UPC. By 1964, the Cameroun government could establish diplomatic relations with the Soviet Union and the East European states;

[12] Though their loans were in both cases smaller than Soviet loans, the Chinese made much of the fact that the Soviets charged interest.

only China and Albania would not recognize the Ahidjo government.[13] The UPC became split, some factions making peace with Ahidjo, some remaining tied to the Chinese.

The Congo crisis contributed more to Sino–Soviet unity than to dissension. After the initial Security Council action, in which the Soviet delegate took a leading part, both Communist powers became disaffected with the UN effort in the Congo, advised African governments to pull their men out of the UN force, and heaped criticism upon both Joseph Kasa-Vubu and Dag Hammarskjold. After Patrice Lumumba had been assassinated, both powers recognized Antoine Gizenga as the legitimate Congo leader, and sought to stabilize his government. Kasa-Vubu, meanwhile, had closed down all Soviet and Chinese consular and other offices, and forced the evacuation of all Communist advisory personnel from Leopoldville. However, after Joseph Mobutu's military action and the eventual suppression of the Katanga secession, Gizenga and the new Premier, Cyrille Adoula, were reconciled temporarily, and the Soviet government quickly dropped its independent support of Gizenga and recognized Adoula's government—as the Chinese did not. The return of Moise Tshombe to Congolese politics, as Premier of the Central government, again alienated the Soviets, and they vied with the Chinese in supporting the rebel movements in the country, until the military coup of Colonel Mobutu.

Early 1964 was a critical time for Chinese fortunes in Africa. The Chinese Premier, Chou En-lai, toured ten African states in December-January, 1963–1964, a tour of seven weeks' duration. At this time, Chinese focus was broadened to incorporate most of the countries of East and Central Africa. Cordial relations were established with several East African governments, and the Chinese, from their new embassy in Dar es Salaam, negotiated several large loans with East African states, including Tanganyika, Kenya and Malawi. Simultaneously, however, the Chinese were making contacts with African rebels almost as fast as they were with African governments. Some of these efforts took place in territories still under colonial rule—particularly the Portuguese colonies of Mozambique and Angola—but some were with rebels from independent African states. Indeed, Premier Chou himself stated that the prospects for revolution were favorable throughout Africa. This policy of support for rebellion, which the Soviets had avoided, was

[13] At one point in the fall of 1962 the Camerounian Economics Minister was being feted in Moscow at the same time that the Vice-President of the UPC was being feted in Peking.

resented by African political leaders. Within two years, Chinese efforts had suffered major setbacks on numerous fronts.

In Zanzibar (now no longer an independent state), Chinese Communists established close relations with the General Secretary of the Zanzibar Nationalist Party, Mohamed Abdul Rahman, known as Babu. When the government of the island state, under the Sultan, was toppled in January of 1964, after a general breakdown of order and widespread rioting, Babu competed with other politicians for control of the *ad hoc* coalition government that replaced the Sultan. Having become External Affairs Minister under the nationalist President Abeid Karume, Babu set about immediately to expand relations between the Zanzibar "People's Republic," as he called it, and China; he soon announced a large grant from Peking. Babu's close association with the Chinese was halted by counteraction on the part of nationalist leaders. Karume and Julius Nyerere, President of Tanganyika and also an ardent nationalist, decided (while Babu was abroad in Peking) to merge their two countries. The Soviet Union recognized the new Republic of Tanzania immediately; China did not.

In the smaller Congo, Congo Brazzaville, the government that had existed since independence was overthrown in August, 1963. The new leaders established diplomatic relations with China early the following year, and the Chinese contingent in the Congo expanded so rapidly that by 1965 it was the largest expatriot group in the country. There were further indications, in 1966, of Cuban advisors, including military personnel, also active in the Congo.

Elsewhere, Chinese officials were ejected from Malawi after President Banda accused them of trying to bribe members of his cabinet; they were accused by the Kenya government of intervening in that country's internal affairs. Most importantly, Chinese and Soviet efforts both were halted in Ghana with the military overthrow of President Nkrumah early in 1966. While Nkrumah was in Peking, Ghanaian army officers effected a swift takeover of the government, and spent months afterward undoing political repression under Nkrumah. Several hundred Soviet and Chinese personnel in the country were ejected, and several secret guerrilla-type training schools sponsored by the Chinese were discovered and disbanded.

On another front, the Communist countries continued to offer attractive opportunities for African students to study abroad. Most of the African students who go to study in Communist countries appear to do so for higher education, not for political training. However, political indoctrination being an integral part of Communist education, these students are inevitably exposed to a considerable amount of it, despite their frequent resentment. In recent years, there has been an increasing number of accounts published by returning students from Communist countries—some ejected by their hosts, others having quit in disgust. These accounts have complained, often bitterly, of the lack of freedom, the hardship conditions, and even of racial discrimination inside Communist states.[14]

Finally, the Communist countries have not been free of cultural prejudices. Propaganda and official literature from Communist sources can be found to contain descriptions of Africans as "tribalist," "feudal," "medieval," and most commonly, "backward."[15] However accurate these terms may seem to their users, they cannot but offend the Africans and renew their determination to find the "African way," free of foreign imitation and influence, Western or Eastern.

African Ideology and Communism

It seems clear, then, that despite minor successes and occasional fears in the West, the "exotic plant of communism" has not done well "flourish[ing] on African soil." Although many or most African leaders have proclaimed a commitment to "African socialism," antipathy to orthodox Communist ideology is quite pervasive. This is the case even with African leaders who have had training in Marxism–Leninism, or who are otherwise identified as "Marxist."[16] No important African leader has proclaimed a belief in Communist ideology.

African leaders have detected disquieting parallels between communism and capitalism, the latter also widely rejected throughout Africa. Communism, it is argued, is as much productive of exploitation and alienation as is capitalism. Touré has equated communism with state capitalism, arguing that in both systems the worker is exploited, whether by private capital or by public capital. Léopold Sédar Senghor, President of Senegal, has been more explicit, as in the following.

[14] See, for example, the works of Amar, Ajao, and Hevi cited in the bibliography at the end of this chapter.

[15] This exists in spite of Communist efforts to discredit Westerners for precisely these sorts of cultural prejudices, and suggests that the Communists are still prisoners of their past, at least back as far as Stalin's "backward countries" view. The traditional Chinese view, that all non-Chinese are "barbarians," is well known.

[16] Those most frequently so identified are Nkrumah and Touré, both of whom admittedly have studied the works of Marx, Lenin, Mao Tse-tung, and others.

> The paradox in the building of socialism in Communist countries, or at least in the Soviet Union, is that it increasingly resembles capitalistic growth in the United States, the American way of life, with high salaries, refrigerators, washing machines, and television sets, but with less art and less freedom of thought.[17]

Communism and capitalism are equally condemned for stressing material and temporal values at the expense of moral, ethical, spiritual, and religious norms. Senghor insists: "We are not Communists for a theoretical reason: Lenin's definition of matter proceeds from a one-sided concept, from a purely materialistic and deterministic postulate. . . ."[18] While proclaiming his deep faith in socialism, Senghor has been, at the same time, a devout Catholic, profoundly influenced by the Jesuit theologian Pierre Teilhard de Chardin. For nearly a decade, throughout the late 1940s and much of the 1950s, Senghor's party was allied with the Mouvement Republicain Populaire, the French Catholic party. Christianity, he insists, is the source of numerous African ideals.

Similar lines of thought are developed by other African leaders. Nobel Prize winner Chief Luthuli, President of the South African ANC, is a devout Christian, as are many leaders throughout Africa.[19] The Mali Minister of Development, Seydou Kouyate, argues that spirituality is "an integral part of man."[20] The Ghanaan, Kofi Baako, has said that "no native of Ghana, or of any other African country, is an atheist. Deep down within him there are hidden spiritual forces . . . [and] his whole being instinctively rejects the idea that the beginning and end of all life is in this world alone. . . ."[21] Nkrumah once described himself as "a nondenominational Christian and a Marxist Socialist."[22]

African rejection of communism is also motivated by a desire to

[17] Léopold Sédar Senghor, *On African Socialism,* translated with an Introduction by Mercer Cook (New York: Praeger, 1964), p. 46.

[18] *Ibid.,* p. 45.

[19] See Albert Luthuli, *Let My People Go* (New York: McGraw-Hill, 1962).

[20] Seydou Kouyate, paper presented at the Dakar Colloquium of December, 1962; excerpts in *Africa Report,* VIII, May, 1963, p. 16.

[21] Quoted in Fritz Schatten, *Communism in Africa* (New York: Praeger, 1965), p. 329.

[22] Kwame Nkrumah, *Ghana: The Autobiography of Kwame Nkrumah* (New York: Nelson, 1957), p. 13 (hereafter abbreviated as *Autobiography*). Just before his downfall, however, Nkrumah seemed to be moving away from religion. See Kwame Nkrumah, *Consciencism: Philosophy and Ideology for Decolonialization and Development with Particular Reference to the African Revolution* (New York: Monthly Review Press, 1964), pp. 13–14 (hereafter abbreviated as *Consciencism*).

forestall the influence of the Soviet Union and other Communist countries. Having expelled Western imperialism, the argument runs, Africans are not about to substitute Communist imperialism in its place. Nkrumah has been most explicit on this point: "As we would not have British masters, so we would not have Russian masters, or any other masters for that matter. It is not our intention to substitute one imperialism for another. We want to be free and independent in the management of our own affairs."[23] This view brings into focus the force of nationalism in contemporary Africa, and underscores ideologies of "Pan-Africanism," *"négritude,"* and "African Personality."

In terms of some of the categories commonly associated with Communist thought, Africans have generally shied away from such conceptions as class struggle, the dialectic, and revolutionary violence. There appears to be substantial agreement that (1) the class struggle is irrelevant to African conditions primarily because there are no clearly defined classes in Africa, or (2) while some "classes," "strata," or "groups" may be identified, the relationships among them are not antagonistic, and do not require violence.

Nearly every important African leader has at some point denied the existence of exploiting and exploited classes in Africa. Nyerere, for example, goes to the point of "doubt[ing] if the equivalent for the word 'class' exists in any indigenous African language"; the concept of class, he insists, is foreign to Africa.[24] Similarly, M. Dia, former Premier of Senegal, maintains that the emergence of a privileged class in the African context would be an "unnatural" phenomenon; African society, he argues, must be based on the "active solidarity" of all elements of its population.[25]

Senghor's position is that while at the moment there are no classes in Africa, "social groups" do exist, and the potentiality for their transformation into antagonistic classes is present. Every effort, therefore, must be made to prevent this occurrence:

> In our Negro-Berber society . . . there are no classes at war, but only social groups struggling for influence. Tomorrow they will be at war with one another unless we are careful, if we allow the intellectuals—

[23] Quoted in Bankole Timothy, *Kwame Nkrumah: His Rise to Power* (London: G. Allen & Unwin, 1955), p. 150.

[24] Julius Nyerere, *Ujamaa: The Basis of African Socialism* (Dar es Salaam, 1962); reprinted in William H. Friedland and Carl G. Rosberg, Jr. (eds.), *African Socialism* (Stanford: Stanford University Press, 1964), p. 246.

[25] Mamadou Dia, closing speech at the Dakar Colloquim of December, 1962; excepts in *Africa Report, op. cit.*, p. 17.

> liberal professionals, civil servants, employees, and even laborers—to form a class that oppresses by misleading peasants, shepherds, and artisans. To prevent this, political parties and government must be vigilant.[26]

It seems clear, however, that Senghor's distinction between "classes" and "groups" is overdrawn. The several groups that he does identify appear to constitute stratification; they would not vanish into thin air merely by calling them "groups." This is not the same as saying, however, that groups and class lines follow the Marxist pattern.

A slightly different position is set forth by Kouyate, who forecasts the eventual emergence of classes in Africa. He writes:

> . . . the attitude which consists of opposing Marxism by citing the absence of classes in Africa is not a solution; it is purely negative. As a matter of fact, our countries are open to foreign private initiative. A proletariat will come about. If classes do not exist today, the workers of tomorrow, born of this private capital, will assume themselves destined to play the historic role of the revolutionary class. The assertion that classes do not exist in Africa is accurate today, but might not hold true tomorrow.[27]

He proceeds to add immediately, however, that the future of African society will not be determined by the proletarian class alone: "other strata of the population" will play a creative role in the historical process.

Perhaps the most wide-ranging position on the question of class is presented by Nkrumah. Until a few years before his downfall, he rejected the revelance of "class" for Africa. As late as 1962, he described "the African social system" as "communistic," in the sense of being wholly classless: "In the African social system the formulation of a pauper class is unknown, nor is there antagonism of class against class."[28]

Shortly thereafter, Nkrumah's position changed. "In every non-Socialist society," he declared, "there can be found two strata which correspond to that of the oppressor and the oppressed, the exploiter and the exploited"; in African society, he went on, colonial penetration gave rise to a middle class:

> In addition to . . .[the cadre of Africans associated with colonial administration], groups of merchants and traders, lawyers, doctors, politicians and trade unionists emerged, who, armed with skills and levels of affluence which were gratifying to the colonial administration, ini-

[26] Léopold Sédar Senghor, *op. cit.,* p. 87.
[27] Seydou Kouyate, *op. cit.,* p. 16.
[28] Kwame Nkrumah, *Consciencism, op. cit.,* p. 144.

tiated something parallel to the European middle class. There were also certain feudal-minded elements who became imbued with European ideals. . . .[29]

By 1964, authoritative Ghanaian sources had begun to speak of "class enemies" and "class struggle." The semiofficial *Ghanaian Times,* in announcing the existence of an antagonistic capitalist class, declared editorially that "Some of our political scientists have served us the false doctrine that Ghana is fortunate to be starting its social revolution without basic class antagonisms." This, the editorial continued, was a "dangerous fallacy"; the capitalist class "must be crushed."[30]

Although little attention has been paid to the class struggle, some African leaders (including Nkrumah, Senghor, and Touré) have made theoretical statements on "contradictions" and the "dialectic." These treatments are not particularly profound, but the striking fact is the common insistence that, although the dialectic may have its utility as a method of analysis or logic, it is not necessarily applicable to Africa. "We shall refuse to believe . . .," Senghor has flatly asserted, "that 'dialectics' solves all problems and dispenses with the need for reflection"; Touré has objected to "the abstract character of a dialectic."[31]

Although the applicability of the dialectic to the internal politics of Africa is rejected, there is an important area of African political thought in which it has found systematic utilization: the analysis of relationships between the African countries and the colonial powers. Thus, for example, Touré does not see conflict in terms of antagonistic *class* forces within society; he does see "contradictions" in the relationships between the colonies and the imperialist states. Within Guinea he recognizes the existence of such contradictions as peasant-landlord, urban-rural, and industrial–agricultural, but these are not formulated as *class* contradictions. Moreover, they are held subordinate to the contradictions involving imperialism and the colonies.

Similarly, Nkrumah has argued that the main contradiction is that between the rich nations and the poor nations, not within African countries. Senghor has expressed the opinion that in modern times contradictions result "from the domination of one country over another." He adds: "The social problem today is less a class struggle within a nation than a global struggle between the 'have' nations (including the Soviet Union) and the proletarian nations (including the Chinese People's

[29] *Ibid.,* p. 69.

[30] Excerpts in *The New York Times,* Jan. 7, 1964.

[31] Léopold Sédar Senghor, *op. cit.,* p. 42; Sékou Touré, "Africa's Future and the World," *Foreign Affairs,* vol. 41, Oct., 1962, p. 142.

Republic), and we are one of these 'have–not' nations."[32] The overriding problem, as he sees it, is not the resolution of class conflict inside Africa, but closing the gap between the developed countries and the underdeveloped countries.

It should be pointed out in this connection that virtually all prominent African leaders appear to accept, in varying degrees, the Leninist analysis of imperialism. This, however, is due less to the fact that the analysis is "Leninist," and more to the fact that it happens to fit in with the conditions of Africa. The special significance of the Leninist theory is that it highlights the plight of the African peoples under colonial rule and reinforces antiimperialist sentiments. Thus Touré notes that during the French occupation of Guinea, the country "experienced forced labor, the compulsion to supply produce, vaxatious proceedings, humiliations, racial discriminations which, moreover, only betokened a policy of exploitation both oppressive and repressive." In such conditions, the only solution is complete "decolonization," i.e., "detecting all that remains of the colonial system and finding a Guinean solution for it."[33] Senghor maintains that colonialism leads to the dependence of one people upon another, is destructive of human freedom, and creates "total alienation."[34]

By far the most explicit analysis of imperialism–colonialism along Leninist lines is in Nkrumah. The argument has been expounded in a series of writings beginning with *Towards Colonial Freedom* in 1947 and ending with *Neo-Colonialism: The Last Stage of Imperialism,* published in 1966. The resemblance of the latter title to Lenin's *Imperialism: The Highest Stage of Capitalism* is too striking to require comment.

In the early work Nkrumah set forth the standard Leninist arguments regarding the nature of imperialism. Imperialism is the carrier of economic and political exploitation; its only interest lies in the colony's raw materials and cheap labor, and in treating its markets as "dumping grounds" for its surplus products; it is the antithesis of individual and national freedom. Nkrumah's commitment to this analysis was so constant that reviewing it a decade later, he could say, "I am not surprised that my views remain the same."[35]

The argument is reiterated and carried forward in later works, in which the focus of Nkrumah's attention is neocolonialism. Neocolonialism, he argues, is more dangerous than colonialism because it is more

[32] Léopold Sédar Senghor, *op. cit.,* pp. 78, 132–133.

[33] Sékou Touré, *Toward Full Re-Africanization* (Paris: Presence Africaine, 1959), pp. 7, 40.

[34] Léopold Sédar Senghor, *op. cit.,* p. 68.

[35] Kwame Nkrumah, *Autobiography, op. cit.,* p. 48.

subtle, more devious; its chief instrument is "balkanization."[36] In the 1966 work, neocolonialism is presented as "imperialism in its final and most dangerous stage." Its essence remains subjugation of one people to another, but in a disguised form. Foreign capital continues to be used for exploitation; foreign investment is geared to increase, rather than decrease, the gap between the rich and the poor nations.

> Neocolonialism is . . . the worst form of imperialism. For those who practise it, it means power without responsibility and for those who suffer from it, it means exploitation without redress. In the days of old fashioned colonialism, the imperial power had at least to explain and justify at home the actions it was taking abroad. In the colony those who served the ruling imperial power could at least look to its protection against any violent move by their opponents. With neocolonialism, neither is the case.[37]

The major conclusion drawn from this was that African independence and unity are the only effective antidotes to neocolonial policies and practices. African unity must find expression and institutionalization at the continental level, and Afro–Asian solidarity must be strengthened.

The Leninist analysis of imperialism has found support throughout Africa not because it represents a statement of Communist dogma, but because it is consistent with the African perception of realities of life on the continent. It helps dramatize the colonial situation, highlight misery and exploitation, and reintensify the feeling of antimperialism. Lenin need not have been its author; it might have been accepted regardless of source. Equally important is the fact that although the Leninist analysis is accepted, the Leninist conclusions are not drawn. Lenin's major conclusion had to do with the inevitability of global conflict as a consequence of imperialist politics, a conflict that would end in the total collapse of capitalism. This conclusion is found nowhere in the writings of African leaders.

Another common category of Communist thought, the autocratic Party, does find expression in some African leaders' thinking, most explicitly in Nkrumah and Touré. Important qualifications, however, are made.

Nkrumah subscribes to a "vanguardist" conception of the party as the chief instrument of national unification and social construction. The rationale is simple: "Mass movements are well and good but they cannot act with purpose unless they are led and guided by a vanguard political

[36] Kwame Nkrumah, *Consciencism, op. cit.*, pp. 102–103; cf. his *Africa Must Unite* (New York: Praeger, 1963), p. 173.

[37] Kwame Nkrumah, *Neo-Colonialism: The Last Stage of Imperialism* (New York: International Publishers, 1966), p. xi.

party."[38] The party, Nkrumah believes, must be well organized, thoroughly disciplined, and directed by a cadre of activists. He proposes a conception of intraparty decision making closely resembling the Leninist scheme of "democratic centralism," including the intolerance of opposition and dissent.

> In our Party all are equal regardless of their race or tribe. All are free to express their views. But once a majority decision is taken, we expect such a decision to be loyally executed, even by those who might have opposed that decision. This we consider and proclaim to be the truest form of Democratic Centralism—decisions freely arrived at and loyally executed. This applies from the lowest to the highest level. None is privileged and no one shall escape disciplinary action.[39]

Touré's conception of the party also stresses the role of a small leadership or "vanguard" group whose authority is "absolute." The party, he has said, symbolizes discipline and control; it "is the brain of our society." There is an explicit commitment to democratic centralism:

> (a) All the party leaders are directly and democratically chosen by the supporters who all enjoy full liberty of conscience and of expression within the party;
> (b) The . . . program of the party is democratically discussed. As long as no decision has been made, each is free to say what he thinks or what he wishes. But when, after extensive discussions in congress or in assembly, a decision has been arrived at by a unanimous vote or by a majority, the supporters and the leaders are bound to apply it correctly;
> (c) The responsibility for leadership is not shared. Only the responsibility for a decision is shared. Thus, no breach of discipline can be permitted.[40]

Touré calls for the practice of "criticism and self-criticism" within the party, because it helps pinpoint responsibility and achieve party unity and control. Without criticism and self-criticism, he writes, "the Party slowly dies."[41]

Both Nkrumah and Touré, then, do subscribe to a "vanguardist" conception of the party and do speak of certain "Communist" practices. However, they are far from putting their conception of the party into the Leninist straightjacket. Unlike the orthodox Communists, both Nkrumah and Touré have proclaimed a commitment to mass-membership parties. Neither Nkrumah nor Touré sees the party as standing for

[38] Kwame Nkrumah, *Autobiography, op. cit.*, p. xv; cf. his *I Speak of Freedom* (New York: Praeger, 1961), pp. 163 ff.

[39] Kwame Nkrumah, *I Speak of Freedom, op. cit.*, p. 164.

[40] Sékou Touré, *Toward Full Re-Africanization, op. cit.*, pp. 46, 91.

[41] *Ibid.*, p. 22.

the interest of any specific group or class; nor is it an instrument of class struggle. On the contrary, the party is seen as embracing the entire nation. Nkrumah writes: "The Convention People's Party is Ghana. Our Party . . . is the custodian which stands guard over the welfare of the whole people." The CPP, he argues, "though imbued with Marxist socialist philosophy," does not follow the Communist pattern: "the C.P.P. has been built up out of our own experiences, conditions and environment."[42] Touré insists that the Partie Democratique de Guinée is a popular, progressive party that unites "all the masses of the country."[43] Toure describes the PDG as a "vanguard democratic party" capable of unifying the entire nation and pursuing the general interest.

Similar conceptions of the party are presented by other African leaders. Kouyate sees the party in Mali as the most important agent of national unification:

> . . . the political organization has been the melting pot where the peasant and the city dweller have met. It has pulled the former out of his isolation, cured the latter of his disdain for the bush, and achieved practically the national unity from which it was drawing its strength.[44]

Senghor, in a similar vein, has written:

> The formula of the dominant party seemed best to us. It rejects violence, which is useless here. It appeals to nationalist sentiment. . . . This is why the dominant party is the party of the masses: a political organization of the nation evolving toward the nation's construction by socialization—in other words, by planning, conceived as integral development, with the nation and each individual citizen progressing from underdevelopment to development.[45]

Thus, although the primacy of the party is everywhere stressed, nowhere has the party been viewed as strictly Marxist–Leninist in character. To be sure, certain Leninist concepts and phrases are used, but no commitment to an explicit Communist formulation has been made.

General African orientation toward peaceful social construction has led to a rejection of the notions of violent revolution and dictatorship of the proletariat. Ideologically, violence is seen as out of context in Africa. Touré, for example, has said that "No task can be well done, no enterprise can endure where there is coercion and force."[46] Nkrumah's notion of "positive action," formulated in the 1940s, was based

[42] Kwame Nkrumah, *I Speak of Freedom, op. cit.*, pp. 161, 209; *Africa Must Unite, op. cit.*, p. 129.

[43] Sékou Touré, *Toward Full Re-Africanization, op. cit.*, p. 16.

[44] Seydou Kouyate, *op. cit.*, p. 16.

[45] Léopold Sédar Senghor, *op. cit.*, p. 145.

[46] Sékou Touré, *Toward Full Re-Africanization, op. cit.*, pp. 50–51.

on "the principle of absolute nonviolence. . . ."[47] Subsequently, as we have seen, he did advocate force, but the rationale was not drawn from Marxism–Leninism:

> There is a tendency to forget that Britain's evolution into democracy was not altogether peaceful. . . . The states of America fought a bitter civil war, whose memories still condition attitudes and thinking, to impose their union. . . .
>
> Conditions in Ghana today are comparable with those prevailing in Britain or France or America at the time when they were struggling to establish a free form of government. . . .[48]

Nkrumah makes a distinction between "communal" and "noncommunal" societies, arguing that only in the latter will transition to socialism take place through revolution and violence.

> . . . from the ancestral line of [African] communalism, the passage to socialism lies in reform, because the underlying principles are the same. . . . But because of the continuity of communalism with socialism, in communalistic societies, socialism is not a revolutionary creed, but a restatement in contemporary idiom of the principles underlying communalism.[49]

This point of view is common throughout Africa. Dia insists, for example, that Africa must at all costs avoid dictatorship, revolution, and violence. Although African development does call for transformation of colonial society into a new society, such transformation, he believes, does not call for the blind use of violence. Similarly, Senghor has written that the notion of the dictatorship of the proletariat is irrelevant to Senegal because there is no proletariat in Senegal: "lacking a bourgeoisie, we Senegalese could have no proletariat." He adds:

> What good is our independence if it is only to imitate European totalitarianism, to replace external colonialism by domestic colonialism. Dictatorship of the proletariat? That is simply gargling a formula: There would have to be a proletariat and a capitalism "at war" in our countries, to use Marx's language.[50]

Under Stalin, whose views Senghor describes as a "major deviation" of communism, the dictatorship of the proletariat "made the state an omnipotent, soulless monster"; it destroyed human freedom, and became "the dictatorship of the Party and State in self-perpetuation."[51]

As a whole, then, one cannot call "Communist" the complex of

[47] Kwame Nkrumah, *Autobiography, op. cit.,* p. 112.
[48] Kwame Nkrumah, *Africa Must Unite, op. cit.,* p. 67.
[49] Kwame Nkrumah, *Consciencism, op. cit.,* p. 74.
[50] Léopold Sédar Senghor, *op. cit.,* p. 87.
[51] *Ibid.,* pp. 45–46.

ideas we have identified. Of the several criteria commonly associated with Communist ideology, only two—the Leninist analysis of imperialism and the vanguardist conception of the Party—are met in the political thought of African leaders, and at that only with qualifications. The Leninist analysis of imperialism is popular in Africa because of all the conceptual alternatives, the Leninist "theory" seems to explain imperialism most satisfactorily, and not because it is Leninist. Even the conception of the party as a "vanguard" is only superficially Leninist, for it lacks the basic Leninist goals and outlook. African leaders have not viewed their parties as a class instrument, or as a vehicle of "Communist society" brought about through violence. All African leaders have endeavored to make their parties mass-membership parties, even aspiring to have their entire citizenry as stalwart members. African parties are viewed as instruments for national unification, economic planning, and social construction; as such, they are more "Socialist" in outlook and purpose. Indeed, "African socialism" is the most widely proclaimed ideological aim of African leaders.

The feeling in Africa is that "socialism" is the most appropriate ideology and that in the absence of a local entrepreneurial class and the necessary capital, only the state possesses the authority and the means to undertake capital development.[52] Thus in almost every African country, planned socialism is seen as the only rational—indeed, the only possible—road to development. According to Nyerere, "I believe that no underdeveloped country can afford to be anything but 'socialist.' I believe, therefore, that we in Africa are bound to organize ourselves on a socialist pattern."[53] Similarly, having rejected both capitalism and communism, Senghor insists that "We stand for a middle course, for a democratic socialism. . . ." He further argues that planned socialism, with its emphasis on the interests of the society as a whole, will prevent the formation of antagonistic classes and the emergence of class struggle.[54]

Conclusions

Essentially, communism as a domestic political factor in the independent states of Africa has been prevented from becoming anything significant

[52] For various expressions of African socialism, see, for example, the works of Brockway, Friedland and Rosberg, Nkrumah, Senghor, and Touré cited in the bibliography at the end of this chapter. See also *Africa Report,* VIII, May, 1963.

[53] Julius Nyerere, "The Second Scramble," speech at the opening of the World Assembly of Youth's second Pan-African Youth Seminar, Aug. 5, 1961.

[54] Léopold Sédar Senghor, *op. cit.,* pp. 46, 129.

because it must operate on grounds that have been preempted by African nationalism. African ideology borrows, uses, and adapts; it necessarily produces certain amounts of parallelism in Marxist–Leninist ideological cant, but this in itself portends nothing about Communist proclivities among African nationalists.

Communist Parties are few and small in Africa, and likely to remain so. Because of the general utility of one-party politics, existing regimes are no more predisposed to tolerate opposition from a Communist Party than they are from any other source. Communist *influence* however, in the sense of policies originating in Moscow or Peking, remains a possibility. In the case of Guinea, the Soviet Union demonstrated its readiness gently to strangle a friendly state into desparate dependence; there, the Guinean government was willing to take the steps to extricate itself while it still could. In Ghana, where Soviet efforts at building the groundwork for influence proceeded more circumspectly, and earned more success, the calamity of terminating Communist-influenced policy was much greater than in Guinea, taking the form of a military revolt which overturned the domestic government itself.

Soviet concerns are multiple and mixed. It is unquestionably of significance to Soviet "African policy" that the Russians operate within the Cold War environment, and have committed themselves to avoiding violent confrontation with Western countries. This is a necessary background against which to understand Soviet policies in Algeria and the Congo, for example. It is a part of the explanation, also, of the Soviet stance toward the option of either supporting nationalist governments or fostering Communist Parties inside African countries. For the present at least, the Soviets appear to have committed themselves to seeking cooperation with the popular nationalist regimes, trying at the same time to keep open the door to possibilities of left-revolutionary tendencies, and even Communist Parties, inside or outside the nationalist organizations. If forced to choose, preference would probably go to the nationalist government. This policy has had ample precedent in the classic example of Egypt, where the Soviet Union curried favor with President Nasser at the very time that Nasser was engaging in a campaign to smash the Egyptian Communist Party. To a degree this same issue was involved in the Soviet Union's policy of abandoning the UPC and establishing relations with the Ahidjo government in the Cameroun.

Another inescapable ingredient of Soviet policy is rooted in Sino–Soviet rivalry in Africa. The Chinese have taken the lead in stressing to Africans how they (the Chinese) differ from the Russians. Claiming solidarity based on underdevelopment, racial affinity, and more consistent revolutionism, the Chinese have not sought favor with all African governments to the exclusion of support for radical revolutionary interests. In the Congo, in the Cameroun, in Zanzibar, and elsewhere, the Chinese have openly worked with real or potential rebel elements—to the great displeasure of the African governments.

It is unwarranted to presume that because they are Communist, totalitarian, etc., the Communist states have nothing but advantages over the West in furthering their interests in Africa. Communist countries, for all their appeal, have not succeeded in overaweing African leaders, as is sometimes feared. While perhaps few Africans are experts on the Communist states, they are not ignorant of the disadvantages of membership in the "Communist Camp." Particularly in the case of the Soviet Union, African leaders are aware of the opportunist and at times hypocritical past of the Comintern. They are aware of the character of totalitarianism. This is more true, of course, among older African leaders than among the younger; and it is most true among those older leaders who have had the longest and closest association with Communists—particularly the South African nationalist leaders. But even among the young men there is the embittered reaction of those students who have left (or have been ejected) from Communist countries.

Moreover, the Communist countries no less than the Western countries, have brought to their involvement with Africa an inadequate understanding of that continent—and here the Chinese are at even greater disadvantage than the Soviets. Sound knowledge of African realities is no older than the independence decade itself—and at that is still not free of ideological bias. Communists encounter the same difficulties as other outsiders when it comes to grasping the essential facets of the African "mentality." And, despite denials, even the (officially) pure-principled Communists have not been free of racial and cultural discrimination and prejudice.

On the other hand, the Communist powers undoubtedly do have some advantages in their attempt to establish influence in Africa. Anti-imperialism remains a most intense issue throughout the continent; and the Communist states, not having a traditional imperialist past, have not failed to capitalize on the political importance of antiimperialist slogans. A certain amount of Western embarrassment in international politics on this issue is, apparently, endemic. The Communist countries have other advantages as well: the greater facility to utilize political motives in economic policies, for example. The West has had difficulty in this respect: trade balances between Western and African countries typically remain quite unfavorable for the latter; investment in capital development projects is difficult to find in the West in cases where the likelihood of substantial economic return—profit—is small or absent. African leaders, in dire need of trading economies and development capital, frequently resent these Western attributes, and find the Communist approach preferable. Still, the bulk of African trade is oriented to the countries of the West, and to alter this remains costly.

Ideologically, African intellectuals have seen neither capitalism nor communism as appropriate for Africa. It is a recurrent theme of African political thought that as a third force in world affairs, Africa must reject both capitalism and communism and choose a midway course. African leaders insist that Africa must adapt from contending ideologies those things most appropriate for Africa, without wholesale imitation. The central question is not whether to stand for capitalism or for communism, but how to maximize the interests of Africa. Accordingly, African leaders have adapted for their own use certain Communist ideas and practices, but this, as we have seen, has not made them "Communist." More specifically, the politicoeconomic content of African ideologies is much closer to socialism—a socialism adapted to the specific conditions and needs of Africa. Socialism has been particularly attractive because, in conformity with traditional African values, it stresses the welfare of the collectivity, communal ownership, cooperation, egalitarianism, and humanism.

Finally, and perhaps most significantly for the future, in those areas of Africa today where the basic issues of coloniasilm are still unresolved, and where, indeed, colonialism appears to be doing its utmost to entrench itself, the continued frustration of the efforts to win freedom and independence carries the possibility that the African peoples may turn in desperation to radical alternatives. South Africa and Rhodesia, and the Portuguese colonies—all Western-oriented regimes—constitute, as Colin and Margaret Legum have pointed out, "a crisis for the West."[55] This crisis may be turned to advantage by the Communists.

SELECTED BIBLIOGRAPHY

Africa Report, vol. VIII, no. 5, May, 1963. Special issue on African socialism. In addition to three articles on ideological, sociological, and economic aspects of African socialism, this issue includes an informative selection of statements by African leaders on the sources, nature, and objectives of socialism in Africa.

[55] Colin & Margaret Legum, *South Africa: Crisis for the West* (London: Pall Mall Press, 1964).

Ajao, Aderogba, *On the Tiger's Back* (Cleveland: World Publishing, 1962). A Nigerian, Ajao spent several years in East Germany, where he was coerced into Communist education and from which he eventually fled. Strongly anti-Communist, it reflects the author's disgust at his experiences inside a Communist country.

Amar, Andrew Richard, *A Student in Moscow* (London: Ampersand Press, 1961). Written by a Ugandan student in Russia, this is a short account of disillusionment over experiences in the USSR.

Brockway, A. Fenner, *African Socialism* (London: The Bodley Head, 1963). Examines the emergence of socialist ideology in Africa and identifies four trends: Communism (Marxism–Leninism), African Marxism, African Pragmatic Socialism, and African Democratic Socialism. Chapters on the socialism of Nasser and Nkrumah.

Brzezinski, Zbigniew (ed.), *Africa and the Communist World* (Stanford: Stanford University Press, 1963). An excellent and scholarly study of the policies of the Communist countries toward Africa. Written by specialists, chapters cover Soviet political policies, Soviet economic policies, Eastern European policies, Yugoslav policies, and Chinese policies.

Cooley, John K., *East Wind Over Africa: Red China's African Offensive* (New York: Walker, 1965). The only book length survey of Communist Chinese activities in Africa. Journalistic rather than scholarly, the work suffers from the conservative bias of the author and a strident and alarmist anticommunism. Nevertheless useful; contains valuable statistical tables and documents in the appendices.

Friedland, William H. and Carl G. Rosberg, Jr. (eds.), *African Socialism* (Stanford: Stanford University Press, 1964). Perhaps the most comprehensive work of its kind, this volume brings together eleven essays by as many specialists on a wide range of subjects relative to African socialism. Seven appendices present original statements by Nkrumah, Nyerere, Padmore, Senghor, and others.

Hevi, Emmanuel, *An African Student in China* (New York: Praeger, 1962). Written by a Ghanaian who went to China as a student, and left in disgust. Disclaiming any liking for the West or for colonialism, the author has written a strongly anti-Communist and anti-Chinese account of his, and other African students', treatment by the Chinese.

Morison, David, *The U.S.S.R. and Africa* (London and New York: Oxford University Press, 1964). A very detailed and carefully documented presentation of Soviet views on Africa from Soviet sources. Morison is editor of the *Mizan Newsletter,* a periodical review of Russian publications on Asia and Africa published by Oxford University's Central Asian Research Center. An invaluable source for Soviet materials on Africa.

Nkrumah, Kwame, *Consciencism: Philosophy and Ideology for Decolonization and Development with Particular Reference to the African*

Revolution (New York: Monthly Review Press, 1964). Nkrumah's philosophical work. "Consciencism" refers to the standpoint stressing the need for fusing the three dominant influences in contemporary Africa: the European, the Islamic, and the Traditional African.

Nkrumah, Kwame, *Neo-Colonialism: The Last Stage of Imperialism* (New York: International Publishers, 1966). Title, contents, and much of the substance closely parallel that of Lenin's *Imperialism: The Highest Stage of Capitalism.*

Padmore, George, *Pan-Africanism or Communism? The Coming Struggle for Africa* (London: Dennis Dobson, 1956). An account of Pan-Africanism generally, written by one of its major participants, who was a West Indian. Personal in style, the book provides excellent material in both theoretical expositions and historical facts not available elsewhere. The chapter, "Communism and Black Nationalism," is invaluable to the study of communism in Africa.

Roux, Edward, *Time Longer Than Rope: A History of the Black Man's Struggle For Freedom in South Africa,* 2nd ed. (Madison: University of Wisconsin Press, 1964). The major work on the history of the African people in South Africa that devotes significant attention to the Communists. Written by a (white) former member of the South African Communist Party, the book is in the style of a memoire, although its documentation is excellent. The author's bias toward the "left" is undeniable, though his standard of historical chronicling is high.

Schatten, Fritz, *Communism in Africa* (New York: Praeger, 1965). A general survey of communism in Africa, this book, written by a German journalist, suffers from a conservative bias and occasional errors of fact. More journalistic than scholarly, the book is valuable as the only survey of its kind.

Senghor, Léopold Sédar, *On African Socialism,* translated and with an Introduction by Mercer Cook (New York: Praeger, 1964). Brings together three separate works written between 1959 and 1962, plus a useful introduction by the translator. The book represents a major statement of the African approach to socialism, and reveals Senghor as a sensitive thinker.

Touré, Sékou, *Toward Full Re-Africanization* (Paris: *Présence Africaine,* 1959). Subtitled "Policy and Principles of the Guinea Democratic Party," this important work touches upon virtually every aspect of life in Guinea. Chapters on decolonization, economic planning, "democracy," etc., provide an overview of the political thought of this major leader.

Woodis, Jack, *Africa: The Lion Awakes* (London: Lawrence and Wishart, 1961). Written by a leading British Communist expert on Africa, this book focuses not on communism directly, but on the anticolonialist revolt on the continent; it provides insights into a Western Communist's perception of Africa.

9

Communism in Southeast Asia

Ruth T. McVey

SOUTHEAST ASIA, the late Indonesian Communist leader D. N. Aidit used to say, has become the center of the world revolutionary struggle.[1] Certainly, that area has witnessed more than its share of upheaval since World War II, one of the latest victims of its seemingly endemic violence being Aidit's own Party. The Southeast Asian instability has been partly a result of circumstances beyond the control of the region's inhabitants: The most powerful political forces in twentieth-century Southeast Asia have been external ones, and in the past generation there has been an extraordinary succession of these. The post-Stalin changes in the Communist world and the 1956 events in Eastern Europe are not, however, to be numbered among them, either in general or even specifically in the case of Communist movements, which, as we shall see, have not been under overwhelming Soviet control. Moreover, the Southeast Asian disorder has rested on social forces at work in the area itself; many of these were generated originally by changes or ideas introduced from outside, but they now have acquired a momentum quite their own. A condition has been created whereby for many people of the area there exists an unbridgeable gap between the mandates of custom and the requirements of reality, or between what actually exists and the vision of what the world should be like. Southeast Asia's cultural variety has meant that this malaise has been felt and expressed in a number of different ways, but the basic problem throughout has been that of determining a response to modernization.

[1] *Harian Rakjat* (Djakarta: official PKI newspaper), Jan. 1, 1964; Aidit's political report to the December, 1963, Central Committee plenum.

There are few areas of Southeast Asia which have not, in one way or another, felt the socioeconomic repercussions of the industrial revolution. In some places this has been indirectly experienced, seeming a distant ripple (though even here its consequences may be profound—consider the effect on social and economic organization of public health measures that raise the population level above what the land can support), and in others it may appear as a tidal wave that sweeps away the traditional social structure and leaves behind little but debris and promises. The promises are implicit in the image of the industrially advanced state that is conveyed to the nascent national elites by the power in whose sphere of influence they fall. The image is one of prosperity and strength; the ideological messages conveyed with it proclaim that this happy estate results from a different ordering of society and a different hierarchy of values than those which their countries had hitherto known.

In general the political elites of Southeast Asia have come to endorse "modernity" as a goal, and in doing so have adopted as their own ideals those several desiderata common to the expressed ideologies of all industrial states: national independence, democracy, and social equality. These concepts are descendants of the French *liberté, ĕgalité,* and *fraternité,* however variously they have come to be interpreted by our century. Some members of the modernizing elites have comprehended them as being the proper aim for all society, the achievement of which only the industrial revolution has made realizable, others as the most efficient instruments for arriving at that rational social order which is most conducive to material progress. The difficulty has lain not so much in securing acknowledgment of modernity or its concomitant but in determining how to go about achieving them. Should the ways of the dominant power be copied directly and without reservation? Should the doors be thrown open wide to outside influence in an effort to transform the country as rapidly and as completely as possible into a modern state? To follow such a course has frequently been the first reaction to the decision that fundamental change is needed; and some individuals or groups who were given the opportunity to imitate the dominant foreign culture and to obtain some of the advantages enjoyed by the aliens resident among them have continued to maintain the belief that in this lies the key to salvation.

For most members of the Southeast Asian elites, imitation has been less possible to accomplish and the advantages of attempting it have appeared less clear, in part because the transformation involved would go against still-respected principles of the traditional order. Moreover, it soon became evident that the unhesitating embrace of everything foreign did not necessarily bring the progress desired. When industrialized and preindustrial societies exist side by side, modernization is a highly ambiguous process, for it may well have consequences carrying the non-industrial state away from rather than towards real economic development. The phenomenon is by now all too familiar: transportation is improved and as a result a budding local textile industry is killed by imported goods; health and sanitation are improved, and a rising population eliminates the margin of income needed for capital investment. Moreover, not only does the process of modernization not necessarily lead to modernity, but the detraditionalization that is a part of it is not reversible. By the time the problem is appreciated and an indigenous elite has obtained the political power that would enable it to check the process, too many new ideas have entered and too many new interests have been created. In many cases, economic changes have taken place which make it physically as well as psychologically impossible to turn back. It is hardly surprising that subjection to a process which is alien in its origin, inexorable in its extension, and uncertain and often negative in its effects should arouse strong resentment, particularly on the part of those who experience it solely as the irretrievable loss of a more meaningful and often more prosperous world. Nor is it surprising that this resentment becomes focussed on the area or group seen as the source of this change.

Because elements and ideas of modernization were initially acquired from foreign conquerors by all Southeast Asian countries save Thailand, arriving at an acceptable attitude towards modernization has been particularly vexing. This difficulty has been exacerbated by the fact that in the past few decades the region has been subjected to a number of severely disruptive shifts in power which have brought with them different ideologies and attitudes: from Western colonial to wartime Japanese regimes, then to an attempted colonial resurgence, and finally to a period of national self-determination qualified by a growing American presence and, still, in the distance, a rising Chinese power. Finally, Southeast Asia has been for more than a decade a prime area for Cold War competition, with the foreign superstates furthering their power interests by aid and advice packaged with ideological recipes for the achievement of modernity. All this has meant that the region has experienced changes which badly eroded or shattered old institutions. A range of new societal patterns has been held before the leadership of the Southeast Asian state; however, each of these alternatives is ticketed with a clear reminder of its foreign derivation.

Relatively Unchanged Societies

As Marx himself pointed out, colonialism is by no means without its progressive aspects from the revolutionary viewpoint, inasmuch as it has served to cripple or destroy the traditional order, create social tensions, and introduce new ideas.[2] It is certainly no accident that the sole Southeast Asian country to have thus far escaped a postwar upheaval more unsettling than an occasional palace coup is the one state, Thailand, that was not subjected to colonial rule. Since the revolution of 1932—itself in reality a *coup d'état*—a military-bureaucratic elite has been able to channel and adjust to the changes imposed by modernization as a process while muffling or reinterpreting the demands of modernity as an ideal, with the result that a highly conservative socioeconomic structure has been successfully maintained. However, in the mid–1960s Thailand entered a period of rapid economic growth, and it may be that the type and rate of the accompanying change will be more than the country's social and political structure can accomodate. Should it fail to adjust, there could take place that widespread alienation which provides the backing for serious ideologies of social revolution. In this communism—which is no stranger to Thailand[3]—has the advantage that the present system of military rule, with its firm suppression of dissent and steady emphasis on communism as an all-purpose bogeyman, runs the risk of giving Marxism, whose support has historically been restricted to the occasional intellectual dissentor, the allure of forbidden fruit in the eyes of a discontented younger generation. Moreover, the Vietnam war has brought to Thailand a swiftly expanding American presence, which has contrasted sharply with the inward, conservative character of the society it has entered, placing it under considerable strain. The rise in elite anti-American sentiment and the occurrence of intermittent violence in the countryside in the mid-1960s reflect the pressures to which Thai society is being subjected. It is not yet possible to say whether these pressures are great enough to support a general insurgency, but certainly they presage an irreversable change from the traditional order of things.

Most current concern for the danger of revolution in Thailand has been devoted to the backward and poverty-stricken region of the north-

[2] Karl Marx, "The British Rule in India," in Marx and Engels, *Selected Writings* (Moscow: 1955), vol. I, p. 351.

[3] The Communist Party of Thailand, represented in parliament from 1946 until the coup of 1947, was a member of the Constitution Front, a "Popular Front" style coalition. *See* David A. Wilson, *Politics in Thailand* (Ithaca: Cornell University Press, 1962), p. 236.

east, an area traditionally isolated from central government interest and control. The strategic location of the northeast with respect to the contest for Laos having drawn attention to the region's importance in the 1960s, intensive efforts were made to link it more closely to central Thailand. In the process it was observed that the region was plagued by violence, with local officials prominent among the victims. Whether this represented a new insurgency, or a tendency to dacoity long endured by the local society, or the clash between private and public law natural to the process of consolidating a frontier area, was hard to say in the general absence of knowledge about the region. At least, however, it pointed to a frangibility in the social structure.[4] The massive buildup of American military bases in the hitherto isolated and economically backward region, which took place in connection with the Vietnam war in the mid-1960s, was unlikely to aid in alleviating violence. Moreover, importance of the area for the Vietnam affair gave Hanoi and Peking reason to devote some effort to the encouragement of insurrection there. In consequence, an area that suffered more from a lack of structure and articulated authority than from positively revolutionizing forces may, by virtue of events and interests outside it, find itself in a revolutionary situation. We shall see a similar development on a larger scale in Laos.

Another country whose structure is, in its way, as conservative as Thailand's is Cambodia, which, having been peripheral to colonial interests, passed relatively undisturbed through the period of foreign rule. To be sure, its conservatism is worn with a difference, for Prince Sihanouk's perception of Cambodia's national interest is such that his country has sought accomodation with China rather than the United States. The latter he viewed as the supporter of Thailand and South Vietnam, two states with active claims on portions of Cambodia's territory.[5] In addition, Sihanouk sought to take the wind out of the domestic oppo-

[4] Some idea of the dimensions of the debate can be gained from the symposium on the Northeast problem published in *Asian Survey,* vol. VI, no. 7, July, 1966. For an excellent analysis, see Charles F. Keyes, *Isan: Regionalism in Northeastern Thailand* (Ithaca, 1967). A principal cause of concern has been that the population of the region is generally Lao-speaking and therefore, it is feared, open to appeals on an ethnic basis. However, there is no Lao political or cultural center towards which Thailand's minority, traditionally oriented toward Bangkok, might reasonably be expected to look. In apparent recognition of this, the anti-government groups that have thus far established with the blessings of Peking and Hanoi have been under auspices of the Thailand Patriotic Front, which, as its name declares, aims at revolutionizing the whole country rather than detaching part of it.

[5] Sihanouk's position toward North Vietnam, while far more cordial than his view of the South, has been cooler than toward China, apparently for fear that

sition's sails by appearing as a champion of progressivism at home and abroad, in the process taking up slogans of socialism as well as anti-imperialism. His attitude to modernization in general and the Marxist–Leninist road to modernity in particular is, at best, ambiguous. It is Sihanouk's announced view that communism represents the wave of the future and at the same time a fate which is so unpleasant as to be postponed as long as humanly possible.[6] His own brand of painless socialism, a combination of Marxist borrowings, prudent politics, and traditional concepts of welfare and the state, is presented as the best means by which to stave off that evil day.

Domestic Cambodian communism, a frail but stubborn flower, is represented by the Pracheachon, a minor party which did not join the Sankum Reastr Viyun, the political machine established by Sihanouk in 1955. Though small and without distinguished leadership, the Pracheachon comprises almost the sole organized opposition to the regime. It is part of an amorphous grouping sometimes given the label Khmer Red, which includes some former adherents of the Democratic Party (once the major opposition group but dissolved into the Sankum in 1957) and other dissidents, mostly younger intellectuals. Their status has thus far been ambiguous, with positions of trust being given to prominent Khmer Red partisans with one hand and light harassment being imposed with the other. Unlike its predecessors of the preindependence period—the Khmer Issarak and the Comité Khmer de Libération Nationale[7]—the opposition of this group has been loyal. It has no mass base, but represents rather a younger educated elite which can find no economic or spiritual place in the existing structure. Precisely because Cambodian government and society have had to alter so little, while at the same time opportunities for modern education and acquaintance with outside ideas have been considerable, a very marked generational schism has occurred within the Cambodian elite. It should be noted that Sihanouk's verbal radicalism helps bridge this gap by giving a progressive and future-oriented cast to what might otherwise seem to impatient youth a hopelessly traditionalist regime.

---

the northern Democratic Republic of Vietnam (DRV) shares the general Vietnamese ambitions regarding Cambodian territory. *See,* for example, *La Dépêche du Cambodge* (Phnom Penh: principal French-language Cambodian newspaper), Nov. 19, 1964 (Sihanouk speech on returning from China and discussions with the North Vietnamese).

[6] For a sample of this argument, see Sihanouk's report to the Sankum Reastr Niyun, Nov. 14, 1964, in *La Dépêche du Cambodge,* Nov. 16, 1964.

[7] For a description of the development of the Khmer Issarak and the related Khmer Committee of National Liberation, see Roger M. Smith, *Cambodia's Foreign Policy* (Ithaca: Cornell University Press, 1965), pp. 24–32.

At the same time, however, the proclamation of radical ideals arouses expectations that strides will be made towards their fulfillment. This, as we shall see in the case of Indonesia, can have consequences of the gravest nature for the incumbent regime. In Cambodia, however, the Prince's youth, his political acumen, and the lack of pressing socioeconomic problems make it seem unlikely that this will be a direct source of early trouble. Rather, the restlessness of the younger elite appears to be a ferment akin to the prewar agitation of disaffected younger intellectuals in Burma or Indonesia—of little immediate impact but of singular importance for the development of future revolutionary leaders.

Though the Cambodian condition appears to offer little hope to a Marxist–Leninist movement, the structure of all Southeast Asian states is sufficiently labile and international intervention in the area sufficiently intense that with a little less strong leadership, and a little more activity by foreign interests, a very different situation could have arisen. An unhappy example of such a development is Laos, which emerged from World War II with a background not unlike Cambodia's. It had been a backwater to European and Japanese regimes and, possessing a relatively stable and uncomplicated socioeconomic structure, was on the face of it not a likely environment for a successful movement on the far left. Nonetheless one arose, due partly to the fact that there was not, as in Cambodia, a paramount figure of traditional authority capable of maintaining a strong grip on the country's affairs, but rather three rival principalities under minimal kingly authority. Moreover, there was in the figure of Prince Souphanouvong, a royal personage of the far left, to which position he had become attracted while a student in France during the "Popular Front" period. His political leanings, coupled with the presence of the other princely rivals and ideologically committed foreign powers with an interest in the region, were to make communism a principal issue in the struggle for the control of Laos.

When less radical leaders of the Lao Issarak independence movement elected to return from their Bangkok exile to a formally independent Laos following the French reoccupation of 1946–1959, Souphanouvong elected to go it alone in a Vietminh-type struggle for complete national liberation. The result was what has become known as the Pathet Lao Movement,[8] which, in spite of efforts to reach a modus vivendi with neutralist and rightist forces, which achieved their

[8] "Pathet Lao" actually refers to the movement's goal, the Nation of Laos. It took the name Neo Lao Issara (Free Laos Front) in 1950; in assuming legal status in preparation for the elections of 1958 it became the Neo Lao Hak Xat (Laos Patriotic Front).

greatest substance in the ill-fated coalition of 1957–1959, has maintained control over its own armed units and territory. Indeed, despite occasional setbacks its territorial and military position showed steady improvement. By 1964 it had extended itself loosely over virtually all the country save the Mekong lowlands. In holding the essentials of Maoist revolutionary strategy—military power and an advantageously located territorial base—the Pathet Lao enjoys a position in Southeast Asia comparable only to that of the revolutionary movement in Vietnam.

A fateful element in the Laotian contest has been the reliance of the rival princes on foreign support. It was hardly necessary to solicit such backing, as both Thailand and Vietnam had longstanding interests in the area, reflecting both general expansionist impulses and a specific desire to secure the vital frontier communications lines of the Mekong River and what is now the Ho Chi Minh trail. These local concerns have been strongly reinforced by great-power desire to control Laos ideologically and militarily for purposes of the Vietnam war. Cambodia, similarly a buffer state between Vietnam and Thailand, was able to prevent foreign-supported insurrectionary movements—the Viet Minh-backed Khmer Committee of National Liberation of the period of the independence struggle and the more recent Thai- and South Vietnamese-succored Khmer Serei—from effectively linking up with domestic political forces of major importance. As a matter of fact, the "exposure" of the foreign allegiances of dissident elements within his own country has served Sihanouk well as a weapon against the legal opposition. In Laos, however, domestic rivalries and foreign interests have tended to reinforce each other, so that the competing factions have been driven farther away from one another and have become more dependent on outside backing.

In spite of international efforts to reduce the Laotian crisis through the Geneva agreements of 1954 and 1962, through third-power intervention (principally that of the Soviet Union), and through attempts at a forceful restoration of a balance such as represented by the Kong Le coup, the over-all trend has been towards a polarization of forces into two camps heavily influenced by foreign interest. A critical development in this process came in April–May, 1964, when, after a rightist military coup, an agreement was reached between the neutralist Souvanna Phouma and the rightist forces which in effect acknowledged the former's command over a government which would carry out the policies of the latter. In the end, the pursuit of compromise or conflict depends much less on Laotian initiative than on the desires of the foreign parties concerned; there is little reason to assume either of the rival princes are pleased with this state of affairs, which essentially places them in pawn to interests allied with states traditionally hostile to the Lao, but there is equally little reason to think they can do much to restore their independence before the settlement of the conflict in Vietnam.

Although the Pathet Lao grew out of a princely rivalry reinforced by foreign intervention, it has since acquired a social base and a set of interests of its own. Given the weak and confused nature of Laotian central authority, the rapid enrichment and cultural transformation of some segments of the elite resulting from the foreign presence, and the general disorganization produced by lengthy and indecisive warfare, it is not surprising that even a society which did not at the outset present marked anomic tendencies should soon acquire them. In spite of its lack of prior organizational or intellectual background, the Pathet Lao has managed to create what is certainly for Laos a complex and widespread organization for the mobilization and control of the population. That it has done so is probably a key ingredient in its success, for a principal attraction of Communist or Communist-type movements in areas experiencing cultural breakdown is their offer of a coherent rationale and structure.

In its mobilization effort the Pathet Lao has pursued a strategy similar to that employed by the Chinese Communists and the Viet Minh in the areas they controlled while not yet everywhere in power; this same strategy has been pressed by the Viet Cong in South Vietnam and by Indonesia's PKI in the parts of rural Java where its peasant organization was well established. Land reform has not been a major issue in Laos, as it was in these other countries, but even in areas where land ownership has been a burning issue the general tendency has been to pursue reform with sufficient energy to reassure the poorer peasants that their interests have not been forgotten while attempting to avoid the alienation of more of the village population than absolutely necessary. Emphasis at stages short of ubiquitous power has been on the maximization of solidarity and support behind the movement. To this end, ideally, thorough studies are made of village socioeconomic relations and attitudes; peasants are carefully introduced to new ways of considering the world and their own condition; and various institutions and activities are organized to demonstrate to the villagers that they, when properly led, are capable of changing their own lives. The faith and energies so mobilized are directed against an enemy which is as obvious and alien to the village as possible: gentry, absentee landlords, and moneylenders, in the immediate vicinity; further removed, a corrupt and uncomprehending government; or, as the optimum foe, a foreign oppressor.

A second point in which the Pathet Lao's approach has been similar to that employed successfully elsewhere in Southeast Asia has been in its use of cultural minority groups. Soon after its inception as a dissident movement in independent Laos it bid for the support of the minorities living in the mountainous regions that cover the great part of the north and east. The attention paid these people was amply rewarded, giving the Pathet Lao a lasting hold on areas vital to a guerrilla campaign. Similarly, the Viet Minh and Viet Cong solicited the support of the mountain minorities, while in the latter days of its expansion the PKI sought and received response from the interior peoples of Kalimantan (Borneo) and the eastern islands. That such movements could find the loyalties of groups whose cultures were less "advanced" than that of the main cultural body should not be surprising, for belief systems newly penetrating an area commonly find their first adherents among such groups. People to whom the majority culture seems meaningless, or who are denied access to it, may well seek to make up for this lack by adopting a new and therefore presumably truer revelation. Or, on the other hand, such a group may feel the old beliefs inadequate in a rapidly changing world; they do not wish to lose their identity as a separate folk by absorbing the impinging majority culture, and they therefore adopt an ideology proffered from outside as an alternative. The motives for receptivity to a new belief can be many, and initially may have very little to do with the interests the new faith claims to represent: thus, traditional emnity between cultural groups may result in the new faith's espousal by one people almost automatically bringing firm rejection by another, to the comfort of the organizers of counterinsurgency.

If one can speak of a distinctive feature of the Communist proselytizing of minorities in Southeast Asia, it has been that (with the possible exception of Thailand) it did not get its hold first among minority groups but was successful initially among the cultural majority and then extended itself by successfully persuading other groups that it appreciated and would respect their unique contribution to the national whole. Moreover, communism has not been visibly popular among the foreign minorities of the Southeast Asian states—the Chinese population of Malaysia excepted, but it can hardly be considered a proper minority. This is striking in view of the fact that members of the two largest such groups, the Vietnamese (in Cambodia, Laos, and Thailand) and the Chinese (in all countries) tend in their majority to look to Ho Chi Minh and Mao Tse-tung as the symbols of their respective countries of origin. Traditionally, however, these groups have been passive in local politics, their efforts being concentrated largely on making themselves as inconspicuous as possible to the authorities. Moreover, many of them are engaged in trade and finance, and this has not endeared them to the peasant population. The Chinese have tended to occupy a vital economic position, particularly in island Southeast Asia, which makes them a prominent target for jingoist sentiment.

To be rich, alien, and defenseless is to be in a dangerous position, and the foreign minorities have not had an easy time of it in the post-colonial era. Their troubles, however, have come primarily from nationalistic governments and indigenous rivals for their economic position rather than from a left which finds them a convenient target against which to rally popular wrath. One reason for this circumstance is probably the Marxist ideological bias against racism; moreover, it has probably seemed inadvisable to embark on campaigns that might divert popular attention from the main opponents of the movement and that might promote the fortunes of an indigenous enterpreneurial group, which would probably take a more active and antileftist political role. The Chinese and Vietnamese commercial minorities have frequently been charged by their enemies with supplying funds to the Communist forces; in various cases money probably has changed hands in order to preserve leftist tolerance and to encourage, where needed, the balance between indigenous right and left—the situation in which the minority group is most likely to be left undisturbed. However, the commercial minorities in Southeast Asia are by force of circumstances involved in the almost constant payment of "protection money" and bribes to officials and political leaders. It is unlikely that in most cases the left benefits more from their presence than the right.

Changing Societies, Conservative Elites

Thus far, the principal illustrations presented here have been from those countries whose colonial experience was relatively superficial and which therefore did not possess from the start of their independence the deep contradictions which have provided the fundamental fuel for the Communist fire in Southeast Asia. For those that were more directly affected by colonialism, the most important result of the experience was the severe alteration it brought in their local structures. Economic changes working largely in the direction of sharp delineation between "modern" commercial and "native" subsistence sectors, were the most far-reaching and irreversible of these, but bureaucratic and other consciously modernizing reforms were also of considerable importance. Second—with the exception of the Philippines and, in part, Malaysia—

colonial policies in these countries acted to shore up the traditional hierarchies, for reasons of convenience and control, so that instead of those structures conforming to their changing environment they became increasingly rigid and irrelevant. Third, the modern education and outside ideas to which at least the urban elite was exposed introduced concepts of the proper organization of human affairs which comprised a radical criticism of the traditional order and, more, a recommendation for its overthrow. These externally-introduced factors created deep schisms within the societies of the countries involved, opening them to ideologies of radical transformation, and, with the apparent exception of the Philippines, left them without socioeconomic elites capable of successfully replacing the colonial regimes as holders of stable political power.

Those who inherited political control from the colonial regimes of Vietnam, Burma, Indonesia, Malaysia, and the Philippines have had four major foreign indicators from which to choose when setting out on the path to modernization. These might be classified as the Western liberal, Marxist, Japanese, and Communist Chinese. It should be understood that reference to these as examples does not mean that they were taken as models to be emulated in toto, but rather that there has been a tendency to draw for inspiration on certain elements perceived as essential to the success of the system or state concerned. Because the Western example meant a fairly unqualified imitation of the former ruling power, its appeal was primarily to those who had been permitted to enjoy considerable advantages under the colonial regime and who were interested in modernity but not in social revolution. The major groups of this sort were the Philippine and Malayan Chinese elites.

Though the United States had established its rule in the Philippines by crushing what was in effect the first national liberation movement in Southeast Asia, its subsequent ambivalence toward both the political and economic aspects of colonial possession had allowed the development of an indigenous structure in these areas oriented more or less along modern lines. As a result, the end of the American occupation saw the existence of a Filipino elite that was familiar with and had a vested interest in a future not far different from that envisioned by its former rulers. Even so, the hegemony of that elite was not assured, for the Japanese occupation had provided an opportunity for the rise of a movement representing social as well as national revolution. The occupation served to divide the elite and discredit, at least temporarily, those who served the wartime regime; this, combined with the inability of the Japanese to exert strong control over outlying areas, allowed the creation of a revolutionary movement which possessed something of a territorial base and a military-governmental structure. This was the People's Anti-Japanese Army (Hukbalahap), which drew its principal support from the tenant farmers of Central Luzon, who had long chafed at their service under the great estate owners of the area and had recently begun to organize under radical Socialist sponsorship in alliance with the small, urban-oriented Communist Party.[9]

Together with the Malayan People's Anti-Japanese Army (MPAJA) and the Viet Minh, the Hukbalahap was the first of the Southeast Asian movements to possess the arms and territorial control necessary for a Maoist-style struggle for power.[10] While all three of the above groups proclaimed national liberation as their goal, both the Philippine and Malayan forces lost their determination to fight for it before World War II was out. The Huks, apparently, did not believe they could extend their appeal to the country as a whole—they remained essentially a rural class movement and did not actively proselytize in groups and areas beyond their original center of strength—and they did not consider themselves able to battle the American forces, which returned in strength on the heels of the Japanese. The Huk leader Luis Taruc later declared this to have been a grave error;[11] and doubtless it was, in view of the fact that the movement failed to find an acceptable peaceful role for itself. By the time it returned to the field, it had lost much of its wartime prestige and the Filipino elite was well on the way towards regaining its shaken predominance. Even so the revolt posed a threat to the government that was not overcome before the mid-1950s.

For the Philippines, the postwar period of severe instability came to an end in part through the public confidence generated by the reformist President Magsaysay. The following of the Hukbalahap—to whom a military victory now seemed hopeless while a legal amelioration of their grievances at last appeared possible—declined precipitously; and eventually Luis Taruc surrendered, breaking with the intransigent Communist

[9] Although peasant organizations had been founded in the 1920s it was only a decade later that rural leftism developed any real strength. It then consisted largely of the followers of Pedro Abad Santos, a radical of saintly character and distinguished family whose Socialist Party joined the Communists through a "Popular Front" alliance made in 1937. The principal Huk leader Luis Taruc was a Santos lieutenant rather than a "birthright" Communist.

[10] The Hukbalahap (People's Anti-Japanese Army) was organized in 1942 as a guerilla movement, having as its civilian auxiliary and shadow government the Barrio (Village) United Defence Corps. The MPAJA (Malayan People's Anti-Japanese Army), founded in the same year, had as its civilian arm the Malayan People's Anti-Japanese Union (MPAJU).

[11] Luis Taruc, *Born of the People* (New York: International Publishers, 1953), p. 199.

regulars, who continued a desultory and fugitive resistance. In the decade following the collapse of Huk activity, the resettlement scheme sponsored by Magsaysay for ex-guerrillas and land-hungry peasants largely proved a failure; the land reform law, by promising to exempt land planted to sugar from its provisions, greatly increased the transfer of land from rice to cane growing, and thus reduced the poor tenant to poorer farm laborer. The rural poor of the Philippines grew poorer; and yet, save for the annual discovery of Huk activity by the military at budget time there has been little sign of renewed insurgency.[12] What strength radicalism still has is in the urban centers, particularly the capital—and even there not in labor organizations, where leftist influence has been largely broken through the extension of nonpolitical unions, but in the journalistic and academic world. Here, too, its influence has been much magnified by the fact that it has frequently been equated with anti-Americanism, a force which doubtless will continue to increase in strength as a rising entrepreneurial class seeks the exclusion of foreign interests.

Seen from the mid-1960s, the Philippines was, with the Democratic Republic of Vietnam, the Southeast Asian country whose governing system and course of economic development appeared most stable. Their opposed approaches to the subject apart, they were the two countries of the area which seemed most thoroughly launched, in terms of structure and ideology, on the road to industrial modernity. As for rural interest in the Philippines, it would seem that the "cake of custom"[13] formed from a loss of faith in the possibility of a radical solution, had effectively crusted over the urge to rebellion. Nonetheless, the possibilities for a revolutionary revival remain if development does not proceed at a pace that will enable it to absorb those who can no longer live from the land and those who belong to the rapidly expanding ranks of the educated urban young. Should these groups become sufficiently disaffected

[12] Renewed concern for Huk activity in Central Luzon was expressed by the Philippine authorities in mid-1966. For an interesting journalistic survey of the situation in the Huk heartland at this time, see "The Huk Situation," *Philippine Free Press,* Aug. 6, 1966. The Huk role described here bears more resemblance to the one traditionally played by the Mafia in Sicily than to that of a Communist underground. The Huk remnants are portrayed as shorn of nearly all their ideological accoutrements, living off the local population and in return providing a rough justice and various services which the government itself seems uninterested in granting. Because the Huks are willing and able to provide protection and avenge local wrongs, the populace has come to look to them as a sort of shadow government, according to this account. Local officialdom was also willing to tolerate the Huks, as they did not usually threaten it and could be utilized for strongarm work and various endeavors which the notables might not wish to engage in directly. However, at the beginning of 1966 the central gov-

to combine forces under the anti-American banner a movement of considerable power could arise. The problems confronting a Southeast Asian country beginning industrialization in the mid-twentieth century are, after all, not the same as those faced by England at a similar stage. The European economies did not have to cope with the competition of far more advanced countries; with the effects of a colonial development that had brought high population concentration without corresponding industrial development; and with a massive influx of ideas and goods from outside that served to speed the course of disaffection.

The position of Malaysia's modern-minded but nonrevolutionary elite is far less stable than that of the Philippines, inasmuch as it represents a socially distinct portion of the population. Large-scale immigration of outside labor during the colonial period led eventually to a division of the population along boundaries that were ethnic as well as economic in nature. The principal differentiation was between an agrarian Malay society, which possessed a bureaucratic and aristocratic elite and which, largely bypassed in the colonial development of the country, had experienced few of the frustrations and stimuli of direct European domination, and, on the other hand, a largely urban Chinese population which possessed a commercial and modernizing elite and a mass that was ambitious and oriented towards change. The result of the compromise which enabled the country to hold together in the post-independence period has been a society whose principal leadership confronts the world in a curiously schizophrenic manner, one segment holding political power and being strongly traditionalist and the other having economic power and being equally strongly modernist in its views. Such an arrangement is likely to last only as long as the leaders of both elites are able, in the interest of avoiding mutual destruction, to restrain themselves and their followers from giving in to the frustrations that such coexistence of incompatibles necessarily creates.

---

ernment decided to make an end to this practice of live-and-let-live: a purge of the constabulary and bureaucracy was carried out in the region, and an Anti-Huk Mayors' League was formed, the chairman of which was promptly assassinated. Huk-hunting expeditions were held, in the course of which some peasants were killed and many others badly frightened. The journalists found the population of the area to be generally disillusioned with a government they viewed as distant and uncaring, and pondered whether the result of the new anti-Huk line would serve to isolate the Huks from the peasants and the government or to isolate the government from the peasants and the Huks (cf. articles on pp. 2, 41–42; 3, 69).

[13] The phrase is used by Adam Ulam in *The Unfinished Revolution* (New York: Random House, 1960), pp. 88–90, in describing the process by which the masses of nineteenth-century England were brought to accept the conditions of industrialization. The work offers a stimulating discussion of the general relationship of Marxism to the modernization process.

If the Malayan Chinese elite was attracted to the Western liberal outlook, its opponents within the Chinese community chose the Marxist example. As a result, the Communist movement has had long-standing roots in the country and, in spite of efforts at acquiring an all-national character, has remained essentially an expression of the Chinese working class of Malaya and Singapore. However, in spite of this Chinese identification and the easy access of Singapore to the outside Asian world, relatively few of the principles employed by the Chinese Communists were visibly practiced by the Malayan Communist Party (MCP). The reason for this dichotomy is less likely to have been a lack of regard for CCP policy than the fact that the overwhelmingly urban and communal social base of the MCP did not lend itself to the Chinese program, which essentially aims at agrarian and national revoltuion.

The Chinese peasant population of Malaya was largely limited, because of the reservation of farmland for Malays, to a squatter population which expanded greatly when Chinese fled the cities during the Japanese occupation. The wartime Communist-led Malayan People's Anti-Japanese Army, composed of Chinese from the cities, enjoyed the favor of these squatter peasants because of its anti-Japanese activities. When the MCP took to the hills in 1948, it counted on its ability to exploit what remained of this sympathy as well as the squatters' hopes that the Communists could gain for them secure rights to land. That the true orientation of the Malayan Communists was not agrarian, however, was illustrated in their legal interlude of 1945–1948, when they returned to the cities and operated as an urban movement based on labor and veterans' associations. The great part of the peasant population, being Malay, was from the start hostile to the Communist movement; and the enthusiasm of the Chinese rural population dimmed with the gradual restoration of the war-shaken authority of the Chinese business elite, the identification of the postwar Party with urban labor, and, during the insurrection, the adoption of government measures directed at improving the position of the rural Chinese population while strongly restricting its freedom of movement and areas of settlement. Consequently, the Malayan movement did not really acquire the character of a national liberation movement, as did the Vietnamese and to a lesser extent the Pathet Lao, nor did it represent a peasant revolution, as did the Hukbalahap.[14]

[14] The Malayan Communist guerrillas took the name Malayan Races' Liberation Army in 1949, later changing this again to Malayan National Liberation Army. Similarly, the Hukbalahap became the People's Liberation Army (HMB) in 1950 in an effort to escape the limits of its original appeal.

The MCP insurgents, though still existing as a fugitive band along the Thai-Malaysian border, are no longer the principal vehicle of Malaysian communism, which since the mid-1950s has extended itself chiefly through the general leftist movement in the cities—among student, labor, and political opposition groups, most of which have been subjected to strict but not inhumane suppression. Its most interesting development was in Sarawak, where it became the vehicle for expressing generational schism, a characteristic noted earlier in the case of leftist disaffection in Cambodia.[15] This aspect of the movement reflects the impatience an ambitious younger Chinese generation, finding its career opportunities limited by overpopulation, overeducation, and the Malay domination of the bureaucracy, has felt towards its elders, most of them shopkeepers and journeymen who appear old-fashioned, cautious, and overeager to placate the Malays. Although the phenomenon is most striking in the Borneo territories of Malaysia it is present in all parts of the country, and results in a considerable pressure on the leadership of Singapore and the Chinese community in Malaysia towards a less conciliatory stand vis-à-vis the Malays.

Younger Malay radicals, for their part, chafe at Chinese wealth and sense of superiority, and regard the political advantages given them under the coexistence arrangement as small enough redress for the loss of control over a country which was originally theirs.[16] In their vocal radicalism, their stress on the need to discover a true "national identity," and their simultaneous orientation towards traditional and modern modes of thought, the Malay radicals have shown traits similar to those which became increasingly characteristic for the Indonesian and Burmese political styles.

[15] For a comment on the generational conflict aspect of the Communist movement in Sarawak, see Francis Starner, "Communism in Malaysia," in Robert A. Scalapino (ed.), *The Communist Revolution in Asia* (Englewood Cliffs, N.J.: Prentice-Hall, 1965), pp. 228–229. The leftist movement in Sarawak began during the Japanese occupation with the establishment of the Sarawak Anti-Fascist League (later Races Liberation League). In 1956, after an ephemeral existence involving several changes of organization and name, it became the Sarawak Advanced Youth League, which the Malaysian government prefers to refer to by the more menacing-sounding Clandestine Communist Organization (CCO). In December, 1964, the Malaysian government announced the Communists were responsible for the creation of a North Kalimantan Liberation League, which was to carry out a national united front action; this organization was declared illegal, and such leftist activity as is now openly pursued occurs through the Sarawak United People's Party (SUPP), part of which is of radical inclination and part of which represents local Chinese entrepreneurial interests.

[16] The principal radical Malay organization has been the Malayan National Liberation League (Liga Pembebasan Nasional Malaya); its slogan is "God, Na-

Countries with Radical Nationalist Elites

The national leadership of Burma and Indonesia developed from elites that had not been co-opted satisfactorily into the colonial system and consequently tended to see independence as requiring a fundamental break with the colonial past. They sought an explanation of their people's subservient condition that would place the fault elsewhere than on a native inferiority; and they desired a world view that provided an alternative both to the traditional one that they felt had failed them and to unrevolutionary Western liberalism.

Marxism provided such an alternative; moreover, purporting to be the representative of the most advanced political thinking concerning industrial nations, it seemed to promise greater assurance of success than the ideological examples set by Western bourgeois institutions. As a result, elements of Marxist thought were widely adopted by the radical nationalist leaderships of Southeast Asia. Such acceptance was usually only partial, however. For most radical nationalists the Leninist analysis of imperialism and the goal of a Socialist society—the latter appealing to traditional ideas of a benevolent and all-encompassing state as well as to a desire for the most "modern" form of government—were so welcome as to become ideological truisms. But the prospect of class struggle, or indeed of any class-oriented government in the postcolonial stage, was considered by all but the most extreme groups to be very well for Europe but inappropriate and unacceptable for their own countries. Orthodox Marxists might explain nationalist hesitation on this point with the argument that the revolutionary nationalistic politician derived from exactly that aspiring elite which would be the presumable victim of any postcolonial class conflict; and Western liberals might argue that such opposition to class conflict reflected democratic unwillingness to tread the path towards totalitarianism. Both explanations have some truth, but it must also be pointed out that the nationalist leaders of Burma and Indonesia have tended to come from bureaucratic elites

---

tionality, and Social Justice." Other radical groups are the Malayan Independence Struggle League (LPKM), the Front Anti-Malaysia, and the Free Malaya Union (Kemam). It is with these organizations rather than the Chinese-oriented ones that the Sukarno government and the PKI had contact; the Malayan Communist groups were almost exclusively oriented toward China rather than Indonesia. However, the Indonesian army did give military training of sorts to dissident Chinese youths from Sarawak who made their way over the border to Indonesian Borneo; the Malaysian government claimed the young Chinese were poorly treated by their Indonesian mentors, which, given the Indonesian army's basic attitude towards Communists and Chinese, is readily imaginable.

which had little sympathy for nascent entrepreneurial elements and were hardly threatened by statism; nor was their devotion to constitutional democracy by any means unquestionable.

Another motive for the radical nationalists' opposition to the idea of class conflict may be found in their general ambivalence to modernization, a hesitation more marked than that of either their Westernizing reformist or their Communist contemporaries. Their revolutions have been to restore past glories and good custom as well as to bring about a brave new world. They see the cause of present disorder and uncertainty as an outside force, imperialism, which must be removed in order to restore the lost sense of identity and purpose. Only when this has been done can the direction of the country's further development be determined. For who can decide where he should go if he does not yet know who he is? If the end of colonial rule does not bring clarity, this must be the result of continuing imperialist manipulation, and indeed, Marxist–Leninist theoreticians have obligingly produced the theory of neocolonialism to demonstrate that this was so.

In an effort to escape this continuing alien intervention, Burma fled into hermitic isolation, while Indonesia assumed an ever more combative antiimperialist stand. In the end, failures and frustrations led to a schizophrenic political development, whereby increasingly revolutionary postures were assumed while at the same time growing attention was paid to the restoration of traditional usage and the justification for the continuance in office of the postrevolutionary elite. In this development the Japanese example, interestingly enough, has helped play a reinforcing role. It has not been the image of an industrializing Japan, for that has been too undefinable to provide a formula and too closely linked with characteristics peculiar to Japanese society for it to be effective as an inspiration for much beyond the very important idea that Asians could in fact equal the West. The predominating image has rather been that of the wartime military regime—one of power achieved not by systems or institutions but through iron discipline, patriotism, and unshakeable will. This has served to reinforce romantic and nativist inclinations and, ultimately, to make it easier for the military of Burma and Indonesia—a considerable portion of whose officer corps received their first training and indoctrination under the wartime Japanese—to see themselves as the sources of national salvation.

It has been difficult for the Burmese and Indonesian Communists to determine effective responses to radical nationalism of this type. Should one oppose it from the outset as protofascist? Or count on the fact that its character has not yet set, that it had already absorbed a good dose of Marxist–Leninist principles, and that the elite it represents should not object to a statist system? To follow the latter seemed to be to court the fate the Chinese Communists had suffered in 1927 as a result of their dependent alliance with the Kuomintang. On the other hand, the radical nationalist stand had widespread appeal among the people on whom the Communists also depended for support. The nationalist leaders were popular and generally recognized as legitimate. In opposing them too early the Communists might only make themselves unpopular; and, in entering a contest of arms against them, they might appear as opponents of the revolution—as indeed happened to the Indonesian Communists in their brief but disastrous clash with government forces in 1948.

There were a variety of Burmese Communist responses to the problem this situation posed. On the insurgent extreme was the Communist Party of Burma (CPB), the Red Flags, which broke off from the regular Burma Communist Party (BCP, White Flags) in 1946 and took up arms against the government, which it has defied ever since. The White Flag Communists began their own rebellion in 1948, but though they initially had considerable rural support and the cooperation of veterans' and dissident minority groups that were similarly engaged in insurrection, they were never able to establish the hegemony over these elements necessary to form a successful national front appeal. In the course of their years in the wilderness some White Flag adherents lost interest and others elected to cooperate with the government; but most held out with the principal BCP leader Than Tun, conducting what has been essentially a holding operation against the day when a new revolutionary opportunity would dawn. A third group, the Burma Workers' and Peasants Party (BWPP, or Red Socialists), was begun in 1951 by those who saw the White Flag rebellion as a political dead end and placed their hope in parliamentary and loyal opposition. They enjoyed some success in the U Nu era, broadening their base to form a National United Front (NUF) coalition in 1956, but were unable to shape this into a united and effective machine. The Ne Win coup of 1962 saw part of the NUF leadership willing to cooperate with the new regime, but this attempt at pursuing the peaceful path into the post-parliamentary period came to an end with the arrest of NUF leaders as well as other civilian politicians in 1963–1964.

So inconsistent an approach to the achievement of power could hardly be expected to impress people with the certitude and unity of Marxism–Leninism, or with the particular capabilities of the Communists to organize and govern. However, the very weaknesses of Burmese communism could in the end prove its strength. Certainly its varied approaches to power have not left it with all its political eggs in one basket. When the parliamentary progress of the NUF was brought to an end, there were still the insurrectionaries in the hills; and should the Ne Win regime's drastic reordering of Burmese life fail to yield much beyond the hitherto prevalent disorganization and demoralization, the possibility of increasing sympathy for Than Tun's long-proferred revolutionary alternative would not be negligible. The Communists have been the only group preferring, at least in theory, an alternative system to both parliamentary and military rule; it will be interesting to see whether a deepening crisis will bring to the rebels the talent and organizational skill that has made possible the elaborate Communist mobilization of the countryside elsewhere in Southeast Asia.

From 1951 to 1965 the Communist Party of Indonesia (PKI) did put all its eggs in one basket: that of legal organization. Its rapid advance demonstrated the advantages that could accrue to a Communist movement that made good use of the possibilities presented by the ambivalence of the above-described kind of radical nationalism. With less than two thousand members in 1952, a black name from the conflict of 1948, and a government leadership generally accepted as legitimate, the Party took the course of assuming an ultrapatriotic stance. It cooperated with the political forces that found it useful—first the National Party of Indonesia (PNI) and increasingly President Sukarno—and built up its mass organizations and popular strength. Social and economic decline brought the PKI massive support within a very few years; but the same circumstances also led to a breakdown in consensus and the consequent collapse of the parliamentary system in the late 1950s. From its wreckage arose the "guided democracy" system, in which the two principal holders of power were the army, which possessed the means of violence, and the president, who possessed legitimacy and immense popularity.

Guided democracy had a good deal more guidance than democracy in it, and initially there was considerable debate within the PKI as to whether to lend support to the system, inasmuch as its strength rested on its ability to agitate among and organize the masses and to put pressure on a government sensitive to public opinion. But by now the movement was a victim of its own success, being too extensive and open to make illegality seem a practical choice. It therefore sought to make itself as invulnerable as possible to attack by the army—whose leadership saw in it a rival for post-Sukarno power—by identifying ever more strongly with Sukarno and taking a jingoist stand on foreign affairs. The latter tactic had the advantage of making it difficult for the army to accuse the Communists of insufficient patriotism or to concentrate on fighting them rather than the imperialist foe. Moreover, it helped alienate Indonesia from the West and thus from the countries which were an important source of moral and material reinforcement for the PKI's enemies. Finally, it was useful in shifting the balance of Indonesian foreign policy toward a source of support for the left via the concept of a Djakarta-Phnompenh-Hanoi-Peking-Pyongyang antiimperialist axis, which emerged at the end of the guided democracy period.

The domestic policy of the PKI under guided democracy is of considerable interest because it illustrated the development, under nonmilitary conditions, of the same sort of activities as were carried out by Communists in China and other parts of Southeast Asia during armed struggles for power. The Party threw most of its efforts into the rural areas, developing a considerable range of agitational and organizational activities based, insofar as possible, on the careful study of local needs and interests and the building of the peasants' capacity and confidence to act for themselves. The edifice of organization and activity that was thus constructed was the more notable because all other civilian institutions, voluntary or governmental, experienced a rapid decline in this period. Its expansion was, in fact, largely a response to that decline, for it filled a need for structure and direction which was sorely felt by a society enduring the agony of cultural breakdown.

The organizational success, self-confidence, and integrity of the Communists made them loom increasingly large in Indonesia's future; and by 1965 it appeared that Sukarno himself had concluded that a peaceful accession of the PKI would be preferable to the only alternative successor which he saw to his rule: a rightist government backed by the military and conservative civilian forces. Given the declining morale and prestige of the army leadership, Sukarno's evident preference, and the Communists' growing momentum, it is possible the late 1960s might have seen a large portion of the military and civilian elite so persuaded of the inevitability of PKI victory that they would have committed themselves to it and blocked any chances for an effective post-Sukarno repression of the Communists.

The Communists might thus have come into office. Whether they would have come into real power is another matter, however. For the draconian measures that would needs be taken by any regime hoping to deal seriously with Indonesia's virtually collapsed economy would be particularly difficult for a government that had come to power, essentially, through the sufferance of what had by now become a tightly integrated bloc of bureaucratic, military, and economic elite interests. In any event, the PKI was spared confrontation with such a prospect by the attempted *coup de force* of October 1, 1965, which both broke Sukarno's psychological grip on the nation and gave the military leadership an opportunity to secure the elimination of its rival by blaming the affair on the PKI.[17] The method chosen to accomplish this, once the military dissidents had been successfully immobilized and Sukarno's activity restricted, was to kill off the Communist cadre and to carry out a general massacre of PKI adherents wherever hostile to the movement. In many cases social tensions had been rising so rapidly under the economic and political strains of late guided democracy that encouragement to communal slaughter was hardly needed, and the problem was one of keeping things in hand, rather than of urging them on.

The PKI, accustomed to relying on Sukarno and general avoidance of violence for its protection, proved totally unable to defend itself. However, the virtual overnight elimination of the Party also removed the principal forces which held the other forces together. Groups and individuals that had been suffocating politically under guided democracy began to push beyond opposition to the PKI alone to urge the complete overturning of the Sukarno system. This, in turn, evoked a reaction from those who feared too radical a departure from the principles and personnel of the former regime, and all of the foregoing combined with severe economic and bureaucratic disintegration.

In the light of this latter over-all decline it will be interesting to see whether, in spite of its massive character, the Indonesian anti-Communist repression will result in the permanent elimination of communism as a contendor for power in that country. If, as has been argued above, the major reason for the expansion of the PKI, as of other significant Southeast Asian Communist movements, has been an anomic condition of the society, it is possible that, should the post-Sukarno regime fail to maintain a necessary minimum of structure, direction, and stability, a resistance will develop in which the teachings, methods, and surviving cadre of the PKI could play a key role. Such a movement, which could hardly be other than insurrectionary, could make good use of such material as the rapid postcoup reversal of Indonesian for-

[17] Much still needs to be done before any firm conclusions can be drawn about the background of the October, 1965, coup. On the basis of the evidence thus far available, however, it appears the Communist involvement in the affair was at best an attempt to jump on the bandwagon, the coup having been launched by a young officer cabal in the army. For some preliminary considerations, see McVey, "Indonesian Communism and China," in Tang Tsou (ed.) *China in Crisis* (Chicago: University of Chicago Press, 1968).

eign policy, the dethronement of Sukarno, the abandonment of such gestures as had been made toward land reform, and the increasingly visible layer of civilian and military newly rich, in order to rally the forces of social and national revolution.

The location, terrain, and island character of Indonesia are not favorable to an insurgent movement, as Aidit himself pointed out in arguing for the peaceful road.[13] The Vietnamese Communists, on the other hand, have not tired of reiterating that their own military situation was far from felicitous from the outset and did not contain the strategic ingredients that seemed vital to Mao's victory in China.[19] Nor, for that matter, did the Chinese conditions resemble those which had secured victory for the Bolsheviks. In fact, if we consider the available instances of unassisted Communist revolutionary victory, we shall see that they took place in countries with very different geographic and strategic characteristics. All, however, occurred in nonindustrial countries that, because of war, prolonged mismanagement, or tension caused by the inability of institutions to respond to ongoing change, were in a state of extreme social disarray. Moreover, there were no viable alternatives to the Communist-led movements, other forces being either too identified with the discredited regimes, too divorced from their own societies to give real leadership, or too overshadowed by the image the Communists had already acquired as the rightful leaders of the revolution.

Of all the countries in Southeast Asia Vietnam most clearly possessed the sociopolitical conditions requisite for revolution at the time its Communists made their bid for power. The Vietnamese Communists, who in 1941 formed the Vietnam Independence League, or Viet Minh, had the great good fortune that the Japanese had run occupied Indochina through a French puppet regime for nearly the entire course of World War II and so did not promote a non-Communist anticolonial native leadership which would claim command of the national revolution—as had happened, for example, in Burma and Indonesia. The Communists were also fortunate in having in Ho Chi Minh an experienced and distinctive personality, who was able to establish his image as the cardinal leader of the independence struggle. Most important, the Vietnamese Communists recognized the importance of acting in order to establish at the outset their claims to this leadership. Under similar circumstances leftists in Malaya and the Philippines failed to do so in spite of the fact that they enjoyed the advantage, which the Viet Minh by and large did

[18] For an example of this argument see D. N. Aidit, *Indonesian Society and the Indonesian Revolution* (Djakarta, 1958), pp. 70–78.

[19] Vo Nguyen Giap, *People's War, People's Army* (Hanoi, 1963), pp. 57–59.

not, of having gained experience, reputation, and arms as anti-Japanese guerrillas in the war years.[20]

The National Liberation Front Approach

The "national liberation front" strategy pursued by the Vietnamese in their armed struggle for power has aimed at securing an identification of the people with the movement in terms of race, language, and shared custom, bonds that seem more real to them than those of solidarity. Moreover, such an appeal has been less disturbing to remaining traditional attitudes towards social hierarchy and conflict; and at the same time it has aided in recruiting the educated and semieducated young, who have been a vital source of cadres though they generally have come from the more privileged classes. The approach has made it possible to appeal simultaneously to modernist and traditionalist rejection of the status quo, for the need for revolution can be argued not only on "scientific" lines but also on the grounds that those in power have abandoned good custom for foreign ways and foreign gold; and the leap into the future represented by their overthrow is thus not a plunge into the totally unknown but a restoration of true order. The Vietnamese Communists have, in short, appropriated for themselves the appeal of national revolution, with the additional favorable factor that all revolutionary forces from the start have been firmly under their control. The national liberation movement should also, in theory, mix social reform with the antiforeign struggle. However, in the effort to rally all forces against the alien enemy the class struggle is not always pushed with vigor—as was witnessed in Vietnam in the early years of the anti-French struggle[21]—but even so particular attention is paid to cultivating the interest and support of the peasant masses.

A "National Liberation Front" approach requires an incumbent state leadership that is at best regarded by the populace with suspicion. A regime that clearly has an alien life style and cultivates foreign contacts makes a still more suitable enemy; and one that is openly foreign-dominated is easiest of all to mobilize support against. Inasmuch as

[20] The Viet Minh was one of several exile groups created in southern China in 1941, but it did not begin military action in north Vietnam until December, 1944, a Free Zone comprising six provinces being proclaimed in June, 1945. See *Thirty Years of Struggle of the Party* (Hanoi, 1960), pp. 81–88.

[21] Truong Chinh, *The August Revolution* (Hanoi, 1962), pp. 46–47, provides an early (1946) criticism of the Viet Minh's neglect of the "antifeudal" struggle in the countryside. Despite such exhortations, there was not much stress on rural class warfare in the first five years of the revolution.

regimes closely associated with foreign governments usually command more fire-power than nonaligned ones, it is often to be observed that the weaker a regime is politically, the stronger it is militarily, and vice versa. Generally, the political advantage outweighs the military, because whereas an unallied government may attempt to make itself more acceptable to the masses in order to broaden its base of support, a foreign-linked one is more likely to seek sanctuary in an even closer relationship with its sponsor.

The National Liberation Front strategy proved successful in the Viet Minh war against the French, and it also generally held during the Viet Cong drive. The South Vietnamese regimes became increasingly rigid and dependent on the American presence; urban elements grew demoralized and disaffected, and, in the countryside, the rapid wartime disintegration of order and institutions resulted in the widespread emergence of a Communist-style ideological and organizational system. Moreover, the Viet Cong insurgents have found themselves faced with a foreign power which appeared both willing and able to maintain its presence, for reasons of its perceived international stature, regardless of whether the regime it supports possesses any power, popularity, or real presence of its own. In order to meet this challenge, the insurrectionaries have drawn increasingly on outside support, so that the struggle has finally acquired such scale and international character that it has been extremely difficult for the Viet Cong to maintain the flexibility and the half-political, half-military approach of a National Liberation Front strategy.

This National Liberation Front concept is a descendant of the program of national and agrarian revolution which formed the ideological basis for Mao's victory in China. At about the time the CCP assumed power, this "Chinese way" was given the then still-important imprimatur of the international Communist movement as the path for Asian communism.[22] And although Soviet opinion soon decided it was safer not to portray China as the light of Asia, the image of that example continued to loom large in Southeast Asia. China's proximity has, of course, been a major reason for this. Moreover, the Chinese revolutionary experience has shown, far more clearly than the Soviet, how a Communist movement can draw strength from an overwhelmingly rural society and how, once in power, it can organize such a society for rapid

[22] The public adoption of this view occurred at a conference of the World Federation of Trade Unions in Peking in November, 1949, official Soviet opinion having developed towards an acceptance of this analysis over the preceding two years. For a description of this theoretical evolution, see John Kautsky, *Moscow and the Communist Party of India* (Cambridge, Mass.: The MIT Press, 1956), pp. 16–34, 86–99.

modernization. Again, the Chinese Communist revolution occured within a few years of the independence of most Southeast Asian states and within the lifetime of most contemporary Southeast Asians. Communist China's progress relative to their own thus serves as a measure of the success of the system China represents, and inasmuch as that country has advanced from a near-cipher in Southeast Asian political considerations to America's major challenger for influence in the region, the Chinese Communist image has come to loom large indeed. The most far-reaching effect of this is likely to be its influence on the way Southeast Asians—especially those of the younger generation—envision the future: what they see as ideal and as possible, and what methods they hold appropriate for achieving their aims. To the extent that the looming Chinese image succeeds in presenting Marxist categories of thought and Maoist modes of organization and struggle to people in countries where communism is unfamiliar or anathema, it makes it possible for them to "think the unthinkable" regarding an alternate sort of future; to the extent that it presents itself in countries where Marxist ideas have already been widely espoused, it strengthens the tendency to accept them as truths—and in the process, lessens the possibility of seeing other ways of dealing with the world.

Adoption of a "Chinese" ideological position by Southeast Asian Communists has not necessarily been paired, however, with a political commitment to the Chinese People's Republic. The Party whose philosophy of struggle most closely resembles the Chinese, North Vietnam's Lao Dong, has followed what one observer has titled a "straight zigzag line"[23] in its handling of the Sino–Soviet dispute, alternating support for the Chinese and the Soviets; for the Vietnamese have had little desire to forego Soviet aid in their war or to become overly dependent on their country's traditional foe. The Party with the most affinity for the Soviet position in terms of its method of seeking power, Aidit's PKI, became instead a staunch supporter of a China alliance in international affairs; but, at the same time, it was careful to nominate North Korea as the country-most-worthy-of-emulation,[24] for China's proximity and power has been, for nationalistically-oriented Southeast Asian Communists, a two-edged sword.

The strong nationalist element characteristic of Southeast Asian Communist movements has not been only a function of their perception of opportunity or power but has also been a response to the develop-

[23] Bernard Fall, *The Two Viet-Nams* (New York: Praeger, 1964), pp. 387, 403.

[24] *Harian Rakjat,* Oct. 4 and 5, 1963 (report by Aidit on returning from a trip to Moscow and Peking aimed at reconciling Sino-Soviet differences.)

ment since World War II of a generation of radicals who have sought a "modern" future not in the mirror imitation of outside examples but in the adjustment of received ideas to the environment and culture at hand. In theory this position is quite different from the radical nationalist attitude described earlier: the former involves a firm commitment to economic and social modernism, debating only the question of style; the latter, though it may also make heavy use of Marxist–Leninist terminology, is ambivalent as to the content of modernity itself. In practice, of course, the difference may be much harder to determine; for the commitment of groups and individuals may change over time, and the specific nature of their dedication may not be always immediately apparent. The Hukbalahap, for example, was less Communist in terms of ultimate commitment to Marxism–Leninism than the Viet Minh, though it pursued a program of class struggle which the Viet Minh initially ignored. Similarly, Thakin Soe's Red Flag Communists in Burma take what is undoubtedly the most extreme position of any Southeast Asian Party in their social revolutionary slogans, but their movement resembles the following of a traditional messianic leader far more than a contemporary Communist *apparat.*

The passage of time, and with it the continuing development of a younger generation less ambiguous in its attitude toward modernization and at the same time familiar with the revolutionary process in its own country, should lessen some of these anomalies by reducing the tension between the exogenous universalist ideology and the attachment to local circumstances and traditions. This, however, would not necessarily alleviate conflict between Communist and anti-Communist domestic forces in Southeast Asia. On the contrary, removal in time from the colonial and revolutionary periods should cause memories of the common struggle to fade; and, in cases where the postrevolutionary elites have become entrenched and incapable of absorbing new members, opportunities for such conflict should broaden. In the end it is on the felt need for radical social change that movements of revolutionary dissent depend; and inasmuch as the transformation which Southeast Asia is undergoing is by no means at an end, the regimes it has thus far acquired by no means stable, and the exacerbating international pressures by no means abating, it is not likely that communism has reached the limits of its appeal in that region.

SELECTED BIBLIOGRAPHY

General

Brimmell, J. H., *Communism in Southeast Asia* (London: Oxford, 1959).

A general survey, tending to lean a bit heavily on the international-plot aspect. Good especially for Malaysia.

Kahin, George McTurnan (ed.), *Governments and Politics in Southeast Asia* (Ithaca: Cornell University Press, 1964). For background on the political and socioeconomic environments in which the Southeast Asian Communist movements have developed; useful bibliographies.

Scalapino, Robert A. (ed.), *The Communist Revolution in Asia* (Englewood Cliffs, N.J.: Prentice-Hall, 1965). Includes important essays on North Vietnam, the Pathet Lao, Malaysia, Indonesia, and Burma, plus an interesting introductory chapter by the editor.

Trager, Frank N. (ed.), *Marxism in Southeast Asia* (Stanford: Stanford University Press, 1959). Worthwhile particularly for the essays on Burma, Thailand, and Vietnam.

Vietnam

Burchett, Wilfred, *Vietnam: Inside Story of the Guerilla War* (New York: International Publishers, 1965). A left-wing journalist's view into Viet Cong organization and activities. Highly interesting.

Fall, Bernard B., *The Two Viet-Nams: A Political and Military Analysis* (New York: Praeger, 1962). A solid and well-written study by a leading student of Vietnam.

Ho Chi Minh, *Selected Writings* (Hanoi: Foreign Langauges Publishing House, 1962, 4 vols). One of a number of major theoretical selections, published in English by this Hanoi firm.

Honey, P. J., *Communism in North Vietnam: Its Role in the Sino-Soviet Dispute* (Cambrige, Mass.: The MIT Press, 1963). Intrigue and ambition in darkest North Vietnam.

Honey, P. J. (ed.), *North Vietnam Today: Profile of a Communist Satellite* (New York: Praeger, 1962). A helpful collection of essays on various aspects of the DRV. Political emphasis.

Pike, Douglas, *Viet Cong* (Cambridge, Mass.: The MIT Press, 1966). A very useful study of National Liberation Front organization and strategy, with much documentation.

Tanham, George K., *Communist Revolutionary Warfare* (New York: Praeger, 1962). A consideration of the Viet Minh and Viet Cong rebellions from a counterinsurgency point of view.

Tran Van Giau and Le Van Chat, *The South Viet Nam National Liberation Front* (Hanoi: Foreign Languages Publishing House, 1962). Communist description and analysis of the early Viet Cong insurgency and the social and political factors that went into it.

Indonesia

Aidit, D. N., *Problems of the Indonesian Revolution* (Peking? 1963?). Selected writings of the late PKI chairman. A number of major PKI documents on general strategy and the problems of the international movement were also published in English by Jajasan Pembaruan, the PKI publisher, and by the Foreign Languages Publishing House in Peking.

Brackman, Arnold, *Indonesian Communism: A History* (New York: Praeger, 1963). A journalist's account, notable more for emotion than analysis or accuracy.

Hindley, Donald, *The Communist Party of Indonesia* (Berkeley: University of California Press, 1964). An excellent study of the organizational development of the movement under Aidit's regime.

van der Kroef, Justus M., *The Communist Party of Indonesia* (Vancouver: University of British Columbia Press, 1965). Discussions of various aspects of PKI development, especially in the guided democracy period.

Malaya

The Danger Within (Kuching: Sarawak Information Service, 1963). A government account of the development of the Sarawak leftist insurgency. A number of reports on the Malaysian movement have been published by the information services of Sarawak, Singapore, and Malaya. Intended as exposés, they naturally incline to stress intrigue and far-reaching conspiracy, but they are very useful sources for otherwise unavailable information.

Hanrahan, Gene Z., *The Communist Struggle in Malaya* (New York: Institute of Pacific Relations, 1954). An account of the historical development of the movement.

The Malayan Monitor (periodical). Unofficial spokesman for Malaysian communism, published in London. Various Malayan Communist Party statements have also been published in English as pamphlets by the Foreign Languages Publishing House in Peking; they are mostly taken over from the *Malayan Monitor,* and concern questions of the international movement.

Pye, Lucien W., *Guerrilla Communism in Malaya* (Princeton: Princeton University Press, 1956). An original and stimulating investigation of the social why and how of the insurgency.

Philippines

Hoeksema, Renze, *Communism in the Philippines* (unpublished Doctoral dissertation, Harvard University, 1956). Available on microfilm. Written from a militantly anti-Communist viewpoint, this is one of the best historical accounts so far of a Southeast Asian Communist movement, and certainly of the Communist Party of the Philippines. Well researched, utilizing many scarce or unpublished documents.

Pomeroy, William J. *The Forest* (New York: International Publishers, 1963). An account of life among the insurgent Huks by an American Communist who served with them. Rather disappointingly uninformative.

Scaff, Alvin. *The Philippine Answer to Communism* (Stanford: Stanford University Press, 1955). An account centering about the Philippine army project to resettle former Huks in Mindanao. Superficial.

Taruc, Luis. *Born of the People* (New York: International Publishers, 1953). Autobiography of the Huk leader (some would say biography, as William Pomeroy is reputed to have been the actual writer of it).

10

Communism in Western Europe

Pio Uliassi

FIFTY YEARS after the October Revolution, the Communist Parties of Western Europe are sometimes viewed, at least from America, as political anachronisms of only marginal importance in the Communist movement and in the politics of their own countries. After World War II, as political scholars broke away from their conventional emphasis on Western studies and as the main centers of domestic and international instability shifted from Europe, the attention of most American scholars also shifted to the more exotic variants of communism. As a result, there is now a tendency to consider the Communist Parties, if not alien conspiracies, then infantile disorders of the developmental process and thus historic residues, at most, in Western industrial societies well launched toward consensual politics.

There is of course considerable justification for this attitude. A great deal in the Western European Communist Parties *is* archaic and even moribund. Their ideology has suffered the fate of more orthodox Marxism generally in failing to provide a fully satisfying guide to political life—in the advanced countries, whatever may be true elsewhere.[1] The Parties' organizational arrangements are conspicuously maladapted to the evolving structures of unprecedentedly mobile and prosperous

[1] But the history of Western European Marxism is hardly at an end and in France especially there is serious intellectual work by Marxists, including some still active in the Communist Party. See George Lichtheim, *Marxism in Modern France* (New York: Columbia University Press, 1966). The author knows of no comparable contemporary work in English for other Western European countries, or for Western Europe generally.

societies. Their strategies are a strange blend of revolutionary rhetoric, revisionist doctrine, and reformist practice. Their goals seem increasingly confused in a world dominated by the examples of Communist states which they cannot wholly reject and those of welfare states which they cannot wholly embrace. The Western European Communists, in short, are struggling through a crisis of identity created by the diminishing congruence between their traditional philosophies, operational codes, and objectives, on the one hand, and the exigencies of politics in modern industrial countries with relatively efficient democratic institutions, on the other.

Still, this is hardly the whole story. And—to borrow David Caute's remark about some critics of Marxism—those who tend to assume that it is also tend to sound two distinctive notes: confidence that Western European communism must soon wither away and marked irritation that it has not already done so. It would be a mistake to conclude too rapidly that communism in Western Europe has no future in societies so comfortably entrenched in prosperous modernity that they have no tolerance for ideology and no use for radical dissent.

If the Communist Parties of Western Europe were sufficiently set in their ways to resist any inner transformation, they could with some assurance be relegated to the dustbin of history. But perhaps the most striking characteristic of the Western European Parties in the past decade has been their effort to "renovate" and in the process to shed, more or less rapidly and consciously, most of the features that once stamped them as "Communist." A high official of the largest of the Western European Parties has even suggested publicly that "neither of the two solutions available to the working class of the capitalist countries of Western Europe in the last fifty years, the social democratic and the Communist solution, has up to this point shown itself valid for the goal of accomplishing a Socialist transformation of society"—and has called for a "new party" that would fuse the bankrupt branches of the traditional left without regard to "ideological presuppositions."[2] The remarkably open debate provoked by this heretical "hypothesis" shows, if nothing else, that Western European Communists are rethinking their politics, not only their tactics but also some of their basic ideas about the world they live in and how to cope with it.

There are, in fact, some trends in Western European communism that mark a fairly clear break with the past. The first and most obvious trend is the growing independence of the Parties, their cautious but

[2] Giorgio Amendola of the Italian Communist Party, in the ideological weekly *Rinascita* (Rome), Nov. 28, 1964, p. 8.

ultimately unequivocal rejection of any extranational source of authority or control, including a strictly regional one. The revolutionary implications of this change have only partly been tempered or camouflaged by appeals to "unity in autonomy and diversity." The unity of the movement now appears to be little more than a myth incapsulating historical memories, vestigial loyalties, and fading ideals. The autonomy of the Parties, in contrast, is real enough already, and this has enabled the Western European Communists to erase some of the stigma of subservience to foreign interests.

Even more important, it has created the conditions for a more basic alteration in the very nature of the European variants of communism, distinguishing it from most other sectors of the almost shattered movement. There are obviously places around the world where the erosion of international solidarity has not altered the Parties' doctrinal rigidity, their revolutionary zeal, their hegemonial ambitions, and their chiliastic hopes—all aspects of the historical character of communism that are more or less responsive to the felt needs of politicized elites and masses in modernizing societies. But Western Europe is another matter. There, industrial development has solved many historical problems and created new ones which challenge the Communists (as well as others) in unexpected ways. Moreover, in most countries of the region the Communist Parties operate in a political culture that includes liberal values and institutions and traditions of rational thought sufficiently well rooted to command their respect and some measure of adaptation. As a result, the second trend in Western European communism is an evolution in theory and practice that is more than faintly reminiscent of the revisionist transformation of the mainstream of continental socialism.

The third trend follows from the others: The progressive and probably irreversible transformation of communism stimulates changes in the poltical roles and expectations of the Parties. Although Communists have long been a conspicuous part of the European scene, until recently they have been treated almost always and everywhere as subversives threatening the democratic institutions, if not the independence, of their countries and since the late 1940s they have been rather effectively isolated from other political forces and relegated to permanent opposition. Not surprisingly, the gradual acculturation of the Communist Parties is reducing habitual suspicions and animosities toward them and in a number of countries they (or their successors and rivals where evolution results in organizational breaks) are winning more widespread acceptance as legitimate participants in the political process. Finland provides an illustration: "It is important for the peaceful development of our society," President Urho Kekkonen said in 1967, "that we accept the [Communists'] rights in principle to take part in the government and equally with others to influence the course of the state's affairs," but he cautioned that this presupposed their willingness to "abide by the mutually agreed rules of the game."[3]

These common tendencies naturally overlay considerable differences among the Parties, in such things as the patterns of their formation, their readiness to engage in a basic reappraisal, and their political weight in their respective countries. Strictly speaking, there is no "Western European communism"—in the sense of a movement bound by an ideological consensus, maintaining some organizational ties among its national units, and developing a common strategy—but only a collectivity of Parties sharing an ambiguous legacy and working in roughly comparable circumstances. If they are considered only as the inheritors of original Communist political ideas and practices, these Parties are undoubtedly anachronistic in contemporary Europe—perhaps they always were in some respects, and that explains their failures. But they are also rapidly changing and lively participants in whatever remains of the international movement and in a few countries they are and seem destined to remain, in one form or another, the preferred instruments for channeling widespread popular and intellectual hostility to the established order.

Thus they are important, not only because they provide intellectually fascinating case studies in the partial "deradicalization" of some components of the Communist movement, but also because they still mean something in the practical politics of Western Europe.

Polycentrism Unlimited

Historically, all the Western European Parties have been affected by a persistent tension between their dual roles as sections of an international movement looking to the Soviet Union for legitimacy, material aid, and policy guidance and as national Parties anxious to meet the expectations of their actual or potential domestic supporters and partners.

For a time during the years of the "Popular Front" and again during and immediately after World War II, the Communists were able to reconcile these two roles remarkably well and they reached the apex of their influence and power; but soon after the war they ran into

[3] Helsinki, domestic radio service, Feb. 4, 1967.

difficulties and lost much of the popular sympathy they had won during the years of resistance to the Nazis. In a number of countries, plans for fusions of Communist and Socialist Parties were abandoned and indeed the consultations that did take place usually strengthened the suspicions of Socialists that the Communists viewed the proposed mergers simply and cynically as means for imposing their own control over the democratic left.[4] In 1947 and 1948, the Communists were everywhere eased out of coalition governments in which they had won a place during the last stages of the war or soon after it.[5] The smaller Parties suffered badly from these setbacks; the larger ones managed to carry on, and even to increase their electoral strength, but even they suffered from the ostracism imposed upon them by virtually all other parties of any significance. The postwar pattern of isolation was set.

Some of the Communists' problems were rooted in domestic issues that had been submerged during the war, when the most disparate political groups temporarily buried their differences and made common cause against Nazi Germany and its satellites. Others, however, stemmed directly from the Parties' close ties to Moscow, which had several consequences. For one thing, the advent of the Cold War unmasked the Communists as servile defenders of Soviet interests and policies and this undermined the Communists' own efforts to accommodate themselves to nationalist and even chauvinist sentiments in their countries. In addition, the Parties' ties to Moscow helped to strengthen and perpetuate precisely those features of communism which (though based partly on indigenous traditions) conflicted with Western liberal ideals, and thus cut the Parties off from the democratic groups whose tolerance and cooperation they needed if their moderate strategies were to have any chance of success. The Soviet Union's influence or control also frequently compelled the Parties to take positions that were incompatible with their own immediate interests, either in the adoption of a general strategy or in the formulation of positions on particular issues.

[4] For example: In Norway, negotiations looking toward the organizational union of the Communist and Labor Parties were broken off in May, 1946. In Finland, the Social Democratic Party refused even to cooperate with the Communists in the first postwar elections in March, 1945, although a number of Socialists broke with their party to join or support the Communist-dominated electoral front, the Finnish People's Democratic League (SKDL). The French Communists' efforts to unite the political forces that had been active in the Resistance collapsed in 1945 and by 1946 even the Socialists who had formerly regarded the Communists as electoral allies had become their bitter adversaries. The Italian Communists and Socialists also gave up their long-planned fusion in 1946, although the two Parties remained linked through "unity of action" agreements for ten more years.

[5] At the end of the war, Communists served in coalition governments in Denmark, Norway, Iceland, Finland, Belgium, Luxembourg, France, and Italy.

All this had also been true in the past, of course, and though it could and did lead to defections and expulsions, it had never seriously shaken the Communist Parties' acceptance of Moscow's guidance and control. Although the Parties' setbacks after 1945 created a great deal of internal tension, there was never any serious question, at that time, about their official commitment to "proletarian internationalism," which in practice meant submission to Moscow on fundamental questions, at least. As suggested elsewhere,[6] this quasimonolithic phase of communism was the product of several factors: the internationalist sentiments of the Communists, who inherited and developed (or, more correctly, distorted) a tradition common to much of the European left; their apotheosization of the Soviet Union as the first land of "socialism"; and their psychological and political submission to the Soviet Union resulting from the early weaknesses and defeats of the Western Parties. Nevertheless, the postwar experiences of the Western European Communists influenced their positions on the issues that eventually confronted the movement so dramatically.

The conventional dividing line is 1956 and indeed Khrushchev's first so-called "revelations" about the Stalinist regime did break the established pattern of Communist public discourse and allowed the autonomist tendencies that had been repressed during the preceding decade to assert themselves more openly and strongly. Developments since 1956 suggest that the Soviet Union's authority in the Communist movement has been almost shattered by the interaction of several factors. Traditional Marxist internationalism in Western Europe has been weakened and partly replaced with nationalist sentiments stimulated and exploited by the Communists themselves[7] and with a technocratically oriented (though sometimes politically motivated) internationalism expressing itself largely in European forms.[8] The Soviet Union's prestige as a

[6] See Chapter 3.

[7] The "nationalization" of the Communist Parties began in the Popular Front period in the mid-1930s, with a new emphasis on national values and the defense of the national state, and continued into the war and postwar period. That the Communist use of nationalist appeals was largely instrumental hardly affected the result: an erosion, or at least a modification, of traditional attitudes and views. See, for example, David Caute, *Communism and the French Intellectuals* (New York: Macmillan, 1964), pp. 197–201.

[8] It is doubtful that "Europeanism" as an ideology has significantly reduced the appeal of Communist internationalism among the faithful; but the development of the European Community has certainly forced Communist labor and political leaders to accommodate their views and policies to the "realities" of trans-national institutions and programs, although the French especially have done so reluctantly. See Kevin Devlin, "Workers of the World, Disunite!" *Orbis,* vol. X, no. 3, Fall, 1966. Also the chapter on "The Common Market Controversy" in Donald L. M. Blackmer, *Unity in Diversity—Italian Communism and the Communist World* (Cambridge, Mass.: The MIT Press, 1968).

model Socialist state had declined both because of its own failures[9] and because of the unanticipated successes of Western Europe in developing free, prosperous, and apparently stable societies that hardly fit conventional Marxist and particularly Leninist analysis. In practical terms, too, Communist ties to the Soviet Union have become more of a burden than an advantage: for if subordination to the USSR once seemed an acceptable price for political survival and relevance, these now require, as many leading Communists now say openly, the independence of the national Parties. Increasingly open criticism of Communist regimes and the strong resistance of half a dozen Western European Parties to Soviet pressures for an international conference provide ample evidence of the changed outlook.

On the other hand, the Communists, even the most "revisionist" of them, have not broken completely with their past. Much of the Communist heritage continues to engage the emotional loyalty and the intellectual commitment of Western Europeans. Marxist habits of thought, substantial alienation from the established social and political order, and continuing hopes (if not expectations) of revolutionary change are still evident on the far left; the radical impulse, in short, outlasts the particular forms it took under Soviet inspiration and control, and the impulse includes a lingering attachment to the Soviet Union as a Socialist society, however flawed. Moreover, apart from such basic continuities, the Parties' evolution, their emancipation from the Leninist and even from the Stalinist past, is retarded by a number of prudential constraints: like most political leaders of every persuasion, Communists are inclined to avoid a rapid and fully explicit public reversal or reappraisal of their doctrines and practices that might threaten personal reputations, provoke internal Party divisions, or compromise the movement's standing with its supporters. Thus even the assertion of Party autonomy is linked with reaffirmations of Socialist internationalism, although it is far from clear what operational forms such internationalism may take.

[9] European Communist criticism of the Soviet Union are often prompted in part, at least, by the desire to disassociate the Parties from embarassing institutions and policies. Note, for example, the French Communist Louis Aragon's public reaction to the trial of Soviet writers Daniel and Sinyavsky: "It must be feared, indeed, that the thought could arise that this type of procedure is inherent in the nature of communism and that the judgment pronounced today foreshadows what justice will be in a country that has abolished the exploitation of man by man. It is our duty to proclaim that this is not the case and will not be the case in France, at least, where it is part of our responsibility." *L'Humanité* (Paris), Feb. 16, 1966. Other prominent Western European Communists were equally outspoken.

What *is* clear, however, is that Communist unity seems every day more of a political chimera. The "world" movement, whether led and dominated by Moscow or (as seemed possible for a brief moment) directed by a council of equals, has been shattered, and most Western European Communists have been conspicuously suspicious of proposals for a general conference or other central institution that might restrict their own responses to national traditions and needs or define a new Communist orthodoxy. The Western European Communists have even failed to develop "polycentrism" in the direction apparently originally intended by the late Italian leader Palmiro Togliatti, toward a regional cluster of Parties with a fairly high level of integration and reciprocal support Meetings of Western European Parties in Brussels (in 1965), Vienna (in 1966), and a more inclusive assembly of East and West European parties at Karlovy Vary (in April, 1967) were notable for their less than full attendance, their inconclusive resolutions, and the almost complete lack of immediate practical results in terms of coordinated policy. A Swedish leader expressed the general mood of the Western European Communists when he commented on his Party's decision to send only an "observer" to the Karlovy Vary conference on European security: "We feel that it is more normal for each Party to formulate its own decisions on such political questions."[10]

The evolution of a once-monolithic movement, sustained by the utopian idea of a natural harmony of interest among Communist Parties and states, into something less cohesive and centralized probably was an inevitable as anything in history, or so it now seems in retrospect. The distinctive contribution to this process of the more prestigious European Parties—which are, after all, among the oldest and were once the most faithful daughters of the Moscow church—has been to help rationalize and legitimate the idea of an international movement retaining a measure of unity while respecting the autonomy of its parts. Whether or not it was originally meant to do so, this formula serves mainly to protect the Parties from the trauma of a sudden and total rupture with their own past while they grope for a new political character more attuned to the current realities of Europe.

The New Varieties

As communism disintegrates as a unitary world movement, its component parts undergo a more or less rapid differentiation. What

[10] Carl-Henrik Hermansson, Communist Party secretary, as reported by *Agence France Presse,* Apr. 20, 1967.

this means, essentially, is that each Party becomes more nearly identified with the dominant political culture of its immediate environment, more fully absorbed by its role in the existing domestic political system, and more sensitive to the demands of local circumstance. It has fewer inhibitions about taking on the style of its native land. In some developing countries, especially, where a total transformation of society may still seem to Communists desirable and possible, the resulting changes may be minimal; even completely independent Parties may retain the violently totalitarian features associated with the movement so far, because these features still have a functional relationship to perceived local realities and possibilities. In Western Europe, on the other hand, differentiation involves a more thorough transformation and an abandonment of "communism" in the historic meaning of the term; the alternative would seem to be current irrelevance and ultimate decay.

This is so because the Western European Communists are, in various degrees, subject to strong pressures which, projected far enough, will probably drive them toward some form of leftwing democratic socialism. There are several more or less obvious reasons for this. The Parties now operate in highly developed industrial societies that constantly challenge the more simplistic orthodoxies of their economic creed.[11] In addition, most of the Western European Parties work in countries with strong democratic traditions and institutions, though exceptions of course can be found, most conspicuously in such places as Germany, Italy, and the Iberian states. Finally, the Communists in Western Europe almost everywhere face the competition and usually the opposition of Socialist and laborite parties (and in places Catholic parties also) with strong ties to the very classes that are the objects of Communist appeals. In a sense, even the tactical adjustments of the Parties over the years—such as the calls for popular fronts, the nationalistic slogans of the war years, and the incipient "national roads to socialism" of the immediate postwar period—may be seen as acculturation

[11] The Italians were the first and most outspoken malcontents to respond to this as to so many other problems. An early, somewhat dated but still valuable survey of Communist economic revisionism may be found in Giuseppe Tamburrano, "Lo sviluppo del capitalismo e la crisi teorica dei comunisti italiani," in *Tempi Moderni* (Rome), July–Sept., 1962. A more recent transalpine example of accommodation comes from the Austrian Party, whose Franz Marek lectured members of the Soviet Academy of Sciences, of all people, on the vigor of the Western European capitalist economies and the need to pursue gradual "structural reforms" within the existing system both as a practical imperative and as means of preserving and expanding "bourgeois" liberties. See Franz Marek, "Probleme der Kommunistischen Parteien West-europas," in *Weg und Ziel* (Vienna), Nov., 1965.

processes that transcended the immediate instrumental motives of their advocates.

The transformation involves drastic revisions in the two components of Communist ideology that are most directly political and that are examples of what have been called the "transfer" and the "goal" cultures of revolutionary movements—the code of conduct or grand strategy, designed to change a social system and the utopian image of what is to replace the established order.[12]

Traditionally, the transfer culture of the Communist movement has involved: (1) an almost complete skepticism about the possibility of an evolutionary transformation of the "capitalist" system into a "Socialist" one; (2) a conviction that an elite vanguard Party was the indispensable instrument of revolutionary change; and (3) a belief that the "dictatorship of the proletariat" was a necessary transitional stage toward the ultimate goal of the movement (and of history). A rough measure of Communist revisionism can be taken along these three dimensions of the movement's transfer culture. So far as the Western European Parties are concerned, the results are striking: the trends include a new faith in "structural reforms" of the existing social system as an alternative to violent revolution; a serious questioning of the role and nature of the Leninist Party in advanced industrial societies with well-functioning democratic institutions;[13] and considerable debate over the meaning and value of the dictatorship of the proletariat.

These developments conform to an expected pattern. For revolutionary movements out of power, important changes in political ideology are likely to occur first in their transfer culture because this comes into daily contact with "reality" and must somehow adjust to it, even if the adjustment is, at first, only a tactical one.[14] The goal culture, in contrast, is a set of ideals which normally remain relatively stable in their abstract (prerevolutionary) form and become controversial and unstable more rapidly when a revolutionary movement comes to power,

[12] The terms come from Anthony F. C. Wallace, *Culture and Personality* (New York: Random House, 1961). For a discussion of Wallace's view of revolutionary or "revitalization" movements, see Chalmers Johnson, *Revolutionary Change* (Boston and Toronto: Little, Brown, 1966), especially pp. 105–111.

[13] The Swedish Communists have virtually abolished democratic centralism by tolerating open factionalism, allowing Party members in trade unions and government councils almost complete freedom to adopt personal positions, and opening Party meetings to the public. In Italy the trend is in the same direction but has not gone nearly far enough to constitute a real break with the Leninist tradition.

[14] For an elaboration of this point, see Robert C. Tucker, "The Deradicalization of Marxist Movements," *The American Political Science Review*, vol. LXI,

gives them some institutional expression, and thus provides a concrete basis for measuring accomplishment against aspiration.

But in Western Europe, the Communist Parties are also experiencing a prerevolutionary crisis in their goal culture, which illustrates another and more novel aspect of their revisionism. One of the strengths of the Communist movement in the past has been its opportunity to point to the Soviet Union as the embodiment of the ideal goals of the movement and thus to sustain hope in the practicality and the ultimate victory of the new order. The Soviet Union provided the movement with the model of a real rather than a merely hypothetical or historically immanent utopia. At the same time, the Communists have had to pay a price for such concreteness: The contrast between the ideal goal culture of the movement and its actual implementation in the Soviet Union has been a classic source of conflict within the Parties, leading to disillusionment, despair, and defections. The very concreteness of the Communist goal culture forced attention to a component of revolutionary ideology which does not usually become the focus of doubt and controversy before the conquest of power. This is probably the central meaning of the de-Stalinization experience since 1956 in its impact on the Western Parties especially.

The progress of Communist revisionism in Western Europe has not been even or uncontested. There naturally are some common trends, but they have hardly asserted themselves equally strongly in all Parties. The Italian and Swedish Parties have gone furthest in revising both their transfer and goal cultures, and have done it with a candor unusual in Communist history. The others have followed more or less willingly and rapidly. Although the details differ from country to country, the revisionist forces in all the Parties must contend with a double constraint: the inertia, if not the outright opposition, of conservatives still tied to old habits; and the open attacks of radicals who, in their ardent

no. 2, June, 1967, pp. 334–358. Tucker argues that "deradicalization must be the eventual fate of all radical movements, whether or not they achieve political power" (p. 346) and that "deradicalization signifies a subtle change in the movement's relation to the social milieu. Essentially, it settles down and adjusts itself to existence within the very order that it officially desires to overthrow and transform. . . . it becomes 'reformist' in the sense that it accepts the established system and its institutionalized procedures as the framework for further efforts in the direction of social change" (p. 348). Deradicalization may at first involve an actual intensification of "ideological rhetoric" and "verbal protestations of fidelity to Communist ideas" at the same time that there is a "revision of the tactical doctrine, changes in the official conception of the *means* by which the ultimate goals may be achieved" (p. 355).

commitment to a total reconstruction of society, reject both the Stalinism of the past and the once heretical revisionism that has become the dominant mood, if not everywhere the explicit creed, of the European movement. The former are mostly political relics, old Party bureaucrats who are gradually, in the Italian phrase, being relegated to the "elephants' graveyard" when they are not expelled or do not leave their Parties altogether. The latter are mostly young rebels who have constructed an array of miniscule "Marxist-Leninist" groups throughout Europe, but they have had little impact on Party activists intent on proving their respectability and little appeal to electorates who find the parent Parties already heady enough for their tastes.

In their own ways, all of the Communist Parties of Western Europe are searching for a new identity, a political nature that will be different both from that of communism and that of social democracy, as these two mainstreams of the European Socialist tradition have developed during the past fifty years and more. For most Western European Communist revisionists, the rejection of the Soviet or Chinese model does not mean an unqualified acceptance of the welfare state system, which they consider the political expression of "neocapitalism" in the more advanced industrial societies; but in practice they show considerable accommodation to the status quo. For most of them also, the abandonment of hopes or plans for violent revolution does not imply a complete acceptance of the parliamentary system as the exclusive domain of political action; but the trend toward a reformist politics based largely on an effective parliament is already well marked in practice.

Perhaps the European Communists are more accurately characterized (to use an old phrase) as irresolute Marxists rather than resolute revisionists. But even the Communists seem destined to share the fate of democratic mass revolutionary parties: "Once parliamentary activity becomes enjoyable and habitual," as one author has observed, "theoretical orthodoxy is subordinated to vote-getting: the road to opportunism is paved with parliamentary success."[15]

Roles and Expectations

Changes in the political roles and expectations of the Western Parties can be traced to the idea that "socialism" can be achieved through "peaceful" means, a notion that had a long history in Western

[15] Peter Gay, *The Dilemma of Democratic Socialism—Eduard Bernstein's Challenge to Marx* (New York: Collier Books, 1962), p. 111.

Communist habits and attitudes even before it gained full legitimacy, in a sense, from PC XX of the CPSU in 1956. In time the idea, which perhaps originated as a temporary expedient, gained ascendancy over two other, more or less covert, elements in the transfer culture of the Western European Parties: the expectation that communism could be achieved only through domestic violence or only through external (Soviet) military intervention.[16] The shift from a predominantly revolutionary to an increasingly reformist orientation gave new importance to two old Communist problems—the problem of each Party's own direct strength as measured not by the standards of an elite Leninist organization but by standards more appropriate to conventional parties working in a parliamentary setting, and the problem of alliances.

So long as the Communists considered the use of existing political and governmental institutions simply as an interim or at best an auxiliary strategy of power, faith in their ultimate success could survive electoral weakness and parliamentary impotence. But once they adopted seriously the idea of a nonviolent and essentially parliamentary transition to socialism, electoral and parliamentary strength became a uniquely critical measure of their success or failure and their prospects. And the measure is, as the accompanying table indicates, largely one of failure. There is a new urgency, consequently, in the Communists' efforts to increase their electoral appeal and, of course, their role in local and

[16] A prominent Italian Communist, Valdo Magnani, noted the prevalence of the latter view just before his expulsion from the PCI in 1951: "There is a common opinion among our comrades that revolution can advance only through war and it must be said that this opinion is well tolerated in our Party. . . . The campaign for peace is considered by some only a kind of cover. It is thought . . . nothing more nor less, that in the present phase of struggle in the world the revolution can succeed only on the bayonets of an army which crosses our frontier. I know these comrades are thinking of the Red Army or of the forces of the People's Democracies. . . . This is a political error. . . . It tends to make the Party an alien body in our national life." See Valdo Magnani and Aldo Cucchi, *Dichiarazioni e documenti* (Bologna: Luigi Parma, 1951), pp. 10–17, as quoted in Giorgio Galli, *Storia del Partito Comunista Italiano* (Milan: Schwarz, 1958), pp. 307–308. Magnani returned to the PCI in 1962.

A similar observation about the French Communist Party was made by George Lichtheim in a recent review article: "It is only since [Thorez's] death in 1964 that the PCF has partially come to terms with the real world. This has meant renouncing not just the more eccentric notions of 'proletarian revolution,' but the (secret and confidential) doctrine that France (like other West European countries) would one day have to be 'liberated' by the Soviet Army. For *this* and nothing else was the long-term strategy to which the leadership had committed the party. But now these expectations have been quietly buried, and the party of Waldeck Rochet is busy acquiring a social-democratic image." *The New York Review of Books,* July 13, 1967, p. 34.

West European Communist Parties Electoral and Parliamentary Strength (by countries)

	Country	Date of Last Election Prior to Jan. 1, 1967	Votes		Parliamentary Seats	
			No.	%	No.	%
Proscribed parties	West Germany[a]	9/19/65	343,188	1.3	—	—
	Spain	—	—	—	—	—
	Portugal	—	—	—	—	—
Minor legal parties	Austria[b]	3/6/66	18,638	0.4	—	—
	Belgium[c]	5/23/65	260,236	5.1	6	2.8
	Denmark[d]—CP	11/22/66	21,536	0.8	—	—
	—SPP		304,234	10.9	20	11.43
	Iceland[e]	6/9/63	14,274	16.0	9	15.0
	Ireland	8/7/65	183	0.01	—	—
	Luxembourg	6/7/64	330,909	12.5	5	8.9
	Netherlands	2/15/67	248,008	3.6	5	3.3
	Norway[d]—CP	9/12/64	29,450	1.4	—	—
	—SPP		121,900	6.0	2	1.3
	Sweden	9/20/64	221,746	5.2	8	3.4
	Switzerland	10/63	21,008	2.2	4	2.0
	Great Britain	3/31/66	62,112	0.2	—	—
Major legal parties	Finland[f]	3/20–21/66	502,812	21.2	41	20.5
	France	3/12/67	5,029,808	22.46	73	15.0
	Italy	4/28–29/63	7,763,854	25.3	166	27.5

[a] Figures are for the Communist-front German Peace Union.

[b] The Communist Party of Austria did not contest the 1966 election on a nation-wide basis but asked its supporters to vote for Socialist Party candidates. The Party ran only one one candidate, Party Chairman Franz Muhri, who was defeated.

[c] The figures for Belgium include votes cast for the major Communist Party and a group of dissidents.

[d] Initials represent the parent Communist Parties and the Socialist People's Parties.

[e] Figures are for the Communist-dominated electoral front, the Labor Alliance.

[f] Figures are for the Communist-dominated electoral front, the Finnish People's Democratic League.

SOURCE: Adapted from U.S. Department of State, Bureau of Intelligence and Research, *World Strength of the Communist Party Organizations,* 1967 ed.

national representative bodies.[17] They are doing this mainly by appealing opportunistically, in the best manner of "conventional" parties, to particular and often marginal groups whose support (lacking conscious ideological commitment) contributes to the so-called "protest" vote. But this is old and routine. More novel and interesting is the Communists' effort to create a new image of themselves that they hope will overcome the ideologically rooted hostility of intellectuals and middle-class voters (including many with serious grievances against the existing social system) toward Parties cast in the Soviet mold. The results are mixed, but the modest electoral gains of some Parties seem to be attributable partly to their tactical virtuosity on particular issues and to the greater attractiveness of their somewhat refurbished image.[18]

Electoral gains are not enough to satisfy political ambitions, though, even for the strongest of the Western European Parties, because none of them has the slightest hope of coming to power, or even of having a measure of positive influence[19] on national affairs, without strong allies. As a result, almost all Communists are absorbed by the problem

[17] It should be noted, however, that one of the important themes of debate even among revisionist Communists in Western Europe centers precisely on "parliamentarism." Does the national and nonviolent road to socialism mean a full and exclusive reliance on existing political institutions, especially parliament? Some Communists answer with an unequivocal yes and thus place themselves flatly on social-democratic ground. Others are more ambiguous and consider parliament essentially as a political institution which "offers the triple inconvenience of having lost much of its former importance, of not enjoying great prestige among the masses and of being . . . a shock absorber and therefore an extremely effective instrument of integration" and which, by giving the masses "the illusion that they have a share in power," absorbs and neutralizes their radical impulses. For the more radical revisionists, parliamentary action must be supplemented by "mass actions" which will provide more intimate forms of political participation and give a truer expression of the "concrete needs" of the masses. These passages come from an Italian Socialist ideolog who is a major advocate of a "New Left" will avoid the "opportunisms" of both Communist and democratic Socialist Parties. The remarks were made at a conference sponsored by the Gramsci Institute of the Italian Communist Party. See Lelio Basso, "Perspectives on the European Left," *Studies on the Left,* vol. 7, no. 2, 1967.

[18] In Sweden, for instance, the Communist Party, rejuvenated under Hermansson, won 6.4 percent of the vote in the 1966 municipal elections, as compared to 3.8 percent four years earlier. The French Communist Party accumulated 22.5 percent of the votes in the first round of the 1967 legislative election, which almost (but not quite) brought it back to the position it held before de Gaulle's return to power in 1958; and politically—if not electorally—the Party is stronger than it was ten years ago, when it struggled in not-so-splendid isolation. Elsewhere the picture is more ambiguous, but it now seems that if some form and degree of revisionism is no guarantee of electoral success, its absence is almost certainly a harbinger of stagnation or failure.

[19] The qualification is important, because the larger Parties in opposition, of course, do influence policy—negatively perhaps—by the very fact of their *permanent* exclusion from the decision-making orbit, which means that some social and

of establishing working relations with other parties, and the most outspoken of these Communists—the Amendolas, Hermanssons, Mareks, and others—now say openly that these relations must be based on tolerance for ideological diversity and respect for the achievements and liberties of "bourgeois" democracies. There is nothing new in the Communists' attempts to find collaborators among those of other political persuasion; what is new is the extent to which the Communists are willing to accommodate their own doctrines, practices, and policy goals to win acceptance as legitimate parties in a pluralistic system—and the moderately favorable responses of other groups.

There are many indications, in fact, that European non-Communists interpret recent changes in Western communism as evidence of a gradual partial deradicalization of the Parties which justifies a cautious modification of the policy of ostracism adopted almost universally during the early years of the Cold War. Among these indications, several are worth noting briefly. First, public opinion in some countries, most strikingly in France,[20] is evidently more willing than it has been for almost twenty years to accept the Communists as somewhat deviant but useful members of the body politic. Second, both non-Communist trade union leaders and some governments have relaxed their opposition or hostility to labor unions dominated or led by Communists.[21] Last, but

---

political measures demanded by sizeable publics simply cannot find the necessary support within the restricted number of parties theoretically eligible to enter government coalitions. Thus demands for social reform have been "frozen" when channeled through Communist Parties.

[20] French polls show a steady rise in favorable attitudes and in early 1967 about 40 percent of respondents favored Communist participation in the government. This prompted the London *Economist,* no friend of communism or gaullism, to comment: "The most interesting lesson to be drawn from the numerous public opinion polls recently carried out is that most Frenchmen are no longer frightened by the prospect of Communists within a ruling parliamentary coalition, or even within a government. Have the Communists mellowed or is the change due mainly to a different international climate? Undoubtedly the gaullists, who had hoped to gain communist votes through their better relations with Moscow, have contributed to the repainting of the red peril pink." *Economist,* Feb. 25, 1967.

[21] For example, both the British Trade Union Congress and the General Federation of Belgian Workers announced after their 1965 congresses that they favored consultations between Communist and non-Communist unions in Western Europe. At the governmental level, the French government permitted the Communist-led General Confederation of Labor (CGT) to be represented in the International Labor Organization on an equal basis with other French labor organizations. Neither the CGT nor the Communist-dominated Italian General Confederation of Labor (CGIL) is yet represented on the Economic and Social Committee of the European Community. However, the Italian government recently included three Socialist leaders of the CGIL among Italian representatives to the Committee in their "personal" capacities.

certainly not least, the Communists have made a beginning in opening or extending a "dialog" with the two political formations that hold the key to their full domestic legitimation, the Catholics and the democratic Socialists. It is true that exchanges with Catholics have so far been limited mostly to the ideological level and have had almost no visible impact on day-to-day politics.[22] But the dialogue with Socialists has already gone far beyond friendly doctrinal seminars toward practical collaboration.[23]

In short, the political climate is changing in Western Europe and the change affects, in a variety of ways, the prospects both of the minor Communist Parties (the great majority) and the three Communist Parties with a large mass base.

The Minor Parties[24]

In most of Western Europe, communism is simply a congeries of minor Parties, many of them floundering in the micropolitics of sects cut off from the main currents of national life. These Parties, illegal or small and relatively ineffective, are usually dismissed as fading vestiges or as pathological formations in otherwise healthy political bodies; but they do have a place in European life and in a few cases their potential roles are quite important, partly as a result of changes encouraged, if not caused, by the erosion of Soviet authority.

The Parties of West Germany, Spain, and Portugal constitute a special case as the only Western European Parties operating as illegal, largely underground and exile, organizations. The Communist Party of Germany (KPD) is essentially a relic. Despite its enormous (and disastrous) influence during the Weimar years, the Party had already be-

22 For a useful survey, see Kevin Devlin, "The Catholic-Communist 'Dialogue,'" in *Problems of Communism,* May–June, 1966. Devlin reports the amused comment of one observer on the warm courtship of the Catholics carried out by the Italian Communists during their 1966 congress: "Is this a Communist congress or an ecumenical council?"

23 But Communist-Socialist relations still vary enormously from place to place. For instance: In Iceland and Italy, the Communists remain closely linked to segments of the Socialist movement that have always been "pro-Communist" in their fashion, but relations with the main Socialist parties are, if anything, deteriorating. In Austria, the tiny revisionist Party has an unrequited passion for collaboration with the Socialists. The Communists have been most successful in Finland (where they now hold cabinet posts) and in France (where they have troubled but apparently lasting electoral and other agreements with the Federation of the Democratic and Socialist Left, which was formed to support François Mitterrand against de Gaulle in the 1965 presidential elections).

24 Defined as parties that are proscribed or that regularly win less than 20 percent of all votes in national elections.

come an insignificant force in West German affairs—sharing the fate of all the smaller political formations crushed between the Christian Democratic and Social Democratic giants—when it was finally proscribed by the federal Constitutional Court in August 1956. In West Germany, communism has been weakened by the general decline of radicalism and discredited by its association with the Soviet Union and the Pankow regime. The Party—that is, its illegal apparatus and its still-active miniscule fronts—survives mainly as an offshoot of the East German Socialist Unity Party (SED) and its fortunes seem linked more to the course of relations between the divided halves of the country than to any vitality within its own ranks or to any latent popular appeal. In the Federal Republic, as one observer has said, "communism is a ghost that broods over calamitous errors and tragedy from which a once-proud movement could not recover."[25]

Iberian communism presents an entirely different picture. On balance, the Spanish and Portuguege Parties are working in what is probably the most promising environment in all of Western Europe for a revolutionary movement and the scant evidence available suggests that they have been less seriously influenced by revisionist forces than most of the legal Parties and less debilitated by blunder and circumstance than the German Party. The Iberian Communists have long histories of opposition to conservative authoritarian regimes and thus claim to be the bearers of progressive and even liberal values. Both the Spanish and Portuguese Parties are committed to unity of action with other opposition groups (including Catholics), which are, on the whole, suspicious of close collaboration with communism but perhaps less adamantly hostile to it than in the past. Both Parties clearly rest their hopes for growing influence on a crisis of regime succession that may enable them to emerge as major forces in societies torn by internal problems of social change and lacking constitutional and political traditions promising a stable democratic consensus.

In seven other countries of Western Europe (Austria, Belgium, Ireland, Luxembourg, the Netherlands, Switzerland, and Great Britain) minor Communist Parties present a confusing array of tendencies. Some Parties (notably the Austrian and British) have moved boldly toward revisionist positions; others (notably the Dutch Party) have resisted ideological change. Some seem to have lost all capacity for electoral growth (again the Austrian Party provides an example); others (especially the Belgian Party) have made modest but perceptible electoral gains

[25] Joseph R. Starobin, "Communism in Western Europe," *Foreign Affairs,* vol. 44, no. 1, Oct., 1965, p. 62.

in recent years. Some (for example, the Irish Party) are utterly insignificant; others (the Belgian, Luxembourg, and British Parties) have some influence in intellectual circles or sectors of the labor movement, although more direct political influence at the national level eludes even the strongest of them. None of these minor Parties, however, has been able to combine an inner transformation with a successful appeal to potential supporters and allies, which seems to be the indispensable condition for a long-range change in political roles.[26]

This combination is, in contrast, characteristic of the Scandinavian Communist or neo-Communist Parties. The two related trends in Nordic communism are an evolution toward left-wing socialism and a closer involvement in national politics and government. The manner in which the ideological component of this transformation is taking place varies. In Denmark and Norway, it has involved splits in the Communist Parties and the rise of small but remarkably vigorous Socialist People's Parties that have virtually replaced the parent movements. In Sweden, the revisionists, under Hermansson, a popular leader who became chairman in 1964, have taken control of the Communist Party itself, with only minor defections on the Party's extreme left wing. In Iceland (and in Finland, which is covered in the next section), the struggle for change is taking place largely within a front organization created by the Communists for electoral purposes— the Labor Alliance in Iceland (and the Finnish People's Democratic League in Finland).[27] As a result

[26] In the short run, however, there is no invaraibly unilinear connection between revisionism and political success. The Austrian Party, despite its new look under a new chairman, Franz Muhri, lost votes in the 1966 election. The British Party has gone to great lengths to create a mellower image (including a change in the name and format of its paper, transformed from *Daily Worker* to *Morning Star*), but this has not significantly affected the solid indifference of Laborite voters or the hostility of most Laborite leaders to it. The Belgian Communists, despite their modest intellectual contribution to the evolution of Western European communism, have managed to increase their electoral strength by appealing to disaffected supporters of the Socialist party. The Dutch Party, although its old chairman, Paul de Groot, almost symbolizes unreconstructed Stalinism, recently has gained both votes and respectability (e.g., representation on some parliamentary committees formerly closed to Communists). But the Dutch Party, though conspicuously rigid on ideological matters, has also become one of the most nationalist of Western European Parties: it sent only a low-level delegation to PC XXIII of the CPSU, refused to sign the final resolution issued by Western European Parties meeting in Brussels in June, 1965, and completely boycotted the Vienna meeting of Western European Parties in May, 1966, and the all-European Karlovy Vary conference in April, 1967.

[27] The most comprehensive account in English of recent developments in Scandinavian communism is found in William E. Griffith (ed.), *Communism in Europe: Continuity, Change, and the Sino-Soviet Dispute,* vol. 2 (Cambridge, Mass. and London: The MIT Press, 1966), which includes chapters on Sweden, Norway, and Finland.

of these developments, the Nordic Communist Parties (or their successors in Denmark and Norway) have generally improved their electoral positions and strengthened their claims on other parties for a share of government power.[28]

The Giants

The larger Communist Parties of Western Europe face—and present to their respective countries—problems of entirely different dimensions. Despite the reverses they suffered a few years immediately after World War II, the Communists of Finland, France, and Italy continued to operate as formidable subversive oppositions—too weak, as it turned out, to really endanger the existing systems, but too powerful also to be ignored (as the smaller Parties could be ignored) as irrelevant eccentrics. These Communist Parties (or their electoral front in Finland) all continue to get between a fifth and a quarter of the votes in national elections. Thus whatever the Communists do in these countries is bound to affect the pattern of politics in a fundamental way, and under some circumstances may even affect the constitutional system. All three Parties are in considerable ferment and all three are anxious to participate in coalition governments, but their immediate prospects are very dissimilar.

In 1948 the Finnish Communist Party seemed for a time on the verge of power, only to be locked in opposition after an abortive coup. The result was a long period in the political wilderness, made less desolate by the companionship of a substantial number of dissident Socialists who joined them in an electoral front called the Finnish People's Democratic League (SKDL). Ironically, the SKDL leadership, long dominated by rather dogmatic Communists, was captured in 1965

[28] In Denmark, the minority Social Democratic government remained in power for a time only with the support of the Socialist People's Party, as a result of a parliamentary alliance formed in early 1967. The Norwegian Socialist People's Party made substantial gains and increased its representation in the councils of Oslo and Bergen in late 1967. In late 1966, the Swedish Communists almost doubled their votes in the municipal elections, and some members of the ruling Social Democrats, sensitive to defections from their own left to the Communists, are apparently considering a "Danish" solution, that is, a government supported by the Communists in parliament. In the meantime, the Communist Party of Sweden used the occasion of its PC XXI in 1967 to add a symbol of change to the substance and now calls itself Left Party—Communists, which may be a half-way point to a complete elimination of traditional nomenclature. In Finland, the Communists entered the government in 1966 through their electoral front, the Finnish People's Democratic League. The Icelandic Communists, however, suffered a setback in early 1967 when *their* electoral front, the Labor Alliance, was split by the defection of its chairman.

by a non-Communist, Ele Alenius, who proceeded to give it a democratic socialist orientation and to use it to encourage revisionists within the Communist Party itself. About the same time, the Finnish Social Democrats underwent a minor revolution of their own and, under new leaders, modified their traditional hostility to both the Soviet Union and the local Communists. These developments paved the way for the Communists' entry into a coalition government with the Social Democrats and the Center (formerly Agrarian) Party in May, 1966.

The French Communists fall somewhere between their Finnish and their Italian comrades in their accommodation to other parties. In Gaullist France, they are not, of course, in any coalition government, but they have emerged in the least few years as active partners in a more or less united left. The main lines of development are simple. Long one of the most sclerotic of Western Parties, the PCF has showed unexpected capacity for modifying its ideological and political views and for liberalizing its internal practices in recent years. This placed it in a more favorable position to negotiate an alliance with the newly-formed Federation of the Left in 1965 and subsequently. In turn, the demands of the Federation, and especially of its Socialist leader Mitterrand, accelerated revisionist trends within the Party. The result has been a series of remarkable electoral successes for the Communists and a virtually complete escape from the political isolation that had plagued them for twenty years. Mitterrand recently predicted that prospective agreements between the PCF and his Federation "will be sufficient not merely to preserve the union of the Left but even to give it a new boost."[29]

The fortunes of politics, in contrast, have not favored the Italian Communists recently. For a long time, while other European Communists were effectively contained within political ghettos, the PCI had a "unity of action" pact with the Italian Socialist Party (PSI) of Pietro Nenni. The alliance not only gave the PCI considerable influence in public affairs but also contributed to its image as the most moderate and "open" Communist Party on the European scene and the one most likely to reach the seats of national power. Instead, the Socialists slowly loosened their ties to the PCI after 1956, eventually joined a "center-left" coalition dominated by the Christian Democrats, and most recently formed a reunified party with the Social Democrats. Although Socialists still collaborate with Communists in labor unions, cooperatives, and many local governments, the PCI has not been able to reverse the trend toward increased isolation. The Communists' inability either

[29] Interview with Edward Mortimer, *The Times* (London), Dec. 19, 1967.

to overthrow the center-left coalition, or to propose an alternative that appeals to the democratic left, or to join the government itself has increased intra-Party frustrations and dissent, despite its electoral vigor.

All of which underscores the importance of local circumstances for the prospects of each Party. "It is ironical," one observer has noted, "that just at the time European communism was beginning to acquire a consistent 'Italian' look, the PCI itself was running into a political impasse more serious than any it had faced since 1956."[30]

The Prospects

What, if anything, can be said about the future of communism in Western Europe? Unless there is a complete reversal of current trends, it is certain that the Communist Parties of tomorrow will bear as little resemblance to the historically classic models as the Socialist parties of today do to their own forebears. Beyond this, it is possible to sketch the probable lineaments of the "new communisms," their place in Europe, and impact on the established social and political order.

It now seems likely that most Communists will become increasingly parochial, more completely absorbed in their domestic environment, and responsive to internationalism only as a somewhat romantic myth with no definite ideological components or operational imperatives. There may be pragmatic accords among some Parties. Thus the French and Italian Communists, after years of bickering, have now established machinery for coordinating Party and trade union matters. Similarly, the Icelandic, Swedish, and Finnish Communists have established close relations with the Socialist People's Parties of Norway and Denmark—to the dismay of the orthodox Communists in the latter countries, who have been publicly dismissed as irrelevant by their own Scandinavian comrades. But such regional arrangements are a far cry from the system of values, the organizational links, and the political demands of old–fashioned proletarian internationalism. And they fall short of Togliatti's "polycentrism."

The shift to a predominantly domestic perspective will probably accelerate the deradicalization of most Parties. The process is already well advanced among most of the legal Parties and probably also affects the clandestine groups of West Germany, Spain, and Portugal—although revisionism can hardly be considered the inevitable wave of the future by the underground and exiled Iberian Parties facing authoritarian regimes. But elsewhere the trend is unmistakable. Small groups

[30] Donald L. M. Blackner, *op. cit.*, p. 405.

of militants will probably always be around to argue the merits of more orthodox Marxist or Leninist perspectives, but it seems unlikely that they will have much influence. On the other hand, it does not follow that most Communists will sooner or later become moderate Socialists indistinguishable from the variety now dominant in the West. Although Western European Communists seem thoroughly disillusioned with many orthodoxies of their own past, they are also seriously concerned about being engulfed by "reformist opportunism," which remains, in their view, the cardinal sin of social democratic parties.

This suggests something that is often overlooked by those who concentrate too exclusively on the Communists' own crisis of identity: The Communists' difficulties are part of a more general crisis of the European left, a widespread disillusionment with *all* the major parties that are the present bearers of the socialist tradition. We can only allude to the evidence: In many places revisionist Communist Parties, as in Sweden and France, and post-Communist radical Socialist parties, as in Norway and Denmark, have considerable power of attraction for dissatisfied social democrats and for young people. The Communist Parties may of course simply be absorbed and tamed by the societies they want so desperately to change; but they—or some of their members—may also contribute to the creation of a New Left that is more attuned to Western values than traditional communism and more charged with radical idealism than reformist Socialists now seem to many Europeans. In this limited sense, communism does have a future in Western Europe.

One final observation must be made more cautiously. The Western European Communists are not now capable (if they ever were), and most of them are probably not anxious, to overturn the liberal-democratic systems in which they operate. Thus their participation in parliamentary or government coalitions is no longer the subversive threat it once might have been. This is certainly true of most of the minor Parties (the Iberian Parties are the only real unknowns), which obviously have no conceivable chance of threatening the liberal-democratic institutions of their respective countries. It is less certain of the larger Parties—partly because they *are* larger and partly because the countries in which they prosper are still suffering from major social cleavages. But the Finnish case indicates that so long as the constitutional system is firmly based, it can survive the access of Communists to the centers of power—and even convert them into slightly discontented establishmentarians.

SELECTED BIBLIOGRAPHY

Almond, Gabriel A., *et. al., The Appeals of Communism* (Princeton: Princeton University Press, 1954). A pioneer study of the "susceptibility" to communism in France, Italy, Britain, and the United States, somewhat marred by its heavy reliance on interviews with disaffected former Party members.

Blackmer, Donald L. M., *Unity in Diversity—Italian Communism and the Communist World* (Cambridge, Mass.: The MIT Press, 1968). A finely-written and perceptive review of the PCI's influence on, and responses to, international Communist developments. Similar in focus, though superior in analysis, to Fejtö's book on the French Party noted below.

Borkenau, Franz, *European Communism.* (New York: Harper & Row, 1953). An old, polemical, but still useful introduction to the European Parties.

Cammet, John M., *Antonio Gramsci and the Origins of Italian Communism* (Stanford: Stanford University Press, 1964). A superior work of scholarship on the intellectual and political work of one of the founders of the PCI, later a victim of the Fascist regime. Particularly useful because of the continuing, and growing, ideological influence of Gramsci on Italian communism and the left generally.

Cantril, Hadley, *The Politics of Despair* (New York: Basic Books, 1958). A study of Communist "protest voters" in France and Italy; valuable for its psychological analysis but shallow in its political understanding of the historical and situational roots of the mass appeals of communism in the two countries.

Caute, David, *Communism and the French Intellectuals, 1914–1960* (New York: Macmillan, 1964). A sympathetic but critical study of the French Communist Party's policies toward intellectuals and—in greater detail—of French intellectuals' responses to Marxism, in general, and the Communist movement in particular.

Delzell, Charles F., *Mussolini's Enemies: The Italian Anti-Fascist Resistance* (Princeton: Princeton University Press, 1961). A thorough and balanced account of the organized opposition to the Fascist regime, Delzell's study throws considerable light on the historical reasons for the enormous influence of the PCI after World War II.

Einaudi, Mario, Jean-Marie Domenach, and Aldo Garosci, *Communism in Western Europe* (Ithaca: Cornell University Press, 1951). An elementary introduction to the French and Italian Parties, not to European communism generally, as the title wrongly implies. The sections by Domenach and Garosci, especially, are still useful after more than 15 years.

Fejtö, François, *The French Communist Party and the Crisis of International Communism* (Cambridge, Mass. and London: The MIT Press, 1967). A review and assessment of the PCF's role in, and hesitant adjustment to, post-Stalin developments in the international movement, by the leading journalistic authority on the French Party.

Griffith, William E. (ed.), *Communism in Europe: Continuity, Change, and the Sino-Soviet Dispute,* 2 vols. (Cambridge, Mass. and London: The MIT Press, 1964 and 1966). The most comprehensive current survey of Communist Parties in Eastern and Western Europe. Volume I contains a good chapter on the Italian Party. Volume II, however, is far more valuable because its four chapters on the Scandinavian Parties are virtually unique in the English-language literature on European communism.

Hodgson, John H., *Communism in Finland* (Princeton: Princeton University Press, 1967). A short and straightforward history of the Finnish Party from its origins to 1945, with a brief epilogue summarizing post World War II developments. Though sketchy, it provides a useful introduction to the analysis of recent developments contained in volume II of the Griffith work noted above.

Labedz, Leopold (ed.), *Revisionism: Essays on the History of Marxist Ideas* (New York: Praeger, 1962). Though the individual contributions vary in quality, the book provides an excellent survey of the main "revisionist" themes in Socialist and Communist theory. Several chapters cover the "New Left" in contemporary Britain, France, Italy, and Germany.

Lichtheim, George, *Marxism in Modern France* (New York: Columbia University Press, 1966). An historical survey and critique of French Marxist thought, Socialist and Communist.

Micaud, Charles A., *Communism and the French Left* (New York: Praeger, 1963). A wide-ranging but uneven book on French politics described by the author as "an essay on the crisis of French democracy." The sections on the organization of the Communist Party and its appeals to various social groups are especially good.

Tarrow, Sidney, *Peasant Communism in Southern Italy* (New Haven: Yale University Press, 1967). The author takes issue with some conventional views of the model Communist Party as a "vanguard" or "combat" organization through a detailed study of communism in a particular social setting.

Overview and Projection

Dan N. Jacobs

IT WAS JUST over a century ago that the full view of Karl Marx's vision of reality and Utopia was uncovered to the world. It was just over a half a century ago that power was seized in the name of that vision. To be sure, that power was achieved through the vehicle of revolution, as Marx had foreseen, but other than in this respect the circumstances of that revolution and coming to power were contrary to Marx's anticipations. For the revolution did not break out in the country of the highest development of capitalism or, hencely, of the greatest contradictions of capitalism, or where the proletariat was the greater part of the population or where almost any of the myriad conditions prescribed by Marx prevailed.

And having occurred contrary to Marx, the revolution developed, in almost all ways, contrary to Marx, as well. Marx had forecast that the revolution, having occurred in one country of antique capitalism would soon break out in other states, as well. The fact of one revolution would facilitate and accelerate the outbreak of other revolutions, but each nation, would individually have to undergo the process of capital building and capital disintegration, though with each succeeding foreign revolution, presumably, the possibility of shortening the capitalist period in other lands would improve. But no matter how much Lenin and his lieutenants expected other revolutions and regardless of the efforts expended to bring them about, they did not occur or were stillborn, in the few instances where they did. The Communist power did not spread during the Civil War in Russia, nor for over two decades. And when it did extend to other countries it did so not by means of the dynamic of the revolution, not through proletarian upsurge, but as a result of Soviet Russian armed might.

Although Karl Marx had within him a strain of German chauvinism, albeit unconscious, he certainly did not contemplate that communism was to become the exclusive preserve of any one people—and certainly not the Russians. Communism, on the contrary, was to erase the artificial boundaries and distinctions that divided nations. But shortly after 1917, communism and Russia became identified, certainly in the eyes of the Bolsheviks and their foes, and, in increasing degree, in the view of the rest of the world. For the initiated, Russian experience became duplicable. What had worked in Russia in 1917, in 1921, in 1927, and so forth, would work in Munich, or Peking, or Prague, five years, a decade, three decades later. The faith that the Russian experience could be duplicated quickly grew into the rule that revolutionary activity in all countries must follow the Russian example. The Russian leadership of the international movement so ordered, and their orders were regularly carried out, regardless of their misassessments, regardless of the doubts the recipients may have had about them, regardless of the fiascos to which they contributed.

So it was to a very great extent through much of the first thirty years of the Soviet state—so long as there was only one Communist state. The rub developed when the uniqueness of Soviet existence became forfeit. In dialectical manner, the fashioning of the postwar Soviet Empire carried with it the seeds of its own destruction.

For a time, the considerable prestige of Russian success and power was able to maintain Russian authority, but only for a time. In those newly become Communist countries, whose leadership commanded national support and had come to power largely through their own as opposed to Russian efforts, there was distress at being made the object of Soviet paranoia and the victim of the Soviet requirement to rebuild Russia's ruined industrial plant as speedily as possible, even at the expense of cannibalizing the remaining industrial strength of the new fraternal powers. And, increasingly, there was unwillingness and an inability to accept the dogmas based on Russian experience as being binding in all situations.

In the case of Yugoslavia, Stalin, grown unaccustomed to even the most minor intransigence, confident that he could soon bring Tito *et cie.* to their knees, determined to pursue a course of excision. While there would be no similar major unheavals in the Soviet domains for another eight years, in a large sense it was true that beginning in 1948, certainly in 1956, the world of communism would be shaped more by the Yugoslav than by the Soviet experience.

For—aided and abetted by the successful Yugoslav defiance, by the accretion to communism of a second potentially major world power, China, in numbers the earth's largest nation, by the Polish October and Hungarian November, by nuclear stalemate, by Chinese disappointments, frustrations and ambitions, by the denigration of the authority of the Russian Party and by the increasing bourgeoisation of Eastern European Communism—the recent history of international Communism has been writ large in letters spelling out "disintegration."

Almost without exception, in any facet of the international movement which may be examined, that nationalism—designated by Marx to be outmoded, but nevertheless continuously present and never very far from the surface—has vigorously asserted itself. A variety of factors have, to a greater or less degree, sometimes made it possible for, sometimes forced, the Parties of the camp, in power and out, to reassess the relationship of their own Parties and countries to the camp and to the Soviet Union and its Party. And while, in most instances, they still value the ties that bind they have also come to realize not only the desireability, but the necessity, if they are to maintain or come to power, of loosening those ties, which often are better described as fetters.

With increasing frequency particularly in the early 1960s Communist leaders the world over awakened to the fact that they stood alone with their own people in their own country; that whether they succeeded or failed depended not on what Moscow did, but on what they themselves did; that the determining of their political futures was to be found not in Moscow, but within the borders of the national entities which they headed. If they wanted to stay in power, they had to please the people back home. As the Bolsheviks of the early 1920s suddenly awoke to find themselves alone with the Russian masses, in a somewhat analogous fashion, the leaders of the non-Russian Parties have found themselves in varying degrees alone with their own peoples, with the knowledge that Soviet leaders, often preoccupied with their own domestic problems, would not or could not do much to help them. But, conversely, the USSR would not interfere with their efforts to help themselves, unless they were to "help" themselves out of the Warsaw Pact.

In power or out, Communist leaders have increasingly realized that the future of themselves and their own Parties depends more upon what they can do for themselves than what the Russian can or would do for them. Certainly in many instances, particularly in the case of Parties out of power, this is, in fact, not an especially new development. But the widespread grasping of the fact and the willingness and ability to act upon it is new. Thus, the decade of the sixties has seen such unlikely phenomena as Communist Parties seeking accommodation with the Roman Catholic church, denying the universal applicability of the revolutionary solution, and favoring non-Communist parties at the expense of Communist ones.

Whether in dealing with the people of one's own country or with a foreign Party or country, Communist or not, Communist leadership has come to be guided by its own conception of national interest. For the USSR, of course, this is not new, but for the non-Russian Parties, so long used to acting in Soviet interest, it is a marked departure. However, this by no means indicates that the non-Soviet Parties feel free to completely disregard the Soviet Union in their calculations. The USSR, though increasingly tolerant, probably would not permit itself to be completely shunted aside by the ex-satellites. And the latter, in many instances, continue to covet Soviet guarantees against German revanchism. Moreover, Soviet power and prestige still remain important to Parties not in power. The Soviet Union and the Russian Party must still be regarded. However, no longer as the only factor, but as one of several, in some areas more important than in others.

This then is where the international movement is at today. Togliatti dubbed it the time of "polycentrism," seeing and foreseeing the number of "centers" that have developed. In a slightly different perspective it may be seen as the age of "local" communism, with each Party defining its own theoretical and tactical interests and acting thereon. The Communist Holy Roman Empire has been brought to an end; local chieftains have taken over, still united by the concept of Rome, but each sees it from the point of view of his own fiefdom. And each is so consumed in the day-to-day job of ruling that he has only an occasional moment to be concerned about the glorious unity that was ancient Rome's and *is no more,* no matter how many Party editorials may be written to the contrary.

All of which brings us to what might be the end, except that, in volumes such as this, it seems to be expected that something be said about the future, it apparently not being enough to have suggested where we are and that we have travelled from there to here. It is also apparently required to indicate where we are going, as well.

Certainly anyone conversant with Marxism is aware of the pitfalls of prognosis. Both Marx's advocates and detractors have often behaved as though the totality of his work must stand or fall on the accuracy of his forecasts. On the one hand there have been extraordinary efforts to make the ever-changing present conform to Marx's developmental prognosis. And on the other, the failure of highly developed capitalism to conform *à la* Marx has caused Marx's often valuable insights into pre-capitalist and capitalist societies to be dismissed. The failure to predict correctly about tomorrow does not necessarily invalidate one's understanding of today—I hope.

Again, because the locomotive of history appears to be travelling in a certain direction, this is no guarantee that it will ever reach the apparent goal. Side tracking to the right or left is always imminent, as is disaster. A wheel on one of the cars may become overheated, a coupling may become unfastened, a bridge may be washed away by a sudden downpour—followed by catastrophe. But, it will be said, if the railroaders had been more careful, more observant, these "accidents" would not have occurred. And if our scholarship had been better, we would have *known* that the "monolith" could not have endured, that the Sino–Soviet split was inevitable, and so forth. We *would* have known, we *should* have known—but I doubt that we ever will.

Certainly we could tell a great deal more about the future of international communism if we knew such things as what kinds of forces are going to succeed Mao? What political side effects will the economic changes being carried out in the Soviet Union have? How long will the unleashed power of nationalism persist? and on and on. If we had answers to those and dozens of similar questions we might be able to do something valuable in anticipating the future. But even then we would have to deal with the ubiquitous unexpected.[1]

Having made the above comments and added the information printed on all political scientist membership cards that we are "scientists" and not prognosticators, I will proceed to make some statements, entirely my own, without benefit or responsibility of co-authors, about the future of international communism(s).

It does, then, within the preceding context, appear likely that the changes embarked upon inside the Soviet Union and the satellites will continue. There is no reason not to expect a still greater reliance upon material incentives. The central power will only reluctantly surrender its economic controls, but faced with unacceptable alternatives, it will

[1] It is to be noted that I crave no special indulgences because these are "Soviet" and "Communist" situations with which we are concerned and thereby less fathomable and predictable. The unexpected is to be found in the politics of every country, not least those of the United States. How many "observers," specialists or nonspecialists, in November, 1964, after the landslide Johnson victory at the polls seriously expressed the possibility that within two years Johnson would be running behind both Nixon and Romney in the Gallup Poll race for the Presidency in 1968, or that he would drop out as a candidate months before the nominating convention?

slowly do so, although always looking for some way of avoiding the ultimate step. This being so, the progress towards a "freer' economy is more likely to follow Lenin's "two steps forward, one step back," than to be linear. But given no cataclysmic events, such as war or revolution in the satellites, such changes are likely to continue.

In the area of human freedom, the future seems more indefinite. Political freedom never having been easily gained and/or maintained, there must always be those who are prepared to stick their necks out for their "rights." As yet, there is no evidence that such groups or individuals exist in any sizeable numbers in the USSR. Traditions of struggle for freedom have had generations of nurture in countries like Hungary, Poland and Yugoslavia. But in the case of the Soviet Union itself there are few traditions of meaningful popular opposition to governmental authority. The peasant *bunts* and the Pugachevesque exploits are meaningless in the contemporary context. That there are elements in Russia who desire "freedom," there is no doubt, but that they desire its materialization sufficiently to risk life and position for it is still unknown. The petition assembled by members of the Soviet intelligentsia upon the conviction of Sinyavsky and Daniel was meaningful in this direction as have been several other occurrences. What would be still more meaningful would be, for example, a strike in a large enterprise, suppressed, then followed by sympathy strikes elsewhere—the engaging of low status participants in the struggle. It would seem that the Soviet Union has not reached this point.

So long as the current transitional regime remains in control, it is likely that there will be backings and filings on the matter of freedom as some demands will be met and others rejected, often in no clear pattern, but subject to the whim of one bureaucrat or group of bureaucrats or another. And probably so long as the material aspirations of the bulk of the population continue to be titilated and often met, the situation can be handled in this fashion. But it is to be expected that, sooner or later, other demands, such as that for freedom, will come into focus. There is abundant psychological evidence that the satisfaction of demands leading to the raising of the level of life above that of mere subsistence, leads not only to the proliferation of material demands, but to the sharpening of other demands, as well. It could prove to be the case that Soviet citizenry or those who might become the leaders of the "opposition" will be so materially satisfied as to be unwilling or unable to struggle for other values. One doubts this, but there is the clear fact that Russian traditions of struggle for political freedom have been woefully underdeveloped, and the Russian struggle suffers from this handicap and will suffer.

In the foregoing pages, there has been some intimation of what the continuing relationship between Russia and the Eastern European countries is likely to be. Here the determining factors include strong, but varying according to the country, pressures for independence; a rather pervasive fear of a reemerged Germany; and the amount of independence the Soviet Union will be willing to tolerate. Given peace, including a contained Germany, it is likely that the Soviet Union will be willing to tolerate almost any defiance up to the announced renunciation of communism, and conceivably even that under specific circumstances. Most of the ex-satellites, however, will continue to value Russian protection against the Germans. Consequently, it is to be expected that, if "rationality" prevails, the Eastern European countries will continue to strengthen their independence of the Soviet Union, though always within limits. However, considering the flammable quality of Central European and Balkan history, much faith is not to be placed in the prevalence of the rational.

In this connection, certainly one factor of surpassing importance is the developing society of Eastern Europe. The heavy doses of industrialization and urbanization now being administered to the ex-satellites are not only altering the physical landscape of the countries involved but are effecting major changes in the life patterns and hence the attitudes of the masses, as well. Wherever high levels of development have occurred, are occurring and will occur, such is the case. Other pre-existing factors, may modify the new sets, but the industrial and urban influences will not be denied. They represent a preeminent force.

As in the USSR, the USA and Western Europe, these industrializing and urbanizing societies of Eastern Europe are producing a strong drive for material acquisition, for possession of the standard of living elevating products deliverable by advanced technology. For the time being, a Communist regime in Eastern Europe that can to a moderate extent satisfy popular material demands is probably secure. But other demands are not far below the surface. And when these demands are reinforced by traditions of older, successful or unsuccessful, struggles for similar or seemingly similar demands, the potential for instability is considerable. And when further there is added the presence, in whatever degree, of what is still often seen in Eastern Europe as a foreign-installed elite and of foreign "oppressors," the possibility for explosion becomes still greater.

Again, "rationality" might indicate that, for the sake of future increments of material satisfaction, it is well to go along with an "improving" situation. But there is no reasonable assurance that a population will always continue to go along under such circumstances, particularly in Eastern Europe with its long-established patterns of turbulence. Moreover, the situation is such that an outbreak in one country can easily and quickly give rise to similar reactions elsewhere. Irrationality may prevail anywhere at any moment, but particularly in Eastern Europe when there is a strongly felt sense of oppression.

One additional factor, regularly overlooked in the past, but increasingly apparent, is that, in some ways the more highly industrialized, the more complex, the society, the more easily it may be brought to its knees. In the 1950s it was frequently asserted that in industrial societies the possibilities for successful popular revolution were increasingly remote. The relative equality of weapons possible in an earlier century no longer held. Trained elitist forces held machine guns and cannon and flame throwers, tanks and weapons carriers. Against these, rifles and Molotov cocktails must inevitably fail unless there is a break in the government forces. But a highly-developed society is a highly interdependent society. Each part relies upon the other. The refusal of a very small segment of the society to cooperate can bring the activity of the society to a halt—and rather quickly, and under certain conditions, where only a minimum of organization, though considerable determination, on the part of the opposition, may be required. The potential of such a weapon, requiring not the unsheathing of arms but simply a display of inertia, has yet to be fully exploited. It has the disadvantage of not satisfying the urge for violence. It has the advantage of possibly being effective.

As for developments to be anticipated among the non-European, non-Chinese Parties in power, what will happen here will to a large degree depend upon what will happen in China—and that is such an uncertain situation as to make punditing *almost* prohibitive. The potential for violent effective internal opposition is probably less than among the European ex-satellites. The local leadership is native, nationalist and it came to power not with the help of foreign intervention. It is autocratic and well-entrenched. Industrial developments in these areas have been slow and a hastening of that pace with a consequently quickened transformation of society is not to be anticipated at an early date.

As for China, caught up in chaos, there would still appear to be a few firm conclusions that can be drawn. One is that China is not within the next two decades, and probably within the twentieth century, likely to become a major world power. The catastrophic "Great Leap Forward" and the disintegrating "Great Proletarian Cultural Revolution" set China back probably for decades in her development. In his efforts to accelerate the transformation of the Chinese People's Republic into the leading Communist nation, Mao has failed—perhaps at the cost of undermining Chinese political stability for decades to come.

In any event, the speedy development of China does not seem an imminent possibility. Mao's successors will have the same problems to face that have plagued him; underdevelopment and overpopulation—plus the possible addition of territorial dismemberment.

As late as the end of 1966 it might have appeared fatuous to have even chanced the fleeting thought that Mao's successors might not be from within the upper echelons of the longtime Party hierachy. The main discussions in this respect generally concerned themselves with which "generation" would succeed to Mao's power and whether its members would be "more" Maoist or "less" Maoist than Mao. And while it still appears likely that any successor to Mao will dress in Mao's blue uniform and seek succor in his quotations, there is less than at any time since 1949 the assurance that, after Mao, his longtime close comrades in the Party's leading organs will succeed to his power. For in the "Great Proletarian Cultural Revolution," Mao opened a Pandora's box, on which, contrary to the "Hundred Flowers" episode, he could not replace the lid, nor was it apparent that any of his erstwhile cohorts would be able speedily to replace it. But whatever the outcome, whether Mao succeeds in at least keeping power, or whether some other Party leader is able to gain the upper hand or whether a military dictatorship is to be established or chaos is to rule universal, China's pace of development scarcely seems promising.

It also seems apparent that China's internal problems will be reflected in her external relations. While it is clear that the kind of Russian–Chinese brothers-in-armsmanship that never prevailed but was mythicized in the early 1950s can never return, it is not clear that the Sino–Soviet rift is irreversible. Should more moderate Communist leadership gain control in China, it is possible that it would enter into negotiations to reinstitute Soviet aid. Indeed, it is conceivable that it is Soviet assistance that would help the moderates take over. There is the further possibility that some severe external threat experienced by both Parties could also lead to a reconciliation of some degree. However, as against these possibilities there must also be weighed the continuing strong differences in national interests, now clearly evident to both sides, and deep-seated and thoroughly aroused national antagonisms. It is not beyond likelihood that, should more "moderate" Communists take over in China, they would seek assistance *not* from the USSR, but rather from Japan, Western Europe, or even the United States.

An interesting but probably almost fanciful question involves Soviet reaction should a non-Communist domestic leadership take over in China. Though such an eventuality would bring the USSR face to face with the loss to the movement of the most populous country in the world, it is unlikely that the Soviet leadership would willingly become involved in any military action involving Soviet manpower in significant quantity in order to prevent such an occurrence. Both Soviet political and military leadership would fear becoming bogged down in the land mass of East Asia. However, such fears would not preclude the seizure of border areas to provide additional "buffers" and to deny important installations and resources to the new Chinese leadership.

China's indisposition of the late 1960s is assuredly not going to raise her stock abroad. To the Overseas Chinese impressed by the respect and fear with which the new China was regarded internationally and, to a lesser degree, by the progress achieved domestically by the regime, the events of the Cultural Revolution were antagonistic. China was not advancing from strength to strength and, indeed, in some quarters her Maoist leadership was coming to be regarded with ridicule. While such reactions were not limited to the Overseas Chinese—were rather widespread—this did not necessarily indicate a lessening of Maoist influence abroad in all instances. The revolutionary situations which the Chinese Communists would have exploited, still existed. And for those both in Southeast Asia and elsewhere who required external support, China continued to offer an alternative to Soviet or American aid—an alternative that would not be easily surrendered—if available.

It can further be indicated that fear and antagonism to the United States may be no less among Mao's successors than it has been for the Chinese Lenin himself. There may seem to be reason for domestic purposes to maintain anti-American hostility as well as a high level of international revolutionary activity. Consequently, the removal of the current Chinese leadership may not result in lessening of an anti-American position or in the diminution of China's revolutionary role. A more moderate domestic policy, which is what China followed 1959–1965, does not, as it did not, necessarily imply a more moderate international policy. Still, such moderation would be expected.

As for the future of relations among the Communist countries, it may be expected that, if the current trends continue, these relations will ever more closely approximate the normal intercourse of nations. That all are "Communist" may cause a certain amount of cohesiveness to remain, but its significance, unless under external pressure, becomes less and less. For example, Polish and East German fears of West German recrudescense did not prevent Rumanian recognition of the

Bonn government in spring, 1967. Increasingly, traditional and interest factors will take over and the "bloc" will become less determining. Trade and contacts with the rest of the world will expand, though not everywhere with the same smoothness and at the same rate.

All of this will, however, occur in the Communist world within the context of the continuing international dominance of the Russian, Chinese, United States and German presences. A varying combination of fear of and the need for protection against and by these four will limit the freedom of action of each less-than-principal Communist state in contact with other similar states as it will in contact with the chief Communist forces. In the relations of the ex-satellites with China, it may be expected that the latter will extend to them the particular bitterness of the true believer for apostates.

For those Communist Parties not in power, the post-1956 decade was filled with uncertainty and indecision. With the exception of the Italian, French and Indonesian Parties, the other CPs had rarely been numerically significant. Their leaderships, voluntarily or involuntarily, but mostly voluntarily, were at Moscow's command. Being the local link to Moscow whether in Asia or Latin America or Western Europe brought prestige and funds. In those areas where the Communist Party was legal, the various Party functionaries at the end of decades of struggle often could and did settle down to a bourgeois existence as the leaders of also-ran Parties.

But for several reasons, dominated by a principal one, the picture sketchily suggested above has had its limitations. For not all leaders have been satisfied to be also-runs. Whether unreconstructed revolutionaries of advanced year or fire brands of the post-World War II revolutionary generation, they have aspired to the seizure of power. But for the first time in over three decades there was the realization that, if they were to succeed, they would have to depend chiefly upon themselves, certainly not upon the USSR.

Although a few Parties in developed countries continue to adhere closely to Moscow in almost all matters, others pursue a nationalistic course. It would seem that in the future, given peace, this growing independence of Moscow's lead would continue and, undoubtedly, in some areas to good effect from the point of view of communism's extension. Under certain circumstances, the nationalization of communism has and will rehabilitate communism in certain countries and refurbish its status. Communism will not necessarily or likely be brought to power as a result, but the chances of its being considered as a viable alternative when new crises arise will be much improved.

The problems of Communist leardership in Parties out of power in less highly developed countries have some analogies to the situation in more highly developed areas, but there are important differences, as well. Here, it is particularly important to note the dangers of generalization for there are all kinds of underdeveloped countries, some old, some new, some politically stable, some for whom stability is seemingly almost indefinitely unattainable, and so forth. In some of these countries, there have been Communist movements for nearly half a century; in other, Marxist ideology is a rather recent importation. But whatever the case, the survival of the plant will depend upon how well it adapts to local conditions, upon the answers it provides to local questions. The prestige of Moscow is no longer sufficient to develop strong movements, if indeed that is Moscow's goal. If communism is to have a viable future in underdeveloped areas it must be able to consistently deal with local problems on an on-the-scene basis and not be faced with the constant requirement of formulating solutions that will satisfy Moscow or of implementing solutions that have been dictated by Moscow for purposes of Russian national interest.

In some areas where Parties and leadership are of long-standing, the switch-over to local initiative will prove impossible. Moscow will not insist upon it and men of advanced age, satisfied with the security they have attained as venerated revolutionaries, will show themselves unwilling or unable to undertake it. In such countries, when the call for revolution is still sounded with considerable force, the established Communist Party will probably not, in most instances, be the vehicle for the revolutionary drive. Instead, where the movements seek external associations, these will be secured from the Cubans or the Chinese or some not-yet-but-to-be-successful revolution achievers or aspirers.

What the decade after 1956 made clear as to Russian revolutionary aspirations is highly unlikely to be reversed by later events. Russian interest in revolution has been institutionalized and nostalgicized. Ideologically, the Soviets are concerned with the spread of revolution, but in practice the priority of that concern has a near nadir quality. On the other hand, in China and Cuba, the dedication to continuing revolution is much stronger and the need to have revolutionary movements and revolutions is keenly felt on the most elementary level of national security. Both the Chinese and the Cubans appear convinced that their respective territorial integrities and freedom of action depend upon the United States being engaged in military actions in other areas, thus leaving them alone to pursue their own policies. More than this, both the Chinese and the Cubans have the need to experience revolutionary comraderie, to be reassured that they do not stand alone (more important for the Cubans than the Chinese); to receive some confirmation that the movements led by them have more than local importance—that they are of world historical significance. For the Chinese, there is the additional consideration of gaining support in the struggle with the USSR to control the international movement. Accordingly, it may be expected that both China and Cuba will continue to seek to export revolution, though not always with the same fervor.

In many areas—despite the prevalence of strong local nationalist sentiments, despite the often negative example of previous Russian domination of the revolutionary scene at the expense of local objectives —association with the Chinese and Cuban external revolutionizing forces is and will be welcomed. Both the Chinese and the Cubans enjoy the prestige of having conducted successful revolutions. Their advice, if given unprovocatively and with no attaching of strings, could be valued. Their weapons and money undoubtedly would be. Racial, geographic, economic and other factors surely will limit the widespread availability, utilization and effectiveness of Chinese and Cuban assistance, but, under certain conditions, it may be very important in the developing of revolutions.

In considering the pervasiveness and effectiveness of the Chinese and Cuban export of revolution, there remain other significant conditioning factors to be taken into account, including the rising material expectations of the masses of the less highly developed nation. If current leadership can provide direction, organization and satisfaction, then revolutionary forces, though they may arise, are unlikely to achieve success in seizing power. If revolutionary solutions do, however, develop appeal, then "communism," which has in the past half century seized "revolution" as its own province, is almost certain to move front and center. What is more, the brands of communism, that are likely to achieve the greatest amounts of favor are the Chinese and Cuban—because they are more revolution-oriented than the Soviet brand; because the world power Soviet Union is often committed to regularized diplomatic relations and support of the very governments that the rebels are seeking to unseat; because the level of development and problems with which the Chinese and Cubans have to cope at home are much more akin to those faced by the underdeveloped countries than to those in whose solution the USSR is now involved.

Certainly, in the context of the spread of revolution, the latent emotional appeal that Marxism of whatever variation still possesses, must not be overlooked. In a world more or less at peace, with developing prosperity centered in the West, and the existence of hope everywhere, with the bourgeoisation of the Soviet Union and the ex-satellites, the failure of China, the exposure of Stalinist brutality and the disintegration of the international movement, communism is often spoken of as though it is dead—or nearly so. And well it may be, so long as there is peace, prosperity and hope. But should bad days arrive, then a new generation, seeking a way out of its anguish, may again turn to Marx, to the exhilarating and edifying promises of the "Manifesto" and the exhaustive argumentation of *Das Kapital,* and be filled with the dreams assured of fulfillment that inspired earlier decades. Then the exhaustive philosophical and psychological indictments drawn up against Marxism—communism by the intellectuals of the past five score and more years will be disregarded. The even more damning indictment of a half century of experience in power will be explained away—Russia was not ready; Stalin betrayed the promise; Mao was impractical and so forth. And only the promise will remain: earthly paradise, the brotherhood of man, peace—and Marxism–communism as the vehicle for fulfillment.

Index

70 71 72 73 7 6 5 4 3